Readings in Social Psychology:
The Art and Science of Research

EIGHTH EDITION

Saul Kassin
Williams College

Steven Fein
Williams College

Hazel Rose Markus
Stanford University

Prepared by

Steven Fein
Williams College

Saul Kassin
Williams College

WADSWORTH
CENGAGE Learning™

Australia • Brazil • Japan • Korea • Mexico • Singapore • Spain • United Kingdom • United States

ISBN-13: 978-0-8400-3300-0
ISBN-10: 0-8400-3300-1

Wadsworth
20 Davis Drive
Belmont, CA 94002-3098
USA

Cengage Learning is a leading provider of customized learning solutions with office locations around the globe, including Singapore, the United Kingdom, Australia, Mexico, Brazil, and Japan. Locate your local office at: **www.cengage.com/global**

Cengage Learning products are represented in Canada by Nelson Education, Ltd.

To learn more about Wadsworth, visit
www.cengage.com/wadsworth

Purchase any of our products at your local college store or at our preferred online store
www.CengageBrain.com

Printed in the United States of America
1 2 3 4 5 6 7 14 13 12 11 10

Contents

INTRODUCTION V

PART 1: INTRODUCTION

READING 1 – *WHO I AM DEPENDS ON HOW I FEEL: THE ROLE OF AFFECT IN THE EXPRESSION OF CULTURE,*
ASHTON-JAMES, MADDUX, GALINSKY, AND CHARTRAND (2009)...................................... 1

READING 2 – *SOCIAL INFLUENCE ON POLITICAL JUDGMENTS: THE CASE OF PRESIDENTIAL DEBATES,*
FEIN, GOETHALS, AND KUGLER (2007) 13

PART 2: SOCIAL PERCEPTION

READING 3 – *FIRST IMPRESSIONS: MAKING UP YOUR MIND AFTER A 100-MS EXPOSURE TO A FACE,*
WILLIS AND TODOROV (2006) 33

READING 4 – *THE CONSEQUENCES OF RACE FOR POLICE OFFICERS' RESPONSES TO CRIMINAL SUSPECTS,*
PLANT AND PERUCHE (2005) 45

READING 5 – *STEREOTYPE THREAT AND THE INTELLECTUAL TEST PERFORMANCE OF AFRICAN AMERICANS,*
STEELE AND ARONSON (1995) 51

PART 3: SOCIAL INFLUENCE

READING 6 – COGNITIVE CONSEQUENCES OF FORCED COMPLIANCE,
FESTINGER AND CARLSMITH (1959) 77

READING 7 – *THE CHAMELEON EFFECT: THE PERCEPTION–BEHAVIOR LINK AND SOCIAL INTERACTION,*
CHARTRAND AND BARGH (1999)... 87

READING 8 – *BEHAVIORAL STUDY OF OBEDIENCE,*
MILGRAM (1963) 119

READING 9 – *BRINGING IN THE EXPERTS: HOW TEAM COMPOSITION AND COLLABORATIVE PLANNING JOINTLY SHAPE ANALYTIC EFFECTIVENESS,*
WOOLLEY, GERBASI, CHABRIS, KOSSLYN, AND HACKMAN (2008)............................... 131

PART 4: SOCIAL RELATIONS

READING 10 – *THE NATURE AND PREDICTORS OF THE TRAJECTORY OF CHANGE IN MARITAL QUALITY FOR HUSBANDS AND WIVES OVER THE FIRST 10 YEARS OF MARRIAGE,*
KURDEK (1999).. 147

READING 11 – *GROUP INHIBITION OF BYSTANDER INTERVENTION IN EMERGENCIES,*
LATANÉ AND DARLEY (1968).. 171

READING 12 – *Effects of Songs with Prosocial Lyrics on Prosocial Thoughts, Affect, and Behavior*,
Greitmeyer (2008)..181

READING 13 – *Weapons as Aggression-Eliciting Stimuli*,
Berkowitz and LePage (1967)..191

READING 14 – *Stand by Your Man: Indirect Prescriptions for Honorable Violence and Feminine Loyalty in Canada, Chile, and the United States*,
Vandello, Cohen, Grandon, and Franiuk (2009) 199

PART 5: APPLYING SOCIAL PSYCHOLOGY

READING 15 -- *Reconstruction of Automobile Destruction: An Example of the Interaction Between Language and Memory*,
Loftus and Palmer (1974) 221

READING 16 – *The Social Psychology of False Confessions: Compliance, Internalization, and Confabulation*,
Kassin and Kiechel (1996)..227

READING 17 – *Looking Deathworthy: Perceived Stereotypicality of Black Defendants Predicts Capital-Sentencing Outcomes*,
Eberhardt, Davies, Purdie-Vaughns, and Johnson (2006)..................................235

READING 18 – *Equity and Workplace Status: A Field Experiment*,
Greenberg (1988) 243

READING 19 – *Sociability and Susceptibility to the Common Cold*,
Cohen, S., Doyle, W.J., Turner, R., Alper, C.M., & Skoner, D.P. (2003)...............257

Introduction

THE PURPOSE OF THIS BOOK

One of the most rewarding aspects of teaching social psychology is that most students are interested in social psychological issues. Most of us—students as well as instructors—are interested in explaining the causes of others' behaviors, in predicting how people will react in various situations, and in understanding the attraction or hostility between people. But this interest can also present an important challenge to instructors. When people learn social psychological theories or findings that are at odds with their own intuition or personal observations, they may be too quick to dismiss these theories or findings as wrong or unrepresentative. Then when they learn other theories or findings that are consistent with their own intuition or personal observations, they may disparage the first theories and findings as mere common sense.

The difference between the discipline of social psychology and people's intuitions and observations is empirical research. Intuition and common sense can be frustratingly accommodating. One can, for example, cite, "Absence makes the heart grow fonder," to explain the continued success of a romantic relationship after the couple has been forced to spend some time apart from each other, and yet also cite, "Out of sight, out of mind," to explain the failure of a different couple to endure a similar amount of time apart. Social psychology, in contrast, cannot have it so easy. Social psychological theories must be more rigorous, and they must be supported by the results of systematic, methodically sound research. To fully understand and appreciate social psychology, therefore, one must understand and appreciate the research on which the field of social psychology has been, and will continue to be, based. Your textbook, the *Eighth Edition of Social Psychology* by Saul Kassin, Steven Fein, and Hazel Rose Markus, explains much of this research clearly, concretely, and compellingly. The authors have made it a point to make this research come alive to students, to give students enough information so that they can imagine what it would be like to be a subject in many of these studies.

This book of readings was designed to take this emphasis a step further by presenting a diverse sample of important, unabridged, original research articles. Whereas a textbook and class lectures can offer summaries of a number of studies, only a sample of representative studies can give valuable insight into the process as well as the content of social psychology. The goal is to encourage students not only to learn the important theories and principles of the field, but also to think critically about them—to see where they came from, how they have been supported, why they have been supported, and what their potential flaws are. This kind of critical thinking not only makes the material more interesting and compelling but also leads to a deeper understanding of the material.

Another goal of this book of readings is to illustrate the creativity involved in designing studies to test one's hypotheses. In this process, social psychologists often are challenged to combine elements of theater and science. Their experiments must be controlled and precise; procedures should be identical across conditions, with the exception of the manipulated independent variable(s); and potential alternative explanations should be anticipated and ruled out. Within these constraints, however, researchers often need to create an artificial but very real world for their subjects. They need to anticipate the thoughts, feelings, and reactions of the people who participate in their studies, and they must create situations that are realistic and meaningful. "Doing" social psychology, therefore, often involves acting like a playwright; in conducting research, the social psychologist often must create characters, dialogue, and interactions among characters, must place these characters into various situations, and must create a setting, all with the intention of drawing the participants into this fabricated reality so that their reactions and responses are real and spontaneous.

Not all social psychological experiments require this level of creativity. Some studies are, by necessity, simple, whereas others are quite elaborate. Some involve a great deal of deception; others involve no deception. Some elicit strong emotional reaction; others are quite mundane. Some are conducted in a laboratory; others are conducted in the field. But whatever the level of complexity, the process that begins with a set of hypotheses and proceeds through the execution of a study to test these hypotheses is creative and enjoyable. We hope that the enjoyment of this process will become evident to the reader in this set of articles.

THE SELECTION OF ARTICLES

In keeping with the goals outlined above, we have selected readings that we feel will help (1) inspire critical thinking about several of the most important issues raised in the textbook, (2) produce a better understanding of various important social psychological principles and findings, and (3) illustrate the creativity of the science of conducting social psychological research. Thus these readings not only present important findings, but they also describe interesting designs, procedures, or settings. We chose psychology journal articles that were written well and concisely and that can be understood and appreciated by people not familiar with all of the literature cited or details given. This is particularly significant because we wanted to present these readings in their entirety, unabridged, as the original authors wrote them. We emphasize this for a number of reasons. We feel there is no substitute for reading these important works firsthand, without the articles being diluted or filtered by anyone else. These are, after all, papers that have helped change the field of social psychology. In addition, an entire article can meet a variety of needs. Readers who want only the gist of the article and readers who want to study and learn the details of the research—such as exactly how some construct was measured or exactly why the researchers believed their results supported their hypothesis—can get what they want from the articles presented in this book. Perhaps most importantly, all students who read these articles must organize and synthesize the information for themselves—whether this means abstracting out the gist or outlining all of the important points and procedures—and this is an excellent way to improve understanding and retention of the information.

These articles include both classic articles that have withstood the test of time and contributed to the development of social psychology, and contemporary articles concerning research that has already made important contributions to the field and that is likely to inspire the research that will help reshape social psychology for years to come. The selection of both classic and contemporary articles can give students a sense of how the field has changed, and continues to change. For example, contemporary articles tend to feature more sophisticated methods and statistical analyses. Another difference is the language used in these articles. Some of the classic articles contain language that would be considered sexist by today's standards, whereas contemporary articles must conform to the American Psychological Association's guidelines for nonsexist language. Yet another example concerns the ethics of the research. Research today must be approved by a review board, and social psychologists today are more sensitive to the needs of those who participate in their research than they were in the past.

This is by no means an exhaustive set of the most important articles in social psychology. Rather, it is a sample of important classic and contemporary articles that report original, empirical research and that are readable and interesting. Moreover, these articles concern the variety of topics covered in Kassin, Fein, and Markus's *Social Psychology*. Like the text, they are divided into five parts: Introduction, Social Perception, Social Influence, Social Relations, and Applying Social Psychology. These readings concern issues raised in every chapter of the textbook.

We have briefly introduced each article to set the article in its proper context, including the sections in the textbook to which the article is most relevant.

NOTE TO STUDENTS: HOW TO READ THE READINGS

Several of the readings in this book were written in a style with which you are likely to be unfamiliar. They were written for psychology journals that have a particular format and set of norms. When approaching these readings, therefore, DO NOT BE INTIMIDATED. We selected articles that even those unfamiliar with the literature cited, jargon used, and statistical analyses reported should be able to understand without much trouble. The key is to know how to read these articles, such as what to read carefully and what to skim. Unless your instructor indicates otherwise, you don't need to understand all of the details.

The Four Major Sections of Many Articles

Many, but not all, of these articles share a particular structure. They begin with an Introduction, followed by a Method section, followed by a Results section, followed by a Discussion section. Articles that describe more than one study begin with a general Introduction and conclude with a General Discussion section; in between, each study reported is introduced with its own brief Introduction, has its own Method and Results sections, and may have its own Discussion section. The complete references of the literature cited in each article are listed at the very end of the article. Many of these articles also have a brief abstract, or summary of the entire article, before the Introduction.

In the Introduction, the purpose of the research is explained and placed into a general context, and hypotheses are developed. By the end of the Introduction, the research that was conducted to test these hypotheses is explained in rather broad detail. The Method section presents the specific details of how the research was conducted. The purpose of this section is to allow the readers to see exactly how the research was done so that they can evaluate the validity of the research and, if they so desire, try to replicate the study themselves. The Results section usually is the most detailed section. It reports the results of the statistical analyses that were used to determine to what extent the data collected were consistent or inconsistent with the hypotheses. The Discussion section summarizes these results and discusses such things as *why* the research found what it did, what the implications of the research may be, and what questions remain unanswered.

These articles can be described as having an hourglass shape: they start out relatively broad, usually by making general statements about a particular problem, then become more and more focused as they introduce the specific research conducted and results found, and then become more and more broad again as the Discussion section first summarizes the results and then discusses the broader implications of these results.

A Suggested Order in Which to Read the More Difficult Articles

To the extent, then, that some of these articles include details that are difficult to understand, how should you read them? First of all, you should be sure to have read Chapter 2 in your textbook carefully, particularly the sections concerning hypothesis, theory, basic research, and applied research; correlations; the essential features of experiments; the language of research, including independent variables, dependent variables, statistical significance, main effect, and interaction; and evaluating research.

Although you should check with your instructor, the way we suggest reading the more difficult (or less "user friendly") articles is to first read the sections that set the context and summarize the research most clearly, and then read the sections that provide more details. Thus, if the article begins with a brief abstract, or summary, begin by reading this carefully. Because of the jargon used, it is sometimes necessary to reread the abstract a few times until you understand the general purpose and findings of the research. Then read the Introduction. If the Introduction ends with a description of the research design and hypotheses, read this description carefully. Next, you may want to skip to the first few paragraphs of the Discussion section toward the end of the paper (this might be called the General Discussion section if there are multiple studies reported). The first paragraphs usually summarize the main points of the research findings. Once you understand these principal findings, you have the context needed to go back and read the rest of the article.

Next, read the Method section. As you read this section, it's often a good idea to jot down notes so you can keep track of the conditions of the study. Try to imagine yourself as a participant in this study. What would you be experiencing? What would you be thinking? Also, imagine yourself as the experimenter. What would you be saying to participants? How would you be observing or measuring their responses? If you come across jargon or references that you don't understand, don't worry about it. You may want to make a note of it and ask your instructor about it, but if you read ahead you should be able to understand the central idea. After you read the Method section, think about the predictions or hypotheses stated in the Introduction. Anticipate how participants will react differently in the different conditions of the study. You may want to go back to the end of the Introduction section where the hypotheses or predictions were stated and explained.

Reading the Results Section

Skim the Results section as best you can. Remember to familiarize yourself with each of the following from Chapter 2 of your textbook: correlations, independent variables, dependent variables, statistical significance, main effects, and interactions. In some of these articles, a number of statistical analyses will be reported that will be difficult, if not impossible, to understand. We'll give you a few guidelines in the following paragraphs to help you with these, but if you can't understand the Results section, you shouldn't be too concerned because you should be able to understand the most important results by reading the Discussion section and, if available, the Abstract.

As you read the results, go slowly and keep in mind the different conditions of the study and the hypotheses for these different conditions. Researchers are often interested in measuring the "average" response of participants in each condition. Suppose 20 participants in one condition were asked to rate how attractive some other person was, and 20 participants in another condition were asked the same thing. The researchers are interested in determining if the *average* rating given by the 20 participants in one condition was different than the *average* rating given by the 20 participants in the other condition. Whenever differences between conditions are reported, try to get a sense of the averages for each condition. The averages for each condition may be depicted in a table or figure, or they may be reported in parentheses, as in ($M = 3.47$), which should be read as "the mean, or average, of this condition is 3.47."

The next thing to look for is whether the differences between the averages of the various conditions are significant. As Chapter 2 indicates, the convention in psychology is to say that a difference between two conditions is statistically significant if the analyses suggest that the probability that this difference could have occurred by chance alone is less than 5 out of 100. For example, if you toss a coin 100 times, you may find that the coin landed on heads 53 times and tails 47 times. Is this difference significant? It is not significant because there is a very high likelihood that the difference reflects nothing more than a random outcome. What if you divide people into different conditions and have each of them rate something on a 100-point scale, and you find that the average response is 53 for the participants in one condition and 47 for the participants in the other condition? Is this significant? There is no way to determine whether this difference is significant without performing some statistical analyses.

The probability that a difference occurred by chance alone is usually reported as a number that comes after the phrase $p<$, where p means the probability. Thus, if $p< .05$, the probability that this difference occurred by chance is less than .05, or 5 out of 100, and so the difference is considered significant. Whenever differences between conditions are reported, you should try to get a sense of the averages for each group, and then see if the p level is less than .05.

When there is more than one independent variable in a study, researchers are interested not only in whether the average of one condition differs from that of another, but also in whether the independent variables interact with each other to create different patterns of results. Be sure to reread the section on interactions in Chapter 2.

In addition to differences between conditions, correlations also can be statistically significant or not. A correlation is an association between two variables that vary in quantity. It is positive when both variables increase or decrease together; it is negative when one variable increases as the other variable decreases. Chapter 2 explains and gives various examples of correlations. A correlation can occur by chance alone, such as if you flip a coin and roll some dice at the same time and find that rolling higher numbers with the dice was correlated with the coin landing on tails. This most likely was just a fluke. What if there is an association between watching a lot of television and being very aggressive? Is this a significant correlation? To the extent that the association between these two variables is a reliable one, it is more likely to be considered statistically significant. But if the probability that this association occurred by chance is less than .05, or 5 out of 100, it is considered statistically significant.

Again, it is important to keep in mind that if you begin to get lost in the details of the results, step back and gain perspective by rereading the Abstract and the beginning of the Discussion section.

READING 1

Who I Am Depends on How I Feel: The Role of Affect in the Expression of Culture

As discussed in Chapter 3 (The Social Self), the self-concept is heavily influenced by cultural factors. Two contrasting cultural orientations are individualism and collectivism, though these should not be viewed as simple opposites on a continuum. That is too simplistic. The researchers of this study, Ashton-James, Maddux, Galinsky, and Chartrand, considered the role of affect in the expression of culture. Through four experiments, they explored how positive and negative affect moderated the expression of "culturally normative cognitions and behaviors." Experiment 1 addressed self-expression. Experiment 2 examined cultural consistency of actual behavior (rather than self-reported beliefs). Experiment 3 focused on the impact of affective cues on self-construal. Experiment 4 examined whether the interaction between affect and culture would also affect an implicit, behavioral measure of self-construal which, in this experiment, was seating distance. Their results showed a difference between Westerners and East Asians. When Westerners experienced positive affect, they valued self-expression less. East Asians, however, after experiencing positive affect, valued and expressed individuality and independence more. Their conclusion demonstrated "a robust moderation of the expression of culture by affective state," which contradicts prior research that found that culture *predicted* affective responses. These four experiments show that affect can also *determine* the expression of culture.

WHO I AM DEPENDS ON HOW I FEEL: THE ROLE OF AFFECT IN THE EXPRESSION OF CULTURE

Claire E. Ashton-James

University of British Columbia

William W. Maddux

INSEAD

Adam D. Galinsky

Northwestern University

Tanya L. Chartrand

Duke University

Claire E. Ashton-James, William W. Maddux , Adam D. Galinsky, Tanya L. Chartrand , "Who I Am Depends on How I Feel: The Role of Affect in the Expression of Culture" *Psychological Science,* Vol. 20, No. 3, pp. 340-346

Address correspondence to Claire E. Ashton-James, University of British Columbia, School of Psychology, 2136 West Mall, Vancouver, British Columbia, Canada V6T 1Z4, e-mail: cajames@psych.ubc.ca.

ABSTRACT—*We present a novel role of affect in the expression of culture. Four experiments tested whether individuals' affective states moderate the expression of culturally normative cognitions and behaviors. We consistently found that value expressions, self-construals, and behaviors were less consistent with cultural norms when individuals were experiencing positive rather than negative affect. Positive affect allowed individuals to explore novel thoughts and behaviors that departed from cultural constraints, whereas negative affect bound people to cultural norms. As a result, when Westerners experienced positive rather than negative affect, they valued self-expression less, showed a greater preference for objects that reflected conformity, viewed the self in more interdependent terms, and sat closer to other people. East Asians showed the reverse pattern for each of these measures, valuing and expressing individuality and independence more when experiencing positive than when experiencing negative affect. The results suggest that affect serves an important functional purpose of attuning individuals more or less closely to their cultural heritage.*

Who people are often depends on how they feel: A confluence of research suggests that diffuse positive and negative affective states significantly influence attitudes, thoughts, and behaviors. For example, feeling good is associated with more positive evaluations, more creative thought, and more novelty-seeking behavior, whereas feeling bad is associated with more negative evaluations, more rigorous or systematic thinking, and more cautious behavior (for a review, see Schwarz & Clore, 2007). In this article, we build from and extend these previous investigations by exploring whether affective states influence the expression of individuals' core self as constructed by their culture. Taking a social functionalist perspective of affective states, we hypothesized that diffuse positive and negative feelings can significantly influence those values, thoughts, and behaviors normally anchored in the deep fabric of one's cultural heritage.

THE ROLE OF AFFECT IN COGNITION AND BEHAVIOR

Overall, research suggests that diffuse positive and negative affective states, including moods, feelings, and temperament (Frijda, 1986), play an important social function, alerting people to the adaptive value of their current thinking and behavior (Schwarz, 1990). For example, positive affect seems to serve as a psychological and physiological marker of well-being, security, and progress toward one's goals (Carver & Scheier, 1990; Fredrickson, 2001; Higgins, 1996; Kahneman, 1999; Schwarz & Clore, 2007). In contrast, negative affect tends to signal that one's current mode of thinking and behaving is maladaptive or that something in one's immediate environment is problematic and requires one to search for restorative solutions (e.g., Schwarz, 1990).

These broad and diffuse affective states direct subsequent cognition and behavior in predictable ways. For example, positive affect leads individuals to become more open to new experiences, and more willing to approach and explore novel objects, people, thoughts, and behaviors (Cacioppo, Gardner, & Berntson, 1999; Fredrickson, 2001). By contrast, negative affect leads individuals to be more cautious when assessing risk (Johnson & Tversky, 1983), to be more prevention focused (Higgins, 1997), and to prefer familiar people, situations, and objects over novel ones (Raghunathan & Pham, 1999).

AFFECT AND THE EXPRESSION OF CULTURE

Taken together, these results suggest that positive affect increases the likelihood of unfamiliar or nonnormative responses, whereas negative affect produces an enhanced propensity for familiar or normative actions (cf. Gable & Harmon-Jones, 2008). However, the behaviors that are considered typical or normative vary significantly across cultures (e.g., Markus & Kitayama, 1991; Triandis, 1995). In Western cultures, independence and individuality are highly valued and consistently reinforced as predominant social goals, and behaviors that assert independence and individuality are considered normative in Western cultural contexts. By contrast, the predominant social goals in Eastern cultures are interdependence and maintenance of interpersonal harmony (Markus & Kitayama, 1991), and interdependence-promoting behaviors are considered normative and appropriate in Eastern cultural contexts. Thus, different behavioral repertoires are socially reinforced as normative or appropriate in different cultures.

Given such cultural influences, we tested the hypothesis that positive and negative affective states produce divergent behavioral responses that depend on the individual's cultural background. In particular, because positive affect encourages individuals to explore what is novel and adopt alternative behaviors and cognitions and negative affect increases reliance on the familiar and normative, we predicted that, on the one hand, individuals from Western cultural backgrounds would value the expression of individuality less and show an increased preference for conformity with other individuals when experiencing positive (relative to negative) affect. On the other hand, we hypothesized that individuals from East Asian cultural backgrounds would value the expression of individuality more and show a decreased preference for conformity when experiencing positive (relative to negative) affect.[1]

Thus, the research reported in this article investigated for the first time whether affective states influence the expression of culturally consistent thoughts, behaviors, and self-expressions. Experiments 1 and 2 explored whether affect moderates the expression of culturally consistent values and behaviors. Experiments 3 and 4 tested whether affect moderates Western and Eastern participants' self-construals both explicitly (Experiment 3) and implicitly (Experiment 4). Across the experiments, we manipulated affect using four different procedures and measured the expression of culturally consistent values and behaviors in four different paradigms, with the hope of demonstrating the robustness of the link from affect to the expression of culture. Specifically, we predicted that participants would express more culturally inconsistent values, behaviors, and self-construals when experiencing positive, as compared with negative, affective states.

Experiment 1

Experiment 1 investigated the impact of affect and culture on the value that people place on self-expression. Such values vary significantly across cultures (Kim & Sherman, 2007), with people from Western cultural backgrounds tending to value the expression of their internal beliefs and attributes more than people from East Asian backgrounds (Kim & Markus, 2002). We hypothesized that Westerners (Europeans and European Canadians) in a positive affective state would value self-expression less than Westerners in a negative affective state, but that East Asians (Asians and Asian Canadians) in a positive affective state would value self-expression more than East Asians in a negative affective state.

Method

Participants and Design. One hundred forty-six students from the University of British Columbia (74 Asian and Asian Canadian students, 72 European and European Canadian students) volunteered to participate. The participants were either Canadians from European or East Asian backgrounds or international students from European (i.e., Germany, Ireland, England) or East Asian (i.e., Taiwan, Korea, China, Japan) nations. Experiment 1 had a 3 (affect: positive vs. neutral vs. negative) × 2 (culture: Western vs. East Asian) between-subjects design

Procedure. Students were approached on campus and were asked to participate in a study on "feelings and beliefs." Participants first completed an autobiographical memory task designed to induce positive, neutral, or negative affect. In the positive-affect condition, participants recalled a life experience that made them feel extremely positive, uplifted, or happy. In the negative-affect condition, participants recalled a time they felt extremely negative, down, or sad. Participants in the neutral-affect condition were asked to recall their actions of the current day. In all conditions, participants were then asked to describe the image that was most vivid about the experience, to list five feelings that they felt at the time, and to rate the intensity of the emotion that they felt at the time on a 10-point scale (1 5 not at all intense, 10 5 extremely intense).

---

[1]   In the present research, we made hypotheses about, and experimentally manipulated, diffuse positive and negative affective states (e.g., feelings or moods; Frijda, 1986; Schwarz & Clore, 2007), rather than more specific emotions such as joy, surprise, anger, or fear (Gable & Harmon-Jones, 2008; Lerner & Keltner, 2001).

Participants then completed the Value of Expression Questionnaire (VEQ; Kim & Sherman, 2007), which measures the extent to which one values self-expression (e.g., ''Freedom of expression is one of the most important rights that people should have''). Participants responded to the items using a 9-point scale ranging from 1 (strongly disagree) to 9 (strongly agree). Finally, participants completed an affect manipulation check and reported their gender, race or ethnicity, and nationality.

Results

Manipulation Check. The manipulation was effective. Participants who recalled a positive life event reported the most positive affect ($M = 5.78$, $SD = 1.70$), followed by participants in the neutral-affect condition ($M = 5.55$, $SD = 1.40$); participants in the negative-affect condition expressed the least positive affect ($M = 4.66$, $SD = 1.39$), $F(2, 139) = 7.32$, $p = .001$.

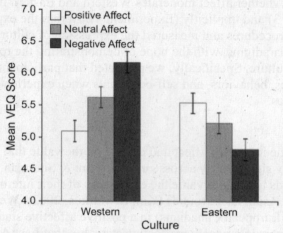

Fig. 1. Mean Value of Expression Questionnaire (VEQ) score as a function of culture and affect (Experiment 1). Error bars represent ±1 *SEM*.

Self-Expression. The VEQ scores were submitted to a 3 (affect: positive, neutral, or negative) × 2 (culture: Western or East Asian) analysis of variance. Results were consistent with Kim and Sherman's (2007) findings in that there was a significant main effect of culture, with Western participants scoring significantly higher ($M = 5.64$, $SD = 0.94$) than East Asian participants ($M = 5.17$, $SD = 0.83$), $F(1, 144) = 10.531$, $p = .002$, $\eta_p^2 = 066$. This main effect was qualified by a significant interaction between affect and culture, $F(2, 144) = 16.142$, $p = .001$, $\eta_p^2 = 186$ (see Fig. 1).

As predicted, Western participants' scores on the VEQ were lower (i.e., less endorsement of individual expression) in the positive-affect condition than in the negative-affect condition, $F(1, 49) = 19.99$, $p < .001$, $\eta_p^2 = 294$, and the neutral-affect condition, $F(1, 45) = 4.769$, $p 5 .03$, $\eta_p^2 = .098$. In contrast, Western participants affirmed self-expression to a greater extent in the negative-affect condition than in the neutral-affect condition, $F(1, 47) = 5.204$, $p = .02$, $\eta_p^2 = 102$.

Also as predicted, East Asians' VEQ scores were higher (i.e., less culturally consistent) in the positive-affect condition compared with the negative-affect condition, $F(1, 53) = 12.36$, $p = .001$, $\eta_p^2 = 194$. Although the VEQ scores of East Asians in the neutral-affect condition were not significantly different from the VEQ scores of East Asians in the positive-affect ($p = .21$) or negative-affect ($p = .07$) condition, a significant linear trend confirmed that East Asians experiencing positive affect obtained the highest VEQ scores (reported the least culturally consistent beliefs), followed by East Asians in the neutral-affect condition, and then by those in the negative-affect condition, $t(71) = 3.45$, $p = .001$ (see Fig. 1).

Experiment 1 provided the first evidence that affect can influence culturally normative beliefs. The values expressed by Westerners and East Asians were less consistent with their cultural norms when participants were in a positive affective state (relative to a neutral affective state) and were more consistent with their cultural norms when participants were in a negative affective state (relative to a neutral affective state).

Experiment 2

Experiment 2 examined the impact of positive and negative affect on the cultural consistency of actual behavior, rather than self-reported beliefs. Previous research has shown that Westerners and East Asians show distinct preferences for choosing objects that reflect uniqueness versus conformity (Kim & Markus, 1999; Kim & Sherman, 2007).[2] For example, Kim and Markus (1999) demonstrated that when asked to choose a single pen from a group of five, one or two of which were a different color from the rest, Westerners tended to choose the pen with the uncommon color, whereas East Asians tended to choose the pen with the common color. In Experiment 2, we adopted this procedure to examine the impact of affect on the tendency to show culturally normative choice behavior. We predicted that participants would show less culturally normative behavior in the positive-affect condition than in the negative-affect condition.

Method

Participants and Design. Sixty-three participants from the University of British Columbia (33 Asians and Asian Canadians, 30 Europeans and European Canadians) volunteered to participate in the study in return for a ballpoint pen. Experiment 2 had a 2 (affect: positive vs. negative) x 2 (culture: Western vs. East Asian) between-subjects design.

Procedure. Participants completed a survey on ''Music and Feelings.'' For this survey, they used headphones to listen to approximately 3 min of classical music chosen to induce either positive (Mozart's Serenade in G Major, K. 525, ''Eine Kleine Nachtmusik'' 1. Allegro) or negative (Rachmaninov's Vocalise in E Minor, Opus 34, No. 14) affect and then were asked to write down what they were feeling as they listened, using two 7-point rating scales (*happy, sad*; 1 = *not at all*, 7 = *extremely*). Next, participants reported their gender, nationality, and race or ethnicity.

After participants returned the completed questionnaire, a pen was offered as payment. Pens were always presented in a set of five, with one or two pens (counterbalanced) a different color from the rest (blue or black, counterbalanced). Our main dependent measure was whether participants chose the pen that had an uncommon color.

Results

Manipulation Check. Participants in the positive-affect condition felt more positive ($M = 4.70$, $SD = 1.05$) than participants in the negative-affect condition ($M = 3.33$, $SD = 5\ 0.97$), $F(1, 61) = 28.686$, $p < .001$.

Choice Behavior. A log-linear analysis of pen choice revealed a significant interaction between affect and culture, $\chi^2(1, N = 63) = 8.247$, $p = .004$. As we hypothesized, Western participants were less likely to choose the uncommon pen in the positive-affect condition (13%) than in the negative-affect condition (60%), $\chi^2(1, N = 30) = 7.033$, $p = .008$. In contrast, East Asian participants showed a trend in the opposite direction, with those in the positive-affect condition more likely to choose the uncommon pen (33%) than those in the negative-affect condition (13%), $\chi^2(1, N = 33) = 1.782$, $p\ 5\ .18$.

---

2   An alternative explanation for this finding (Yamagishi, Hashimoto, & Schug, 2008) is that cultural norms, rather than preferences, drive this effect. However, this interpretation is also consistent with our overall hypothesis that affective states moderate culturally normative behaviors and cognitions.

Experiment 2 found that Westerners were less likely to choose an uncommon pen when they felt positive than when they felt negative, whereas East Asians' behavior exhibited a trend in the opposite direction, that is, a greater preference for uncommon pens in the positive-than in the negative-affect condition.

Experiment 3

The purpose of Experiment 3 was twofold. First, we wanted to examine the impact of affective cues on self-construal, one of the most fundamental manifestations of culture (Markus & Kitayama, 1991). Second, we wanted to demonstrate the automaticity of this process by examining the impact of implicit affect on the cultural consistency of self-construals. To this end, we manipulated affective state (positive vs. negative) through a facial feedback paradigm (Strack, Martin, & Stepper, 1988) and then had participants complete a measure of self-construal. On the basis of research demonstrating that Westerners tend to construe the self in independent terms, whereas East Asians have a predominantly interdependent self-construal (e.g., Markus & Kitayama, 1991), we predicted that Westerners experiencing positive affect via implicit facial feedback would express a more interdependent self-construal than Westerners experiencing negative affect via implicit facial feedback, and that East Asians experiencing positive affect via implicit facial feedback would express a more independent self-construal than East Asians experiencing negative affect via implicit facial feedback.

Method

Participants and Design. Ninety-one undergraduate students (44 female, 47 male) from Duke University were paid $7 for their participation. Sixty-six percent of the participants ($n = 60$) identified themselves as being from a Western cultural background, and 34% ($n = 31$) of the sample identified themselves as being from an East Asian cultural background.[3] The experiment had a 2 (facial feedback: smiling vs. frowning) × 2 (culture: Western vs. East Asian) between-subjects design.

Procedure. Following Strack et al. (1988), we told participants that they would be participating in a study on ''psychomotoric coordination.'' Participants were randomly assigned to a facial feedback condition (positive or negative) and asked to hold a pen between their teeth or lips while they completed the Twenty Statements Test (TST; Kuhn & McPartland, 1954). In the positive-affect condition, participants were instructed to hold the pen between their teeth, which activates the zygomatic muscles involved in smiling. In the negative-affect condition, participants were instructed to hold the pen between their lips, which activates the corrugator facial muscles associated with frowning.

The TST (Kuhn & McPartland, 1954) is a measure of self-construal in which participants are presented with an open-ended probe question, ''Who am I?'' They respond to this question 20 times with reference to themselves (e.g., Cousins, 1989; Gardner, Gabriel, & Lee, 1999). Following Gardner et al. (1999), two raters (blind to hypotheses and experimental conditions) coded a response as representing an independent self-construal if it described a personal attribute (trait, ability, physical attribute, or attitude: e.g., ''I am intelligent''; ''I am athletic'') and as representing an interdependent self-construal if it described a social role, relationship, or group membership (''I am a team captain''; ''I am a sister''). Coders were instructed to exclude responses that were neither independent nor interdependent (e.g., ''I am hungry''). Interrater reliability was acceptable ($a = .79$). Given that the proportions of independent and interdependent self-construals were almost perfectly complementary, we used the proportion of independent self-construals as the dependent variable.

Results

The proportion of independent self-construals was submitted to a 2 (facial feedback: smiling vs. frowning) × 2 (culture: Western vs. East Asian) analysis of variance. A significant two-way interaction emerged, $F(1, 87) = 15.55$, $p = .001$, $\eta_p^2 = 152$. As predicted, Western participants in a positive

---

[3]   Nationalities of participants were not recorded in this study

affective state (i.e., smiling) listed proportionately fewer independent self-construals compared with Western participants in a negative affective state (i.e., frowning), $F(1, 87) = 4.58$, $p = .035$, $\eta_p^2 = 05$. Furthermore, East Asian participants experiencing positive facial feedback expressed proportionately more independent self-construals than those experiencing negative facial feedback, $F(1, 87) = 11.001$, $p = .001$, $\eta_p^2 = 112$ (see Fig. 2). Manipulating affective state via facial feedback influenced the cultural construction of the self. Results were consistent with the pattern of results for values and behaviors in Experiments 1 and 2. Smiling (positive affect) participants expressed fewer culturally consistent self-construals than frowning (negative affect) participants.

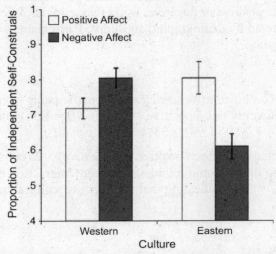

Fig. 2. Proportion of independent self-construals as a function of culture and affect (Experiment 3). Error bars represent ± 1 SEM.

Experiment 4

In Experiment 4, we examined whether the interaction between affect and culture would also affect an implicit, behavioral measure of self-construal, namely, seating distance (see Ashton-James, van Baaren, Chartrand, & Decety, 2007; Holland, Roeder, van Baaren, Brandt, & Hannover, 2004). We predicted that Western participants in a positive affective state would sit closer to other people (reflecting a more interdependent self-construal) than would Western participants in a negative affective state, whereas East Asians in a positive affective state would sit farther from other people (reflecting a more independent self-construal) than would East Asians in a negative affective state.

Method

*Participants and Design.*Thirty-five (13 female, 22 male) undergraduate students from Duke University (17 European Americans, 18 East Asians) participated in return for $3.

Procedure. Two experimenters, one Westerner and one East Asian, recruited participants on campus. Western participants were recruited by the East Asian experimenter, and East Asian participants were recruited by the Western experimenter. The nonactive experimenter served as a confederate, sitting at one end of a bench (ostensibly on a break) when participants approached the experimental area.[4] Thus, the confederate was always of the same ethnic background as the participant. This served as a control for the influence of possible in-group/out-group effects (e.g., individuals may sit further from people of a different ethnicity).

---

[4] African American and Latino participants who approached the experimenter were allowed to participate, but were not included in the final analyses.

Participants were told that the experiment concerned a ''media survey.'' They were first asked to examine 10 positive or 10 negative media images (the affect manipulation). The positive images depicted popular tourist destinations, cute and friendly animals, and candies. The negative images depicted objects, places, and events such as needles, prison, a funeral, and dangerous animals.

Participants were then asked to sit down on the bench to complete a survey. We had placed a sign advertising the study directly in front of the bench, and the experimenter unobtrusively recorded the number of characters and spaces between the resting experimenter and the seated participant. The sign (''PARTICIPATE IN A STUDY FOR $3!!!'') contained a total of 32 evenly spaced characters and spaces (3 in. per character or space). The questionnaire asked participants to indicate the extent to which their affective state was positive or negative, using two unipolar 9-point scales. This manipulation check was followed by demographic questions. Participants were then paid, debriefed, and thanked for their participation.

Results

Manipulation Check. On the combined affect rating scales, participants who viewed the positive media images reported feeling significantly more positive ($M = 6.0$, $SD = 1.36$) than participants who saw the negative media images ($M = 4.4$, $SD = 1.90$), $t(33) = 2.735$, $p < .01$.

Seating Distance. We conducted a 2 (affect: positive vs. negative) × 2 (culture: Western vs. East Asian) analysis of variance on seating distance and found a significant interaction between affect and culture, $F(1, 31) = 8.893$, $p = .006$, $\eta_p^2 = 223$, indicating that participants' cultural background moderated the

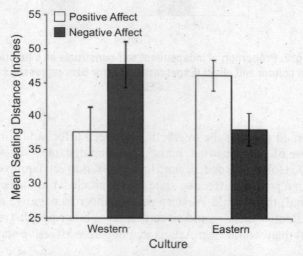

Fig. 3. Mean seating distance (in inches) from the resting experimenter as a function of culture and affect (Experiment 4). Error bars represent ±1 SEM.

effect of affect on seating distance. The pattern of results supported our hypotheses. Western participants in a positive affective state sat closer to the confederate than Western participants in a negative affective state, $F(1, 31) = 5.26$, $p = .026$, $\eta_p^2 = 145$ (see Fig. 3). However, East Asians in a positive affective state sat further from the confederate than East Asians in a negative affective state, $F(1, 31) = 3.67$, $p = .06$, $\eta_p^2 = 106$. Experiment 4 found that affect influenced an implicit measure of self-construal, how close to a confederate participants sat. As in the previous experiments, participants acted in a less culturally consistent manner when experiencing positive affect than when experiencing negative affect.

General discussion

Across four experiments, we found support for the moderating influence of affect on the expression of culturally normative cognitions and behaviors. Experiments 1 and 2 found that Westerners and East Asians who were experiencing positive affect expressed values and behaviors that were less consistent with their culture than did Westerners and East Asians who were experiencing negative affect. Experiments 3 and 4 demonstrated that affect also fundamentally shifts an individual's mode of self-representation toward or away from culturally based self-construals, with Westerners expressing more interdependent self-construals when they experienced positive rather than negative affect, and Easterners expressing more independent self-construals when they experienced positive rather than negative affect. The same pattern of results occurred regardless of how affect was manipulated (music, pictures, recall task, or facial feedback) or how cultural expressions were measured. Thus, these experiments demonstrate a robust moderation of the expression of culture by affective state.

This study provides the first evidence that positive affect encourages individuals to explore ideas and behaviors that are inconsistent with those prescribed as culturally normative. These results also show that the tendency to "broaden and build" when in a positive affective state (Fredrickson, 2001) extends to the self-concept: Individuals not only expand their thought and behavior repertoires, but also demonstrate self-expansion by incorporating culture-inconsistent representations into their self-concept. Our results also contribute to research demonstrating the functional utility of negative affect as a cue that one needs to reaffirm "tried and true" modes of relating to the social world because one's current thoughts or behaviors are not adaptive (Baumeister & Leary, 1995; Frijda, 1986; Lazarus, 1991; Schwarz, 1990; Tesser, 1988, 2000). However, the present experiments go beyond previous research by demonstrating for the first time that negative affect leads to the expression of culturally consistent thoughts, behaviors, and even self-construals, suggesting that affect may serve the functional purpose of attuning individuals more or less closely to their cultural heritage.

Unanswered Questions and Future Directions

One potentially interesting future direction is to examine whether or not allowing participants a chance to express culturally consistent values or behavior actually serves to reduce the experience or intensity of negative affect. A second important direction for future research is to explore the impact of specific emotions (e.g., happiness, sadness, anger, fear) on culturally normative behaviors. Although the present research showed a clear and robust effect for general positive and negative affective states, previous research has shown that inducing very specific emotions of similar valence, such as anger and fear, may produce different behavioral responses (e.g., Lerner & Keltner, 2001). Thus, future research should examine how specific emotions may differentially affect culturally normative behavior.

We believe our findings also speak to the notion of the phenomenal self—the parts of the self that are viewed and experienced in the moment (Jones & Gerard, 1967). Whereas previous research has highlighted the impact of situations and motivations on the moment-to-moment construction of the self (Rhodewalt & Agustsdottir, 1986), the present research has shown that the phenomenal self is also influenced by the combination of affective state and culture. The self is not a static state but a dynamic force, constructed from the situation, from one's culture, and from one's affective state.

The Link Between Culture and Affect

Although prior research has found that culture predicts affective responses (Markus & Kitayama, 1994), the current findings have established the reverse causal direction, showing that affect can also determine the expression of culture. These reciprocal forces between affect and culture create the current self: Who one is— one's behaviors, cognitions, and self-construals—at any given point in time depends on the fundamental interplay between affect and culture.

REFERENCES

Ashton-James, C. E., van Baaren, R., Chartrand, T. L., & Decety, J. (2007). Mimicry and me: The impact of mimicry on self-construal. *Social Cognition, 25*, 410–427.

Baumeister, R. F., & Leary, M. R. (1995). The need to belong: Desire for interpersonal attachments as a fundamental human motivation. *Psychological Bulletin, 117*, 497–529.

Cacioppo, J. T., Gardner, W. L., & Berntson, G. G. (1999). The affect system has parallel and integrative processing components: Form follows function. *Journal of Personality and Social Psychology, 76*, 839–855.

Carver, C. S., & Scheier, M. F. (1990). On the origins and functions of positive and negative affect. *Psychological Review, 97*, 19–35.

Cousins, S. D. (1989). Culture and self-perception in Japan and the United States. *Journal of Personality and Social Psychology, 56*, 124–131.

Fredrickson, B. L. (2001). The role of positive emotions in positive psychology: The broaden-and-build theory of positive emotions. *American Psychologist, 56*, 218–226.

Frijda, N. H. (1986). *The emotions.* Cambridge, England: Cambridge University Press.

Gable, P., & Harmon-Jones, E. (2008). Approach-motivated positive affect reduces breadth of attention. *Psychological Science, 19*, 476–482.

Gardner, W. L., Gabriel, S., & Lee, A. Y. (1999). ''I'' value freedom, but ''we'' value relationships: Self-construal priming mirrors cultural differences in judgment. *Psychological Science, 10*, 324–330.

Higgins, E. T. (1996). Ideals, oughts, and regulatory focus: Affect and motivation from distinct pains and pleasures. In P. M. Gollwitzer & J. A. Bargh (Eds.), *The psychology of action: Linking cognition and motivation to behavior* (pp. 91–114). New York: Guilford Press.

Higgins, E. T. (1997). Beyond pleasure and pain. *American Psychologist, 52*, 1280–1300.

Holland, R. W., Roeder, U., van Baaren, R. B., Brandt, A., & Hannover, B. (2004). Don't stand so close to me: Self-construal and interpersonal closeness. *Psychological Science, 15*, 237–242.

Johnson, E., & Tversky, A. (1983). Affect, generalization, and the perception of risk. *Journal of Personality and Social Psychology, 45*, 20–31.

Jones, E. E., & Gerard, H. B. (1967). *Fundamentals of social psychology.* New York: John Wiley and Sons.

Kahneman, D. (1999). Objective happiness. In D. Kahneman, E. Diener, & N. Schwarz (Eds.), *Well-being: Foundations of hedonic psychology* (pp. 3–25). New York: Russell Sage Foundation Press.

Kim, H. S., & Markus, H. R. (1999). Deviance or uniqueness, harmony or conformity? A cultural analysis. *Journal of Personality and Social Psychology, 77*, 785–800.

Kim, H. S., & Markus, H. R. (2002). Freedom of speech and freedom of silence: An analysis of talking as a cultural practice. In R. Shweder, M. Minow, & H. R. Markus (Eds.), *Engaging cultural differences: The multicultural challenge in liberal democracies* (pp. 432–452). New York: Russell Sage Foundation.

Kim, H. S., & Sherman, D. K. (2007). ''Express yourself'': Culture and the effect of self-expression on choice. *Journal of Personality and Social Psychology, 92*, 1–11.

Kuhn, M. H., & McPartland, T. S. (1954). An empirical investigation of self-attitudes. *American Sociological Review, 19*, 68–76.

Lazarus, R. S. (1991). *Emotion and adaptation.* Oxford, England: Oxford University Press.

Lerner, J. S., & Keltner, D. (2001). Fear, anger, and risk. *Journal of Personality and Social Psychology, 81*, 146–159.

Markus, H. R., & Kitayama, S. (1991). Culture and the self: Implications for cognition, emotion, and motivation. *Psychological Review, 98*, 224–253.

Markus, H. R., & Kitayama, S. (1994). The cultural construction of self and emotion: Implications for social behavior. In S. Kitayama & H.R. Markus (Eds.), *Emotion and culture: Empirical studies of mutual influence* (pp. 89–130). Washington, DC: American Psychological Association Press.

Raghunathan, R., & Pham, M. T. (1999). All negative moods are not created equal: Motivational influences of anxiety and sadness on decision making. *Organizational Behavior and Human Decision Processes, 79*, 56–77.

Rhodewalt, F., & Agustsdottir, S. (1986). Effects of self-presentation on the phenomenal self. *Journal of Personality and Social Psychology, 50*, 47–55.

Schwarz, N. (1990). Feelings as information: Informational and motivational functions of affective states. In E.T. Higgins & R.M. Sorrentino (Eds.), *Handbook of motivation and cognition: Vol. 2. Foundations of social behavior* (pp. 527–561). New York: Guilford Press.

Schwarz, N., & Clore, G. L. (2007). Feelings and phenomenal experiences. In E.T. Higgins & A. Kruglanski (Eds.), *Social psychology: A handbook of basic principles* (2nd ed., pp. 385–407). New York: Guilford Press.

Strack, F., Martin, L. L., & Stepper, S. (1988). Inhibiting and facilitating conditions of the human smile: A nonobtrusive test of the facial feedback hypothesis. *Journal of Personality and Social Psychology, 54*, 768–777.

Tesser, A. (1988). Toward a self-evaluation maintenance model of social behavior. In L. Berkowitz (Ed.), *Advances in experimental social psychology* (Vol. 21, pp. 181–227). New York: Academic Press.

Tesser, A. (2000). On the confluence of self-esteem maintenance mechanisms. *Personality and Social Psychology Review, 4*, 290–299.

Triandis, H. C. (1995). *Individualism and collectivism*. San Francisco: Westview Press.

Yamagishi, T., Hashimoto, H., & Schug, J. (2008). Preferences versus strategies as explanations for culture-specific behavior. *Psychological Science, 19*, 579–584.

Social Influence on Political Judgments: The Case of Presidential Debates

As discussed in Chapter 7 (Conformity) of the text, informational conformity is a form of social influence that occurs in ambiguous situations when people seek to imitate others because they are not sure about what to do and they don't want to do the wrong thing. The researchers of this study, Fein, Goethals, and Kugler, suggest that presidential debates are such ambiguous situations, too complex for most people to understand on their own. They therefore theorized that participants who were asked to view and evaluate presidential debates would look to others for informational clues and conform to others' thinking. Four experiments were carried out to test that hypothesis. In the first and second experiments, participants watched the 1984 Reagan-Mondale debate unedited, or with either the "sound bites" or the audience's reaction to them deleted. In the third experiment, participants received false feedback about the reaction of others in the room to the same debate. Finally, in the fourth experiment, participants viewed the 1992 Bush-Clinton presidential debate on the day it was aired, in two groups, in the company of confederates who loudly supported either Bush or Clinton and jeered the other. In all four studies, there was clear evidence for informational conformity, with participants being influenced by the audience reactions, the false feedback, or the confederates in the room.

SOCIAL INFLUENCE ON POLITICAL JUDGMENTS: THE CASE OF PRESIDENTIAL DEBATES

Steven Fein

Williams College

George R. Goethals

University of Richmond

Matthew B. Kugler

Princeton University

Four experiments investigated the extent to which judgments of candidate performance in presidential debates could be influenced by the mere knowledge of others' reactions. In Experiments 1 and 2 participants watched an intact version of a debate or an edited version in which either "soundbite" one-liners or the audience reaction to those soundbites were removed. In Experiment 3 participants saw what was supposedly the reaction of their fellow participants on screen during the debate. Participants in Experiment 4 were exposed to the reactions of live confederates as they watched the last

Steven Fein, George R. Goethals, and Matthew B. Kugler, "Social Influence on Political Judgments: The Case of Presidential Debates," Political Psychology, Vol. 28, No. 2, pp. 165-192. Reprinted with permission of Blackwell Publishing, Inc. 0162-895X © 2007 International Society of Political Psychology
Published by Blackwell Publishing. Inc., 350 Main Street, Malden, MA 02148, USA, 9600 Garsington Road, Oxford, OX4 2DQ, and PO Box 378 Carlton South, 3053 Victoria Australia

debate of an active presidential campaign. In all studies, audience reactions produced large shifts in participants' judgments of performance. The results illustrate the power of social context to strongly influence individuals' judgments of even large amounts of relevant, important information, and they support the categorization of presidential debates as ambiguous stimuli, fertile ground for informational social influence.

KEYWORDS: presidential debates, conformity, ambiguity, informational social influence, political communication

Ronald Reagan leans back and enjoys the moment. It is the second of his two presidential debates with Walter Mondale as they near the finish line to the 1984 U.S. presidential election. He has just delivered his famous line: "I will not make age an issue of this campaign. I am not going to exploit, for political purposes, my opponent's youth and inexperience." The question had been a difficult one, asking about Reagan's advanced age and the concerns raised by his performance in the first debate, but his answer has satisfied the audience and they are cheering. The moderator, Henry Trewhitt, says "I'd like to head for the fence and try to catch that one before it goes over." The newspapers soon report that Reagan's response has erased concerns over his age. Reagan's declining poll numbers quickly returned to their previously high levels. He wins reelection in 1984 in a 49-state landslide.

The above events could all be seen as independently stemming from Reagan's answer. The audience heard it, and applauded; the moderator heard it, and praised him; the newspapers heard it, and stopped discussing the age issue; the public heard it, and voted for him. But these events could also be seen as describing a causal path. The audience heard it and they applauded, the moderator heard the applause and praised Reagan's answer, and so on. The difference between these two ways of looking at what happened is that one, the latter, does not give the actors much credit. After the initial applause, everyone is part of the herd, running smoothly down preset tracks, conforming to the example set by a small studio audience that was neither better nor wiser than they. In American culture, great value is set on independence. One of the primary sources of enthusiasm for debates is the belief that they help the public makes up its own mind by allowing them to cut through the superficial. Our second, uncharitable, interpretation of these events is quite worrisome from this individualistic perspective, but that does not mean it is wrong.

While many studies have examined conformity in basic laboratory settings, none exists that explore how it may affect assessments of such complex and important real world events as presidential debates. Millions of people watch debates, discuss them, and read and watch analyses of the candidates' performances. They have been shown to play a role in the outcome of every campaign in which they have been held, and they may have been decisive in several (e.g., 1960, 1980, 1992, and 2000). Is conformity an important determinant of people's reactions to them?

While we do not know whether potential voters simply conform to the reactions of other viewers, we do know that contextual features of debates—for example, what network commentators say about them and whether citizens watch them on television or listen to them on the radio—make a difference (Kaid & Bystrom, 1999; Schroeder, 2000). An overall conclusion from Kraus's (1962) volume on *The Great Debates* of 1960 between John F. Kennedy and Richard M. Nixon was that the debates mattered whether people watched them or not. There was so much discussion, especially of Kennedy's performance in the first of the four debates, that a social reality took shape holding that Kennedy had "won" the debates, and this perception very likely was an important factor in the outcome of a very close election. Similarly, media commentary following the Ford-Carter foreign policy debate in 1976 contributed substantially to both the salience and negative evaluation of Ford's statement that there was no Soviet domination of Eastern Europe (Steeper, 1978). McKinnon, Tedesco, and Kaid (1993) showed that network commentary after the 1992 debates between George Bush, Bill Clinton, and Ross Perot lessened Clinton's perceived margins of victory, and McKinnon and Tedesco (1999) showed that network commentary following the 1996 debates raised perceivers' assessments of both Bill Clinton and Bob Dole. While it is not entirely predictable how commentators' appraisals might affect voter opinion, it seems clear that they can and do.

Considering the influence of audience reaction specifically, some elements of the social influence literature suggest that they would produce little conformity in judging presidential debates. First, social influence often produces public compliance (Kiesler & Kiesler, 1969) through normative social influence, where people conform essentially to be liked by their peers. Debate evaluations poorly fit that mold. There is little normative pressure to conform to debate audiences; viewers are not threatened for failing to cheer when their fellows do, especially not when the fellows in question are a studio audience on the other side of the country. And debates are important in that they can affect private voting behavior on Election Day, when people will be answering to no one but themselves. When considering voting behavior, we must limit ourselves primarily to informational social influence, conformity that works on a person's desire to be right, not their desire to be liked (Deutsch & Gerard, 1955).

Debate audiences supply little fodder for informational social influence. Their reactions do little more than provide knowledge of others' judgments. They do not present arguments or reasons for those judgments. This stands in contrast to the separate processes of pre- and post-debate spin, which do provide at least some argumentation and analysis. Thus audience reactions provide information about the judgments of other people, but not the reasons for their judgments, and, as noted above, they apply little normative pressure to conform to or to adopt those judgments. In such situations, the actions of the others provide only information about the typical or predominant response to the situation and, therefore, what the appropriate response for the individual might be.

How likely is it that this seemingly limited form of social influence can affect a real-world judgment, one that we assume not only is important but also that most people believe is important? While we are intuitively drawn to doubt that people would conform on important tasks, conformity research does show that not only trivial laboratory judgments about the length of lines (Asch, 1951) or the movement of lights (Sherif, 1936), but also substantially more important, real-world questions, such as whether New Jersey is really being invaded by Martians (Cantril, 1940), can be heavily influenced by other people's reactions. Still, most of the research on social influence concerns judgments made in the laboratory and its external validity is often unknown. And even laboratory experiments show that conformity is often reduced when judgments are made more consequential (Baron, Vandello, & Brunsman, 1996). In a somewhat related vein, theory and research supporting the Elaboration Likelihood Model of persuasion indicate that individuals are less likely to be influenced by factors peripheral to the content of a message when the issue is an important one (Petty & Cacioppo, 1986).

With these considerations in mind, the literature suggests that conformity to studio audiences in debates should be weak. As noted, there is little interpersonal or normative pressure, no explanations are provided to explain the audience behavior, and the judgment is important, giving the participant every reason to work for accuracy. Is there any reason to think this limited form of social influence could affect such important judgments?

The results of McKinnon et al. (1993)'s research concerning the 1992 presidential debates suggested that viewers may typically process the debates at a relatively shallow, heuristic level. To the extent that this is the case, individuals are more likely to be susceptible to social influence and other factors peripheral to the content of the debate. Another reason is suggested by a finding in the Baron et al. study cited above. They showed that importance reduces conformity on clear-cut judgments, but not when the judgment is ambiguous. Are presidential debates clear stimuli? In reconstructing debates, people often see them as having clear outcomes. Commentators tell narrative-style stories explaining how candidates won or lost: Michael Dukakis as the unnatural "Iceman" in 1988, George H. W. Bush as the disconnected elitist in 1992, John Kennedy as the unexpected professional in 1960. After the tales are told enough times, it becomes hard to imagine that things could be seen any other way.

It is not obvious, though, that we should accept this retrospective consensus as good evidence that debates are clear stimuli. As noted above, audience and media reactions that accompany debates are a major part of the unfolding political stories. While it could be that the debates really are clear, it could also be that perceptions of debates are instead largely a function of how studio audiences, debate panelists, and various professional commentators respond and the narratives they construct. Would Lloyd Bentsen telling Dan Quayle that he was "no Jack Kennedy" in the 1988 vice-presidential debate (Germond & Witcover, 1989) have been as memorable if the audience hadn't reacted loudly? Polls show, for example, that Al Gore in 2000 (Jamieson & Waldman, 2002) and Gerald Ford in 1976 (Sears & Chaffee, 1979) both won debates in their immediate aftermath but lost them in the post-debate spin wars, Ford to Eastern European immigrants who felt quite sure that their homelands were under Soviet domination and Gore to parodies of him on the television show *Saturday Night Live*.

A critical question, then, is whether presidential debates constitute an ambiguous stimulus. Certainly debates provide a rich and substantial physical reality. Therefore individuals might not be much influenced by other people's reactions. Furthermore, people may have strong candidate preferences going into a debate and, often, strong expectations that their candidate will win, with the result that they have clear perceptions of exactly who won (their candidate) and little susceptibility to social influence. Sigelman and Sigelman's study (1984) on the Carter-Reagan debates found many people do exactly that, as did Sears and Chaffee's (1979) review of studies on the 1976 debates. On the other hand, the complex physical reality of debates might be difficult to interpret, leaving participants open to outside "help" as has been seen in studies of pre- and post-debate spin (Fein, Frost, Goethals, & Kassin, 1994; Kugler & Goethals, 2005; Norton & Goethals, 2004). This perspective suggests a high potential for conformity effects. Because of the influence of debates in our modern political arrangements, it seems important to find out.

Four experiments are reported below. In the first three experiments, participants watched parts or all of the second 1984 Mondale-Reagan debate, approximately a decade (from 9 to 12 years) after the debate occurred. In the first of these studies, participants watched parts of the debates under one of three conditions: a pure, unaltered format; with two "soundbites" deleted; or with the soundbites remaining but the audience reaction to them deleted. With this design, we could isolate the effects of the content of the soundbites versus the effects of the audience reaction to those soundbites. Experiment 2 used a similar design, but in this study participants saw the entire 90-minute debate, rather than excerpts from the debate. Participants in Experiment 3 watched the excerpts from this debate, but saw superimposed on the video screen alleged real-time tracking of other people's reactions. The fourth experiment we report was actually conducted before the first three, in October of 1992 on the night of the third debate between George Bush, Bill Clinton, and Ross Perot. It is reported last because it addresses a key "external reality" question lurking in the background of the first three. That is, can real voters be influenced by the reactions of others when watching a debate in real time, when it is actually broadcast, when there are real levels of engagement and resistance? In this study, participants watched the debate either in the presence of several confederates who cheered for pro-Bush remarks, in the presence of several confederates who cheered for pro-Clinton remarks, or with no confederates.

In all four experiments, the main dependent variables were participants' judgments of each candidate's overall performance and personal qualities. Because we believe that presidential debates are, in fact, rather ambiguous stimuli and ripe for social influence, we predicted for all these experiments that the cues from the studio audience or from the participants' peers around them would significantly influence participants' judgments and that this social influence would emerge despite the large amount of relevant content expressed by the candidates during the debate.

Experiment 1

With recent presidential debates including the presence of a live studio audience, political commentators have suggested that too often debates turn on simpleminded soundbites, one-liners, slogans, and canned mini-speeches designed to elicit resounding applause (Sigelman, 1992; Zarevsky, 1992). In 1980, Ronald Reagan buried Jimmy Carter in a televised debate the moment he shook his head and, with a tone of sorrow in his voice, delivered the fatal blow, "There you go again." Four years later, with concerns being raised about his age and mental acumen, Reagan turned around his faltering campaign with his one-liner noted above: "I am not going to exploit...my opponent's youth and inexperience." Then in 1988, Lloyd Bentsen stopped Dan Quayle in his tracks by responding to Quayle's self-comparison to John F. Kennedy with the unforgettable line, "You're no Jack Kennedy." In all instances, live audiences loudly erupted with some combination of cheers, laughter, boos, and applause.

Our first experiment addressed two questions. First, how much impact do such memorable moments really have on people's judgments of a candidate's overall performance? It is part of the political lore that debate outcomes, and perhaps elections as well, may turn on these isolated moments. However, it may be that because one-liners constitute only a tiny fraction of what transpires in a debate, they actually have little effect on overall evaluations. To answer this question our first experiment presented a 40-minute debate segment either with or without one-liners and the audience reaction they generated. Second—and in the context of issues about social influence, perhaps a more interesting question—is it the content of the one-liners themselves, or just the audience reaction to them, that is responsible for any impact the soundbite moments might have? To answer this question we included a condition in which the candidate's remarks, but not the reaction to them, were presented. Thus we compared an unedited 40-minute segment with two edited variations—one that deleted the soundbite exchanges in their entirety and one that deleted just the audience reaction to the relevant one-liners.

Method

Participants and Design. Fifty-three introductory psychology students participated in exchange for course credit. By random assignment, participants saw one of three versions of a debate. One tape included two soundbites and the positive reactions they had drawn from the audience. In a second version, the soundbites and reactions were both deleted from the tape. In a third version, the soundbites were included but the audience reactions to them were not.

Procedure. Participants completed a brief pre-debate questionnaire in which they described their own party affiliation, level of involvement, and political orientation.[1] Next they were shown a 40-minute segment of the second (and final) 1984 debate between Reagan and Mondale. The focus of this debate was on foreign policy. Participants were randomly assigned to watch one of three versions of the videotape. In the *control* condition, the tape included two remarks by Reagan, both of which drew loud cheers and laughter from members of the live audience (each remark-reaction segment lasted for

---

[1] In each of the four studies, we analyzed the main and interactive effects of a variety of individual differences, including participants' gender, political party affiliation, degree of involvement and interest in politics, and so forth. In these studies, there were approximately equal numbers of men and women (all were undergraduates at Williams College). In each study, the majority of the participants identified themselves as Democrats (ranging from 51% of the sample to 57%; the percentage identifying themselves as Republican ranged from 12% to 26%, with the remaining identifying themselves as Independent or having no party affiliation). In less than half the analyses across the four studies, a significant main effect for party affiliation emerged, but in the slight majority of analyses, there was no significant difference as a function of party. No significant interactions between party affiliation and any of our independent variables emerged. In each study, there were no reliable gender differences, nor reliable differences as a function of any of the other measures of individual differences that we took. We therefore do not report the analyses as a function of these subject variables in the Results sections of these studies.

approximately 30 seconds). The first remark concerned a TV ad in which Mondale projected an image of strength by standing on the deck of the Aircraft Carrier Nimitz. Reagan quipped, "If he had had his way when the Nimitz was being planned, he would have been deep in the water out there, because there wouldn't have been any Nimitz to stand on. He was against it." Later, in response to an expected question concerning his age and mental competence, Reagan delivered the memorable remark with which we opened this paper: "I will not exploit, for political purposes, my opponent's youth and inexperience." In the *soundbite-deleted* condition both one-liners—as well as the reactions they had elicited—were deleted. In the *reaction-deleted* condition, Reagan's remarks were included but the audience's reactions were deleted.[2]

Following the tape, participants rated the two candidates for their overall performance on 0–100-point scales. They were also asked to indicate which candidate (or neither) they thought won the debate. Participants then answered additional questions concerning each candidate's handling of key substantive issues (Central America policy, the Middle East, and national defense) and personal character (sense of humor, intelligence, likeability, strength, competence, sincerity, and leadership). Finally, participants were asked if they were transported back in time to the 1984 campaign, who they thought they would have voted for.

Results and Discussion

Overall Performance. A series of one-way analyses of variance (ANOVAs) on the ratings of each candidate's performance, as well as the difference between these ratings, revealed significant effects as a function of condition. As can be seen in Fig. 1, participants in the control condition tended to rate Reagan's performance much more positively than they rated Mondale's, reflecting the popular opinion of the debate back in 1984. Indicating the importance of the two brief soundbites, however, Fig. 1 illustrates that this advantage enjoyed by Reagan disappeared and was even slightly reversed when the soundbites were deleted (Reagan's 7.50-point advantage in the control condition switched to a 7.63 disadvantage in the soundbite-deleted condition), $F(1, 50) = 6.82$, $p < .02$. Most interestingly, the reversal is even more pronounced in the condition in which the content of the soundbites was left in, but the audience reaction to them was deleted (Reagan's average rating was 23.57 points below Mondale's), $F(1, 50) = 24.29$, $p < .0001$. The results switched from an apparent victory for Reagan in the control condition to a decisive victory for Mondale in the condition in which the *content* was identical to the control condition but the audience reaction to the soundbites was eliminated.

Examining the ratings of each candidate independently, ratings of Reagan's performance varied significantly as a function of our manipulation, $F(2, 50) = 4.71$, $p < .02$. It is interesting to note that relative to the ratings in the control condition of Reagan's performance ($M = 66.25$), the ratings in the soundbite-deleted condition did not drop significantly ($M = 65.40$, $F < 1$), but the ratings in the reaction-deleted condition did decrease significantly ($M = 49.29$, $F(1, 50) = 7.89$, $p < .008$). It was the audience reaction to Reagan's soundbites, rather than the soundbites themselves, that made the critical difference in judgments of his performance.

Although the soundbites were made by Reagan, evaluations of Mondale were also significantly affected by our manipulations; in this case with participants rating Mondale more positively in the soundbite-deleted and reaction-deleted conditions than in the control condition ($Ms = 73.03$, 72.86, and 58.75, respectively), $F(2, 50) = 8.59$, $p < .001$. The effects of the manipulation on ratings of Mondale's performance were similar conceptually to results from other research illustrating the implicit effects on a candidate whose opponent is the target of spin (Kugler & Goethals, 2005; Norton & Goethals, 2004).

---

[2] There was occasional, very brief audience applause sprinkled in with the candidates' responses during other parts of the debate, but the reaction was always mild and fleeting. No sustained applause, jeering, or any other reactions could be heard anywhere on the tape, with the exception of the two soundbites in the control condition.

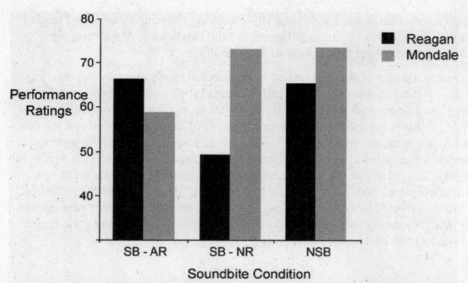

Fig. 1. Post-debate performance ratings of Reagan and Mondale in Experiment 1 as a function of whether the clips contained the soundbites and the audience reaction (SB-AR), the soundbites with no audience reaction (SB-NR), or no soundbites (NSB).

Participants in this study also responded to the question of which candidate they thought won the debate. Here again the manipulation had a significant effect on participants' responses, X^2 (2, $N = 53$) = 17.75, $p < .002$. A majority of the participants in the control condition thought Reagan won the debate (60% versus 15% for Mondale and 25% judging that neither won), whereas most participants in the soundbite-deleted condition thought either neither won (42.11%) or Mondale won (42.11%), and, even more striking, a large majority in the reaction-deleted condition thought Mondale won (71.43% versus 7.14% for Reagan and 21.43% for neither).

For the question of who they would have voted for, there was not a significant difference between the control and the soundbite-deleted conditions, but there was a dramatic difference between these conditions and the reaction-deleted condition, with the percentage of participants indicating they would have voted for Reagan dropping from 51.28% to 14.29%, and those indicating they would have voted for Mondale increasing from 33.33% to 71.43% (and the remaining participants indicating no preference), X^2 (2, $N = 53$) = 6.85, $p < .04$.

Candidates' Qualities. The presence of the soundbites and audience reactions also affected perceptions of each candidate's personal character. On a composite measure that combined mean ratings of intelligence, likeability, leadership, sense of humor, strength, competence, and sincerity ($\alpha = .91$), Reagan was viewed less favorably in the reaction-deleted condition than in the control and soundbite-deleted conditions ($Ms = 61.22$ compared to 70.25 and 72.23, respectively), $F(2, 50) = 2.81$, $p < .07$—a pattern of results that was strongest on ratings of Reagan's sense of humor ($M = 83.50$ in the control condition, 75.79 in the soundbite-deleted condition, 63.21 in the reaction-deleted condition; $F(2, 50) = 6.11$, $p < .005$) and intelligence ($Ms = 67.75$ versus 71.16 versus 55.71, respectively; $F(2, 50) = 4.67$, $p < .02$). As with overall performance ratings, evaluations of Mondale's personal character ($\alpha = .87$) were also significantly affected by soundbites and audience reactions, $F(2, 50) = 4.56$, $p < .02$—particularly on ratings of his leadership, $F(2, 50) = 5.30$, $p < .005$. Remarkably, participants perceived Mondale as having significantly less leadership ability when they watched the original control debate ($M = 62.75$) than when they saw the tape without Reagan's soundbites ($M = 75.53$) or without positive audience reactions ($M = 75.00$).

Summary. Participants' ratings of the candidates' overall performance and specific qualities were affected significantly by our manipulation. Reagan was seen as the clear victor in the debate in the unedited, control condition, but this victory was lost with the deletion of the two brief, but apparently critical, soundbites. Deleting the reaction to the soundbites while keeping the soundbites intact tended to have a much bigger effect on participants' relative judgments of the candidates, illustrating the relative importance of the social context over the content of the soundbite.

Relative to the control conditions, ratings of Reagan tended to be affected much more by the deletion of the audience reaction than the deletion of the soundbite itself, whereas ratings of Mondale tended to be affected equally by these two conditions. Although it is only speculation, perhaps the content of the soundbites affected ratings of Mondale more because he was the target of them, particularly of the one in which Reagan mocked Mondale's record on defense. That soundbite may have presented a strong negative for Mondale, although it may not have counted for ratings of Reagan himself all that much. In any case, and most importantly, it is clear that the relative ratings of Reagan and Mondale were influenced strongly by both independent manipulations, and that, overall, the deletion of the audience reaction had a particularly strong effect. The content of Reagan's responses may have hurt perceptions of Mondale, but it was only with the strong validation of the responses by the audience and moderator that they made participants see Reagan much more positively.

Experiment 2

The results of Experiment 1 indicated that viewers of the 1984 debate between Reagan and Mondale were highly influenced not only by two remarks in the context of a substantive 40-minute debate excerpt, but also by others' reactions to those remarks. When the remarks were heard but the audience reactions taken out, the validation of these remarks as a significant "home run" for Reagan appeared to evaporate.

In light of the provocative implications of these results, a second experiment was designed to replicate these results and to address further three questions. One question is whether these effects would emerge in the context of the full 90-minute debate. With so much information presented in a full 90 minutes of debate, would the effects of two brief soundbites, or the reactions to these soundbites, be strong enough to influence participants' ultimate judgments? Moreover, we felt that using the full debate would increase the study's external validity. A second question addressed in this experiment was whether participants perceived the soundbites to be memorable and noteworthy in the absence of audience reactions. That is, was the content of Reagan's remarks really effective and meaningful in the context of the entire debate, or did they become so in part because of the snowballing reaction of the moderator and audience? To examine this question, we added an item to the post-debate questionnaire asking the participants to list several key moments in the debate.

Third, we worried that having participants sit through an entire 90-minute-long debate would cause the participants to get antsy and stop paying attention after a while. We thought it might help to interrupt the tape halfway through and ask the participants some questions about the debate, and then resume the tape after that break. This both would provide a break and would remind the participants that we would be asking them questions about the debate. We worried, though, that this could reduce the external validity of the study, and, perhaps, have some carry-over effects on the final measures. To allay these concerns, we randomly assigned half the participants to watch the entire debate without interruption, whereas the other half were asked questions approximately midway through the debate.[3]

---

[3] We originally had a fourth question in mind when designing this experiment: Would individual differences in need for cognition moderate our effects? Prior research suggested that audience reaction is a peripheral cue, influencing only participants who are low in involvement or in the need for cognition (Axsom, Yates, & Chaiken, 1987). This same study, however, did not find such a limitation on effects concerning participants' perceptions of a persuasive speaker, as distinct from that speaker's message. We administered Cacioppo and Petty's (1982) Need for Cognition Scale in Experiment 2 in order to determine whether individual differences in need for cognition would moderate our effects. As with the other measures of individual differences that we used in the various

Method

Participants and Design. One hundred and seven introductory psychology students participated in this experiment for course credit. Participants were randomly assigned to one of six cells produced by a 3 (control versus no soundbite-deleted versus no reaction-deleted) × 2 (mid-debate ratings versus post-debate ratings only) factorial design.

Procedure. The procedure was similar to that of Experiment 1 with four exceptions. First, as explained in footnote 3, participants filled out the Need for Cognition Scale as part of their pre-debate questionnaire. Second, participants were shown a videotape of the entire 90-minute debate rather than the 40-minute excerpt previously used. Third, for half the participants, we stopped the debate at the halfway point and had the participants make ratings of the candidates' performance up to that point, explaining to them that these ratings were only their sense of how the debate was going thus far and that their final judgments may or may not be quite different from them. After a brief break, the rest of the debate was shown, after which participants filled out the complete set of ratings. Fourth, to examine whether participants were aware of the impact of the soundbites (i.e., for self-report purposes), they were asked on the final questionnaire to describe two or three "highlights" of the debate. We also shortened the final questionnaire a bit from the first study, in part to give the participants more time to complete this new question.

Results and Discussion

The manipulation of whether or not participants completed mid-debate ratings had no effect on any of the results. We therefore report only the main effects of the manipulation of the presence or absence of the soundbites and audience reaction.

Overall Performance. As in our previous study, the post-debate ratings of each candidate's performance constituted the primary dependent measure. Consistent with the results of Experiment 1, the relative ratings of the candidates in this study varied as a function of our manipulation. As can be seen in Fig. 2, in this study Reagan's and Mondale's performances were judged virtually equally in the control condition, but Reagan tended to be rated more negatively than Mondale in the other two conditions—particularly in the condition in which the soundbite remained but the audience reaction was deleted.

The ratings of each candidate's performance were subjected to separate 3 (soundbite manipulation) × 2 (obtaining measures twice versus only after the debate) ANOVAs. The ANOVA revealed a significant main effect for the soundbite manipulation on ratings of Reagan, $F(2, 101) = 3.12, p < .05$. More specifically, Reagan received significantly higher ratings in the control condition than in the reaction-deleted condition (Ms = 59.32 & 48.09, respectively; $p < .05$ via Newman-Keuls test; $M = 52.81$ in the soundbite-deleted group). In contrast to Experiment 1, however, ratings of Mondale's performance were not significantly affected by the manipulation, $F < 1$.

Candidates' Qualities. As in Experiment 1, our manipulation influenced ratings of Reagan's character. On the same composite measure used in our prior studies (combined ratings of intelligence, sense of humor, likeability, leadership, strength, competence, sincerity), there was a significant main effect, $F(2, 101) = 3.21, p < .05$, as Reagan was viewed more favorably in the control condition than in the reaction-deleted condition (Ms = 65.94 and 55.85, respectively; $p < .05$ via Newman-Keuls test; $M = 62.03$ in the soundbite-deleted condition). This pattern was particularly strong in ratings of Reagan's intelligence, sense of humor, and likeability. Once again in contrast to the results of Experiment 1, the effect of the soundbites on evaluations of Mondale's character was not statistically significant, $F(2, 101) = 2.79, p < .10$.

---

studies, we did not find any significant relationship between participants' scores on this measure and their ratings of the candidates.

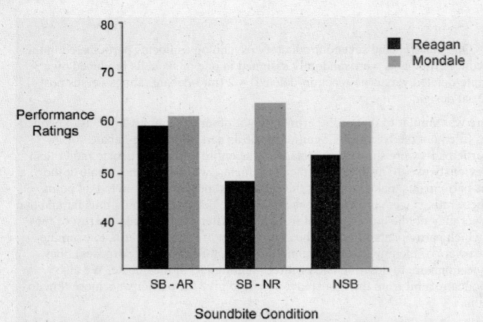

Fig. 2. Post-debate performance ratings of Reagan and Mondale in Experiment 2 as a function of whether the clips contained the soundbites and the audience reaction (SB-AR), the soundbites with no audience reaction (SB-NR), or no soundbites (NSB).

Were Soundbites Perceived as Significant?. Finally, participants were asked on the post-debate questionnaire to describe two or three highlights from the debate. These free-response data were coded for whether or not the participants included a soundbite on the list. The result was informative. Demonstrating the profound importance of audience reactions, 78% of all participants in the control condition included a soundbite among the highlights, compared to only 15% of those in the reaction-deleted condition, X^2 (2, $N = 74$) = 29.17, $p < .001$. In short, participants were impressed by the soundbites only when the remarks were followed by the strong reactions from the audience.

Summary. Supporting the results of the first experiment, participants in this study tended to offer very different relative ratings of the two candidates as a function of the presence or absence of the soundbites and the reaction to them. Although the results are more muted than in the first study, perhaps due to the extra 50 minutes of material—much of it quite dry—diluting the impact of these critical moments, it was still the case that participants' relative judgments were affected significantly. Whereas participants in the control condition perceived a very close debate, those in the condition in which the reactions to Reagan's two soundbites were deleted—representing less than a minute of time in a 90-minute debate about some of the most important issues facing the country—saw Mondale clearly outperforming Reagan. Moreover, absent the applause, laughter, and general approval of Reagan's one-liners, these responses were not seen as particularly noteworthy by the participants. With these audience reactions intact, however, the majority of the participants saw them as a highlight of the debate.

Experiment 3

Although pivotal soundbites stand out remarkably well in debate lore, they are rare, and often debates are won or lost in their absence. In the past several election cycles it is hard to locate defining moments in debates, even in debates with clear winners. The first Bush-Kerry debate of 2004, for example, was judged a clear Kerry win despite its lack of "zingers." Kerry's successes were seen holistically (as were his opponent's foibles). The same could be said of Kennedy's performance in the first debate of 1960. Therefore, conformity should also be examined in the—arguably more common—context of these victories by attrition.

Experiment 3 used segments of the 1984 debate in that light using a 10-minute tape that excludes the critical soundbites from the previous two experiments. Unlike in Experiments 1 and 2, this study did not use studio audience behavior as the independent variable. Rather, participants received false feedback concerning the alleged reactions of their peers in the room with them as they watched the debate together in a group.

The feedback was administered using a technology first displayed during the televised debates of 1992. For those events, the cable television news network, CNN, showed viewers continuous, real-time responses of focus-group members who were watching the debate in an auditorium and using hand-held response dials to record their changing impressions of the event. This computer-based technology thus provided TV viewers with real-time, public-opinion poll data. We used this technology to consistently insert audience feedback into each participant group, with participants being told that the displayed "data" were their own. This procedure enabled us to assess whether judgments of the candidates would be influenced by exposure to the group norm.

Method

Participants and Design. Ninety-four introductory psychology students participated in this study for course credit. Participants were run in groups of approximately 15–20 students. The groups were randomly assigned to either a pro-Reagan or pro-Mondale false feedback condition.

Procedure. The stimulus tape used in this study was a 10-minute segment consisting of excerpts of the second 1984 presidential debate between Reagan and Mondale. Upon their arrival at the laboratory, participants completed a brief pre-debate questionnaire and were then each given a wireless hand-held dial. Each dial was equipped with a digital display that indicates the current numerical setting—in this case, it was set to range from 0 (with the dial hand pointed to the far left) to 100 (with the dial hand pointed to the far right), and having a midpoint of 50 (with the hand pointed up at a 90-degree angle). Participants were told that they would see videotaped excerpts of a presidential debate and were instructed to set the dial at 50 and move it up or down to varying degrees to indicate their changing opinions during the debate. Before seeing the debate, participants got some practice using their dials, which also served to allay potential suspicions they may have had about the validity of these dials—as the experimenters demonstrated how they could tell what each participant's dial was set to at any given moment.

Participants in both groups were informed that they would receive continuous real-time feedback about their group's average opinion in the form of a line graph superimposed over the debate videotape. In fact, the feedback they received was false, pre-programmed to indicate that Reagan or Mondale was gaining in support over the other. In both groups, participants saw the same line graph begin at the neutral midpoint of 50 and move gradually, in a fluctuating pattern, to a final value of 85. For those in the pro-Reagan group, the 0–100 point response scale was defined in such a way that 50 meant that neither candidate was outperforming the other, that numbers higher than 50 meant that Reagan was outperforming Mondale, and that numbers lower than 50 meant that Mondale was outperforming Reagan; for those in the pro-Mondale condition, the scale was reversed. To guard against the possibility that a participant would turn his or her dial down to 0 or up to 100 and become suspicious of the false feedback manipulation when it appeared not to affect the group's average, participants were told that the most extreme high and low scores would always be excluded from the computation.[4]

After watching the tape, participants completed the same post-debate questionnaire as that used in the first experiment.

---

[4] It perhaps should be noted that participants found these dials to be easy to use and did not find them, or the superimposed graph, to be particularly distracting. The first author has used this technology in several studies in subsequent years (e.g., Fein, Hoshino-Browne, Davies, & Spencer, 2003), and it is extremely rare for any participants to be suspicious of or very distracted by it.

Results and Discussion

Overall Performance. Supporting the results of the first two studies, the results of Experiment 3 indicated that others' reactions can have a significant effect on individuals' judgments of the candidates' overall performance and personal qualities. As can be seen in Fig. 3, participants who saw a graph suggesting that their peers saw Reagan as winning the debate rated Reagan's performance more than 15 points better than Mondale's, whereas they rated Reagan's performance more than 20 points worse than Mondale's if they saw a graph suggesting that their peers saw Mondale perform better, resulting in a net difference of about 36 points, $F(1, 92) = 51.74$, $p < .0001$.

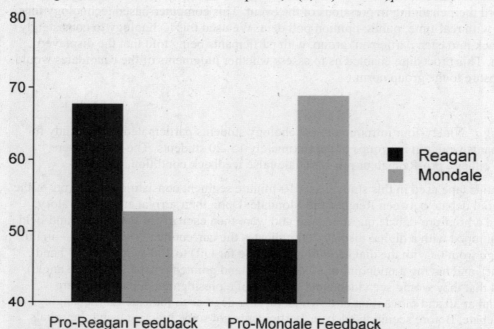

Fig. 3. Post-debate performance ratings of Reagan and Mondale in Experiment 3 as a function of whether participants were exposed to pro-Reagan or pro-Mondale feedback.

On ratings of each candidate's debate performance, the results again supported the hypothesis that participants would be influenced by the false normative feedback concerning the opinions of others in the room. Reagan's performance ratings were significantly higher in the pro-Reagan feedback condition than in the pro-Mondale condition ($Ms = 67.98$ versus 48.81), $F(1, 92) = 31.67$, $p < .001$. In contrast, Mondale's ratings were significantly higher in the pro-Mondale condition than in the pro-Reagan condition ($Ms = 69.17$ versus 52.69), $F(1, 92) = 30.03$, $p < .0001$.

A chi-square analysis on participants' responses to the questions of who won the debate (Reagan, Mondale, or neither) yielded additional support for our hypothesis. Participants in the pro-Reagan condition were significantly more likely to judge Reagan to be the winner of the debate (67.31% versus 7.69% for Mondale and 25% for neither) than were participants in the pro-Mondale condition (11.91% versus 71.43% for Mondale and 16.67% for neither), $X^2 (2, N = 94) = 43.61$, $p < .0001$.

Further indicating the strength of the audience reaction effect was that there was also a significant and sizable difference on the key question, "who do you think you would have voted for?" (Reagan, Mondale, or neither), $X^2 (2, N = 94) = 9.88$, $p < .008$. Participants in the pro-Reagan condition were significantly more likely to indicate they would have voted for Reagan (46.15% versus 34.62% for Mondale and 19.23% for neither) than were participants in the pro-Mondale condition (16.67% versus 61.91% for Mondale and 21.43% for neither).

Candidates' Qualities. As in the first two studies, audience reaction also had a marked effect on perceptions of each candidate's personal characteristics. On a composite measure that combined mean ratings of intelligence, likeability, leadership, sense of humor, strength, competence, and sincerity ($\alpha = .91$), participants evaluated Reagan more favorably in the pro-Reagan feedback group than in the pro-Mondale group ($Ms = 67.02$ versus 58.57), $F(1, 92) = 7.18$, $p < .009$. Similarly, Mondale ($\alpha = .86$) was rated more favorably in the pro-Mondale condition than in the pro-Reagan group ($Ms = 65.50$ versus 56.58), $F(1, 92) = 14.52$, $p < .0003$. Indicating the broad range of effects produced by audience reaction, individual analyses revealed that the two groups differed significantly in their ratings of Reagan's likeability, leadership, and sense of humor, and in their ratings of Mondale's likeability, leadership, intelligence, competence, strength, and sincerity (all at $p < .05$). On estimates of how well the two candidates fared among voters in general, audience reaction also affected mean estimates of Reagan's popularity ($Ms = 74.23$ and 57.98, respectively, in the pro-Reagan and pro-Mondale groups), $F(1, 92) = 35.58$, $p < .0001$, as well as Mondale's ($Ms = 61.55$ and 44.33, respectively, in the pro-Mondale and pro-Reagan groups), $F(1, 92) = 37.56$, $p < .0001$.

Self-Reported Effects of Feedback. Finally, participants rated the extent to which their evaluations of the candidates were influenced by the online normative feedback (i.e., on a 0–100 point scale, whether it led them to favor Reagan or Mondale, where 50 = no effect). Interestingly, the pro-Reagan and pro-Mondale conditions did not differ on this measure, $F(1, 92) = 1.47$, *ns*. With a combined mean rating of 51.20, it appears that participants in general believed that they were not influenced by the feedback. This self-reported lack of influence thus contrasts sharply with all of the above results.

Summary. The results of Experiment 3 indicated that evaluations of the 1984 presidential candidates were significantly influenced by fabricated real-time feedback in the form of a line graph allegedly indicating the opinions of their peers in the room with the participants. For example, seeing the graph of their peers' alleged reactions changed the percentage of participants who thought Mondale had, in their own minds, won the election from fewer than 8% to more than 71%. Overall, these results, which were striking in their breadth and magnitude, suggest that the practice of presenting TV viewers with continuous focus-group data (or, as can be expected in upcoming elections, the practice of seeing others' real-time reactions on the internet as people watch the debate) constitutes a powerful source of social influence information.

Experiment 4

The previous experiments all showed significant conformity effects. However, the 1984 presidential election took place years before these studies were run. The participants knew the outcome of the election, and their concern about the accuracy of their judgments might not have been particularly high. One might presume that when citizens are watching an actual debate live, and sizing up the candidates in order to decide how to vote, they may be much less influenced by the apparent evaluations of others. Furthermore, there are other factors that might reduce conformity effects in this situation—viewers may have well-formed impressions of candidates, been subjected to months of pre-debate spin, been influenced more strongly by personal biases, etc. In short, there may be something fundamentally different about a debate preceding an election in which one will actually vote. Experiment 4 was intended to address this concern by having research participants evaluate a presidential debate on the night it actually took place, during the height of the campaign. If strong conformity effects were found under these circumstances, a host of potential concerns relating to external validity could be dismissed.

Method

Participants and Design. Sixty-one introductory psychology students participated in exchange for course credit. Participants were randomly scheduled to appear in one of three classrooms to watch the third and final presidential debate of that year's campaign. By random assignment, one room was designated as pro-Bush, a second as pro-Clinton, and a third as neutral.[5]

Procedure. The stimulus tape used in this study was the third and final 1992 presidential debate involving George Bush, Bill Clinton, and Ross Perot. Upon recruitment, all participants were asked to refrain from watching the debate live that evening, as they would see it just minutes after its conclusion as part of the study (indeed, they were scheduled to come to the lab several minutes before the debate would conclude). This was a mere 15 days prior to the election. As soon as they arrived at their assigned room, all participants completed a brief pre-debate questionnaire. The entire 90-minute debate tape was then played simultaneously in the three rooms. Afterward, all participants were administered a post-debate questionnaire, fully debriefed, and thanked for their participation.

In this study, social influence was manipulated via audience reactions. In a *pro-Bush* group, 21 participants watched the debate in the company of 13 student confederates who had been instructed to quietly but audibly applaud statements by Bush and disapprove (hiss, jeer) statements by Clinton. In a *pro-Clinton* group, 20 participants were joined by 12 confederates who were told similarly to applaud Clinton and disdain Bush. All confederates were rehearsed to react in ways that seemed natural. Their reactions increased gradually during the course of the debate, but they were cautioned not to interfere with the participants' ability to hear the tape. In a third *control group*, there were 20 participants and no confederates.

The dependent measures were similar to those used in the previous experiments, with the notable exception that in this study, at the end of the post-debate questionnaire participants were asked also to estimate the mean 0–100 point rating that each candidate would receive (1) from the other participants in the room, and (2) from viewers all over the country. The participants were asked to indicate which of the candidates, if any, they planned to vote for on Election Day.

Results and Discussion

Overall Performance. As shown in Fig. 4, the effect of audience reaction on the relative performance ratings of Clinton and Bush was striking. In the control group, Clinton's rating was 23 points higher than Bush's (and, indeed, Clinton was seen as the convincing winner of the debate by analysts and opinion polls). Yet the difference was up to 51 points in the pro-Clinton group and down to only 6 points in the pro-Bush group, $F(2, 58) = 20.59, p < .0001$.

On ratings of each candidate's debate performance, the results indicated that the effects of audience reaction were significant. Specifically, Clinton's ratings were higher among participants in the pro-Clinton audience ($M = 82.75$) than in the pro-Bush ($M = 67.14$) and control groups ($M = 69.50$), $F(2, 58) = 12.99, p < .0001$. In contrast, Bush's ratings were higher in the pro-Bush audience ($M = 60.95$) than in the pro-Clinton ($M = 31.50$) and control groups ($M = 46.25$), $F(2, 58) = 9.94, p < .0002$.

Participants' post-debate voting preferences were relatively consistent with these results, but the chi-square did not approach significance, $X^2 (8, N = 61) = 6.95$, *ns*, perhaps in part because there were five rather than only two options for participants to choose—for Clinton, for Bush, for Perot, did not know, or did not plan to vote.

---

[5] Although he also participated in the debate, third-party candidate Ross Perot was not considered to have a reasonable chance of even coming close to winning the 1992 election, and so we focused our manipulations on the two major candidates.

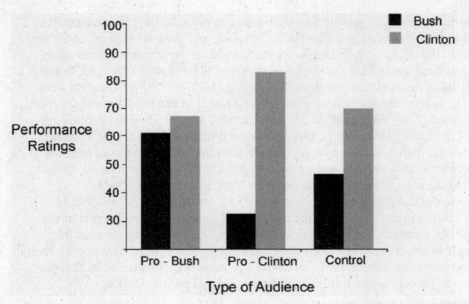

Fig. 4. Post-debate performance ratings of Bush and Clinton in Experiment 4 as a function of whether confederates were exposed to pro-Bush, pro-Clinton, or no (Control) confederates.

There were two additional and interesting results on these overall evaluations of the candidates. First, questionnaires were administered to the 13 pro-Bush and 12 pro-Clinton confederates, and an analysis of their responses indicated that they too were significantly influenced by audience reaction in their ratings of both Bush, $F(1, 23) = 10.91$, $p < .01$, and Clinton, $F(1, 23) = 6.93$, $p < .02$. Despite knowing that audience reaction was systematically manipulated—indeed, despite the fact that they themselves had to vary their behavior according to instruction— the confederates exhibited the same effect. Second, although we manipulated audience reactions only to Bush and Clinton, ratings of Perot's performance were also affected somewhat by the manipulation, $F(2, 58) = 2.63$, $p < .09$. Reflecting the unanticipated fact that Perot had aligned himself more with Clinton in this debate than with Bush, ratings of Perot were higher in the pro-Clinton group ($M = 76.75$) than in the pro-Bush or control conditions ($Ms = 65.00$ and 66.10, respectively), $F(1, 58) = 5.21$, $p < .02$.

Candidates' Qualities. On the more specific evaluation measures, the results followed a similar pattern as the overall performance ratings. Combining each candidate's performance ratings on the economy, foreign affairs, education, health care, and crime, results showed that Bush's mean ratings ($\alpha = .83$) were higher in the pro-Bush group than in the other conditions, $F(2, 58) = 3.70$, $p < .05$, although no comparable difference was found in ratings of Clinton on this same constellation of issues ($F < 1$). It is interesting that although audience reactions had no effect on the Clinton composite measure ($\alpha = .73$), participants did rate Clinton more favorably on economic issues in the pro-Clinton group than in the other conditions, $F(2, 58) = 5.17$, $p < .01$. In fact, the effect of audience reaction on ratings of Bush was also strongest on his economy performance, $F(2, 58) = 9.41$, $p < .001$. Although this pattern was not predicted, the likely reason for it is that the debate focused primarily on economic issues.

Overall, audience reaction effects were even more pronounced on ratings of each candidate's personal characteristics. Participants in the pro-Bush condition, relative to those in the pro-Clinton and control groups, saw Bush as more trustworthy ($F(2, 58) = 3.60$, $p < .05$), more intelligent ($F(2, 58) = 9.64$, $p < .001$), more caring ($F(2, 58) = 3.51$, $p < .05$), and as having a better sense of humor ($F(2, 58) = 3.22$, $p < .05$). Similarly, participants in the pro-Clinton condition relative to those in other groups saw Clinton as more trustworthy ($F(2, 58) = 5.64$, $p < .005$), more intelligent ($F(2, 58) = 9.59$, $p < .001$), more likeable ($F(2, 58) = 4.91$, $p < .01$), and more mature ($F(2, 58) = 2.98$, $p < .05$).

Estimates of Others' Perceptions. Finally, participants were asked to estimate the mean ratings that each candidate would receive from the other participants in the room, and from all viewers nationwide. On the first of these measures, the effect was striking in its magnitude, as participants estimated the highest Bush rating in the pro-Bush group and the lowest in the pro-Clinton group (Ms = 59.76 and 11.50, respectively; M = 41.00 in the control condition), $F(2, 58) = 51.50, p < .0001$. The data were similar for ratings of Clinton, as participants estimated his highest rating in the pro-Clinton group and his lowest in the pro-Bush group (Ms = 89.75 and 62.38, respectively; M = 73.75 in the control condition), $F(2, 58) = 33.20, p < .0001$. Essentially, these results served as a check on the audience reaction manipulation. However, there was also a highly significant effect on estimates of how the candidates fared more generally among viewers across the country. On this measure as well, those in the pro-Bush group projected the rest of the country to be much more positive about Bush's performance ($M = 60.38$) than did those in the control ($M = 53.75$) or pro-Clinton conditions ($M = 40.00$), $F(2, 58) = 7.85, p < .001$. Similarly, those in the pro-Clinton group projected the rest of the country to be much more positive about Clinton's performance ($M = 78.25$) than did those in the control ($M = 69.50$) or pro-Bush conditions ($M = 63.33$), $F(2, 58) = 11.53, p < .0001$. Thus, even though all participants saw the same debate (which included an actual live audience), they inferred that the reactions of the confederates in their sessions were diagnostic of national public opinion.

Summary. The results from Experiment 4 revealed that manipulated peer audience reactions to a presidential debate strongly influenced participants' judgments of each candidate's overall performance, performance on the focal substantive issue, and personal characteristics, even under the most realistic circumstances possible. The magnitude of this effect was astonishing (it produced a 45-point shift in the relative ratings of Bush and Clinton), and was obtained not only with naive participants who were low in political involvement, but with high-involvement participants—and even confederates who knew that the cheers and jeers were experimentally manipulated. This effect occurred even though the stimulus event was a heated 90-minute presidential debate and despite the presence of a live, reactive (i.e., at the debate) audience. Indeed, our manipulation led participants not only to alter their own judgments of the candidates, but to infer that these judgments were diagnostic of national public opinion, as was also seen in Experiment 3.

General Discussion

The results of the four studies reported here were highly consistent. In each of them participants' judgments about debate performance were strongly influenced by their mere exposure to other people's reactions. The magnitude of these effects is striking. Our participants made very different judgments about debate performance as a function of the information we manipulated concerning the reactions of others in the audience. In Experiment 1, participants watched Mondale and Reagan. In one condition the audience reaction to Reagan's winning "one-liners" was removed. Compared to the control condition where the audience reaction was presented intact, Reagan's ratings relative to Mondale's declined by 31 points. The results of Experiment 2 were also significant despite the fact that the manipulation was embedded within the full 90-minute debate. In Experiments 3 and 4, participants saw what they believed to be the reactions of their peers who were watching the debate with them. In Experiment 3, as a function of this false group feedback, Reagan's ratings relative to Mondale's varied by 30 points. In Experiment 4, participants' judgments about overall performances in a 1992 Bush-Clinton-Perot debate, on the night of the live debate itself, were strongly influenced by whether they watched the debate with pro-Clinton or pro-Bush confederates who audibly vocalized their opinions. On a 101-point scale, Clinton's advantage over Bush increased by 45 points across conditions. Taken together, these studies all demonstrated that mere exposure to the judgments of others strongly influenced our participants.

One striking feature of the results is that they were highly similar across a number of dimensions. First, information about others' judgments was presented in a variety of ways: the recorded laughter and cheers of audiences attending actual debates, the visual fabricated feedback of other group members, or the vocal reactions of live confederates. Second, audience reactions significantly affected perceptions of candidate performance across a broad range of participants, including Democrats and Republicans, those who defined themselves as politically involved or uninvolved, and those who were high or low in need for cognition. In each case there were similar effects for the different kinds of participants.[6] Third, effects were obtained across a range of dependent measures, including overall performance ratings as well as perceptions of specific qualities such as intelligence and likeability. Fourth, participants' judgments about a presidential debate in a current campaign cycle were influenced as much as, or even slightly more than, their judgments about debates that took place nearly a decade earlier. The consistency of the influence effects is striking.

Our participants seemed to exhibit informational social influence and internalized conformity, reflecting, in Insko, Drenan, Solomon, Smith, and Wade's (1983) terms, a desire to be right rather than a desire to be liked. Their judgments were given privately and anonymously. In Experiments 1 and 2 the source of influence was simply a videotaped audience from a debate which had taken place years earlier. In those cases, participants had no reason to be concerned about pressure from others or others' opinions about them. Importantly, then, the influence we obtained seems to be informational social influence affecting privately held judgments. This is precisely the kind of influence one would expect in a situation where physical reality is ambiguous but social reality is clear. Our participants probably believed that there was in fact a right answer to questions about how the candidates performed—and that the reactions of others signaled that clear answer.

What is a likely account of the process by which informational social influence was produced in these studies? It may be that the identification and interpretation of specific behaviors in debates were influenced by others' reaction. When Ronald Reagan responded to a very serious question about his energy and intellectual capacity by joking that he would not exploit his opponent's youth and inexperience, there was room for considerable interpretation. Observers could identify his reply as a feeble or even disgraceful attempt to dodge the issues or as a deft and masterful turning of a hostile question to his advantage. The audience reaction of strong approval did not recognize Reagan's quip as a knockout punch so much as it made it one. Throughout a 90-minute debate there are numerous segments of behavior (Newtson, 1976), each of which can be framed and defined by the reactions of others. Furthermore, once a particular expectation is adopted about how each candidate is performing in a debate, individual behaviors can be interpreted within that framework (Fiske & Taylor, 1991; Kelley, 1950; Kugler & Goethals, 2005; Norton & Goethals, 2004). Positive or negative moments can therefore define entire debates, or even campaigns.

It is perhaps worth underlining the fact that the audiences who produced the influence in these studies were most likely perceived as having no intent to influence. This is most clearly the case in Experiments 1 and 2 where the audience's reactions were televised years before. Earlier studies of overheard communications suggest that they are perceived as not being designed to persuade and for this reason often have more credibility and influence than communications delivered with intent to persuade (Brock & Becker, 1965). They also generate less psychological reactance (Brehm, 1966).

---

[6] It should be noted that the participants in our studies all were college undergraduates, and therefore we cannot know whether older samples of people would respond similarly. We have conducted one study in a different line of work concerning social context and presidential debates in which our participants came from a large sample of public-school teachers, and the results were similar to those we found with undergraduate samples. It is clear, though, that including older and broader samples of participants should be an important goal for future research.

What are the policy issues that are suggested by this research? Perhaps the most fundamental is that those who stage, sponsor, and broadcast political debates should take steps to minimize social influence, or psychologists should take steps to publicize that influence, or both. Within the current debate format there are at least three sources of influence that are under virtually no control. The first is the reactions of live audiences. Since 1984 live audience reaction has been part of the mix. In the vice-presidential debate in 1988 Lloyd Bentsen partisans laughed and cheered at his "You're no Jack Kennedy" put-down of Dan Quayle, while the latter's supporters competed with a loud chorus of boos. In several of the recent debates, the moderator has strongly admonished the audience to remain quiet. Since audience reaction has such a strong effect on viewers, this warning is well justified.

A second possible source of influence is the behavior of the commentators who moderate debates and ask questions. In 1984 journalist Henry Trewhitt commented on Reagan's age quip by saying "I'll try to run to the fence to catch that one before it goes out," just in case anyone missed the fact that Reagan had hit a home run. In 1988, Jim Lehrer implicitly supported Bush's attempts to make light of his persistent errors by quoting and endorsing the vice-president's "nobody's perfect" response to Michael Dukakis' derisive response to Bush's misstatements. Also in 1988, NBC newsman Tom Brokaw's headshakes and nods influenced Dan Quayle's response as he walked into Lloyd Bentsen's "You're no Jack Kennedy" put-down. Broadcasters should exercise caution and restraint over the subtle ways in which they guide, diminish, or enhance a debater's remarks.

Third, networks now report on the results of instant polls and focus groups that may have a significant effect on people's judgments about how candidates performed and who won. Some networks also give high-ranking campaign officials free reign to apply their "spin" to the evening's debate performances. All this information is consumed by viewers before they have had a chance to consolidate, deliberate, and make up their own minds about the large amount of content they have just seen. The potential for influence is therefore all the stronger. In this regard, the news media might be more thoughtful about their role in channeling social realities to viewers. While the news media may have no conscious intent to influence, our research suggests that they may have great influence nonetheless. Their good intentions aside, the power of the networks needs to be considered.

We can expect in future debates that communication via the internet will play an increasingly important role. It is easy to imagine that very large numbers of citizens, particularly younger voters, will provide spontaneous audience reactions, along the lines of what we manipulated in Experiments 3 and 4, by posting to blogs, electronic forums and boards, and so on. The normative information that will be provided in this manner has tremendous potential to influence the perceptions and decisions of many individuals. When information such as this, or such as the immediate post-debate spins presented by analysts and campaign officials, bombards individuals before they have had the chance to reach their own interpretations and conclusions independently, individual voters may be unaware that the privacy of their voting booth has been compromised by the long reach of the opinions of a great many friends and strangers.

In conclusion, we have shown that people's judgments of presidential debates can be strongly influenced by their knowledge of other people's reactions. These debates appear to be highly ambiguous events. For people to develop their own independent opinions, great care must be taken on the part of organizers and sponsors to limit the impact of irrelevant cues like the ones discussed herein. One potentially useful direction for future research is to examine the factors that would make people less vulnerable to such effects. Would being educated about the results of studies such as the present ones reduce individuals' susceptibility to the kind of informational social influence we have documented? Of course, other people can and often do provide important, useful, and even correct information. In the theater of political campaigns, however, with spin-doctors, hand-picked audiences, and highly charged emotions galore, this may be less likely to be the case than is usual. The often-adaptive practice of checking in with social reality can be a trap in these orchestrated contexts. What is especially important, therefore, is for individuals to look at the social context around these debates with vigilance and caution.

Acknowledgements

We would like to thank Amelia Cottrell, Jessica Cross, Leigh Frost, C.J. Gillig, and Lauren Parkhill for their help in collecting the data presented in this paper. We would also like to thank Columbia Information Services for their assistance with the Perception Analyzer technology used in Experiment 3. Correspondence concerning this article should be addressed to Steven Fein, Department of Psychology, Williams College, Williamstown, MA 01267, or Al Goethals, Jepson School of Leadership Studies, University of Richmond, Richmond, VA 23173. E-mail: sfein@williams.edu and ggoethal@richmond.edu.

REFERENCES

Asch, S.E. (1951). Effects of group pressure upon the modification and distortion of judgments. In H. Guetzkow (Ed.), *Groups, leadership, and men*. Pittsburgh: Carnegie Press.

Axsom, D., Yates, S., & Chaiken, S. (1987). Audience response as a heuristic cue in persuasion. *Journal of Personality and Social Psychology, 53*, 30–40.

Baron, R.S., Vandello, J.A., & Brunsman, B. (1996). The forgotten variable in conformity research: Impact of task importance on social influence. *Journal of Personality and Social Psychology, 71*, 915–927.

Brehm, J.W. (1966). *A theory of psychological reactance*. New York: Academic.

Brock, T.M., & Becker, L.A. (1965). Ineffectiveness of "overheard" counterpropaganda. *Journal of Personality and Social Psychology, 2*, 654–660.

Cacioppo, J.T. & Petty, R.E. (1982). The need for cognition. *Journal of Personality and Social Psychology, 42*, 116–131.

Cantril, H. (1940). *The invasion from Mars*. Princeton: Princeton University Press.

Deutsch, M., & Gerard, H.B. (1955). A study of normative and informational social influences upon individual judgment. *Journal of Abnormal and Social Psychology, 51*, 629–636.

Fein, S., Frost, L.A., Goethals, G.R., & Kassin, S.M. (1994). *The effects of expectations on perceptions of presidential debate performance*. Presented at the 102nd meeting of the American Psychological Association, Los Angeles.

Fein, S., Hoshino-Browne, E., Davies, P.G., & Spencer, S.J. (2003). Self-image maintenance goals and sociocultural norms in motivated social perception. In S.J. Spencer, S. Fein, M. Zanna, & J.M. Olson (Eds.), *Motivated social perception: The Ontario symposium* (vol. 9, pp. 21–44). Mahwah, NJ: Erlbaum.

Fiske, S.T., & Taylor, S.E. (1991). *Social cognition*. New York: McGraw-Hill.

Germond, J.W., & Witcover, J. (1989). *Whose broad stripes and bright stars? The trivial pursuit of the presidency 1988*. New York: Warner.

Insko, C.A., Drenan, S., Solomon, M.R., Smith, R., & Wade, T.J. (1983). Conformity as a function of the consistency of positive self-evaluation with being liked and being right. *Journal of Experimental Social Psychology, 19*, 341–358.

Jamieson, K.H., & Waldman, P. (2002). *The press effect: Politicians, journalists, and the stories that shape the political world*. Cambridge: Oxford University Press.

Kaid, L.L., & Bystrom, D.G. (1999). *The electronic election: Perspectives on the 1996 campaign communication*. Mahwah, NJ: Erlbaum.

Kelley, H.H. (1950). The warm-cold variable in first impressions of persons. *Journal of Personality, 18*, 431–439.

Kiesler, C.A., & Kiesler, S.B. (1969). *Conformity*. Reading, MA: Addison-Wesley.

Kraus, S. (1962). *The great debates: Background, perspectives, effects*. Bloomington: Indiana University Press.

Kugler, M.B., & Goethals, G.R. (2005). *Trait-focused spin in presidential debates: Surviving the kisses of death*. Unpublished manuscript, Williams College.

McKinnon, L.M., & Tedesco, J.C. (1999). The influence of medium and media commentary on presidential debate effects. In L. L. Kaid & D. G. Bystrom (Eds.), *The electronic election: Perspectives on the 1996 campaign communication* (pp. 191–206). Mahwah, NJ: Erlbaum.

McKinnon, L.M., Tedesco, J.C., & Kaid, L.L. (1993). The third 1992 presidential debate: Channel and commentary effects. *Augmentation and Advocacy*, 30, 106–118.

Newtson, D. (1976). Foundations of attribution: The perception of ongoing behavior. In J. H. Harvey, W.J. Ickes, & R.F. Kidd (Eds.), *New directions in attribution research* (pp. 223–247). New York: John Wiley and Sons.

Norton, M.I., & Goethals, G.R. (2004). Spin (and pitch) doctors: Campaign strategies in televised political debates. *Political Behavior, 26*, 227–248.

Petty, R.E., & Cacioppo, J.T. (1986). *Communication and persuasion: Central and peripheral routes to attitude change*. New York: Springer-Verlag.

Schroeder, A. (2000). *Presidential debates: Forty years of high-risk TV*. New York: Columbia University Press.

Sears, D.O., & Chaffee, S.H. (1979). Uses and effects of the 1976 debates: An overview of the empirical studies. In S. Kraus (Ed.), *The great debates: Carter versus Ford, 1976*. Bloomington: Indiana University Press.

Sherif, M. (1936). The psychology of social norms. New York: Harper.

Sigelman, L. (1992). There you go again: The media and the debasement of American politics. *Communication Monographs, 59*, 407–410.

Sigelman, L., & Sigelman, C.K. (1984). Judgments of the Carter-Reagan debate: The eyes of the beholders. *Public Opinion Quarterly, 48*, 624–628.

Steeper, F.T. (1978). Public response to Gerald Ford's statements on Eastern Europe in the second debate. In G.F. Bishop, R.G. Meadow, & M. Jackson-Beeck (Eds.), *The presidential debates: Media, electoral, and policy perspectives* (pp. 81–101). New York: Praeger.

Zarevsky, D. (1992). Spectator politics and the revival of public argument. *Communication Monographs, 59*, 411–414

READING 3

First Impressions: Making Up Your Mind After a 100-Ms Exposure to a Face

Are quick, first impressions reliable and how long do you need to see a face before you can decide if you trust or like the person, if he or she is attractive, competent, or aggressive? In five experiments, Willis and Todorov found that when participants were allowed only 100 milliseconds, they made comparable judgments to others who rated the faces without any time constraints. When exposure time increased to 500 milliseconds, judgments became more negative and participants expressed more confidence in their decisions. Further increasing the time to 1,000 milliseconds produced no change in judgments but only an additional boost in confidence. To emphasize the importance of inferring traits from the briefly glimpsed appearance of photographs of people's faces, the authors cite their earlier study showing that they were able to accurately predict outcomes of US congressional elections simply by asking participants to choose the more competent-looking of two candidates. As you read this study and consider the research presented in Chapter 4 (Perceiving Persons) of the text, think of other arenas where facial appearance is used to infer trait characteristics and other information about the person.

FIRST IMPRESSIONS: MAKING UP YOUR MIND AFTER A 100-MS EXPOSURE TO A FACE

Janine Willis and Alexander Todorov

Princeton University

ABSTRACT—*People often draw trait inferences from the facial appearance of other people. We investigated the minimal conditions under which people make such inferences. In five experiments, each focusing on a specific trait judgment, we manipulated the exposure time of unfamiliar faces. Judgments made after a 100-ms exposure correlated highly with judgments made in the absence of time constraints, suggesting that this exposure time was sufficient for participants to form an impression. In fact, for all judgments—attractiveness, likeability, trustworthiness, competence, and aggressiveness—increased exposure time did not significantly increase the correlations. When exposure time increased from 100 to 500 ms, participants' judgments became more negative, response times for judgments decreased, and confidence in judgments increased. When exposure time increased from 500 to 1,000 ms, trait judgments and response times did not change significantly (with one exception), but confidence increased for some of the judgments; this result suggests that additional time may simply boost confidence in judgments. However, increased exposure time led to more differentiated person impressions.*

Address correspondence to Alexander Todorov, Department of Psychology, Green Hall, Princeton University, Princeton, NJ 08544-1010, e-mail: atodorov@princeton.edu.

Janine Willis and Alexander Todorov, "First Impressions: Making Up Your Mind After a 100-Ms Exposure to a Face," Psychological Science, Vol. 17, No. 7, pp. 592-598. Reprinted with permission of Blackwell Publishing, Inc.

Lavater's (1772/1880) *Essays on Physiognomy*, which was written in 1772 and reprinted in more than 150 editions by 1940, described in minute detail how to relate facial features to personality traits (e.g., "the nearer the eyebrows are to the eyes, the more earnest, deep, and firm the character," p. 59). Although these ideas strike most people today as ludicrous and bring to mind phrenology, empirical evidence shows that the effects of facial appearance on social outcomes are pervasive. In almost every significant domain of life, attractive people get better outcomes than unattractive people (Hamermesh & Biddle, 1994; Zebrowitz, 1999). The effects of baby-faced appearance are as pervasive as are the effects of attractiveness (Montepare&Zebrowitz, 1998; Zebrowitz, 1999). For example, baby-faced individuals are less likely to receive severe judicial outcomes than mature-faced individuals (Zebrowitz & McDonald, 1991).

From the structure of the face, people form not only global impressions, but also specific trait impressions (Hassin & Trope, 2000). For example, we showed that inferences of competence, based solely on facial appearance, predicted the outcomes of U.S. congressional elections in 2000, 2002, and 2004 (Todorov, Mandisodza, Goren, & Hall, 2005). Although we measured impressions on a variety of traits, including attractiveness, trustworthiness, and likeability, the trait inference that predicted the election outcomes was competence. Competence was also rated as the most important attribute for a person running for a public office. This finding suggests that personal attributes that are important for specific decisions are inferred from facial appearance and influence these decisions.

From both the standard-intuition and the rational-actor points of view, trait inferences from facial appearance should not influence important deliberate decisions. However, to the extent that these inferences occur rapidly and effortlessly, their effects on decisions may be subtle and not subjectively recognized. Using the terms of dual-process theories (Chaiken & Trope, 1999; Kahneman, 2003), we have argued that trait inferences from faces can be characterized as fast, intuitive, unreflective System 1 processes that contrast with slow, effortful, and deliberate System 2 processes (Todorov et al., 2005). We provided preliminary evidence for this proposal by showing that inferences of competence based on 1-s exposure to the faces of the winners and the runners-up for the Senate races sufficed to predict the election outcomes.

In this article, we report a series of studies in which we systematically manipulated the exposure time of faces to further explore the minimal conditions under which people make trait inferences from facial appearance. Research on visual processing has shown that high-level object representations can be constructed very rapidly from visual scenes (Grill-Spector & Kanwisher, 2005; Rousselet, Fabre-Thorpe, & Thorpe, 2002; Thorpe, Fize, & Marlot, 1996). It is possible that inferences about socially significant attributes are also rapidly extracted from facial appearance. We conducted five experiments, each focusing on a different judgment from facial appearance: attractiveness, likeability, competence, trustworthiness, and aggressiveness. Among the studied traits, attractiveness is the only one that is unambiguously related to facial appearance; that is, it is a property of facial appearance. In this respect, judgments of attractiveness provide a benchmark for judgments of character traits. Liking is a global affective response that may require minimal inferential activity (Zajonc, 1980). In contrast to attractiveness and liking, trustworthiness, competence, and aggressiveness are specific traits that have clear behavioral manifestations. These traits are also important for both social and economic interactions.

In all the experiments, faces unfamiliar to the participants were presented for 100 ms, 500 ms, or 1,000 ms. For each face, participants were asked to make a trait judgment and then to express their confidence in that judgment. We tested three hypotheses: (a) that a 100-ms exposure to a face is sufficient for making a trait judgment, (b) that additional exposure time increases confidence in trait judgments without necessarily changing the judgments, and (c) that additional exposure time allows for more differentiated trait impressions.

If trait inferences from faces can be characterized as System 1 inferences, minimal exposure time should be sufficient for trait inferences to occur. In order to obtain criterion judgments, we asked a large group of participants to make trait judgments of the faces in the absence of time constraints. If a 100-ms exposure to a face is sufficient for making a trait inference, then trait judgments made after 100-ms exposure should correlate with judgments made in the absence of time constraints. In contrast, if 100 ms is insufficient, these judgments should be uncorrelated, and only judgments made after longer exposures should correlate with judgments made in the absence of time constraints.

We were also interested in how additional exposure time affects trait judgments and confidence in these judgments. If people commit to a judgment early in time, additional time can serve only as a justification of this judgment. If this is the case, confidence should increase as a function of exposure time, but there should be no corresponding change in judgment. For example, if 500-ms exposure is sufficient for participants to form stable trait judgments, little change in judgments should be observed with additional exposure time. However, additional exposure time may boost confidence in judgments.

Even if trait impressions can be formed after minimal exposure time, additional time may allow for more differentiated impressions. For example, it is possible that after 100-ms exposure, people perform a coarse affective discrimination of faces, such that judgments of different traits are highly correlated. Additional time may allow for more fine-grained impressions based on specific trait attributions, in which case judgments of different traits would be less correlated. We tested these predictions using factor analysis.

Method

Participants. A total of 245 undergraduate students from Princeton University participated in the studies either for payment or for partial course credit. One hundred twenty-eight participated in a preliminary study in which we obtained measures of trait inferences from facial appearance in the absence of time constraints. One hundred seventeen participated in the five main experiments; 20 were asked to make attractiveness judgments, 25 to make liking judgments, 23 to make competence judgments, 24 to make trustworthiness judgments, and 25 to make aggressiveness judgments.

Stimuli. In all the studies, we used a database of photographs of 70 amateur actors, 35 females and 35 males between 20 and 30 years of age (Lundqvist, Flykt, & Öhman, 1998). In the pictures, all actors wore gray T-shirts, and there were no beards, mustaches, earrings, eyeglasses, or visible makeup. We used frontal head-shot photographs of individuals with neutral expressions. Of the 70 photographs, 2 photographs of males were excluded because of poor quality; we also excluded 2 photographs of females in order to have equal numbers of male and female photographs.

To obtain reliable measures of trait inferences from facial appearance, we presented participants in the preliminary study with the photographs and asked them to judge the degree to which the person in each picture was attractive, likeable, competent, honest or trustworthy, aggressive, extraverted or enthusiastic, sympathetic or warm, dependable or self-disciplined, calm or emotionally stable, open to new experiences or complex, and ambitious. The judgments on the first five dimensions provided the criterion judgments for the five experiments. In the preliminary study, each face was presented on a separate questionnaire page, and the order of the trait judgments was fixed. All judgments were made on a 9-point scale ranging from 1 (not at all) to 9 (extremely). The photographs were randomly divided into three groups, each one containing the same number of males and females, and for each group of photographs, we generated two random orders. Participants were randomly assigned to one of the six sets of photographs (3 groups_ 2 orders) and completed the task at their own pace. Each photograph was rated by 42 or 43 participants. The trait judgments were highly reliable. For the three groups of photographs, the Cronbach alphas were .97, .96, and .95 for attractiveness; .94, .91, and .89 for likeability; .92, .92, and .92 for trustworthiness; .85, .91, and .96 for competence; and .87, .75, and .89 for aggressiveness.

The mean trait judgments across participants served as the criterion judgments for the experiments. To the extent that limited exposure time is sufficient for people to form trait impressions from faces, the experimental judgments made under time constraints would be expected to correlate with the criterion judgments. It should be noted that, for two reasons, this procedure underestimated the true correlation between judgments made in the absence of time constraints and judgments made with time constraints: The two sets of judgments were measured on different scales (see Procedure) and were made under different conditions (paper-and-pencil questionnaire vs. computer-controlled presentation).

Procedure. All five experiments followed the same procedure. Participants were told that this was a study about first impressions and that they should make their decisions as quickly as possible. The instructions emphasized that photographs would be presented for very brief periods of time and that we, the experimenters, were primarily interested in participants' first impressions, or gut feelings. Each experiment started with three practice trials in order to familiarize participants with the task.

For the experimental trials, the 66 faces (33 males and 33 females) were randomly divided into three sets of 22 such that each group had the same number of male and female faces. We created three experimental versions of the stimuli by counterbalancing the exposure time assigned to each set (100, 500, or 1,000 ms). For example, each face from the first set was presented for 100 ms in the first version, for 500 ms in the second version, and for 1,000 ms in the third version. Participants were randomly assigned to one of the three experimental versions. For each participant, 22 of the faces were presented for 100 ms, 22 were presented for 500 ms, and 22 were presented for 1,000 ms. Because we were interested in first impressions, each face was presented only once. Thus, the total number of trials was 66 per participant. The order of trials was randomized for each participant y the computer (i.e., the levels of exposure time were randomly intermixed).

Each trial started with a fixation point (+) presented for 500 ms at the center of the screen. Then a photograph was presented for 100 ms, 500 ms, or 1,000 ms. Immediately afterward, a question appeared in the location of the photograph (e.g., "Is this person competent?"). The only difference among the studies was the trait judgment that participants were asked to make. Participants responded using the computer keyboard, pressing the "/" (slash) key, which was labeled "yes," or pressing the "Z" key, which was labeled "no." Given the limited exposure times, we decided to use dichotomous trait judgments because they are simpler than continuous trait judgments. Further, in the correlation analyses (see the next paragraph), the criterion judgments were correlated with the proportions of trait attributions across participants (i.e., continuous scores; the probability of trait attribution). Following this yes/no judgment, the next screen asked participants to rate how confident they were in their judgment. This rating was made on a 7-point scale, ranging from 1 (*least confident*) to 7 (*most confident*). Participants responded by using the number keys at the top of the keyboard. The intertrial interval was 1,500 ms.

To test whether judgments made under limited exposure time correlate with judgments made in the absence of time constraints, we correlated the proportions of trait attributions for each face (at each exposure time) with the mean criterion judgments for that face. Further, for each experiment, we analyzed the proportions of trait attributions, the response times for the trait judgments, and the mean confidence in judgments as a function of exposure time. We removed response time outliers by deleting response times that were 3 standard deviations above the participant's mean. In all experiments, less than 2% of the trials were excluded.

Results and Discussion

Correlation of Time-Constrained With Time-Unconstrained Judgments

As shown in Table 1, even after 100-ms exposure to a face, trait judgments were highly correlated with judgments made in the absence of time constraints. Although the correlations for all judgments but attractiveness increased with the increase in exposure from 100 to 1,000 ms, none of these changes was significant.

We compared the correlations at 100 and 500 ms, at 500 and 1,000 ms, and at 100 and 1,000 ms using Williams's test for dependent correlations (Steiger, 1980). None of these tests reached significance.

| | Exposure time | | | | | |
| | 100 ms | | 500 ms | | 1,000 ms | |
Trait judgment	Zero-order correlation	Partial correlation	Zero-order correlation	Partial correlation	Zero-order correlation	Partial correlation
Trustworthiness	.73	.63	.66	.59	.74	.69
Competence	.52	.39	.67	.58	.59	.50
Likeability	.59	.40	.57	.46	.63	.50
Aggressiveness	.52	.52	.56	.58	.59	.61
Attractiveness	.69	—	.57	—	.66	—

TABLE 1

Correlations Between Time-Constrained Trait Judgments From Facial Appearance and Judgments Made in the Absence of Time Constraints

Note. The partial correlations control for judgments of attractiveness made after the same exposure time. All correlations were significant, $p < .001$, prep > .98.

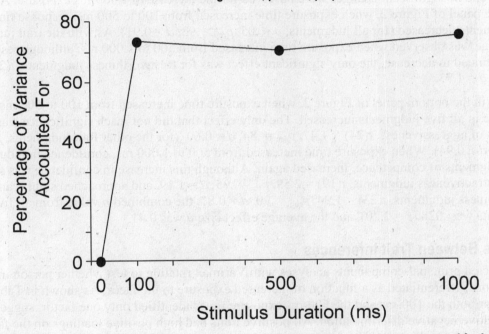

Fig. 1. Percentage of variance in judgments made in the absence of time constraints accounted for by time-constrained trait judgments.

We expected that we would find the highest correlation for judgments of attractiveness. Attractiveness, after all, is a property of facial appearance. However, the correlations for judgments of trustworthiness were slightly higher. We also conducted partial correlation analyses, controlling for judgments of attractiveness, to rule out the possibility that the judgments made after limited exposure time simply reflected an attractiveness halo effect. Although the correlations were reduced (Table 1), they remained highly reliable for all judgments. Comparing the difference between the zero-order and the partial correlations at the different levels of exposure time suggests that the effect of attractiveness on trait judgments was reduced with increased exposure to the faces. The partial correlations increased with increased exposure time, but as in the case of the zero-order correlations, none of the changes reached significance.

How much of the variance in time-unconstrained judgments can be accounted for by time-constrained judgments? To answer this question, we conducted three regression analyses (one for each level of exposure time) in which time-unconstrained judgments (5 types of judgment × 66 faces) were regressed on time-constrained judgments and dummy variables controlling for the type of judgments (4) and the face stimuli (65). As shown in Figure 1, with the increase in exposure from 100 to 1,000 ms, the variance accounted for increased only 2.2%. Although we did not include conditions in which participants were exposed to faces for more than 1,000 ms, it is reasonable to assume that the explained variance could not be improved with longer exposures. Assuming that the average reliability of the judgments is .90, the ceiling of the explained variance should be, on average, 81.0%. Given that the procedures for collecting the time-constrained judgments and the time-unconstrained (criterion) judgments were different and that these differences could have increased the error variance, the accounted-for variance at 1,000-ms exposure (74.9%) seems very close to the possible ceiling.

Analysis Within Experiments

All judgments showed the same pattern as a function of exposure time. As shown in the top panel of Figure 2,[1] when exposure time increased from 100 to 500 ms, judgments became more negative (for all judgments, $p < .05$, $p_{rep} > .91$, $d > 0.85$). Faces were perceived as less attractive, less likeable, less trustworthy, less competent, and more aggressive. The mean level of judgments stabilized at the 500-ms exposure, and no significant changes were observed for the increase to 1,000-ms exposure. As shown in the middle panel of Figure 2, when exposure time increased from 100 to 500 ms, response times for all five judgments decreased (for all judgments, $p < .05$, $p_{rep} > .93$, $d > 0.91$). As with the trait judgments, little change was observed when exposure time increased from 500 to 1,000 ms; although response times continued to decrease, the only significant effect was for trustworthiness judgments, $t(23) = 4.14$, $p_{rep} = .99$, $d = 1.73$.

As shown in the bottom panel of Figure 2, when exposure time increased from 100 to 500 ms, confidence in all five judgments increased. The only effect that did not reach significance was for judgments of aggressiveness, $t(24) = 1.47$, $p_{rep} = .84$, $d = 0.60$ (for the other four judgments, $p < .05$, $p_{rep} > .93$, $d > 0.94$). When exposure time increased from 500 to 1,000 ms, confidence in judgments, except judgments of competence, increased again. Although this increase in confidence was significant only for attractiveness judgments, $t(19) = 2.59$, $p_{rep} = .95$, $d = 1.19$, and approached significance for trustworthiness judgments, $t(23) = 1.94$, $p_{rep} = .90$, $d = 0.81$, the combined p value from all five experiments was .028 ($z = 2.20$), and the average effect size d was 0.41.

Relations Between Trait Inferences

We conducted principal-components analyses with Varimax rotation to test whether person impressions became more differentiated as a function of increased exposure to the faces. As shown in Table 2, the analyses for both the 100-ms and the 500-ms exposure times identified only one factor, suggesting a coarse positive/negative discrimination. All positive traits had high positive loadings on the factor, and aggressiveness had a high negative loading. This factor accounted for 62.5% of the variance in judgments made after 100-ms exposure and 58.3% of the variance in judgments made after 500-ms exposure. The difference in the explained variance suggests that judgments made after 100-ms exposure were more correlated than judgments made after 500-ms exposure.

---

[1] The analyses we report here were conducted at the level of participants (i.e., analyzed the mean judgments across faces). We conducted the same analyses at the level of faces (i.e., analyzed the mean judgments across participants) and obtained identical results.

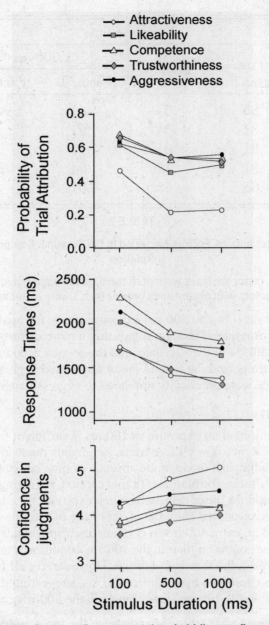

Fig. 2. Probability of trait attribution (top panel), response time (middle panel), and confidence in trait judgment (bottom panel) as a function of the trait being judged and exposure time. The probability of trait attribution of aggressiveness is reversed (i.e., higher probability means fewer attributions of aggressiveness) so that for all traits, higher probabilities reflect more positive valence. Confidence judgments were made on a 7-point scale, ranging from 1 (least confident) to 7 (most confident). Error bars show within-subjects standard errors.

| | Exposure time | | | |
| Trait judgment | 100 ms: Factor 1 | 500 ms: Factor 1 | 1,000 ms | |
			Factor 1	Factor 2
Trustworthiness	.85	.83	.61	.61
Competence	.81	.84	.91	.06
Likeability	.81	.81	.79	.33
Attractiveness	.81	.72	.84	.00
Aggressiveness	−.66	−.58	−.01	−.96

TABLE 2

Factor Loadings of Trait Judgments on Factors Identified in the Principal Components Analysis With Varimax Rotation

Note. For each exposure time, factor analyses were performed on the aggregated judgments for each face. Only factors with eigenvalues greater than 1 were extracted.

In contrast to the analyses for the 100- and 500-ms exposure times, the analysis for the 1,000-ms exposure time identified two orthogonal factors, suggesting a more differentiated person impression. The first factor accounted or 50.5% of the variance, and the second accounted for 27.8%. The first factor comprised all positive traits, and the second factor contrasted aggressiveness and trustworthiness. Attractiveness and competence were practically unrelated to aggressiveness in this factor solution.

General Discussion

Our findings suggest that as minimal an exposure as 100 ms is sufficient for people to make a specific trait inference from a stranger's face. For all five traits, judgments made after 100-ms exposure to a face were highly correlated with judgments made in the absence of time constraints. In fact, additional exposure time did not increase these correlations. In this context, revisiting the response times for the judgments is informative. Response times decreased when exposure time increased from 100 to 500 ms. However, response times were measured from the offset of the face to the response. Thus, in the 500-ms condition, participants had an extra 400 ms to compute their judgments. If participants computed the judgments faster in the 500-ms condition than in the 100-ms condition, the response times should have decreased by more than 400 ms in the former condition. However, for all five judgments, the response times in the 500-ms condition decreased by less than 400 ms, suggesting that the judgments were computed as fast, if not faster, in the 100-ms condition as in the 500-ms condition.

Although judgments were formed after 100-ms exposure to the faces, participants' trait judgments shifted systematically as a function of increased exposure time. When exposure time increased from 100 to 500 ms, judgments became more negative. The positivity in judgments made after 100-ms exposure shows that the person positivity bias (Sears, 1983) may be particularly pronounced under conditions of minimal information in a safe experimental environment. When exposure time increased from 500 to 1,000 ms, none of the judgments shifted significantly, which suggests that a 500-ms exposure was sufficient for participants to create a subjectively satisfying trait impression. This interpretation is consistent with the findings for confidence. The increase in confidence was larger when exposure time increased from 100 to 500 ms than when it increased from 500 ms to 1,000 ms. Although judgments did not change when exposure time increased from 500 to 1,000 ms, confidence in judgments did increase for four of the five judgments. These findings suggest that minimal exposure to faces is sufficient for people to form trait impressions, and that additional exposure time can simply boost confidence in these impressions. That is, additional encounters with a person may serve only to justify quick, initial, on-line judgments.

We expected that the highest correlation between judgments made after 100-ms exposure and judgments made in the absence of time constraints would be for judgments of attractiveness. However, trustworthiness judgments showed the highest correlation. In hindsight, this finding is not surprising. Evolutionary psychologists have argued that detection of trustworthiness is essential for human survival (Cosmides & Tooby, 1992). Further, functional neuroimaging studies show that detection of trustworthiness in a face may be a spontaneous, automatic process linked to activity in the amygdala (Winston, Strange, O'Doherty, & Dolan, 2002), a subcortical brain structure implicated in the detection of potentially dangerous stimuli (Amaral, 2002). Work with patients with bilateral amygdala damage shows impaired ability to discriminate between trustworthy and untrustworthy faces (Adolphs, Tranel, & Damasio, 1998). These findings are consistent with the idea that people can be especially efficient in making inferences of trustworthiness, as shown by our findings. In fact, only judgments of attractiveness were as fast as judgments of trustworthiness in the present study.

We showed that a 100-ms exposure to a face suffices for people to make a trait inference, but we did not show that this is the minimum exposure that allows such inferences. Grill-Spector and Kanwisher (2005) showed that object categorization decisions were as fast as object detection decisions, concluding that "as soon as you know it is there, you know what it is." In fact, the accuracy of decisions was above chance for durations as short as 33 ms in their study. Identifying the lower limit of exposure time for inferring socially significant attributes from faces is an important task. Maybe, as soon as a face is there, you know whether to trust it. One implication of the current findings is that different trait judgments can have different time thresholds. For example, trustworthiness in a face may be inferred earlier than competence in a face.

To the extent that people form differentiated person impressions from facial appearance, additional exposure to a face can facilitate the formation of such impressions. The data from the factor analysis are consistent with this hypothesis. With increased exposure time, trait judgments became less correlated, suggesting a more fine-grained discrimination. For example, after 1,000-ms exposure, judgments of aggressiveness were independent of judgments of attractiveness and competence. The partial correlation analysis, showing that the effect of attractiveness on trait judgments decreased with increased exposure time, is also consistent with this hypothesis.

Conclusions

As minimal an exposure time as a tenth of a second is sufficient for people to make a specific trait inference from facial appearance. Additional exposure time increases confidence in judgments and allows for more differentiated trait impressions. However, the judgments are already anchored on the initial inference. Coupled with findings suggesting that inferences from facial appearance may be uncontrollable (Hassin & Trope, 2000, Experiment 4), our findings suggest that trait inferences from facial appearance can be characterized as fast, intuitive, System 1 processes. Lavater (1772/1880) might have been right about one thing: "Whether they are or are not sensible of it, all men [and women] are daily influenced by physiognomy" (p. 9). Not only trait inferences from facial appearance, but more generally inferences about other people may be effortless (e.g., Todorov & Uleman, 2003; Uleman, Blader, & Todorov, 2005). Person impressions are created effortlessly on-line from minimal information.

Acknowledgments—We thank Andy Conway and Ran Hassin for comments on an earlier version of this article and Manish Pakrashi for his help in running the experiments. This research was supported by National Science Foundation Grant BCS-0446846 to Alexander Todorov.

REFERENCES

Adolphs, R., Tranel, D., & Damasio, A.R. (1998). The human amygdala in social judgment. *Nature, 393*, 470–474.

Amaral, D.G. (2002). The primate amygdala and the neurobiology of social behavior: Implications for understanding social anxiety. *Biological Psychiatry, 51*, 11–17.

Chaiken, S., & Trope, Y. (Eds.). (1999). *Dual process theories in social psychology.* New York: Guilford Press.

Cosmides, L., & Tooby, J. (1992). Cognitive adaptations for social exchange. In J.H. Barkow, L. Cosmides, & J. Tooby (Eds.), *The adapted mind: Evolutionary psychology and the generation of culture* (pp. 163–228). London: Oxford University Press.

Grill-Spector, K., & Kanwisher, N. (2005). Visual recognition: As soon as you know it is there, you know what it is. *Psychological Science, 16*, 152–160.

Hamermesh, D., & Biddle, J. (1994). Beauty and the labor market. *The American Economic Review, 84*, 1174–1194.

Hassin, R., & Trope, Y. (2000). Facing faces: Studies on the cognitive aspects of physiognomy. *Journal of Personality and Social Psychology, 78*, 837–852.

Kahneman, D. (2003). A perspective on judgment and choice. *American Psychologist, 58*, 697–720.

Lavater, J.C. (1880). *Essays on physiognomy; for the promotion of the knowledge and the love of mankind* (Gale Document Number CW114125313). Retrieved May 15, 2005, from Gale Group, Eighteenth Century Collections Online. (Original work published 1772)

Lundqvist, D., Flykt, A., & O¨hman, A. (1998). *The Karolinska directed emotional faces* [Database of standardized facial images]. (Available from Psychology Section, Department of Clinical Neuroscience, Karolinska Hospital, S-171 76 Stockholm, Sweden)

Montepare, J.M., & Zebrowitz, L.A. (1998). Person perception comes of age: The salience and significance of age in social judgments. In M.P. Zanna (Ed.), *Advances in experimental social psychology* (Vol. 30, pp. 93–161). San Diego, CA: Academic Press.

Rousselet, G.A., Fabre-Thorpe, M., & Thorpe, S.J. (2002). Parallel processing in high-level categorization of natural images. *Nature Neuroscience, 5*, 629–630.

Sears, D.O. (1983). The person-positivity bias. *Journal of Personality and Social Psychology, 44*, 233–250.

Steiger, J.H. (1980). Tests for comparing elements of a correlation matrix. *Psychological Bulletin, 87*, 245–251.

Thorpe, S., Fize, D., & Marlot, C. (1996). Speed of processing in the human visual system. *Nature, 381*, 520–522.

Todorov, A., Mandisodza, A.N., Goren, A., & Hall, C.C. (2005). Inferences of competence from faces predict election outcomes. *Science, 308*, 1623–1626.

Todorov, A., & Uleman, J.S. (2003). The efficiency of binding spontaneous trait inferences to actors' faces. *Journal of Experimental Social Psychology, 39*, 549–562.

Uleman, J.S., Blader, S., & Todorov, A. (2005). Implicit impressions. In R. Hassin, J.S. Uleman, & J.A. Bargh (Eds.), *The new unconscious* (pp. 362–392). New York: Oxford University Press.

Winston, J., Strange, B., O'Doherty, J., & Dolan, R. (2002). Automatic and intentional brain responses during evaluation of trustworthiness of faces. *Nature Neuroscience, 5,* 277–283.

Zajonc, R.B. (1980). Feeling and thinking: Preferences need no inferences. *American Psychologist, 35,* 151–175.

Zebrowitz, L.A. (1999). *Reading faces: Window to the soul?* Boulder, CO: Westview Press.

Zebrowitz, L.A., & McDonald, S.M. (1991). The impact of litigants' babyfaceness and attractiveness on adjudications in small claims courts. *Law and Behavior, 15,* 603–623.

(RECEIVED 6/17/05; REVISION ACCEPTED 10/10/05; FINAL MATERIALS RECEIVED 11/15/05)

READING 4

The Consequences of Race for Police Officers' Responses to Criminal Suspects

In recent times, there have been several tragic incidents where policemen have fired at suspects thinking that they were carrying a weapon, when they were not. This type of error is most likely to occur when the suspect is a Black male. This is due, according to researchers Plant and Peruche, to the stereotype that Black people are more likely than Whites to be aggressive and criminal. In their study, they successfully employed a video game format to overcome this bias in a group of 48 police officers. The participants viewed photographs of faces of Black or White men with either a weapon or another object, such as a wallet, superimposed on each face. They were instructed to only shoot if there was a weapon. (One computer key was pressed to "shoot," another was designated as the "don't shoot" button.) At first, when playing the game, the policemen demonstrated the bias shooting unarmed Black men more often than unarmed White men. However, after extensive practice, having learned that the weapons were randomly distributed and not linked with race, they corrected for the bias. They learned to focus on the weapon and not on the race of the person whose photo was seen on the screen. This study highlights a form of implicit racism, which is discussed in Chapter 5 (Stereotypes, Prejudice, and Discrimination) of the text.

THE CONSEQUENCES OF RACE FOR POLICE OFFICERS' RESPONSES TO CRIMINAL SUSPECTS

E. Ashby Plant and B. Michelle Peruche

Florida State University

ABSTRACT—*The current work examined police officers' decisions to shoot Black and White criminal suspects in a computer simulation. Responses to the simulation revealed that upon initial exposure to the program, the officers were more likely to mistakenly shoot unarmed Black compared with unarmed White suspects. However, after extensive training with the program, in which the race of the suspect was unrelated to the presence of a weapon, the officers were able to eliminate this bias. These findings are discussed in terms of their implications for the elimination of racial biases and the training of police officers.*

When in the field, police officers face difficult split-second decisions in which they must determine whether criminal suspects are armed and constitute an imminent threat. Tragic events, such as the shooting of Marquise Hudspeth by police officers who mistook the cellular phone that the young Black man was carrying for a weapon, have led people to question whether officers' split-second decisions to

E. Ashby Plant and B. Michelle Peruche, "The Consequences of Race for Police Officers' Responses to Criminal Suspects," Psychological Science, Vol. 16, No. 3, pp. 180-183. Reprinted with permission of Blackwell Publishing, Inc.
Address correspondence to E. Ashby Plant, Department of Psychology, Florida State University, Tallahassee, FL 32306-1270; e-mail: plant@psy.fsu.edu.

shoot may be influenced by the suspects' race. Consider that the stereotype of Black people includes characteristics such as aggressive and criminal (Brigham, 1971; Devine & Elliot, 1995). This stereotype may create expectations that Black people, and particularly Black men, are more likely than White people to be violent criminals, which may lead to racially biased interpretations of suspects' behavior. If police officers possess such expectations, then their split-second decisions about whether or not to shoot at a suspect may be biased and result in more antagonistic responses to Black than White suspects.

Recent research has examined whether race influences people's decisions to shoot criminal suspects (e.g., Correll, Park, Judd, & Wittenbrink, 2002; Greenwald, Oakes, & Hoffman, 2003; Plant, Peruche, & Butz, in press). For example, Correll et al. had undergraduates complete a computer simulation in which they had to determine whether a male suspect who appeared on screen was holding a gun or a neutral object. If the suspect had a gun, they were instructed to shoot by hitting a specified button. If the suspect had a neutral object, they were instructed to hit a specified "don't shoot" button. The participants were more likely to mistakenly shoot (i.e., shoot an unarmed suspect) when the suspect was Black than when the suspect was White (also see Payne, 2001).

However, recent evidence indicates that such biases can be eliminated. Plant and her colleagues (in press) had participants complete a computer simulation similar to the one used by Correll et al. (2002). Undergraduates pretending to be police officers decided whether to shoot Black and White male suspects on the basis of whether a gun was present in the picture. Although the participants were initially more likely to mistakenly shoot unarmed Black suspects than unarmed White suspects, after extensive practice with the program, in which the race of the suspect was unrelated to the presence of a weapon, this racial bias was eliminated both immediately after training and 24 hr later. These findings indicate that repeated exposure to stimuli in which race is unrelated to the presence of a gun can eliminate race bias. Plant et al. argued that over the course of multiple trials, participants came to inhibit the activation of the racial category because race was nondiagnostic of weapon possession. As a result, participants eliminated the automatic influence of race on their responses. Additional findings were consistent with this argument: After training on the program, participants' responses on a word-completion task indicated that they were inhibiting racial concepts.

Given these findings with undergraduate students, it seems possible that police officers' responses to criminal suspects are influenced by the suspects' race, which could have tragic implications. Therefore, it is essential to consider whether police officers in fact have such racial biases and whether these biases can be eliminated with repeated exposure to a simulation in which the suspect's race is unrelated to the presence of a gun. To this end, in the present study, certified police patrol officers completed training with the computer simulation used by Plant et al. (in press). We expected that, as in the previous work with undergraduate participants, the officers' initial responses would reveal a bias toward mistakenly shooting unarmed Black suspects more often than unarmed White suspects. However, we anticipated that these biases would be eliminated after repeated exposure to the program, in which race was unrelated to weapon possession.

Method

Participants

Participants were 50 certified sworn law-enforcement personnel in the state of Florida (83% male; 84% White, 10% Black, 2% Native American, and 4% Hispanic). The mean age of participants was 37 years, and law-enforcement experience ranged from 2 to 30 years ($M = 12$). Two officers made too few valid responses to the computer simulation (i.e., responded to less than 20% of trials within the time limit), leaving a sample of 48 officers.

Permission to recruit officers was initially obtained through the chiefs of police of the police departments. After we received authorization, we asked police officers to voluntarily participate in a project examining object perception. Officers were informed that their responses would remain completely anonymous, and that this anonymity was ensured because they would not be providing their name or any identifying information.

Materials

In order to test the current hypotheses, we used the computer simulation from the previous study by Plant et al. (in press). The program, which uses Inquisit software, instructed participants:

> Today your task is to determine whether or not to shoot your gun. Pictures of people with objects will appear at various positions on the screen. . . . Some of the pictures will have a face of a person and a gun. These people are the criminals, and you are supposed to shoot at these people. Some of the pictures will have a face of a person and some other object (e.g., a wallet). These people are not the criminals and you should not shoot at them. Press the "A" key for "shoot" and press the "L" key on the keyboard for "don't shoot."

The program presented participants with digital color photographs of nine Black and nine White college-age males selected from a set of pictures matched for attractiveness (Malpass, Lavigueur, & Weldon, 1974). A picture of a gun or a neutral object (e.g., wallet, cell phone), formatted to be equivalent in size and background, was superimposed on each of the faces. The gun or other object was positioned with the face still visible, but the location varied so that participants could not predict where the object would appear. Two stimuli were created for each face, one with a gun and one with a neutral object.

On each trial, the computer program randomly selected one of the pictures and displayed it on the screen. So that the program would be challenging, the picture randomly appeared toward the top, middle, or bottom of the screen and toward the right, center, or left of the screen. Each picture appeared on screen until the participant responded or until the 630-ms time limit elapsed. When a participant did not make a correct decision (i.e., hit the wrong key or exceeded the time limit), an error message appeared on screen for a full second. Each participant completed 20 practice trials and 160 test trials.

Procedure

The officers met the experimenter individually in a private office at their department headquarters and were seated at a desk with a laptop computer. They were told that the study was about decisions to shoot and how different factors influence these decisions. Participants read the consent form and agreed to participate, but did not sign the form so that their anonymity would be ensured. The experimenter provided instructions regarding the computer simulation, and the participants completed the program. After the simulation, participants were debriefed and thanked for their participation.

Results

Analyses of the Simulation Task

In order to determine whether participants' performance on the simulation task revealed less bias on the later trials than the earlier trials, we split the trials in half and compared the responses on the first half of the trials with the responses on the second half. The error scores were submitted to a 2 (race of suspect: Black vs. White) × 2 (object: gun vs. neutral) × 2 (trial: early vs. late) repeated measures analysis of variance (ANOVA). This analysis revealed a main effect of trial, $F(1, 47) = 5.70, p < .03$, and a Race of Suspect × Object interaction, $F(1, 47) = 5.35, p < .03$. However, this lower-order interaction was qualified by a Race of Suspect × Object × Trial interaction, $F(1, 47) = 5.84, p < .03$ (see Table 1). Separate Race of Suspect × Object ANOVAs were conducted for the early and late trials in order to explore the nature of this interaction. Analyses of the early trials revealed a Race of Suspect × Object interaction, $F(1, 47) = 10.66, p < .003$. The officers were more likely to mistakenly shoot at an unarmed suspect when the suspect was Black than when the suspect was White, $t(1, 47) = -3.17, p < .002$. In contrast, when the suspect was armed, the officers were somewhat but not significantly more likely to mistakenly not shoot a White suspect than a Black suspect, $t(1, 47) = 1.60, p = .12$.

TABLE 1

Mean Number of Errors as a Function of Trial, Race of Suspect, and Object

Trial half and object	Race of suspect	
	White	Black
Early trials		
Gun	3.63 (2.64)	3.10 (2.27)
Neutral object	2.65 (2.14)	3.63 (2.45)
Late trials		
Gun	3.13 (2.19)	3.27 (2.84)
Neutral object	2.44 (1.91)	2.60 (1.90)

Note. Standard deviations are in parentheses.

Analysis of the error rates in the later trials revealed only a main effect of object, such that participants made more errors on trials with guns ($M = 3.20, SD = 2.52$) than on trials with neutral objects ($M = 2.52, SD = 1.90$), $F(1, 47) = 4.79, p < .04$. There was no interaction between race of suspect and object, $F < 1$.

Signal Detection Analyses

In evaluating responses to the program, it is useful to consider signal detection theory (Green & Swets, 1966; Snodgrass & Corwin, 1988). By examining participants' hits (i.e., shooting an armed suspect) and false alarms (i.e., shooting an unarmed suspect), we calculated the accuracy (i.e., d') of participants' decisions and the criterion that they used to make their decision (c). Decision criteria can range from liberal (e.g., the tendency to shoot) to conservative (e.g., the tendency not to shoot), with a criterion of 0 representing neither tendency.

On the basis of previous findings (e.g., Correll et al., 2002), we anticipated that the race of the suspect would not affect accuracy (d') on the early trials of the computer task; however, we did expect the race of the suspect to influence the decision criterion (c). Specifically, we anticipated that participants would use a more liberal criterion (i.e., be more likely to shoot) when responding to Black compared with White suspects. However, if exposure to the training program eliminated biases, then participants would shift to a more conservative criterion when responding to Black suspects on the later trials.

Participants' d' and c scores were submitted to 2 (race of suspect: Black vs. White) × 2 (object: gun vs. neutral) × 2 (trial: early vs. late) repeated measures ANOVAs. The analysis of d' revealed only a main effect of trial, such that participants responded with higher overall accuracy on the later trials ($d' = 1.89$) than the earlier trials ($d' = 1.55$), $F(1, 47) = 20.87, p < .001$. These findings indicate that the race biases apparent in responses to the early trials were not due to poorer accuracy on trials with Black suspects than on trials with White suspects.

There was also a main effect of trial for c scores, such that participants responded with more conservative criteria for later trials ($c = .05$) than earlier trials ($c = -.05$), $F(1, 47) = 5.20$, $p < .03$. The analysis also revealed a main effect of race of suspect, with participants showing more liberal criteria (i.e., tendency to shoot) for Black suspects ($c = -.06$) compared with White suspects ($c = .06$), $F(1, 47) = 9.63$, $p < .004$. However, this analysis also resulted in a marginal Race of Suspect × Trial interaction, $F(1, 47) = 2.90$, $p < .10$. Planned comparisons revealed that, as predicted, participants responded with more liberal criteria for Black suspects on early trials ($c = -.12$) than for White suspects on early trials ($c = .04$), $t(47) = -4.11$, $p < .001$. However, for the late trials, participants were similarly conservative in response to the Black ($c = .02$) and White ($c = .07$) suspects, $t(47) = -0.96$, $p = .34$. Further, comparison of the criteria across the early and late trials revealed that participants shifted their responses to the Black suspects to be more conservative on the late than the early trials, $t(47) = -2.82$, $p < .008$, but they did not alter their responses to the White suspects, $t(47) = -0.68$, $p = .50$.

Discussion

This experiment investigated police officers' decisions to shoot Black and White criminal suspects in a computer simulation. Examination of the officers' responses revealed that, as in previous work using undergraduate samples (e.g., Correll et al., 2002; Plant et al., in press), the officers were initially more likely to mistakenly shoot unarmed Black suspects than unarmed White suspects. These findings are troubling because racial biases in officers' responses to criminal suspects could have tragic implications if such biases generalize to real-life decisions. However, on a more promising note, after extensive exposure to the program, the officers were able to eliminate this bias. Specifically, although the officers were biased toward mistakenly shooting unarmed Black more than unarmed White suspects on the early trials, this bias was eliminated on the later trials. Thus, exposure to the program, in which the race of the suspect was unrelated to the presence of a weapon, eliminated the racial bias. Unlike much of the previous work demonstrating the existence of racial biases in decisions to shoot and in weapon identification (e.g., Correll et al., 2002; Payne, 2001), the current study is heartening and indicates that, although such biases exist in police officers' responses to computer simulations, they are not inevitable and may be eliminated.

Signal detection analyses demonstrated that exposure to the simulation resulted in a shift in participants' decision criteria for Black suspects, from a liberal bias toward shooting on early trials to a more conservative response on later trials that was consistent with participants' responses to White suspects. It is also worth noting that over the course of the trials, the officers were becoming more accurate in their responses to the simulation (i.e., they were making fewer errors regardless of race and weapon possession). Thus, exposure to the program had the added benefit of reducing all types of mistakes.

Overall, these findings are encouraging and suggest that it may be possible to eliminate racial biases in responses to criminal suspects. However, it is important to note that there is currently no evidence that the elimination of bias in response to the simulation generalizes to other types of responses (e.g., decisions in the field). Indeed, learning is often quite domain specific. Currently, officers train on programs (e.g., Firearms Training Systems, or FATS) that provide realistic simulation environments for officers to practice response accuracy in various "use of force" scenarios. Future work should explore the generalizability of the elimination of racial bias on the computer simulation used in the current work to other types of responses (e.g., FATS, decisions in the field). If responses generalize, training on such simulations may provide an important tool for eliminating racial biases and improving overall accuracy in police officers' decisions to shoot.

Conclusions

The aim of this study was to demonstrate that racial biases in responses to criminal suspects, although present among some police officers, are not inevitable and can be overcome with training on a computer simulation in which race is nondiagnostic. Our hope is that the current work provides a critical first step toward understanding the factors that influence (and potentially eliminate) racial biases in police officers' responses to criminal suspects.

REFERENCES

Brigham, J.C. (1971). Ethnic stereotypes. *Psychological Bulletin, 76*, 15–38.

Correll, J., Park, B., Judd, C.M., & Wittenbrink, B. (2002). The police officer's dilemma: Using ethnicity to disambiguate potentially threatening individuals. *Journal of Personality and Social Psychology, 83*, 1314–1329.

Devine, P.G., & Elliot, A.J. (1995). Are racial stereotypes really fading? The Princeton trilogy revisited. *Personality and Social Psychology Bulletin, 21*, 1139–1150.

Green, D.M., & Swets, J.A. (1966). *Signal detection and psychophysics*. Huntington, NY: Robert E. Krieger.

Greenwald, A.G., Oakes, M.A., & Hoffman, H.G. (2003). Targets of discrimination: Effects of race on responses to weapon holders. *Journal of Experimental Social Psychology, 39*, 399–405.

Malpass, R.S., Lavigueur, H., &Weldon, D.E. (1974). Verbal and visual training in facial recognition. *Perception & Psychophysics, 14*, 285–292.

Payne, B.K. (2001). Prejudice and perception: The role of automatic and controlled processes in misperceiving a weapon. *Journal of Personality and Social Psychology, 81*, 181–192.

Plant, E.A., Peruche, B.M., & Butz, D.A. (in press). Eliminating automatic racial bias: Making race non-diagnostic for responses to criminal suspects. *Journal of Experimental Social Psychology*.

Snodgrass, J.G., & Corwin, J. (1988). Pragmatics of measuring recognition memory: Applications to dementia and amnesia. *Journal of Experimental Psychology: General, 117*, 34–50.

(RECEIVED 3/23/04; REVISION ACCEPTED 7/1/04)

READING 5

Stereotype Threat and the Intellectual Test Performance of African Americans

This article by Steele and Aronson (1995) triggered a wave of research and interest in what soon came to be known as *stereotype threat*—a predicament in which members of stereotyped groups face situations in which they have reason to fear being seen through the lens of negative stereotypes about their abilities in some domain. Many of the studies inspired by this article are discussed in Chapter 5 (Perceiving Groups). In the research presented here, Steele and Aronson test the provocative hypothesis that African American students may perform below their potential on intellectual tests because of this kind of threat. That is, the testing situation may bring to mind negative stereotypes and low expectations concerning African Americans' abilities on these kinds of tests, which makes African American students vulnerable to being undermined by these concerns. What's particularly exciting about this research is how a relatively simple change in the way the test is introduced to the students can eliminate this threat and allow African American students to perform to their potential.

STEREOTYPE THREAT AND THE INTELLECTUAL TEST PERFORMANCE OF AFRICAN AMERICANS[*]

Claude M. Steele

Stanford University

Joshua Aronson

University of Texas, Austin

Stereotype threat *is being at risk of confirming, as self-characteristic, a negative stereotype about one's group. Studies 1 and 2 varied the stereotype vulnerability of Black participants taking a difficult verbal test by varying whether or not their performance was ostensibly diagnostic of ability, and thus, whether or not they were at risk of fulfilling the racial stereotype about their intellectual ability.*

Reflecting the pressure of this vulnerability, Blacks underperformed in relation to Whites in the ability-diagnostic condition but not in the nondiagnostic condition (with Scholastic Aptitude Tests controlled). Study 3 validated that ability-diagnosticity cognitively activated the racial stereotype in these participants and motivated them not to conform to it, or to be judged by it. Study 4 showed that mere salience of the stereotype could impair Blacks' performance even when the test was not ability diagnostic. The role of stereotype vulnerability in the standardized test performance of ability-stigmatized groups is discussed.

Claude M. Steele and Joshua Aronson, "Stereotype Vulnerability and the Intellectual Test Performance of African Americans," Journal of Personality and Social Psychology, 1995, Vol. 69, No. 5, pp. 797-811.

Claude M. Steele, Department of Psychology, Stanford University; Joshua Aronson, School of Education, University of Texas, Austin. This research was supported by National Institutes of Health Grant MH51977, Russell Sage Foundation Grant 879.304, and by Spencer Foundation and James S. McDonnell Foundation postdoctoral fellowships, and its completion was aided by the Center for Advanced Study in the Behavioral Sciences.

We thank John Butner, Emmeline Chen, and Matthew McGlone for assistance and helpful comments on this research.

Correspondence concerning this article should be addressed to Claude M. Steele, Department of Psychology, Stanford University, Stanford, California 94305, or Joshua Aronson, School of Education, University of Texas, Austin, Texas 78712.

Not long ago, in explaining his career-long preoccupation with the American Jewish experience, the novelist Philip Roth said that it was not Jewish culture or religion per se that fascinated him, it was what he called the Jewish "predicament." This is an apt term for the perspective taken in the present research. It focuses on a social-psychological predicament that can arise from widely-known negative stereotypes about one's group. It is this: the existence of such a stereotype means that anything one does or any of one's features that conform to it make the stereotype more plausible as a self-characterization in the eyes of others, and perhaps even in one's own eyes. We call this predicament *stereotype threat* and argue that it is experienced, essentially, as a self-evaluative threat. In form, it is a predicament that can beset the members of any group about whom negative stereotypes exist. Consider the stereotypes elicited by the terms *yuppie, feminist, liberal*, or *White male*. Their prevalence in society raises the possibility for potential targets that the stereotype is true of them and, also, that other people will see them that way. When the allegations of the stereotype are importantly negative, this predicament may be self-threatening enough to have disruptive effects of its own.

The present research examined the role these processes play in the intellectual test performance of African Americans. Our reasoning is this: whenever African American students perform an explicitly scholastic or intellectual task, they face the threat of confirming or being judged by a negative societal stereotype—a suspicion—about their group's intellectual ability and competence. This threat is not borne by people not stereotyped in this way. And the self-threat it causes—through a variety of mechanisms—may interfere with the intellectual functioning of these students, particularly during standardized tests. This is the principal hypothesis examined in the present research. But as this threat persists over time, it may have the further effect of pressuring these students to protectively disidentify with achievement in school and related intellectual domains. That is, it may pressure the person to define or redefine the self-concept such that school achievement is neither a basis of self-evaluation nor a personal identity. This protects the person against the self-evaluative threat posed by the stereotypes but may have the byproduct of diminishing interest, motivation, and, ultimately, achievement in the domain (Steele, 1992).

The anxiety of knowing that one is a potential target of prejudice and stereotypes has been much discussed: in classic social science (e.g., Allport, 1954; Goffman, 1963), popular books (e.g., Carter, 1991) and essays, as, for example, S. Steele's (1990) treatment of what he called *racial vulnerability*. In this last analysis, S. Steele made a connection between this experience and the school life of African Americans that has similarities to our own. He argued that after a lifetime of exposure to society's negative images of their ability, these students are likely to internalize an "inferiority anxiety"—a state that can be aroused by a variety of race-related cues in the environment. This anxiety, in turn, can lead them to blame others for their troubles (for example, White racism), to underutilize available opportunities, and to generally form a victim's identity. These adaptations, in turn, the argument goes, translate into poor life success.

The present theory and research do not focus on the internalization of inferiority images or their consequences. Instead they focus on the immediate situational threat that derives from the broad dissemination of negative stereotypes about one's group—the threat of possibly being judged and treated stereotypically, or of possibly self-fulfilling such a stereotype. This threat can befall anyone with a group identity about which some negative stereotype exists, and for the person to be threatened in this way, he need not even believe the stereotype. He need only know that it stands as a hypothesis about him in situations where the stereotype is relevant. We focused on the stereotype threat of African Americans in intellectual and scholastic domains to provide a compelling test of the theory and because the theory, should it be supported in this context for this group, would have relevance to an important set of outcomes.

Gaps in school achievement and retention rates between White and Black Americans at all levels of schooling have been strikingly persistent in American society (e.g., Steele, 1992). Well publicized at the kindergarten through 12th grade level, recent statistics show that they persist even at the college level where, for example, the national drop-out rate for Black college students (the percentage who do not complete college within a 6-year window of time) is 70% compared to 42% for White Americans (American Council on Education, 1990). Even among those who graduate, their grades average two thirds of letter grade lower than those of graduating Whites (e.g., Nettles, 1988). It has been most common to understand such problems as stemming largely from the socioeconomic disadvantage, segregation, and discrimination that African Americans have endured and continue to endure in this society, a set of conditions that, among other things, could produce racial gaps in achievement by undermining preparation for school.

Some evidence, however, questions the sufficiency of these explanations. It comes from the sizable literature examining racial bias in standardized testing. This work, involving hundreds of studies over several decades, generally shows that standardized tests predict subsequent school achievement as well for Black students as for White students (e.g., Cleary, Humphreys, Kendrick, & Wesman, 1975; Linn, 1973; Stanley, 1971). The slope of the lines regressing subsequent school achievement on entry-level standardized test scores is essentially the same for both groups. But embedded in this literature is another fact: At every level of preparation as measured by a standardized test—for example, the Scholastic Aptitude Test (SAT)—Black students with that score have poorer subsequent achievement—GPA, retention rates, time to graduation, and so on—than White students with that score (Jensen, 1980). This is variously known as the overprediction or underachievement phenomenon, because it indicates that, relative to Whites with the same score, standardized tests actually overpredict the achievement that Blacks will realize. Most important for our purposes, this evidence suggests that Black-White achievement gaps are not due solely to group differences in preparation. Blacks achieve less well than Whites even when they have the same preparation, and even when that preparation is at a very high level. Could this underachievement, in some part, reflect the stereotype threat that is a chronic feature of these students' schooling environments?

Research from the early 1960s—largely that of Irwin Katz and his colleagues (e.g., Katz, 1964) on how desegregation affected the intellectual performance of Black students—shows the sizable influence on Black intellectual performance of factors that can be interpreted as manipulations of stereotype threat. Katz, Roberts, and Robinson (1965), for example, found that Black participants performed better on an IQ subtest when it was presented as a test of eye-hand coordination—a nonevaluative and thus threat-negating test representation—than when it was said to be a test of intelligence. Katz, Epps, and Axelson (1964) found that Black students performed better on an IQ test when they believed their performance would be compared to other Blacks as opposed to Whites. But as evidence that bears on our hypothesis, this literature has several limitations. Much of the research was conducted in an era when American race relations were different in important ways than they are now. Thus, without their being replicated, the extent to which these findings reflect enduring processes of stereotype threat as opposed to the racial dynamics of a specific historical era is not clear. Also, this research seldomly used White control groups. Thus it is difficult to know the extent to which some of the critical effects were mediated by the stereotype threat of Black students as opposed to processes experienced by any students.

Other research supports the present hypothesis by showing that factors akin to stereotype threat—that is, other factors that add self-evaluative threat to test taking or intellectual performance—are capable of disrupting that performance. The presence of observers or coactors, for example, can interfere with performance on mental tasks (e.g., Geen, 1985; Seta, 1982). Being a "token" member of a group—the sole representative of a social category—can inhibit one's memory for what is said during a group discussion (Lord & Saenz, 1985; Lord, Saenz, & Godfrey, 1987). Conditions that increase the importance of performing well—prizes, competition, and audience approval—have all been shown to impair performance of even motor skills (e.g., Baumeister, 1984). The stereotype threat hypothesis shares with these approaches the assumption that performance suffers when the situation redirects attention needed to perform a task onto some other concern—in the case of stereotype threat, a concern with the significance of one's performance in light of a devaluing stereotype.

For African American students, the act of taking a test purported to measure intellectual ability may be enough to induce this threat. But we assume that this is most likely to happen when the test is also frustrating. It is frustration that makes the stereotype—as an allegation of inability—relevant to their performance and thus raises the possibility that they have an inability linked to their race. This is not to argue that the stereotype is necessarily believed; only that, in the face of frustration with the test, it becomes more plausible as a self-characterization and thereby more threatening to the self. Thus for Black students who care about the skills being tested—that is, those who are identified with these skills in the sense of their self-regard being somewhat tied to having them—the stereotypeloads the testing situation with an extra degree of self-threat, a degree not borne by people not stereotyped in this way. This additional threat, in turn, may interfere with their performance in a variety of ways: by causing an arousal that reduces the range of cues participants are able to use (e.g., Easterbrook, 1959), or by diverting attention onto task-irrelevant worries (e.g., Sarason, 1972; Wine, 1971), by causing an interfering self-consciousness (e.g., Baumeister, 1984), or overcautiousness (Geen, 1985). Or, through the ability-indicting interpretation it poses for test frustration, it could foster low performance expectations that would cause participants to withdraw effort (e.g., Bandura, 1977, 1986). Depending on the situation, several of these processes may be involved simultaneously or in alternation. Through these mechanisms, then, stereotype threat might be expected to undermine the standardized test performance of Black participants relative to White participants who, in this situation, do not suffer this added threat.

STUDY 1

Accordingly, Black and White college students in this experiment were given a 30-min test composed of items from the verbal Graduate Record Examination (GRE) that were difficult enough to be at the limits of most participants' skills. In the stereotype-threat condition, the test was described as diagnostic of intellectual ability, thus making the racial stereotype about intellectual ability relevant to Black participants' performance and establishing for them the threat of fulfilling it. In the nonstereotype-threat condition, the same test was described simply as a laboratory problem-solving task that was nondiagnostic of ability. Presumably, this would make the racial stereotype about ability irrelevant to Black participants' performance and thus preempt any threat of fulfilling it. Finally, a second nondiagnostic condition was included which exhorted participants to view the difficult test as a challenge. For practical reasons we were interested in whether stressing the challenge inherent in a difficult test might further increase participants' motivation and performance over what would occur in the nondiagnostic condition. The primary dependent measure in this experiment was participants' performance on the test adjusted for the influence of individual differences in skill level (operationalized as participants' verbal SAT scores).

We predicted that Black participants would underperform relative to Whites in the diagnostic condition where there was stereotype threat, but not in the two nondiagnostic conditions—the non-diagnostic-only condition and the non-diagnostic-plus-challenge condition—where this threat was presumably reduced. In the non-diagnostic-challenge condition, we also expected the additional motivation to boost the performance of both Black and White participants above that observed in the non-diagnostic-only condition. Several additional measures were included to assess the effectiveness of the manipulation and possible mediating states.

Method

Design and Participants This experiment took the form of a 2 × 3 factorial design. The factors were race of the participant, Black or White, and a test description factor in which the test was presented as either diagnostic of intellectual ability (the diagnostic condition), as a laboratory tool for studying problem solving (the non-diagnostic-only condition), or as both a problem-solving tool and a challenge (the non-diagnostic-challenge condition). Test performance was the primary dependent measure. We recruited 117 male and female, Black and White Stanford undergraduates through campus advertisements which offered $10.00 for 1 hr of participation. The data from 3 participants were excluded from the analysis because they failed to provide their verbal SAT scores. This left a total of 114 participants randomly assigned to the three experimental conditions with the exception that we ensured an equal number of participants per condition.

Procedure Participants who signed up for the experiment were contacted by telephone prior to their experimental participation and asked to provide their verbal and quantitative SAT scores, to rate their enjoyment of verbally oriented classes, and to provide background information (e.g., year in school, major, etc.). When participants arrived at the laboratory, the experimenter (a White man) explained that for the next 30 min they would work on a set of verbal problems in a format identical to the SAT exam, and end by answering some questions about their experience.

The participant was then given a page that stated the purpose of the study, described the procedure for answering questions, stressed the importance of indicating guessed answers (by a check), described the test as very difficult and that they should expect not to get many of the questions correct, and told them that they would be given feedback on their performance at the end of the session. We included the information about test difficulty to, as much as possible, equate participants' performance expectations across the conditions. And, by acknowledging the difficulty of the test, we wanted to reduce the possibility that participants would see the test as a miscalculation of their skills and perhaps reduce their effort. This description was the same for all conditions with the exception of several key phrases that comprised the experimental manipulation.

Participants in the diagnostic condition were told that the study was concerned with "various personal factors involved in performance on problems requiring reading and verbal reasoning abilities." They were further informed that after the test, feedback would be provided which "may be helpful to you by familiarizing you with some of your strengths and weaknesses" in verbal problem solving. As noted, participants in all conditions were told that they should not expect to get many items correct, and in the diagnostic condition, this test difficulty was justified as a means of providing a "genuine test of your verbal abilities and limitations so that we might better understand the factors involved in both." Participants were asked to give a strong effort in order to "help us in our analysis of your verbal ability."

In the non-diagnostic-only and non-diagnostic-challenge conditions, the description of the study made no reference to verbal ability. Instead, participants were told that the purpose of the research was to better understand the "psychological factors involved in solving verbal problems. . . ." These participants too were told that they would receive performance feedback, but it was justified as a means of familiarizing them "with the kinds of problems that appear on tests [they] may encounter in the future." In the non-diagnostic-only condition, the difficulty of the test was justified in terms of a research focus on difficult verbal problems and in the non-diagnostic-challenge condition it was justified as an attempt to provide "even highly verbal people with a mental challenge. . . ." Last, participants in both conditions were asked to give a genuine effort in order to "help us in our analysis of the problem solving process." As the experimenter left them to work on the test, to further differentiate the conditions, participants in the non-diagnostic-only condition were asked to try hard "even though we're not going to evaluate your ability." Participants in the non-diagnostic-challenge condition were asked to "please take this challenge seriously even though we will not be evaluating your ability."

Dependent Measures The primary dependent measure was participants' performance on 30 verbal items, 27 of which were difficult items taken from GRE study guides (only 30% of earlier samples had gotten these items correct) and 3 difficult anagram problems. Both the total number correct and an accuracy index of the number correct over the number attempted were analyzed.

Participants next completed an 18-item self-report measure of their current thoughts relating to academic competence and personal worth (e.g., "I feel confident about my abilities," "I feel self-conscious," "I feel as smart as others," etc.). These were measured on 5-point scales anchored by the phrases *not at all* (1) and *extremely* (5). Participants also completed a 12-item measure of cognitive interference frequently used in test anxiety research (Sarason, 1980) on which they indicated the frequency of several distracting thoughts during the exam (e.g., "I wondered what the experimenter would think of me," "I thought about how poorly I was doing," "I thought about the difficulty of the problems," etc.) by putting a number from 1 (*never*) to 5 (*very often*) next to each statement. Participants then rated how difficult and biased they considered the test on 15-point scales anchored by the labels *not at all* (1) and *extremely* (15). Next, participants evaluated their own performance by estimating the number of problems they correctly solved, and by comparing their own performance to that of the average Stanford student on a 15-point scale with the end points *much worse* (1) and *much better* (15). Finally, as a check on the manipulation, participants responded to the question:

> The purpose of this experiment was to: (a) provide a genuine test of my abilities in order to examine personal factors involved in verbal ability; (b) provide a challenging test in order to examine factors involved in solving verbal problems; (c) present you with unfamiliar verbal problems to measure verbal learning.

Participants were asked to circle the appropriate response.

Results

Because there were no main or interactive effects of gender on verbal test performance or the self-report measures, we collapsed over this factor in all analyses.

Manipulation Check Chi-square analyses performed on participants' responses to the postexperimental question about the purpose of the study revealed only an effect of condition, $x^2 (2) = 43.18, p < .001$. Participants were more likely to believe the purpose of the experiment was to evaluate their abilities in the diagnostic condition (65%) than in the nondiagnostic condition (3%), or the challenge condition (11%).

Test Performance The ANCOVA on the number of items participants got correct, using their self-reported SAT scores as the covariate (Black mean = 592, White mean = 632) revealed a significant condition main effect, $F(2, 107) = 4.74, p < .02$, with participants in the non-diagnostic-challenge condition performing higher than participants in the non-diagnostic-only and diagnostic conditions, respectively, and a significant race main effect, $F(1, 107) = 5.22, p < .03$, with White participants performing higher than Black participants.[1] The race-by-condition interaction did not reach conventional significance ($p < .19$). The adjusted condition means are presented in Figure 1.

If making the test diagnostic of ability depresses the performance of Black students through stereotype threat, then their performance should be lower in the diagnostic condition than in either the non-diagnostic-only or non-diagnostic-challenge conditions which presumably lessened stereotype threat, and it should be lower than that of Whites in the diagnostic condition. Bonferroni contrasts[2] with SATs as a covariate supported this reasoning by showing that Black participants in the diagnostic condition performed significantly worse than Black participants in either the nondiagnostic condition, $t(107) = 2.88, p < .01$, or the challenge **condition**, $t(107) = 2.63, p < .01$, as well as significantly worse than White participants in the diagnostic condition $t(107) = 2.64, p < .01$.

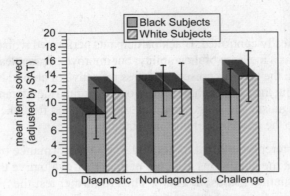

Figure 1. Mean test performance Study 1.

But, as noted, the interaction testing the differential effect of test diagnosticity on Black and White participants did not reach significance. This may have happened, however, because an incidental pattern of means—Whites slightly outperforming Blacks in the nondiagnostic-challenge condition—undermined the overall interaction effect. To pursue a more sensitive test, we constructed a weighted contrast that compared the size of the race effect in the diagnostic condition with that in the nondiagnostic condition and assigned weights of zero to the White and Black non-diagnostic-challenge conditions. This analysis (including the use of SATs as a covariate) reached marginal significance, $F(1, 107) = 3.27, p < .08$. In sum, then, the hypothesis was supported by the pattern of contrasts, but when tested over the whole design, reached only marginal significance.

Accuracy An ANCOVA on accuracy, the proportion correct of the number attempted, with SATs as the covariate, found that neither condition main effect nor the interaction reached significance, although there was a marginally significant tendency for Black participants to evidence less accuracy, $p < .10$. This tendency was primarily due to Black participants in the diagnostic condition who had the lowest adjusted mean accuracy of any group in the experiment, .420. The adjusted means for the White diagnostic, White non-diagnostic-only, White non-diagnostic-challenge, Black non-diagnostic-only, and Black diagnostic-challenge conditions were, .519, .518, .561, .546, and .490, respectively. Bonferroni tests revealed that Black participants in the diagnostic condition were reliably less accurate than Black participants in the non-diagnostic-only condition and While participants in the diagnostic condition, $t(107) = 2.64, p < .01$, and $t(107) = 2.13, p < .05$, respectively.

No condition or interaction effects reached significance for the number of items completed or the number of guesses participants recorded on the test (all $Fs < 1$). The overall means for these two measures were 22.9 and 4.1, respectively.

Self-Report Measures There were no significant condition effects on the self-report measure of academic competence and personal worth or on the self-report measure of disruptive thoughts and feelings during the test. Analysis of participants' responses to the question about test bias yielded a main effect of race, $F(1, 107) = 10.47, p < .001$. Black participants in all conditions thought the test was more biased than White participants.

Perceived Performance Participants' estimates of how many problems they solved correctly and of how they compared to other participants both showed significant condition main effects, $F(2, 106) = 7.91, p < .001$, and $F(2, 107) = 3.17, p < .05$, respectively. Performance estimates were higher in the non-diagnostic-only condition ($M = 11.81$) than in either the diagnostic ($M = 9.20$) or non-diagnostic-challenge conditions ($M = 8.15$). Bonferroni tests showed that Black participants in the diagnostic condition ($M = 4.89$) saw their relative performance as poorer than Black participants in the non-diagnostic-only condition ($M = 6.54$), $t(107) = 2.81, p < .01$, and than Black participants in the nondiagnostic-challenge condition ($M = 6.30$), $t(107) = 2.40, p < .02$., while test description had no effect on the ratings of White participants. The overall mean was 5.86.

Discussion

With SAT differences statistically controlled, Black participants performed worse than White participants when the test was presented as a measure of their ability, but improved dramatically, matching the performance of Whites, when the test was presented as less reflective of ability. Nonetheless, the race-by-diagnosticity interaction testing this relationship reached only marginal significance, and then, only when participants from the non-diagnostic-challenge condition were excluded from the analysis. Thus there remained some question as to the reliability of this interaction.

We had also reasoned that stereotype threat might undermine performance by increasing interfering thoughts during the test. But the conditions affected neither self-evaluative thoughts nor thoughts about the self in the immediate situation (Sarason, 1980). Thus to further test the reliability of the predicted interaction and explore the mediation of the stereotype threat effect, we conducted a second experiment.

STUDY 2

We argued that the effect of stereotype threat on performance is mediated by an apprehension over possibly conforming to the negative group stereotype. Could this apprehension be detected as a higher level of general anxiety among stereotype-threatened participants? To test this possibility, participants in all conditions completed a version of the Spielberger State Anxiety Inventory (STAI) immediately after the test. This scale has been successfully used in other research to detect anxiety induced by evaluation apprehension (e.g., Geen, 1985). We also measured the amount of time they spent on each test item to learn whether greater anxiety was associated with more time spent answering items.

Method

Participants Twenty Black and 20 White Stanford female undergraduates were randomly assigned (with the exception of attaining equal cell sizes) to either the diagnostic or the nondiagnostic conditions as described in Study 1, yielding 10 participants per condition. Female participants were used in this experiment because, due to other research going on, we had considerably easier access to Black female undergraduates than to Black male undergraduates. This decision was justified by the finding of no gender differences in the first study, or, as it turned out, in any of the subsequent studies reported in this article—all of which used both men and women.

Procedure This experiment used the same test used in Study 1, with several exceptions; the final three ana-gram problems were deleted and the test period was reduced from 30 to 25 min. Also, the test was presented on a Macintosh computer (LCII). Participants controlled with the mouse how long each item or item component was on the screen and could, at their own pace, access whatever item material they wanted to see. The computer recorded the amount of time the items, or item components were on the screen as well as the number of referrals between item components (as in the reading comprehension items)—in addition to recording participants' answers.

Following the exam, participants completed the STAI and the cognitive interference measure described for Study 1. Also, on 11-point scales (with end-points *not at all* and *extremely*) participants indicated the extent to which they guessed when having difficulty, expended effort on the test, persisted on problems, limited their time on problems, read problems more than once, became frustrated and gave up, and felt that the test was biased.

Results and Discussion

The ANCOVA performed on the number of items correctly solved yielded a significant main effect of race, $F(1, 35) = 10.04$, $p < .01$, qualified by a significant Race × Test Description interaction, $F(1, 35) = 8.07$, $p < .01$. The mean SAT score for Black participants was 603 and for White participants 655. The adjusted means are presented in Figure 2. Planned contrasts on the adjusted scores revealed that, as predicted, Blacks in the diagnostic condition performed significantly worse than Blacks in the nondiagnostic condition $t(35) = 2.38$, $p < .02$, than Whites in the diagnostic condition $t(35) = 3.75$, $p < .001$, and than Whites in the nondiagnostic condition $t(35) = 2.34$, $p < .025$.

For accuracy—the number correct over the number attempted—a similar pattern emerged: Blacks in the diagnostic condition had lower accuracy ($M = .392$) than Blacks in the nondiagnostic condition ($M = .490$) or than Whites in either the diagnostic condition ($M = .485$) or the nondiagnostic condition ($M = .435$). The diagnosticity-by-race interaction testing this pattern reached significance, $F(1, 35) = 4.18$, $p < .05$. But the planned contrasts of the Black diagnostic condition against the other conditions did not reach conventional

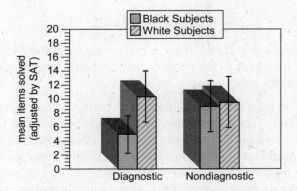

Figure 2. Mean test performance Study 2.

significance, although its contrasts with the Black nondiagnostic and White diagnostic conditions were marginally significant, with ps of .06 and .09 respectively.

Blacks completed fewer items than Whites, $F(1, 35) = 9.35$, $p < .01$, and participants in the diagnostic conditions tended to complete fewer items than those in the nondiagnostic conditions, $F(1, 35) = 3.69$, $p < .07$. The overall interaction did not reach significance. But planned contrasts revealed that Black participants in the diagnostic condition finished fewer items ($M = 12.38$) than Blacks in the nondiagnostic condition ($M = 18.53$), $t(35) = 2.50$, $p < .02$; than Whites in the diagnostic condition ($M = 20.93$), $t(35) = 3.39$, $p < .01$; and than Whites in the nondiagnostic condition ($M = 21.45$), $t(35) = 3.60$, $p < .01$.

These results establish the reliability of the diagnosticity-by-race interaction for test performance that was marginally significant in Study 1. They also reveal another dimension of the effect of stereotype threat. Black participants in the diagnostic condition completed fewer test items than participants in the other conditions. Test diagnosticity impaired the rate, as well as the accuracy of their work. This is precisely the impairment caused by evaluative pressures such as evaluation apprehension, test anxiety, and competitive pressure (e.g., Baumeister, 1984). But one might ask why this did not happen in the near-identical Study 1. Several factors may be relevant. First, the most involved test items—reading comprehension items that took several steps to answer—came first in the test. And second, the test lasted 25 min in the present experiment whereas it lasted 30 min in the first experiment. Assuming, then, that stereotype threat slowed the pace of Black participants in the diagnostic conditions of both experiments, this 5-min difference in test period may have made it harder for these participants in the present experiment to get past the early, involved items and onto the more quickly answered items at the end of the test, a possibility that may also explain the generally lower scores in this experiment.

This view is reinforced by the ANCOVA (with SATs as a covariate) on the average time spent on each of the first five test items—the minimum number of items that all participants in all conditions answered. A marginal effect of test presentation emerged, $F(1, 35) = 3.52$, $p < .07$, but planned comparisons showed that Black participants in the diagnostic condition tended to be slower than participants in the other conditions. On average they spent 94 s answering each of these items in contrast to 71 for Black participants in the nondiagnostic condition, $t(35) = 2.39$, $p < .05$; 73 s for Whites in the diagnostic condition, $t(35) = 2.12$, $p < .05$, and 71 s for Whites in the nondiagnostic condition, $t(35) = 2.37$, $p < .05$. Like other forms of evaluative pressure, stereotype threat causes an impairment of both accuracy and speed of performance.

No differences were found on any of the remaining measures, including self-reported effort, cognitive interference, or anxiety. These measures may have been insensitive, or too delayed. Nonetheless, we lack an important kind of evidence. We have not shown that test diagnosticity causes in Black participants a specific apprehension about fulfilling the negative group stereotype about their ability—the apprehension that we argue disrupts their test performance. To examine this issue we conducted a third experiment.

STUDY 3

Taking an intellectually diagnostic test and experiencing some frustration with it, we have assumed, is enough to cause stereotype threat for Black participants. In testing this reasoning, the present experiment examines several specific propositions.

First, if taking or expecting to take a difficult, intellectually diagnostic test makes Black participants feel threatened by a specifically racial stereotype, then it might be expected to activate that stereotype in their thinking and information processing. That is, the racial stereotype, and perhaps also the self-doubts associated with it, should be more cognitively activated for these participants than for Black participants in the nondiagnostic condition or for White participants in either condition (e.g., Dovidio, Evans, & Tyler, 1986; Devine, 1989; Higgins, 1989). Accordingly, in testing whether test diagnosticity arouses this state, the present experiment measured the effect of conditions on the activation of this stereotype and of related self-doubts about ability.

Second, if test diagnosticity makes Black participants apprehensive about fulfilling and being judged by the racial stereotype, then these participants, more than participants in the other conditions, might be motivated to disassociate themselves from the stereotype. Brent Staples, an African American editorialist for the *New York Times*, offers an example of this in his recent autobiography, *Parallel Time*. He describes beginning graduate school at the University of Chicago and finding that as he walked the streets of Hyde Park he made people uncomfortable. They grouped more closely when he walked by, and some even crossed the street to avoid him. He eventually realized that in that urban context, dressed as a student, he was being perceived through the lens of a race-class stereotype as a potentially menacing Black man. To deflect this perception he learned a trick; he would whistle Vivaldi. It worked. Upon hearing him do this, people around him visibly relaxed and he felt out of suspicion. If it is apprehension about being judged in light of the racial stereotype that interferes with the performance of Black participants in the diagnostic condition, then these participants, like Staples, might be motivated to deflect such a perception by showing that the broader racial stereotype is not applicable to them. To test this possibility, the present experiment measured the effect of conditions on participants' stated preferences for such things as activities and styles of music, some of which were stereotypic of African Americans.

Third, by adding to the normal evaluative risks of test performance the further risk of self-validating the racial stereotype, the diagnostic condition should also make Black participants more apprehensive about their test performance. The present experiment measured this apprehension as the degree to which participants self-handicapped their expected performance, that is, endorsed excuses for poor performance before the test.

The experiment took the form of a 2×3 design in which the race of participants (African American or White) was crossed with diagnostic, nondiagnostic, and control conditions. The diagnostic and nondiagnostic conditions were the same as those described for Study 2, while in the control condition participants completed the critical dependent measures without expecting to take a test of any sort. In the experimental conditions, the dependent measures were administered immediately after the diagnosticity instructions and just before the test was ostensibly to be taken. These included measures of stereotype activation, stereotype avoidance, and, as a measure of general performance apprehension, participants' willingness to self-handicap. Participants in this experiment never took the test. The measures of stereotype activation and stereotype avoidance, we felt, could activate the racial stereotype and stereotype threat among Black participants in both the diagnostic and nondiagnostic conditions, making performance results difficult to interpret.

If test diagnosticity threatens Black participants with a specifically racial stereotype, then Black participants in the diagnostic condition, more than participants in the other conditions, should show greater cognitive activation of the stereotype and ability-related self-doubts, greater motivation to disassociate themselves from the stereotype, and greater performance apprehension as indicated by the endorsement of self-handicapping excuses.

Method

Participants Thirty-five Black (9 male, 26 female) and 33 White (20 male, 13 female) Stanford undergraduates were randomly assigned to either a diagnostic, nondiagnostic, or control condition, yielding from 10 to 12 participants per experimental group.

Procedure A White male experimenter gave a booklet to participants as they arrived that explained that the study was examining the relationship between two types of cognitive processes: lexical access processing (LAP) and higher verbal reasoning (HVR). They were told that they would be asked to complete two tasks, one of which measured LAP—"the visual and recognition processing of words"—and the other of which measured HVR—"abstract reasoning about the meaning of words." Test diagnosticity was manipulated as in Study 1 with the following written instructions to further differentiate the conditions:

Diagnostic: Because we want an accurate measure of your ability in these domains, we want to ask you to try as hard as you can to perform well on these tasks. At the end of the study, we can give you feedback which may be helpful by pointing out your strengths and weaknesses.

Nondiagnostic: Even though we are not evaluating your ability on these tasks, we want to ask you to try as hard as you can to perform well on these tasks. If you want to know more about your LAP and HVR performance, we can give you feedback at the end of the study.

Finally, participants were shown one sample item from the LAP (an item of the same sort as used in the fragment completion task) and three sample items from the HVR—difficult verbal GRE problems. The purpose of the HVR sample items was to alert participants to the difficulty of the test and the possibility of poor performance, thus occasioning the relevance of the racial stereotype in the diagnostic condition.

Participants in the control condition arrived at the laboratory to find a note on the door from the experimenter apologizing for not being present. The note instructed them to complete a set of measures lying on the desk in an envelope with the participant's name on it. The envelope contained the LAP word fragment measure and the stereotype avoidance measure (described below) with detailed instructions. No mention of verbal ability evaluation was made.

Measures *Stereotype activation*. Participants first performed a word-fragment completion task, introduced as the "LAP task," versions of which have been shown to measure the cognitive activation of constructs that are either recently primed or self-generated (Gilbert & Hixon, 1991; Tulving, Schacter, & Stark, 1982). The task was made up of 80 word fragments with missing letters specified as blank spaces (e.g., _ _ C E). Twelve of these fragments had as one possible solution a word reflecting either a race-related construct or an image associated with African Americans. The list was generated by having a group of 40 undergraduates (White students from the introductory psychology pool) generate a set of words that reflected the image of African Americans. From these lists, the research team identified the 12 most common constructs (e.g., lower class, minority) and selected single words to represent those constructs on the task. For example, the word "race" was used to represent the construct "concerned with race" on the task. Then, for each of the words placed on the task, at least two letter spaces were omitted and the word was checked again to determine whether other, non-stereotype-related associations to the word stem were possible. Leaving at least two letter spaces blank in each word fragment greatly unconstrains the number of word completions possible for each fragment when compared to leaving only one letter space blank. This reduces the chance of ceiling effects in which virtually all participants would think of the race-related fragment completion. The complete list was as follows: _ _ C E (RACE); L A _ _ (LAZY); _ _ A C K (BLACK); _ _ O R (POOR); C L _ S _ (CLASS); B R _ _ _ _ _ (BROTHER); _ _ _ T E (WHITE); M I _ _ _ _ _ _ (MINORITY); W E L _ _ _ _ (WELFARE); C O _ _ _ (COLOR); T O _ _ _ (TOKEN).

We included a fairly high number (12) of target fragments so that if ceiling or floor effects occurred on some fragments it would be less likely to damage the sensitivity of the overall measure. To reduce the chance that participants would become aware of the racial nature of the target fragments, they were spaced with at least three filler items between them, and there were only two target fragments per page in the task booklet. Participants were instructed to work quickly, spending no more than 15 s on each item.

Self-doubt activation. Seven word fragments reflecting self-doubts about competence and ability were included in the 80-item LAP task: L O _ _ _ (LOSER); D U _ _ (DUMB); S H A _ _ (SHAME); _ _ _ E R I O R (INFERIOR); F L _ _ _ (FLUNK); _ A R D (HARD); W _ _ K (WEAK). These were generated by the research team, and again included at least two blank letter spaces in each fragment. As with the racial fragments, these were separated from one another (and from the racial fragments) by at least three filler items.

Stereotype avoidance. This measure asked participants to rate their preferences for a variety of activities and to rate the self-descriptiveness of various personality traits, some of which were associated with images of African Americans and African American life. Participants in the diagnostic and nondiagnostic conditions were told that these ratings were taken to give us a better understanding of the underpinnings of LAP and HVR processes. Control participants were told that these measures were being taken to assess the typical interests and personality traits of Stanford undergraduates. The measure contained 57 items asking participants to rate the extent to which they enjoyed a number of activities (e.g., pleasure reading, socializing, shopping, traveling, etc.), types of music (e.g., jazz, rap music, classical music), sports (e.g., baseball, basketball, boxing), and finally, how they saw themselves standing on various personality dimensions (e.g., extroverted, organized, humorous, etc.). All ratings were made on 7-point Likert scales with 1 indicating the lowest preference or degree of trait descriptiveness. Some of these activities and traits were stereotypic of African Americans. For an item to be selected as stereotypic, 65% of our pretest sample of 40 White participants had to have generated the item when asked to list activities and traits they believed to be stereotypic of African Americans. In the activities category, the stereotype-relevant items were: "How much do you enjoy sports?" and "How much do you enjoy being a lazy 'couch potato'?" The stereotype-relevant music preference item was *rap music;* the stereotype-relevant sports preference item was *basketball;* and the stereotype-relevant trait ratings were *lazy* and *aggressive/belligerent.*

Participants also completed a brief demographic questionnaire (asking their age, gender, major, etc.) just before they expected to begin the test. As another measure of participants' motivation to distance themselves from the stereotype, the second item of this questionnaire gave them the option of recording their race. We reasoned that participants who wanted to avoid having their performance viewed through the lens of a racial stereotype would be less willing to indicate their race.

Self-handicapping measure. This measure just preceded the demographic questionnaire. The directions stated "as you know, student life is sometimes stressful, and we may not always get enough sleep, etc. Such things can affect cognitive functioning, so it will be necessary to ask how prepared you feel." Participants then indicated the number of hours they slept the night before in addition to responding, on 7-

point scales (with 7 being the higher rating on these dimensions) to the following questions: "How able to focus do you feel?;" "How much stress have you been under lately?;" "How tricky/unfair do you typically find standardized tests?"

Results

Stereotype Activation A 2 (race) × 3 (condition: diagnostic, nondiagnostic, or control) ANCOVA (with verbal SAT as the covariate: Black mean = 581, White mean = 650) was performed on the number of target word fragments filled in with stereotypic completions. This analysis yielded significant main effects for both race, $F(1, 61) = 13.77, p < .001$, and for experimental condition, $F(2, 61) = 5.90, p < .005$. These main effects, however, were qualified by a significant Race × Condition interaction, $F(2, 61) = 3.30, p < .05$. Figure 3 shows that as expected, the diagnostic condition significantly increased the number of race-related completions of Black participants but not of White participants. Black participants in the diagnostic condition produced more race-related completions ($M = 3.70$) than Black participants in the nondiagnostic condition ($M = 2.10$), $t(61) = 3.53, p < .001$, or for that matter, more than participants in any of other conditions, all $ps < .05$.

Self Doubt Activation It did the same for their self doubts. The number of self-doubt-related completions of self-doubt target fragments were submitted to an ANCOVA (as described above) yielding a main effect of experimental condition, $F(2, 61) = 4.33, p < .02$, and a Race × Condition interaction, $F(2, 61) = 3.34, p < .05$. As Figure 3 shows, Black participants in the diagnostic condition, as predicted, generated the most self-doubt-related completions, significantly more than Black participants in the nondiagnostic condition, $t(61) = 3.52, p < .001$, and more than participants in any of the other conditions as well, all $ps < .05$.

Stereotype Avoidance The six preference and stereotype items described above were summed to form an index of stereotype avoidance that ranged from 6 to 42 with 6 indicating high avoidance and 42 indicating low avoidance (Cronbach's alpha = .65). When these scores were submitted to the ANCOVA they yielded a significant effect of condition, $F(2, 61) = 4.73, p < .02$, and a significant Race × Condition interaction, $F(2, 61) = 4.14, p < .03$. As can be seen in Figure 3, Black participants in the diagnostic condition were the most avoidant of conforming to stereotypic images of African Americans ($M = 20.80$), more so than Black participants in the nondiagnostic condition ($M = 29.80$), $t(61) = 3.61, p < .001$, and/or White participants in either condition, all $ps < .05$.

Indicating Race Did the ability diagnosticity of the test affect participants' tendency to indicate their race on the demographic questionnaire? Among Black participants in the diagnostic condition, only 25% would indicate their race on the questionnaire, whereas 100% of the participants in each of the other conditions would do so. Using a 0/1 conversion of the response frequencies (with 0 = refusal to indicate race and 1 = indication of race) the standard ANCOVA performed on this measure revealed a marginally significant effect of race, $F(1, 61) = 3.86, p < .06$, a significant effect of condition, $F(2.61) = 3.40, p < .04$, and a significant Race X Condition interaction, $F(1, 61) = 6.60, p < .01$, all due, of course, to the unique unwillingness of Black participants in the diagnostic condition to indicate their race.

Self-Handicapping Four measures assessed participants' desire to claim impediments to performance. Because participants in the control conditions did not complete this measure, these responses were submitted to separate 2(race) × 2(diagnosticity) ANCOVAs. Cell means are presented in Table 1. Framing the verbal tasks as diagnostic of ability had significant effects on three of the four measures.

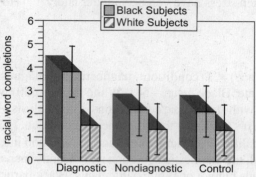

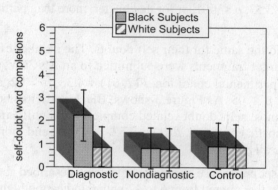

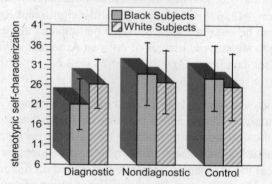

Figure 3. Indicators of stereotype threat.

For the number of hours of sleep, the ANCOVA yielded a significant effect of race, $F(1, 39) = 8.22$, $p < .01$, and a significant effect of condition, $F(1, 39) = 6.53$, $p < .02$. These effects were qualified by a significant Race × Condition interaction, $F(1, 39) = 4.1$, $p < .01$. For participants' ratings of their ability to focus, a similar result emerged: main effects of race, $F(1, 39) = 7.26$, $p < .02$, and condition, $F(1, 39) = 10.67$, $p < .01$, and a significant qualifying interaction, $F(1, 39) = 5.73$, $p < .03$. And finally, the same pattern of effects emerged for participants' ratings of how tricky or unfair they generally find standardized tests to be: a race main effect, $F(1, 39) = 13.24$, $p < .001$, a condition main effect, $F(1, 39) = 13.42$, $p < .001$, and a marginally significant, qualifying interaction, $F(1, 39) = 3.58$, $p < .07$. No significant effects emerged on participants' ratings of their current stress.

Discussion

We had assumed that presenting an intellectual test as diagnostic of ability would arouse a sense of stereotype threat in Black participants. The present results dramatically support this assumption. Compared to participants in the other conditions—that is, Blacks in the nondiagnostic condition and Whites in either condition—Black participants expecting to take a difficult, ability-diagnostic test showed significantly greater cognitive activation of stereotypes about Blacks, greater cognitive activation of concerns about their ability, a greater tendency to avoid racially stereotypic preferences, a greater tendency to make advance excuses for their performance, and finally, a greater reluctance to have their racial identity linked to their performance even in the pedestrian way of recording it on their questionnaires. Clearly the diagnostic instructions caused these participants to experience a strong apprehension, a distinct sense of stereotype threat.

TABLE 1
Self-Handicapping Responses in Study 3

| | Experimental condition | | | |
| | Diagnostic | | Nondiagnostic | |
Measure	Blacks $(n = 12)$	Whites $(n = 11)$	Blacks $(n = 11)$	Whites $(n = 10)$
Hours of sleep	5.10_a	7.48_b	7.05_b	7.70_b
Ability to focus	4.03_a	5.88_b	5.85_b	6.16_b
Current stress	5.51_a	5.24_a	5.00_a	5.02_a
Tests unfair	5.46_a	2.78_b	3.14_b	2.04_b

Note. Means not sharing a common subscript differ at the .01 level according to Bonferroni procedure. Means sharing a common subscript do not differ.

So far, then, we have shown that representing a difficult test as diagnostic of ability can undermine the performance of Black participants, and that it can cause in them a distinct sense of being under threat of judgment by a racial stereotype. This manipulation of stereotype threat—in terms of test diagnosticity—is important because it establishes the generality of the effect to a broad range of real-life situations.

But two questions remain. The first is whether stereotype threat itself—in the absence of the test being explicitly diagnostic of ability—is sufficient to disrupt the performance of these participants on a difficult test. That is, we do not know whether mere activation of the stereotype in the test situation—without the test being explicitly diagnostic of ability—would be enough to cause such effects. A second question is whether the disruptive effect of the diagnosticity manipulation was in fact mediated by the stereotype threat it caused. Showing first that test diagnosticity disrupts Black participants' performance and then, separately, that it causes in these participants to be threatened by the stereotype, does not prove that the effect of test diagnosticity on performance was mediated by the stereotype threat it caused. The performance effect could have been mediated by some other effect of the diagnosticity manipulation. We conducted a fourth experiment to address these questions, and thereby, to test the replicability of the stereotype threat effect under different conditions.

STUDY 4

This experiment again crossed a manipulation of stereotype threat with the race of participants in a 2 × 2 design with test performance as the chief dependent measure. We addressed the first question above by representing the test in this experiment as nondiagnostic of ability. If stereotype threat then depressed Black participants' performance, we would know that stereotype threat is sufficient to cause this effect even when the test is not represented as diagnostic of ability. We addressed the second question by taking from Study 3 a dependent measure of stereotype threat that had bee significantly affected by the diagnosticity manipulation, and manipulating that variable as an independent variable in the present experiment. If this manipulation then affects Black participants' performance, we would know that at least one aspect of the stereotype threat caused by the diagnosticity manipulation was able to impair performance. This would mean that the effect of that manipulation on performance was, or could have been, mediated by the stereotype threat it caused.

The variable that we manipulated in the present study was whether or not participants were required to list their race before taking the test. Recall that in Study 3, 75% of the Black participants in the diagnostic condition refused to record their race on the questionnaire when given the option, whereas all of the participants in the other conditions did. On the assumption that this was a sign of their stereotype avoidance, we reasoned that having participants record their race just prior to the test should prime the racial stereotype about ability for Black participants, and thus make them stereotype threatened. If this threat alone is sufficient to impair their performance, then, with SATs covaried, these participants should perform worse than White participants in this condition.

In the non-stereotype-threat conditions, the demographic questionnaire simply omitted the item requesting participants' race and, otherwise, followed the nondiagnostic procedures of Studies 1 and 2. Without raising the specters of ability or race-relevant evaluation, we expected Black participants in this condition to experience no stereotype threat and to perform (adjusted for SATs) on par with White participants.

Method

Design and Participants This experiment took the form of a 2×2 design in which participants' race was crossed with whether or not they recorded their ethnicity on a preliminary questionnaire. Twenty-four Black (6 male, 18 female) and 23 White (11 male, 12 female) Stanford undergraduates were randomly assigned to either the race-prime condition or the no-race-prime condition. Data from two Black participants were discarded because they arrived with suspicions about the racial nature of the study. One White student failed to provide her SAT score and was discarded from data analyses. These participants were replaced to bring the number of participants in each of the four conditions to 11.

Procedure The procedure closely paralleled that of the nondiagnostic conditions in Studies 1 and 2. After explaining the purpose and format of the test, the experimenter (White man) randomly assigned the participant to the race-prime or no-race-prime condition by drawing a brief questionnaire (labeled "personal information") from a shuffled stack. This questionnaire comprised the experimental manipulation. It was identical for all participants—asking them to provide their age, year in school, major, number of siblings, and parents' education—except that in the race-prime condition the final item asked participants to indicate their race. Because this questionnaire was given to the participant immediately prior to the test, the experimenter remained blind to the participant's condition throughout the pretest interaction. After ensuring that the participant had completed the questionnaire, the experimenter started the test and left the room. Twenty-five minutes later he returned, collected the test, and gave the participant a dependent measure questionnaire.

Dependent Measures This experiment used the same 25-min test used in Study 2, but in this experiment it was administered on paper. During the test, participants marked their guesses, and after the test, they indicated on 11-point scales (with end points *not at all* and *extremely*) the extent to which they guessed when they were having difficulty, expended effort on the test, persisted on problems, limited their time on problems, read problems more than once, became frustrated and gave up, and felt that the test was biased.

Participants also completed a questionnaire aimed at measuring their stereotype threat, by expressing their agreement on 7-point scales (with endpoints *strongly disagree* and *strongly agree*) with each of eight statements (e.g., "Some people feel I have less verbal ability because of my race," "The test may have been easier for people of my race," "The experimenter expected me to do poorly because of my race," "In

English classes people of my race often face biased evaluations," "My race does not affect people's perception of my verbal ability").

As a measure of academic identification, nine further items explored the effect of conditions on participants' perceptions of the importance of verbal and math skills to their education and intended career (e.g., "verbal skills will be important to my career," "I am a verbally oriented person," "I feel that math is important to me," etc.). Participants responded to these items on 11-point scales with end-points labeled *not at all* and *extremely*.

Results

Test Performance A 2 (race) × 2 (race prime vs. no race prime) ANCOVA on test performance with self-reported SATs as a covariate (Black mean = 591, White mean = 643) revealed a strong condition

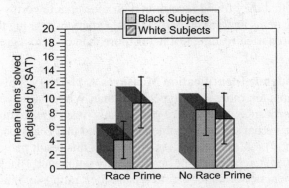

Figure 4. **Mean test performance Study 4.**

interaction in the predicted direction. As Figure 4 shows, Blacks in the race-prime condition performed worse than virtually all of the other groups, yet in the no-race-prime condition their performance equaled that of Whites, $F(1, 39) = 7.82$, $p < .01$. Planned contrasts on these adjusted scores revealed that, as predicted, Blacks in the race-prime condition performed significantly worse than Blacks in the no-race-prime condition, $t(39) = 2.43$, $p < .02$, and significantly worse than Whites in the race-prime condition, $t(39) = 2.87$, $p < .01$. Black participants in the race-prime condition performed worse than Whites in the no-race-prime condition, but not significantly so. Nonetheless, the comparison pitting the Black race-prime condition against the three remaining conditions was highly significant, $F(1, 39) = 8.15$, $p < .01$.

Accuracy The ANCOVA for this index—the percent correct of the items attempted for each participant—with participants' SATs as the covariate revealed a significant tendency for participants in the race-prime condition to have poorer accuracy, $F(1, 39) = 4.07$, $p = .05$. The adjusted means for the Black and White participants in the race-prime condition were .402 and .438 respectively, while those for the Black and White participants in the no-race-prime condition were .541 and .520 respectively. Condition contrasts did not reach significance, although the difference between the Black participants in the race-prime and no-race-prime conditions was marginally significant, $p < .08$. Again, these data suggest that lessened accuracy is part of the process through which stereotype threat impairs performance.

Number of Items Completed An ANCOVA (again with SATs removed as a covariate) revealed only a significant Race × Race Prime interaction for the number of test items participants completed, $F(1, 39) = 12.13$, $p < .01$. In the race-prime condition Blacks completed fewer items than Whites, $t(39) = 3.83$, $p < .001$. The adjusted means were 11.58 and 20.15 respectively. In the no-race-prime condition, however, Blacks and Whites answered roughly the same number of problems. The adjusted means were 15.32 and 13.03, respectively.

Performance-Relevant Measures Although participants' postexam ratings revealed no differences in the degree to which they thought they guessed on the test ($F < 1$), the ANCOVA performed on the actual number of guesses participants indicated on their test sheet revealed a Race $\times$ Race Prime interaction, $F(1, 39) = 5.56, p < .03$. Black participants made fewer guesses when race was primed ($M = 1.99$) than when it was not ($M = 2.74$), whereas White participants tended to guess more when race was primed ($M = 4.23$) than when it was not ($M = 1.58$). No significant condition effects emerged for participants' self-reported effort where, on an 11-point scale with 11 indicating *extremely hard* work, the overall mean was 8.84.

Participants' estimates of how well they had performed, taken after the test, showed no condition effects (the overall mean was 7.4 items). Neither were there condition effects on participants' ratings (made during the postexperimental debriefing) of how much having to indicate their ethnicity bothered them during the test (or *would* have bothered them in the case of participants in the no-race-prime condition). The overall mean was 3.31 on an 11-point scale for which 11 indicated the most distraction. Participants often stated in postexperimental interviews that they found recording their race unnoteworthy because they had to do it so often in everyday life. Of the items bearing on participants' experience taking the test, only one effect emerged: Black participants reported reading test items more than once to a greater degree than did White participants, $F(1, 39) = 8.62, p < .01$.

Stereotype Threat and Academic Identification Measures A MANOVA of the stereotype threat scale revealed that Black participants felt more stereotype threat than White participants, $F(9, 31) = 8.80, p < .01$. No other effects reached significance. Analyses of participants' responses to questions regarding the personal importance of math, verbal skills, and athletics revealed that Black participants reported valuing sports less than Whites, $F(1, 39) = 4.11, p < .05$. As in Study 3, this result may reflect Black participants distancing themselves from the stereotype of the academically untalented Black athlete. Correlations between participants' numerical performance estimates and their ratings of the importance of sports, showed that for Blacks, the worse they believed they performed, the more they devalued sports—in the no-race-prime condition ($r = .56$), and particularly in the race-prime condition ($r = .70$).

Discussion

Priming racial identity depressed Black participants' performance on a difficult verbal test even when the test was not presented as diagnostic of intellectual ability. It did this, we assume, by directly making the stereotype mentally available and thus creating the self-threatening predicament that their performance could prove the stereotype self-characteristic. In Studies 1, 2 and 3, the stereotype was evoked indirectly by describing the test as diagnostic of an ability to which it was relevant. What this experiment shows is that mere cognitive availability of the racial stereotype is enough to depress Black participants' intellectual performance, and that this is so even when the test is presented as not diagnostic of intelligence. Also— because we know from Study 3 that the diagnosticity manipulation strongly affects participants' willingness to record their race—this finding shows that the performance-depressing effect of the diagnosticity manipulation in the earlier experiments was, or could have been, mediated by the effect of that manipulation on stereotype threat—as opposed to some other aspect of the manipulation.

Still, we had expected Black participants in the race-prime condition to show more stereotype threat (as measured by the stereotype threat and stereotype avoidance measures) than Black participants in the no-race-prime condition—reflecting the effect of the manipulation. Instead, while Blacks showed more stereotype threat than Whites, Blacks in the race-prime condition showed no more stereotype threat

than Blacks in the no-race-prime condition. Nor did these groups differ on the identification measures. This may have happened for several reasons. These measures came after the test in this experiment, not before it as in Study 3. Thus, after experiencing the difficult, frustrating exam, all Black participants may have been somewhat stereotype threatened and stereotype avoidant (more so than the White participants) regardless of their condition. Also, the lack of a condition difference between Black participants on the stereotype threat and identification items may have occurred because these items asked participants to respond in reference to settings (e.g., English classes) and attitudes (e.g., about how one's race is generally regarded) that are beyond their immediate experience in the experiment.

Compared to participants in the other conditions, Black participants in the race-prime condition did not report expending less effort on the test; they were not more disturbed at having to list their race; and they did not guess more than other participants. Also, Black participants in both conditions reread the test items more than White participants. Such findings do not fit the idea that these participants underperformed because they withdrew effort from the experiment.

To establish the replicability of the race-prime effect and to explore the possible mediational role of anxiety, we conducted a two-condition experiment which randomly assigned only Black participants to either the race-prime or no-race-prime conditions described in Study 4. We also administered the test on computer to enable a measure of the time participants spent on the items, and gave participants an anxiety measure at the end of the experiment. Replicating Study 4, race-prime participants got significantly fewer items correct ($M = 4.4$) than no-race-prime participants ($M = 7.7$), $t(18) = 2.34$, $p < .04$; they were marginally less accurate ($M = .334$) than no-race-prime participants ($M = .395$), $p = .10$; and they answered fewer items ($M = 13.2$) than no-race-prime participants ($M = 20.1$), $t(18) = 2.89$, $p < .01$. Race-prime participants spent more time on the first five test items (the number which all participants completed) ($M = 79$ s) than no-race-prime participants ($M = 61$ s), $t(18) = 2.27$, $p < .04$, and they were significantly more anxious than no-race-prime participants, $t(18) = 2.34$, $p < .04$. The means on the STAI were 48.5 and 40.5 respectively, on a scale that ranged from 20 (indicating *low anxiety*) to 80 (*extreme anxiety*). These results show that a race prime reliably depresses Black participants' performance on this difficult exam, and that it causes reactions that could be a response to stereotype threat—namely, an anxiety-based perseveration on especially the early test items, items that, as reading comprehension items, required multiple steps.

GENERAL DISCUSSION

The existence of a negative stereotype about a group to which one belongs, we have argued, means that in situations where the stereotype is applicable, one is at risk of confirming it as a self-characterization, both to one's self and to others who know the stereotype. This is what is meant by stereotype threat. And when the stereotype involved demeans something as important as intellectual ability, this threat can be disruptive enough, we hypothesize, to impair intellectual performance.

In support of this reasoning, the present experiments show that making African American participants vulnerable to judgment by negative stereotypes about their group's intellectual ability depressed their standardized test performance relative to White participants, while conditions designed to alleviate this threat, improved their performance, equating the two groups once their differences in SATs were controlled. Studies 1 and 2 produced this pattern by varying whether or not the test was represented as diagnostic of intellectual ability—a procedure that varied stereotype threat by varying the relevance of the stereotype about Blacks' ability to their performance. Study 3 provided direct evidence that this manipulation aroused stereotype threat in Black participants by showing that it activated the racial stereotype and stereotype-related self-doubts in their thinking, that it led them to distance themselves from African American stereotypes. Study 4 showed that merely recording their race—presumably by making the stereotype salient—was enough to impair Black participants' performance even when the test was not diagnostic of ability. Taken together these experiments show that stereotype threat— established by quite subtle instructional differences—can impair the intellectual test performance of Black students, and that lifting it can dramatically improve that performance.

Mediation: How Stereotype Threat Impairs Performance

Study 3 offers clear evidence of what being stereotype threatened is like—as well as demonstrating that the mere prospect of a difficult, ability-diagnostic test was enough to do this to our sample of African American participants. But how precisely did this state of self-threat impair performance, through what mechanism or set of mechanisms did the impairment occur?

There are a number of possibilities: distraction, narrowed attention, anxiety, self-consciousness, withdrawal of effort, over-effort, and so on (e.g., Baumeister, 1984). In fact, several such mechanisms may be involved simultaneously, or different mechanisms may be involved under different conditions. For example, if the test were long enough to solidly engender low performance expectations, then withdrawal of effort might play a bigger mediational role than, say, anxiety, which might be more important with a shorter test. Such complexities notwithstanding, our findings offer some insight into how the present effects were mediated.

Our best assessment is that stereotype threat caused an inefficiency of processing much like that caused by other evaluative pressures. Stereotype-threatened participants spent more time doing fewer items more inaccurately—probably as a result of alternating their attention between trying to answer the items and trying to assess the self-significance of their frustration. This form of debilitation—reduced speed and accuracy—has been shown as a reaction to evaluation apprehension (e.g., Geen, 1985); test anxiety (e.g., Wine, 1971; Sarason, 1972); the presence of an audience (e.g., Bond, 1982); and competition (Baumeister, 1984). Several findings, by suggesting that stereotype-threatened participants were both motivated and inefficient, point in this direction. They reported expending as much effort as other participants. In those studies that included the requisite measures—Study 2 and the replication study reported with Study 4—they actually spent more time per item. They did not guess more than non-stereotype-threatened participants, and, as Black participants did generally, they reported rereading the items more. Also, as noted, these participants were strong students, and almost certainly identified with the material on the test. They may even have been more anxious. Stereotype threat increased Black participants' anxiety in the replication study, although not significantly in Study 2. Together then, these findings suggest that stereotype threat led participants to try hard but with impaired efficiency.

Still, we note that lower expectations may have also been involved, especially in real-life occurrences of stereotype threat. As performance falters under stereotype threat, and as the stereotype frames that faltering as a sign of a group-based inferiority, the individual's expectations about his or her ability and performance may drop—presumably faster than they would if the stereotype were not there to credit the inability interpretation. And lower expectations, as the literature has long emphasized (e.g., Bandura, 1977, 1986; Carver, Blaney, & Scheier, 1979; Pyszczynski & Greenberg, 1983) can further undermine performance by undermining motivation and effort. It is precisely a process of stereotype threat fostering low expectations in a domain that we suggest leads eventually to disidentification with the domain. We assume that this process did not get very far in the present research because the tests were short, and because our participants, as highly identified students, were unlikely to give up on these tests—as their self-reports tell us. But we do assume that lower expectations can play a role in mediating stereotype threat effects.

There is, however, strong evidence against one kind of expectancy mediation. This is the idea that lowered performance or self-efficacy expectations alone mediated the effects of stereotype threat. Conceivably, the stereotype threat treatments got Black participants to expect that they would perform poorly on the test—presumably by getting them to accept the image of themselves inherent in the racial stereotype. The stereotype threat condition did activate participants' self-doubts. This lower expectation, then, outside of any experience these participants may have had with the test itself, and outside of any apprehension they may have had about self-confirming the stereotype, may have directly weakened their motivation and performance. Of course it would be important to show that stereotype threat effects are mediated in African American students by expectations implicit in the stereotype, expectations powerful enough to more or less automatically cause their underperformance.

But there are several reasons to doubt this view. For one thing, it isn't clear that our stereotype threat manipulations led Black participants to accept lower expectations and then to follow them unrevisedly to lower performance. For example, they resisted the self-applicability of the stereotype. But most important, as noted, it is almost certain that any expectation formed prior to the test would be superseded by the participants' actual experience with the test items; rising with success and falling with frustration. In fact, another experiment in our lab offered direct evidence of this by showing that expectations manipulated before the test had no effect on performance. Its procedure followed, in all conditions, that of the standard diagnostic condition used in Studies 1 and 2—with the exception that it directly manipulated efficacy and performance expectations before participants took the test. After being told that the test was ability diagnostic, and just before taking the test, the experimenter (an Asian woman) asked participants what their SAT scores were. After hearing the score, in the positive expectation condition, she commented that the participant should have little trouble with the test. In the negative expectation condition, this comment indicated that the participant would have trouble with the test, and nothing was said in a no-expectation condition. Both White and Black participants were run in all three expectation conditions. While the experiment replicated the standard effect of Whites outperforming Blacks under these stereotype threat conditions (participants' SATs were again used as a covariate) $F(1, 32) = 5.12$, $p < .03$, this personalized expectation manipulation had no effect on the performance of either group. For Blacks, the means were 4.32, 6.38, and 6.55, for the positive, negative and no-expectations conditions, respectively, and for Whites, for the same conditions, they were 8.24, 9.25, and 11.23, respectively. Thus in an experiment that was sensitive enough to replicate the standard stereotype threat effect, expectations explicitly manipulated before the test had no effect on performance. They are unlikely, then, to have been the medium through which stereotype threat affected performance in this research.

Finally, participants in all conditions of these experiments were given low performance expectations by telling them that they should expect to get few items correct due to the difficulty of the test. Importantly, this instruction did not depress the performance of participants in the non-stereotype-threat conditions. Thus it is not likely that a low performance expectation, implied by the stereotype, would have been powerful enough, by itself, to lower performance among these participants when a direct manipulation of the expectation could not.

The Emerging Picture of Stereotype Threat

In the social psychological literature there are other constructs that address the experience of potential victims of stereotypes. For clarity's sake, we briefly compare the construct of stereotype threat to these.

"Token" Status and Cognitive Functioning Lord & Saenz (1985) have shown that token status in a group—that is, being the token minority in a group that is otherwise homogeneous—can cause deficits in cognitive functioning and memory, presumably as an outgrowth of the self-consciousness it causes. Although probably in the same family of effects as stereotype threat, token status would be expected to disrupt cognitive functioning even when the token individual is not targeted by a performance-relevant stereotype, as with, for example, a White man in a group of women solving math problems. Nor do stereotype threat effects require token status, as was shown in the present experiments. In real life, of course, these two processes may often co-occur, as for the Black in an otherwise non-Black classroom. They are nonetheless, distinct processes.

Attributional Ambiguity Another important theory, and now extensive program of research by Crocker and Major (e.g., Crocker & Major, 1989; Crocker, Voelkl, Testa, & Major, 1991) examined how people contend with the self-evaluative implications of having a stigmatized identity. Both their theory and ours focus on the psychology of contending with social devaluation and differ most clearly in which aspect of this psychology they attend to. The work of Crocker and Major focused on the implications of this psychology for self-esteem maintenance (for example, the strategies available for protecting self-esteem against stigmatized status) and we have focused on its implications for intellectual performance. There is also a conceptual difference. Attributional ambiguity refers to the confusion a potential target of prejudice might have over whether or not he is being treated prejudicially. Stereotype threat, of course, refers to his apprehension over confirming, or eliciting the judgment that the stereotype is self-characteristic. Again, the two processes can co-occur—as for the woman who gets cut from the math team, for example—but are distinct.

The Earlier Research of the Katz Group We also note that stereotype threat may explain the earlier findings of Katz and his colleagues. They found in the 1960s that the intellectual performance of Black participants rose and fell with conditions that seemed to vary in stereotype threat—for example, whether the test was represented as a test of intelligence or as one of psychomotor skill. A stereotype threat interpretation of these findings was foiled, however, by the lack of White participant control groups. Thus, the finding that manipulations very similar to Katz's depressed Black participants' performance while not depressing White participants' performance makes stereotype threat a parsimonious account of all these findings.

Test Difficulty and Racial Differences in Standardized Test Performance The test used in these experiments is quite difficult, as the low performance scores indicate. As we argued, it may have to be at least somewhat demanding for stereotype threat to be occasioned. But acknowledging this parameter raises a question: Does stereotype threat significantly undermine the performance of Black students on the SAT? And if it does, is it appropriate to use the SAT as the standard for equating Black and White participants on skill level within our experiments? The answer to the first question has to be that it depends on how much frustration is experienced on the SAT. If the student perceives that a significant portion of the test is within his or her competence, it may preempt or override stereotype threat by proving the stereotype inapplicable. When the student cannot gain this perception, however, the group stereotype becomes relevant as an explanation and may undermine performance. Thus we surmise that over the entire range of Black student test takers, stereotype threat causes a significant depression of scores.

And, of course, this point holds more generally. An important implication of this research is that stereotype threat is an underappreciated source of classic deficits in standardized test performance (e.g., IQ) suffered by Blacks and other stereotype-threatened groups such as those of lower socioeconomic status and women in mathematics (Herrnstein, 1973; Jensen, 1969, 1980; Spencer & Steele, 1994). In addition to whatever environmental or genetic endowments a person brings to the testing situation, this research shows that this situation is not group-neutral—not even, quite possibly, when the tester and test content have been accommodated to the test-taker's background. The problem is that stereotypes afoot in the larger society establish a predicament in the testing situation—aside from test content—that still has the power to undermine standardized test performance, and, we suspect, contribute powerfully to the pattern of group differences that have characterized these tests since their inception.

But, for several reasons, we doubt that this possibility compromises the interpretation of the present findings. First, it is unlikely that stereotype threat had much differential effect on the SATs of our Black and White participants since both groups, as highly selected students, are not likely to have experienced very great frustration on these tests. Second, even if our Black participants' SATs were more depressed in this way, using such depressed scores as a covariate in the present analyses would only adjust Black performance more in the direction of reducing the Black-White difference in the stereotype threat conditions. Thus, while a self-threateningly difficult test is probably a necessary condition for stereotype threat, and while stereotype threat may commonly depress the standardized test performance of Black test takers, these facts are not likely to have compromised the present results.

In conclusion, our focus in this research has been on how social context and group identity come together to mediate an important behavior. This approach is Lewinian; it is also hopeful. Compared to viewing the problem of Black underachievement as rooted in something about the group or its societal conditions, this analysis uncovers a social psychological predicament of race, rife in the standardized testing situation, that is amenable to change—as we hope our manipulations have illustrated.

REFERENCES

Allport, G. (1954). *The nature of prejudice*, New York: Addison-Wesley. American Council on Education. (1990). *Minorities in higher education*. Washington, DC: Office of Minority Concerns.

Bandura, A. (1977). Self-efficacy: Toward a unifying theory of behavioral change. *Psychological Review, 84*, 191–215.

Bandura, A. (1986). Fearful expectations and avoidant actions as coeffects of perceived self-inefficacy. *American Psychologist, 41*, 1389–1391.

Baumeister, R. F. (1984). Choking under pressure: Self-consciousness and paradoxical effects of incentives on skillful performance. *Journal of Personality and Social Psychology, 46*, 610–620.

Bond, C. F. (1982). Social facilitation: A self-presentational view. *Journal of Personality and Social Psychology, 42*, 1042–1050.

Carter, S. L. (1991). *Reflections of an affirmative action baby*. New York: Basic Books.

Carver, C. S., Blaney, P. H., & Scheier, M. F. (1979). Reassertion and giving up: The interactive role of self-directed attention and outcome expectancy. *Journal of Personality and Social Psychology, 37*, 1859–1870.

Cleary, T. A., Humphreys, L. G., Kendrick, S. A., & Wesman, A. (1975). Educational uses of tests with disadvantaged students. *American Psychologist, 30*, 15–41.

Crocker, J., & Major, B. (1989). Social stigma and self-esteem: The self-protective properties of stigma. *Psychological Review, 96*, 608–630.

Crocker, J., Voelkl, K., Testa, M., & Major, B. (1991). Social stigma: The affective consequences of attributional ambiguity. *Journal of Personality and Social Psychology, 60*, 218–228.

Devine, P. G. (1989). Stereotypes and prejudice: Their automatic and controlled components. *Journal of Personality and Social Psychology, 56*, 5–18.

Dovidio, J. F., Evans, N., & Tyler, R. B. (1986). Racial stereotypes: The contents of their cognitive representations. *Journal of Experimental Social Psychology, 22*, 22–37.

Easterbrook, J. A. (1959). The effect of emotion on cue utilization and the organization of behavior. *Psychological Review, 66*, 183–201.

Geen, R. G. (1985). Evaluation apprehension and response withholding in solution of anagrams. *Personality and Individual Differences, 6*, 293–298.

Geen, R. G. (1991). Social motivation. *Annual Review of Psychology, 42*, 377–399.

Gilbert, D. T., & Hixon, J. G. (1991). The trouble of thinking: Activation and application of stereotypic beliefs. *Journal of Personality and Social Psychology, 60*, 509–517.

Goffman, I. (1963). *Stigma*. New York: Simon & Shuster, Inc.

Herrnstein, R. (1973). *IQ in the meritocracy*. Boston: Little Brown.

Higgins, E. T. (1989). Knowledge accessibility and activation: Subjectivity and suffering from unconscious sources. In J. S. Uleman & J. A. Bargh (Eds.), *Unintended Thoughts* (pp. 75–123). New York: Guilford.

Jensen, A. R. (1969). How much can we boost IQ and scholastic achievement? *Harvard Educational Review, 39*, 1–123.

Jensen, A. R. (1980). *Bias in mental testing*. New York: Free Press.

Katz, I. (1964). Review of evidence relating to effects of desegregation on the intellectual performance of Negroes. *American Psychologist, 19*, 381–399.

Katz, I., Epps, E. G., & Axelson, L. J. (1964). Effect upon Negro digit symbol performance of comparison with Whites and with other Negroes. *Journal of Abnormal and Social Psychology, 69*, 963–970.

Katz, I., Roberts, S. O., & Robinson, J. M. (1965). Effects of task difficulty, race of administrator, and instructions on digit-symbol performance of Negroes. *Journal of Personality and Social Psychology, 2*, 53–59.

Linn, R. L. (1973). Fair test use in selection. *Review of Educational Research, 43*, 139–161.

Lord, C. G., & Saenz, D. S. (1985). Memory deficits and memory surfeits: Differential cognitive consequences of tokenism for tokens and observers. *Journal of Personality and Social Psychology, 49*, 918–926.

Lord, C. G., Saenz, D. S., & Godfrey, D. K. (1987). Effects of perceived scrutiny on participant memory for social interactions. *Journal of Experimental Social Psychology, 23*, 498–517.

Nettles, M. T (1988). *Toward undergraduate student equality in American higher education*. New York: Greenwood.

Pyszczynski, T., & Greenberg, J. (1983). Determinants of reduction in effort as a strategy for coping with anticipated failure. *Journal of Research in Personality, 17*, 412–422.

Sarason, I. G. (1972). Experimental approaches to test anxiety: Attention and the uses of information. In C. D. Spielberger (Ed.), Anxiety: *Current trends in theory and research* (Vol. 2). New York: Academic Press.

Seta, J. J. (1982). The impact of coactors' comparison processes on task performance. *Journal of Personality and Social Psychology, 42*, 281–291.

Spencer, S. J., & Steele, C. M. (1994). *Under suspicion of inability: Stereotype vulnerability and women's math performance*. Unpublished manuscript, State University of New York at Buffalo and Stanford University.

Stanley, J. C. (1971). Predicting college success of the educationally disadvantaged. *Science, 171*, 640–647.

Steele, C. M. (1992, April). Race and the schooling of black Americans. *The Atlantic Monthly*.

Steele, S. (1990). *The content of our character*. New York: St. Martin's Press.

Tulving, E., Schacter, D. L., & Stark, H. A. (1982). Priming effects in word-fragment completion are independent of recognition memory. *Journal of Experimental Psychology: Learning, Memory, and Cognition, 8*, 336–342.

Wine, J. (1971). Test anxiety and direction of attention. *Psychological Bulletin, 76*, 92–104.

NOTES

1. Because we did not warn participants to avoid guessing in these experiments, we do not report the performance results in terms of the index used by Educational Testing Service, which includes a correction for guessing. This correction involves subtracting from the number correct, the number wrong adjusted for the number of response options for each wrong item and dividing this by the number of items on the test. Because 27 of our 30 items had the same number of response options (5), this correction amounts to adjusting the number correct almost invariably by the same number. All analyses are the same regardless of the index used.

2. All comparisons of adjusted means reported hereafter used the Bonferroni procedure.

Received August 9, 1994

Revision received May 9, 1995

Accepted May 18, 1995

READING 6

Cognitive Consequences of Forced Compliance

Festinger's cognitive dissonance theory states that people seek to maintain a consistency between their beliefs and their actions—and that this motive can give rise to some irrational and sometimes maladaptive behavior. As discussed in Chapter 6 (Attitudes), this theory predicts that under certain conditions, people who find themselves behaving in ways that contradict their beliefs experience an unpleasant state of tension known as cognitive dissonance. To reduce this tension, they often change their attitude to bring it in line with their behavior, exhibiting a process of self-persuasion. The following study by Festinger and Carlsmith (1959) represents the first controlled test of this important theory. In this study, as you will see, people who were given little inducement to lie—compared to those who were highly paid for it—come to believe that lie as a way to justify their behavior.

COGNITIVE CONSEQUENCES OF FORCED COMPLIANCE[*]

Leon Festinger and James M. Carlsmith

Stanford University

What happens to a person's private opinion if he is forced to do or say something contrary to that opinion? Only recently has there been any experimental work related to this question. Two studies reported by Janis and King (1954; 1956) clearly showed that, at least under some conditions, the private opinion changes so as to bring it into closer correspondence with the overt behavior the person was forced to perform. Specifically, they showed that if a person is forced to improvise a speech supporting a point of view with which he disagrees, his private opinion moves toward the position advocated in the speech. The observed opinion change is greater than for persons who only hear the speech or for persons who read a prepared speech with emphasis solely on elocution and manner of delivery. The authors of these two studies explain their results mainly in terms of mental rehearsal and thinking up new arguments. In this way, they propose, the person who is forced to improvise a speech convinces himself. They present some evidence, which is not altogether conclusive, in support of this explanation. We will have more to say concerning this explanation in discussing the results of our experiment.

Kelman (1953) tried to pursue the matter further. He reasoned that if the person is induced to make an overt statement contrary to his private opinion by the offer of some reward, then the greater the reward offered, the greater should be the subsequent opinion change. His data, however, did not support this idea. He found, rather, that a large reward produced less subsequent opinion change that did a smaller reward. Actually, this finding by Kelman is consistent with the theory we will outline below but, for a number of reasons, is not conclusive. One of the major weaknesses of the data is that not all subjects in the experiment made an overt statement contrary to their private opinion in order to obtain the offered reward. What is more, as one might expect, the percentage of subjects who complied increased as the size of the offered reward increased. Thus, with self-selection of who did and who did not make the

[*] SOURCE: Leon Festinger and James M. Carlsmith. 1959. *JOURNAL OF ABNORMAL AND SOCIAL PSYCHOLOGY, 58,* 203–210.

required overt statement and with varying percentages of subjects in the different conditions who did make the required statement, no interpretation of the data can be unequivocal.

Recently, Festinger (1957) proposed a theory concerning cognitive dissonance from which come a number of derivations about opinion change following forced compliance. Since these derivations are stated in detail by Festinger (1957, Ch. 4), we will here give only a brief outline of the reasoning.

Let us consider a person who privately holds opinion "X" but has, as a result of pressure brought to bear on him, publicly stated that he believes "not X."

1. This person has two cognitions which, psychologically, do not fit together: one of these is the knowledge that he believes "X," the other the knowledge that he has publicly stated that he believes "not X." If no factors other than his private opinion are considered, it would follow, at least in our culture, that if he believes "X" he would publicly state "X." Hence, his cognition of his private belief is dissonant with his cognition concerning his actual public statement.

2. Similarly, the knowledge that he has said "not X" is consonant with (does fit together with) those cognitive elements corresponding to the reasons, pressures, promises of rewards and/or threats of punishment which induced him to say "not X."

3. In evaluating the total magnitude of dissonance, one must take account of both dissonances and consonances. Let us think of the sum of all the dissonances involving some particular cognition as "D" and the sum of all the consonances as "C." Then we might think of the total magnitude of dissonance as being a function of "D" divided by "D" plus "C."

    Let us then see what can be said about the total magnitude of dissonance in a person created by the knowledge that he said "not X" and really believes "X." With everything else held constant, this total magnitude of dissonance would decrease as the number and importance of the pressures which induced him to say "not X" increased.

    Thus, if the overt behavior was brought about by, say, offers of reward or threats of punishment, the magnitude of dissonance is maximal if these promised rewards or threatened punishments were just barely sufficient to induce the person to say "not X." From this point on, as the promised rewards or threatened punishment become larger, the magnitude of dissonance becomes smaller.

4. One way in which the dissonance can be reduced is for the person to change his private opinion so as to bring it into correspondence with what he has said. One would consequently expect to observe such opinion change after a person has been forced or induced to say something contrary to his private opinion. Furthermore, since the pressure to reduce dissonance will be a function of the magnitude of the dissonance, the observed opinion change should be greatest when the pressure used to elicit the overt behavior is just sufficient to do it.

The present experiment was designed to test this derivation under controlled, laboratory conditions. In the experiment we varied the amount of reward used to force persons to make a statement contrary to their private views. The prediction [from 3 and 4 above] is that the larger the reward given to the subject, the smaller will be the subsequent opinion change.

PROCEDURE

Seventy-one male students in the introductory psychology course at Stanford University were used in the experiment. In this course, students are required to spend a certain number of hours as subjects (*Ss*) in experiments. They choose among the available experiments by signing their names on a sheet posted on the bulletin board which states the nature of the experiment. The present experiment was listed as a two-hour experiment dealing with "Measures of Performance."

During the first week of the course, when the requirement of serving in experiments was announced and explained to the students, the instructor also told them about a study that the psychology department was conducting. He explained that, since they were required to serve in experiments, the department was conducting a study to evaluate these experiments in order to be able to improve them in the future. They were told that a sample of students would be interviewed after having served as *Ss*. They were urged to cooperate in these interviews by being completely frank and honest. The importance of this announcement will become clear shortly. It enabled us to measure the opinions of our *Ss* in a context not directly connected with our experiment and in which we could reasonably expect frank and honest expressions of opinion.

When the *S* arrived for the experiment on "Measures of Performance" he had to wait for a few minutes in the secretary's office. The experimenter (*E*) then came in, introduced himself to the *S* and, together, they walked into the laboratory room where the *E* said:

> This experiment usually takes a little over an hour but, of course, we had to schedule it for two hours. Since we have that extra time, the introductory psychology people asked if they could interview some of our subjects. [Offhand and conversationally.] Did they announce that in class? I gather that they're interviewing some people who have been in experiments. I don't know much about it. Anyhow, they may want to interview you when you're through here.

With no further introduction or explanation the *S* was shown the first task, which involved putting 12 spools onto a tray, emptying the tray, refilling it with spools, and so on. He was told to use one hand and to work at his own speed. He did this for one-half hour. The *E* then removed the tray and spools and placed in front of the *S* a board containing 48 square pegs. His task was to turn each peg a quarter turn clockwise, then another quarter turn, and so on. He was told again to use one hand and to work at his own speed. The *S* worked at this task for another half hour.

While the *S* was working on these tasks, the *E* sat, with a stopwatch in his hand, busily making notations on a sheet of paper. He did so in order to make it convincing that this was what the *E* was interested in and that these tasks, and how the *S* worked on them, was the total experiment. From our point of view the experiment had hardly started. The hour which the *S* spent working on the repetitive, monotonous tasks was intended to provide, for each *S* uniformly, an experience about which he would have a somewhat negative opinion.

After the half hour on the second task was over, the *E* conspicuously set the stop watch back to zero, put it away, pushed his chair back, lit a cigarette, and said:

> O.K. Well, that's all we have in the experiment itself. I'd like to explain what this has been all about so you'll have some idea of why you were doing this. [*E* pauses.] Well, the way the experiment is set up is this. There are actually two groups in the experiment. In one, the group you were in, we bring the subject in and give him essentially no introduction to the experiment. That is, all we tell him is what he needs to know in order to do the tasks, and he has no idea of what the experiment is all about, or what it's going to be like, or anything like that. But in the other group, we have a student that we've hired that works for us regularly, and what I do is take him into the next room where the subject is waiting—the same room you were waiting in before—and I introduce him as if he had just finished being a subject in the experiment. That is, I say: "This is so-and-so, who's just finished the experiment, and I've asked him to tell you a little of what it's about before you start." The fellow who works for us then, in conversation with the next subject, makes these points [The *E* then produced a sheet headed "For Group B" which had written on it: It was very enjoyable, I had a lot of fun, I enjoyed myself, it was very interesting, it was intriguing, it was exciting. The *E* showed this to the *S* and then proceeded with his false explanation of the purpose of the experiment.] Now, of course, we have this student do this, because if the experimenter does it, it doesn't look as realistic, and what we're interested in doing is comparing how these two groups do on the experiment—the one with this previous expectation about the experiment, and the other, like yourself, with essentially none.

Up to this point the procedure was identical for *Ss* in all conditions. From this point on they diverged somewhat. Three conditions were run, Control, One Dollar, and Twenty Dollars, as follows:

Control Condition

The *E* continued:

> Is that fairly clear? [Pause.] Look, that fellow [looks at watch] I was telling you about from the introductory psychology class said he would get here a couple of minutes from now. Would you mind waiting to see if he wants to talk to you? Fine. Why don't we go into the other room to wait? [The *E* left the *S* in the secretary's office for four minutes. He then returned and said:] O.K. Let's check and see if he does want to talk to you.

One and Twenty Dollar Conditions

The *E* continued:

> Is that fairly clear how it is set up and what we're trying to do? [Pause.] Now, I also have a sort of strange thing to ask you. The thing is this. [Long pause, some confusion and uncertainty in the following, with a degree of embarrassment on the part of the *E*. The manner of the *E* contrasted strongly with the preceding unhesitant and assured false explanation of the experiment. The point was to make it seem to the *S* that this was the first time the *E* had done this and that he felt unsure of himself.] The fellow who normally does this for us couldn't do it today—he just phoned in, and something or other came up for him—so we've been looking around for someone that we could hire to do it for us. You see, we've got another subject waiting [looks at watch] who is supposed to be in that other condition. Now Professor _____, who is in charge of this experiment, suggested that perhaps we could take a chance on your doing it for us. I'll tell you what we had in mind: the thing is, if you could do it for us now, then of course you would know how to do it, and if something like this should ever come up again, that is, the regular fellow couldn't make it, and we had a subject scheduled, it would be very reassuring to us to know that we had somebody else we could call on who knew how to do it. So, if you would be willing to do this for us, we'd like to hire you to do it now and then be on call in the future, if something like this should ever happen again. We can pay you a dollar (twenty dollars) for doing this for us, that is, for doing it now and then being on call; do you think you could do that for us?

If the S hesitated, the E said things like, "It will only take a few minutes," "The regular person is pretty reliable; this is the first time he has missed," or "If we needed you we could phone you a day or two in advance; if you couldn't make it, of course, we wouldn't expect you to come." After the S agreed to do it, the E gave him the previously mentioned sheet of paper headed "For Group B" and asked him to read it through again. The E then paid the S one dollar (twenty dollars), made out a hand-written receipt form, and asked the S to sign it. He then said;

> O.K., the way we'll do it is this. As I said, the next subject should be here by now. I think the next one is a girl. I'll take you into the next room and introduce you to her, saying that you've just finished the experiment and that we've asked you to tell her a little about it. And what we want you to do is just sit down and get into a conversation with her and try to get across the points on that sheet of paper. I'll leave you alone and come back after a couple of minutes. O.K.?

The E then took the S into the secretary's office where he had previously waited and where the next S was waiting. (The secretary had left the office.) He introduced the girl and the S to one another saying that the S had just finished the experiment and would tell her something about it. He then left saying he would return in a couple of minutes, the girl, an undergraduate hired for this role, said little until the S made some positive remarks about the experiment and then said that she was surprised because a friend of hers had taken the experiment the week before and had told her that it was boring and that she ought to try to get out of it. Most *Ss* responded by saying something like "Oh, no, it's really very interesting. I'm sure you'll enjoy it." The girl, after this listened quietly, accepting and agreeing to everything the *S* told her. The discussion between the *S* and the girl was recorded on a hidden tape recorder.

After two minutes the *E* returned, asked the girl to go into the experimental room, thanked the *S* for talking to the girl, wrote down his phone number to continue the fiction that we might call on him again in the future and then said: "Look, could we check and see if that fellow from introductory psychology wants to talk to you?"

From this point on, the procedure for all three conditions was once more identical. As the *E* and the *S* started to walk to the office where the interviewer was, the *E* said: "Thanks very much for working on those tasks for us. I hope you did enjoy it. Most of our subjects tell us afterward that they found it quite interesting. You get a chance to see how you react to the tasks and so forth," This short persuasive communication was made in all conditions in exactly the same way. The reason for doing it, theoretically, was to make it easier for anyone who wanted to persuade himself that the tasks had been, indeed, enjoyable.

When they arrived at the interviewer's office, the *E* asked the interviewer whether or not he wanted to talk to the *S*. The interviewer said yes, the *E* shook hands with the *S*, said good-bye, and left. The interviewer, of course, was always kept in complete ignorance of which condition the *S* was in. The interview consisted of four questions, on each of which the *S* was first encouraged to talk about the matter and was then asked to rate his opinion or reaction on an 11-point scale. The questions are as follows:

1. Were the tasks interesting and enjoyable? In what way? In what way were they not? Would you rate how you feel about them on a scale from 5 to +5 where −5 means they were extremely dull and boring, +5 means they were extremely interesting and enjoyable, and zero means they were neutral, neither interesting nor uninteresting.

2. Did the experiment give you an opportunity to learn about your own ability to perform these tasks? In what way? In what way not? Would you rate how you feel about this on a scale from 0 to 10 where 0 means you learned nothing and 10 means you learned a great deal.

3. From what you know about the experiment and the tasks involved in it, would you say the experiment was measuring anything important? That is, do you think the results may have scientific value? In what way? In what way not? Would you rate your opinion on this matter on a scale from 0 to 10 where 0 means the results have no scientific value or importance and 10 means they have a great deal of value and importance.

4. Would you have any desire to participate in another similar experiment? Why? Why not? Would you rate your desire to participate in a similar experiment again on a scale from −5 to +5, where −5 means you would definitely dislike to participate, +5 means you would definitely like to participate, and 0 means you have no particular feeling about it one way or the other.

As may be seen, the questions varied in how directly relevant they were to what the *S* had told the girl. This point will be discussed further in connection with the results.

At the close of the interview the *S* was asked what he thought the experiment was about and, following this, was asked directly whether or not he was suspicious of anything and, if so, what he was suspicious of. When the interview was over, the interviewer brought the *S* back to the experimental room where the *E* was waiting together with the girl who had posed as the waiting *S*. (In the control condition, of course, the girl was not there.) The true purpose of the experiment was then explained to the *S* in detail, and the reasons for each of the various steps in the experiment were explained carefully in relation to the true purpose. All experimental *Ss* in both One Dollar and Twenty Dollar conditions were asked, after this explanation, to return the money they had been given. All *Ss*, without exception, were quite willing to return the money.

The data from 11 of the 71 Ss in the experiment had to be discarded for the following reasons:

1.   Five Ss (three in the One Dollar and two in the Twenty Dollar condition) indicated in the interview that they were suspicious about having been paid to tell the girl the experiment was fun and suspected that that was the real purpose of the experiment.

2.   Two Ss (both in the One Dollar condition) told the girl that they had been hired, that the experiment was really boring but they were supposed to say it was fun.

3.   Three Ss (one in the One Dollar and two in the Twenty Dollar condition) refused to take the money and refused to be hired.

4.   One S (in the One Dollar condition), immediately after having talked to the girl, demanded her phone number saying he would call her and explain things, and also told the E he wanted to wait until she was finished so he could tell her about it.

These 11 Ss were, of course, run through the total experiment anyhow and the experiment was explained to them afterwards. Their data, however, are not included in the analysis.

Summary of Design

There remain, for analysis, 20 Ss in each of the three conditions. Let us review these briefly: 1. *Control condition.* These Ss were treated identically in all respects to the Ss in the experimental conditions, except that they were never asked to, and never did, tell the waiting girl that the experimental tasks were enjoyable and lots of fun. 2. *One Dollar condition.* These Ss were hired for one dollar to tell a waiting S that tasks, which were really rather dull and boring, were interesting, enjoyable, and lots of fun. 3. *Twenty Dollar condition.* These Ss were hired for twenty dollars to do the same thing.

RESULTS

The major results of the experiment are summarized in Table 1 which lists, separately for each of the three experimental conditions, the average rating which the Ss gave at the end of each question on the interview. We will discuss each of the questions on the interview separately, because they were intended to measure different things. One other point before we proceed to examine the data. In all the comparisons, the Control condition should be regarded as a baseline from which to evaluate the results in the other two conditions. The Control condition gives us, essentially, the reactions of Ss to the tasks and their opinions about the experiment as falsely explained to them, without the experimental introduction of dissonance. The data from the other conditions may be viewed, in a sense, as changes from this baseline.

How Enjoyable the Tasks Were

The average ratings on this question, presented in the first row of figures in Table 1, are the results most important to the experiment. These results are the ones most directly relevant to the specific dissonance which was experimentally created. It will be recalled that the tasks were purposely arranged to be rather boring and monotonous. And, indeed, in the Control condition the average rating was −.45, somewhat on the negative side of the neutral point.

In the other two conditions, however, the Ss told someone that these tasks were interesting and enjoyable. The resulting dissonance could, of course, most directly be reduced by persuading themselves that the tasks were, indeed, interesting and enjoyable. In the One Dollar condition, since the magnitude of dissonance was high, the pressure to reduce this dissonance would also be high. In this condition, the average rating was +1.35, considerably on the positive side and significantly different from the Control condition at the .02 level[1] ($t = 2.48$).

TABLE 1

Average Ratings on Interview Questions

for Each Condition

Question on Interview	Experimental Condition		
	Control (N = 20)	One Dollar (N = 20)	Twenty Dollars (N = 20)
How enjoyable tasks were (rated from −5 to +5)	−.45	+1.35	−.05
How much they learned (rated from 0 to 10)	3.08	2.80	3.15
Scientific importance (rated from 0 to 10)	5.60	6.45	5.18
Participate in similar exp. (rated from −5 to +5)	−.62	+1.20	−.25

In the Twenty Dollar condition, where less dissonance was created experimentally because of the greater importance of the consonant relations, there is correspondingly less evidence of dissonance reduction. The average rating in this condition is only −.05, slightly and not significantly higher than the Control condition. The difference between the One Dollar and Twenty Dollar conditions is significant at the .03 level ($t = 2.22$). In short, when an S was induced, by offer of reward, to say something contrary to his private opinion, this private opinion tended to change so as to correspond more closely with what he had said. The greater the reward offered (beyond what was necessary to elicit the behavior) the smaller was the effect.

Desire to Participate in a Similar Experiment

The results from this question are shown in the last row of Table 1. This question is less directly related to the dissonance that was experimentally created for the Ss. Certainly, the more interesting and enjoyable they felt the tasks were, the greater would be their desire to participate in a similar experiment. But other factors would enter also. Hence, one would expect the results on this question to be very similar to the results on "how enjoyable the tasks were" but weaker. Actually, the result, as may be seen in the table, are in exactly the same direction, and the magnitude of the mean differences is fully as large as on the first question. The variability is greater, however, and the differences do not yield high levels of statistical significance. The difference between the One Dollar condition (+1.20) and the Control condition (−.62) is significant at the .08 level ($t = 1.78$). The difference between the One Dollar condition and the Twenty Dollar condition (−.25) reaches only the .15 level of significance ($t = 1.46$).

The Scientific Importance of the Experiment

This question was included because there was a chance that differences might emerge. There are, after all, other ways in which the experimentally created dissonance could be reduced. For example, one way would be for the S to magnify for himself the value of the reward he obtained. This, however, was unlikely in this experiment because money was used for the reward and it is undoubtedly difficult to convince oneself that one dollar is more than it really is. There is another possible way, however. The Ss were given a very good reason, in addition to being paid, for saying what they did to the waiting girl. The Ss were told it was necessary for the experiment. The dissonance could, consequently, be reduced by magnifying the importance of this cognition. The more scientifically important they considered the experiment to be, the less was the total magnitude of dissonance. It is possible, then, that the results on this question, shown in the third row of figures in Table 1, might reflect dissonance reduction.

The results are weakly in line with what one would expect if the dissonance were somewhat reduced in this manner. The One Dollar condition is higher than the other two. The difference between the One and Twenty Dollar conditions reaches the .08 level of significance on a two-tailed test ($t = 1.79$). The difference between the One Dollar and Control conditions is not impressive at all ($t = 1.21$). The result that the Twenty Dollar condition is actually lower than the Control condition is undoubtedly a matter of chance ($t = 0.58$).

How Much They Learned From the Experiment

The results on this question are shown in the second row for figures in Table 1. The question was included because, as far as we could see, it had nothing to do with the dissonance that was experimentally created and could not be used for dissonance reduction. One would then expect no differences at all among the three conditions. We felt it was important to show that the effect was not a completely general one but was specific to the content of the dissonance which was created. As can be readily seen in Table 1, there are only negligible differences among conditions. The highest t value for any of these differences is only 0.48.

DISCUSSION OF A POSSIBLE ALTERNATIVE EXPLANATION

We mentioned in the introduction that Janis and King (1954; 1956) in explaining their findings, proposed an explanation in terms of the self-convincing effect of mental rehearsal and thinking up new arguments by the person who had to improvise a speech. Kelman (1953), in the previously mentioned study, in attempting to explain the unexpected finding that the persons who complied in the moderate reward condition changed their opinion more than in the high reward condition, also proposed the same kind of explanation. If the results of our experiment are to be taken as strong corroboration of the theory of cognitive dissonance, this possible alternative explanation must be dealt with.

Specifically, as applied to our results, this alternative explanation would maintain that perhaps, for some reason, the Ss in the One Dollar condition worked harder at telling the waiting girl that the tasks were fun and enjoyable. That is, in the One Dollar condition they may have rehearsed it more mentally, thought up more ways of saying it, may have said it more convincingly, and so on. Why this might have been the case is, of course, not immediately apparent. One might expect that, in the Twenty Dollar condition, having been paid more, they would try to do a better job of it than in the One Dollar condition. But nevertheless, the possibility exists that the Ss in the One Dollar condition may have improvised more.

Because of the desirability of investigating this possible alternative explanation, we recorded on a tape recorder the conversation between each *S* and the girl. These recordings were transcribed and then rated, by two independent raters, on five dimensions. The ratings were, of course, done in ignorance of which condition each *S* was in. The reliabilities of these ratings, that is, the correlations between the two independent raters, ranged from .61 to .88, with an average reliability of .71. The five ratings were:

1. The content of what the *S* said *before* the girl made the remark that her friend told her it was boring. The stronger the *S*'s positive statements about the tasks, and the more ways in which he said they were interesting and enjoyable, the higher the rating.

2. The content of what the *S* said *after* the girl made the above-mentioned remark. This was rated in the same way as for the content before the remark.

3. A similar rating of the over-all content of what the *S* said.

4. A rating of how persuasive and convincing the *S* was in what he said and the way in which he said it.

5. A rating of the amount of time in the discussion that the *S* spent discussing the tasks as opposed to going off into irrelevant things.

The mean ratings for the One Dollar and Twenty Dollar conditions, averaging the ratings of the two independent raters, are presented in Table 2. It is clear from examining the table that, in all cases, the Twenty Dollar condition is slightly higher. The differences are small, however, and only on the rating of "amount of time" does the difference between the two conditions even approach significance. We are certainly justified in concluding that the *S*s in the One Dollar condition did not improvise more nor act more convincingly. Hence, the alternative explanation discussed above cannot account for the findings.

SUMMARY

Recently, Festinger (1957) has proposed a theory concerning cognitive dissonance. Two derivations from this theory are tested here. These are:

1. If a person is induced to do or say something which is contrary to his private opinion, there will be a tendency for him to change his opinion so as to bring it into correspondence with what he has done or said.

2. The larger the pressure used to elicit the overt behavior (beyond the minimum needed to elicit it) the weaker will be the above-mentioned tendency.

A laboratory experiment was designed to test these derivations. Subjects were subjected to a boring experience and then paid to tell someone that the experience had been interesting and enjoyable. The amount of money paid the subject was varied. The private opinions of the subjects concerning the experiences were then determined.

The results strongly corroborate the theory that was tested.

TABLE 2

Average Ratings of Discussion Between Subject and Girl

Dimension Rated	Condition		
	One Dollar	Twenty Dollar	Value of *t*
Content before remark by girl (rated from 0 to 5)	2.26	2.62	1.08
Content after remark by girl (rated from 0 to 5)	1.63	1.75	0.11
Over-all content (rated from 0 to 5)	1.89	2.19	1.08
Persuasiveness and conviction (rated from 0 to 10)	4.79	5.50	0.99
Time spent on topic (rated from 0 to 10)	6.74	8.19	1.80

REFERENCES

Festinger, L. A. *Theory of cognitive dissonance.* Evanston, Ill: Row Peterson, 1957.

Janis, I. L., & King, B. T. The influence of role-playing on opinion change. *J. Abnorm. Soc. Psychol.,* 1954, 49, 211–218.

Kelman, H. Attitude change as a function of response restriction. *Hum. Relat.,* 1953, 6, 185–214.

King, B. T., & Janis, I. L. Comparison of the effectiveness of improvised versus non-improvised role-playing in producing opinion changes. *Hum. Relat.,* 1956, 9, 177–186.

NOTES

1.   All statistical tests referred to in this paper are two-tailed.

Received November 18, 1957

READING 7

The Chameleon Effect: The Perception–Behavior Link and Social Interaction

Over the years, research has shown that as social animals, people are highly influenced by the judgments and behaviors of others, which is an essential theme of much of the research presented throughout the textbook, and most specifically in Chapter 7 (Conformity). Sometimes we conform because we are uncertain of how to react and so we turn to others for guidance. At other times, we conform in our public behavior to avoid standing out as different. But is conformity always the result of a calculated decision, or are people also vulnerable to subtle, almost reflex-like influences—as when we yawn in response to the sight of others yawning or laugh when we hear others laughing? Can this type of mimicry be demonstrated in a controlled experiment? In the following series of studies, Chartrand and Bargh (1999) had participants interact with a partner who exhibited certain motor habits and found that, without even realizing it, the participants imitated these behaviors, a phenomenon they called the "the chameleon effect" after the lizard that changes colors according to its physical environment. Why does this nonconscious form of influence occur? Read on and you will see.

THE CHAMELEON EFFECT: THE PERCEPTION–BEHAVIOR LINK AND SOCIAL INTERACTION*

Tanya L. Chartrand and John A. Bargh

New York University

The chameleon effect *refers to nonconscious mimicry of the postures, mannerisms, facial expressions, and other behaviors of one's interaction partners, such that one's behavior passively and unintentionally changes to match that of others in one's current social environment. The authors suggest that the mechanism involved is the perception–behavior link, the recently documented finding (e.g., J. A. Bargh, M. Chen, & L. Burrows, 1996) that the mere perception of another's behavior automatically increases the likelihood of engaging in that behavior oneself. Experiment 1 showed that the motor behavior of participants unintentionally matched that of strangers with whom they worked on a task. Experiment 2 had confederates mimic the posture and movements of participants and showed that mimicry facilitates the smoothness of interactions and increases liking between interaction partners. Experiment 3 showed that dispositionally empathic individuals exhibit the chameleon effect to a greater extent than do other people.*

> He looked about his surroundings. They had become so familiar to him that, without realizing it, he was beginning to take on some of the mannerisms of the people who lived there.
>
> —Georges Simenon, *Maigret and the Toy Village*

* Tanya L. Chartrand and John A. Bargh, "The Chameleon Effect: The Perception-Behavior Link and Social Interaction," Journal of Personalityand Social Psychology, 1999, Vol. 76, , No. 6, pp. 893-910. Copyright (c) 1999 by the American Psychological Association.. Reproduced with permission.

As the saying goes, "Monkey see, monkey do." Primates, including humans, are quite good at imitation. Such imitation, in all primates, has generally been considered to be an intentional, goal-directed activity—for instance, mimicry helps one to learn vicariously from the experience of conspecifics or to ingratiate oneself to the other person (see Bandura, 1977; Galef, 1988; Heyes, 1993; Piaget, 1946; Tomasello, Savage-Rumbaugh, & Kruger, 1993).

This research was supported in part by National Science Foundation Grants SBR-9409448 and SBR-9809000.

We thank Vinnie Chawla, Catherine Cordova, Elina Geskin, Nora Guerra, Peter Karp, Marianna Moliver, and Christina Ungerer for serving as experimenters and confederates and Annette Lee Chai, Ap Dijksterhuis, Peter Gollwitzer, Katelyn McKenna, and Dan Wegner for helpful suggestions on an earlier version of this article.

Correspondence concerning this article should be addressed to Tanya L. Chartrand, who is now at the Department of Psychology, Ohio State University, 1885 Neil Avenue Mall, Columbus, Ohio 43210, or to John A. Bargh, Department of Psychology, New York University, 6 Washington Place, Seventh Floor, New York, New York 10003. Electronic mail may be sent to tanyac@psych.nyu.edu or to bargh@psych.nyu.edu.

Recently, however, several studies have documented a passive, direct effect of social perception on social behavior, an effect that is unintended and not in the service of any discernible purpose (Bargh, Chen, & Burrows, 1996; Chen & Bargh, 1997; Dijksterhuis, Spears, et al., 1998; Dijksterhuis & van Knippenberg, 1998; Macrae et al., 1998; Mussweiler & Foerster, 1998). These findings suggest that imitation and mimicry effects in humans might often be unintentional (Chen, Chartrand, Lee Chai, & Bargh, 1998). As the popular meaning of the phrase "to ape" is "to intentionally imitate," perhaps the monkey metaphor may not be the most appropriate animal metaphor for the phenomenon.

We believe that the chameleon is a better one. In the motion picture *Zelig*, Woody Allen plays a human chameleon who cannot help but take on the behavior, personality, and values of whomever he is with. Like a chameleon changing its color to match its current surroundings, Zelig's behavior changes to match the norms and values of the group with which he is currently involved. Although Allen's film took this phenomenon to laughable extremes, it is nevertheless a common experience to discover, after the fact, that one has taken on the accent, speech patterns, and even behavioral mannerisms of one's interaction partners. The naturalness and nonconsciousness of this process was frequently commented on by the author Georges Simenon, whose fictional Inspector Maigret (the subject of the opening epigraph) routinely immersed himself in the lives of murder victims as a favorite method for solving the crimes.

Such a "chameleon effect" may manifest itself in different ways. One may notice using the idiosyncratic verbal expressions or speech inflections of a friend. Or one may notice crossing one's arms while talking with someone else who has his or her arms crossed. Common to all such cases is that one typically does not notice doing these things—if at all—until after the fact.

PERCEIVING IS FOR DOING

The Perception–Behavior Link

Throughout the history of psychology, many have argued that the act of perceiving another person's behavior creates a tendency to behave similarly oneself. To begin with, William James's principle of *ideomotor action* held that merely thinking about a behavior increases the tendency to engage in that behavior (James, 1890). This principle is in harmony with the proposed existence of a perception–action link, if one assumes perceptual activity to be one source of behavior-relevant ideation. Making just this assumption, Berkowitz (1984) invoked the principle of ideomotor action in his revised theory of how violence portrayed in the mass media increases the probability of aggression in the viewer. He argued that activation spread automatically in memory from representations of the perceived violent acts to other aggressive ideas of the viewer. This spreading activation to aggressive behavioral representations, he asserted, automatically led the viewer to behave in a more aggressive manner.

Carver, Ganellen, Froming, and Chambers (1983) tested Berkowitz's ideomotor account of modeling effects. They posited that individuals use *interpretive schemas* for perceiving and interpreting behaviors and *behavioral schemas* for producing behaviors. Because these two schemas are assumed to have substantial overlap in their semantic features, they should tend to become active at the same times. Carver et al. predicted that perceiving a hostile behavior in the environment would activate not only one's hostile interpretive schema, but one's hostile behavioral schema as well, so that the mere act of interpreting the behavior as hostile would make the perceiver more likely to behave in a hostile manner. Participants first were primed (or not) with hostile-related stimuli and then, in an ostensibly unrelated study, were to give shocks to another participant each time the latter made an error in a learning task. Results supported the hypothesis: Relative to the control group, participants who had been previously exposed to hostility-related priming stimuli gave longer shocks to the "learner."

Researchers in the area of language acquisition have also posited a "common-coding" principle to account for rapid language acquisition in young children. In a seminal paper, Lashley (1951) asserted that "the processes of language comprehension and language production have too much in common to depend on wholly different mechanisms" (p. 120). Following Lashley, Prinz (1990) hypothesized a common, or shared, representational system for language comprehension and action codes. He further suggested that the coding system for perceiving behaviors in others is the same as for performing those behaviors—and if so, he argued, that code cannot be used simultaneously in the service of perception and of behavior.

In an experimental demonstration of Prinz's (1990) thesis, Muesseler and Hommel (1997) instructed participants to reproduce certain sequences of four left and right arrow key presses as quickly as they could on each trial (the keys were labeled "<" and ">" respectively; thus, on one trial the sequence might be "< < > <" and on another trial "> < > <"). Participants practiced the sequence until they were ready to perform it rapidly. As soon as they made the first keypress of the sequence, however, the computer display briefly presented an additional left or right arrow key that they had been instructed to append to the end of their practiced sequence. The timing of this presentation was such that it occurred precisely when the participant was pressing the second of the four keys in the sequence. Which of the two keys ("<" or ">") was to be pressed at the end of the practiced sequence was manipulated to be either the same or the opposite of the key actually being pressed at that moment. As hypothesized, participants made more errors (i.e., more often pressed the wrong extra key) if the presented symbol corresponded to the one they were pressing at that moment than when it was different. Apparently, the behavior of pressing the right (or left) arrow key interfered with the ability to perceive the right (or left) arrow key symbol, consistent with Prinz's position that the same representation is used for perceiving as for behaving, and cannot be used for both at the same moment in time.

Priming of Social Behavior

The existence of an automatic, unintended, and passive effect of perception on behavior has important ramifications for whether social behavior can occur nonconsciously and without intention. If the effect of perception on behavior is automatic, then direct environmental causation of social behavior could be produced in a two-step process. The first would involve automatic (i.e., not effortful or consciously guided) perceptual categorization and interpretation of social behavior (environment to perception), with this perceptual activation continuing on to activate corresponding behavioral representations (perception to behavior). In this way, the entire sequence from environment to behavior would occur automatically, without conscious choice or guidance playing a role (see Bargh & Chartrand, 1999).

Regarding the first stage of this hypothetical sequence, it is now widely accepted that much of social perceptual activity is automated (i.e., immediate, efficient, and not consciously guided). Many years of research have demonstrated the variety of ways in which (a) behaviors are encoded spontaneously and without intention in terms of relevant trait concepts (e.g., Bargh & Thein, 1985; Carlston & Skowronski, 1994; Uleman, Newman, & Moskowitz, 1996; Winter & Uleman, 1984), (b) contextual priming of trait concepts changes the perceiver's interpretation of an identical behavior through temporarily increasing their accessibility or readiness to be used (see Bargh, 1989; Higgins, 1989, 1996; Wyer & Srull, 1989, for reviews), and (c) stereotypes of social groups become activated automatically upon the mere perception of the distinguishing features of a group member (e.g., Bargh, 1994, 1999; Brewer, 1988; Devine, 1989).

Thus, if the automatic activation of perceptual representations continuously activates behavioral representations, the same priming manipulations that have been shown to influence social perception should also influence social behavior. In support of this prediction, Bargh, Chen, et al. (1996) found that when stereotypes or trait constructs were "primed," or nonconsciously activated in the course of an unrelated task, the participant subsequently was more likely to act in line with the content of the primed trait construct or stereotype. In Experiment 1, in what was ostensibly a language test, participants were exposed to words related to either rudeness (e.g., "rude," "impolite," and "obnoxious"), politeness (e.g., "respect," "considerate," and "polite"), or neither (in the control condition); considerable previous work on impression formation using the same priming method (but with varying trait content; e.g., Banaji, Hardin, & Rothman, 1993; Srull & Wyer, 1979, 1980) had shown it to activate the corresponding perceptual trait constructs. On the basis of the hypothesized perception–behavior link, this activation was expected to continuously activate the behavioral constructs of rudeness or politeness, increasing the likelihood of such behavior.

After completing this priming task, participants encountered a situation in which they could either behave in a rude fashion and interrupt an ongoing conversation or behave in a polite fashion and wait for the conversation to end on its own—without the participant's intervention, the conversation would continue on for 10 min. Results showed that significantly more participants in the rude priming condition (67%) interrupted the conversation than did those in the control condition (38%), whereas only 16% of those primed with the polite condition interrupted it—in other words, fully 84% of participants in the politeness priming condition waited the entire 10 min without interrupting.

Experiment 2 of Bargh, Chen, et al. (1996) extended these findings to the case of stereotype (collections of group-related traits, as opposed to single-trait concepts) activation. Participants were first primed either with words related to the stereotype of the elderly (e.g., "Florida," "sentimental," "wrinkle") or with words unrelated to the stereotype. Importantly, none of the primes was semantically related to slowness or weakness, though these concepts are components of the stereotype. As predicted, priming the stereotype caused participants to subsequently behave in line with the stereotype content; specifically, they walked more slowly down the hallway after leaving the experiment. Experiment 3 conceptually replicated this effect by subliminally presenting faces of young male African Americans to some participants, who then reacted to a provocation with greater hostility (a component of the African American stereotype; see, e.g., Devine, 1989) than did control participants. This latter effect was replicated and extended by Chen and Bargh (1997).

Dijksterhuis and van Knippenberg (1998) have conceptually replicated these findings by demonstrating that priming a stereotype or trait can affect subsequent performance on an intellectual task. In several studies, these researchers primed participants with a positive stereotype ("professor"), a negative stereotype ("soccer hooligans"), a positive trait ("intelligent"), or a negative trait ("stupid"). Those participants primed with either the professor stereotype or the "intelligent" trait showed enhanced performance on a general knowledge scale (similar to Trivial Pursuit), whereas those primed with the hooligan stereotype or the "stupid" trait showed decreased performance.

Mediational Evidence

The Bargh, Chen, et al. (1996) and Dijksterhuis and van Knippenberg (1998) studies showed that priming techniques produce changes in behavior based on the hypothesis of an automatic perception–behavior link. However, these studies (as well as that of Carver et al., 1983) did not provide evidence that perceptual activity mediated the effect of priming on behavior, because perception itself was never manipulated (or measured). It remains possible that environmental events (which priming manipulations simulate) directly activate perception and separately directly activate behavioral tendencies.

One way to show that passive perceptual activity automatically causes behavior would be to show that manipulations known to cause changes in perception and judgment produce corresponding changes in behavior. Dijksterhuis and his colleagues (Dijksterhuis, Aarts, Bargh, & van Knippenberg, 1998; Dijksterhuis, Spears, et al., 1998) have conducted a series of such studies.

Assimilation and contrast effects in automatic behavior Research in social perception has documented two main forms of representation that moderate social judgments: trait categories (e.g., honesty) and exemplars (representations of specific people who exemplify the trait, such as Einstein for intelligence). In general, the evidence shows that activated trait categories usually produce assimilation effects; ambiguously relevant behavior is assimilated into the category rather than contrasted against it. A person whose trait category of honesty is in a heightened state of accessibility or activation is more likely than the average person to consider someone generous when he or she gives money to a charity following his or her boss's request to do so (e.g., Higgins, Rholes, & Jones, 1977; Srull & Wyer, 1979). But if a person is thinking about exemplars of a given trait, such as Einstein for the "intelligent" trait, then ambiguously relevant behaviors (getting a B on a test) are seen as less, not more representative of that trait (Herr, Sherman, & Fazio, 1984; Smith & Zarate, 1992; Stapel, Koomen, & van der Pligt, 1997). The exemplar sets a high standard against which mundane trait-consistent behaviors pale in comparison.

If perception mediates the ideomotor effects of the environment on behavior, then one should find assimilation effects on behavior with category priming and contrast effects on behavior with exemplar priming—the same effects one obtains on perceptual and judgmental dependent measures. Confirming this prediction, Dijksterhuis, Spears, et al. (1998) showed that priming (without specific examples) the stereotype of professors versus that of supermodels (the latter group being stereotypically viewed as unintelligent by the participant population) produced assimilation effects on behavior. Those participants primed with the professor stereotype gave more correct answers on a subsequent knowledge test than did those primed with the supermodel stereotype. But when specific exemplars of the two categories served as the priming stimuli (e.g., Albert Einstein and Claudia Schiffer), the opposite pattern was obtained; that is, contrast effects on behavior were observed.

Amount of experience mediates perception–behavior effects Another approach to gaining positive evidence of mediation by perceptual activity is to assess individual differences regarding how much contact the individual has had with that group. The more contact, the stronger and more automatic the perceptual representation, and thus the stronger and more likely the behavioral effect. Dijksterhuis, Aarts, et al. (1998) assessed how much contact college-age experimental participants had per week with the elderly. It was assumed that greater amounts of contact with the elderly would correspond to stronger perceptual associations between being elderly and having relatively poor memory. In the course of a lexical decision task, it was shown that the greater the participant's amount of contact with the elderly, the stronger the association between the concepts of the elderly and of forgetfulness. Moreover, a subsequent memory test for all of the target stimuli in the lexical decision task showed that greater amounts of contact with the elderly were related to poorer memory performance. Most importantly, however, the effect of contact on memory was entirely mediated by the strength of the perceptual association between the concepts *elderly* and *forgetful*. There was no direct effect of amount of contact on behavior that was not mediated by the strength of the perceptual representation.

RESEARCH ON BEHAVIORAL COORDINATION

Observations of and theories about nonconscious mimicry have a long history (see Bandura, 1977; Bavelas, Black, Lemery, & Mullett, 1987; Koffka, 1925; Piaget, 1946). Interestingly, most of the early writers on the topic conceptualized mimicry in terms of empathy. Adam Smith (1759/1966), for example, posited that reflexive imitation occurs after one takes the perspective of the other and realizes what he or she must feel, and Charles Darwin (1872/1965) used the term sympathy to refer to imitation based on reflex or habit. In fact, according to Gordon Allport (1968), the original meaning of the term empathy was "objective motor mimicry"; it was only in the latter half of the 20th century that it came to be used as a global term encompassing vicarious emotion, role taking, and the ability to understand others.

Research on nonconscious mimicry began after a seminal paper by Scheflen in 1964. He observed that postural configurations were a source of information about an ongoing social interaction, as they communicated messages about liking and understanding. Moreover, individuals were said to utilize this postural information unconsciously to orient themselves within a group. Three basic lines of research on behavioral coordination developed thereafter (see Bernieri & Rosenthal, 1991). Research on rhythmic synchrony has included work on the precise synchronization between the speech and body movements of the two interaction partners (Bernieri, 1988; Condon & Ogston, 1966; Condon & Sander, 1974; Dittmann & Llewellyn, 1968, 1969; Kendon, 1970; cf. McDowall, 1978). Facial mimicry research has focused on neonates' mimicry of adult facial expressions (Meltzoff & Moore, 1977, 1979, 1983; cf. Kaitz, Meschulach-Sarfaty, Auerbach, & Eidelman, 1988). However, no consensus developed from this research as to the mechanisms responsible for the effect (Anisfeld, 1979; Jacobson & Kagan, 1979; Masters, 1979).

Facial mimicry has also been found in adults (Dimberg, 1982; Vaughan & Lanzetta, 1980; Zajonc, Adelmann, Murphy, & Niedenthal, 1987), although it is not clear from these studies whether the observers actually experience the same emotions as the other person or simply mimic his or her facial expressions. The Zajonc et al. finding that couples grow to resemble each other the longer they are together is especially intriguing given the present hypothesis of a perception–behavior link, because one reason for the increased resemblance could be the similar facial lines left by many years of unconsciously mimicking the perceived facial expressions of the partner.

The third type of behavioral coordination research, and the one that most closely resembles the chameleon effect, is that on behavior matching, which occurs when people mimic behavior patterns by adopting similar postures or showing similar body configurations (La France, 1979, 1982; La France & Broadbent, 1976). The main focus of this research has been to link posture similarity in naturalistic settings to rapport, which (though rarely operationalized the same way twice) often includes measures of involvedness, togetherness, being "in step," and compatibility (see also Bavelas, Black, Chovil, Lemery, & Mullett, 1988; Bavelas, Black, Lemery, & Mullett, 1986, 1987).

Despite the considerable amount of research on mimicry and behavioral coordination, there has been relatively little attention given to the mechanism responsible for it. The consensus position appears to be that behavioral coordination is in some way related to empathy, rapport, and liking, although some see mimicry as the cause and others see it as the effect of empathic understanding. That mimicry and behavioral coordination are said to serve the adaptive function of facilitating social interaction and interpersonal bonding does not, however, answer the question of how these effects are produced.

Four critical elements are missing from these observational studies. First, although moderate posture sharing has been reported, there has been no baseline or control group with which to compare the amount of mimicry observed; without this, one cannot determine whether it occurs more often than chance would predict. In fact, La France (1982) has stated that "posture mirroring is not constant nor ubiquitous" (p. 290), and the results of one statistical test of its existence suggested that it did not occur more often than would be predicted by chance (Bernieri, 1988). Although there is wide agreement that posture and body movement mimicking do occur, it nonetheless remains an experimentally unproven observation.

Second, there has been no test of the minimal conditions under which behavior matching occurs. As noted before, research has shown that there is greater posture similarity when the interactants like each other and feel more rapport (Charney, 1966; La France, 1979; La France & Broadbent, 1976; Scheflen, 1964). However, there has been no compelling test of whether there is significant mimicry among unacquainted interaction partners. If the perception–behavior link is the mechanism underlying behavior matching, then it should occur even among strangers. Furthermore, the chameleon effect is hypothesized to be an entirely passive and preconsciously automatic process (i.e., it does not depend on the concurrent operation of an intentional goal, such as ingratiation, during the interaction; see Bargh, 1989). Thus, not only should it occur among strangers, but it should occur even without an active goal to get along with and be liked by the interaction partner. To date, there have been no tests of whether posture and behavior mimicry occur under such minimal conditions.

Third, the previous studies were correlational and did not manipulate the postures and mannerisms of either interactant.[1] This lack of experimental control over which mannerisms are done and how long they are engaged in precludes one from inferring causation. That is, one cannot conclude from these studies that Person X was mimicking Person Y; rather, one can only say that Persons X and Y were displaying the same mannerisms or postures at a given time. For one thing, there could be other, third factors that could spuriously lead to these shared behaviors (e.g., a hot room causing all present to fan their face). For a valid demonstration of the chameleon effect, one would need to show that Person X first engages in a particular behavior, and then Person Y mimics that behavior, without intending or having any reason to do so.

Finally, just as chameleons change their coloring to blend in with their current environment, an experimental demonstration of a behavioral chameleon effect should incorporate, as a within-subjects factor, variability in the behavior of interaction partners, to show that the participant's behavior changes accordingly. Again, to date, there has been no demonstration of such passive behavior adaptations to multiple interaction partners.

THE CHAMELEON EFFECT AS CAUSE OF INTERPERSONAL RAPPORT AND EMPATHY

We propose that the chameleon effect is the mechanism behind mimicry and behavioral coordination and thereby is the source of the observed smoother social interaction and interpersonal bonding produced by the (nonconscious) mimicry. In relating these formerly disparate areas of research, we hypothesize that the perception of another's behavior (be it facial expression, body posture, mannerism, etc.) increases the tendency for the perceiver to behave in a similar manner, and that this is an entirely passive and nonconscious phenomenon. Thus, we argue that the perception of another's behavior does not require or depend on the perceiver having any interpersonal goal, such as ingratiation, toward the person being perceived, nor does perception require the two interaction partners to have an already established relationship (i.e., a preexisting state of rapport). Unlike the prior correlational accounts of mimicry and rapport, we posit a directional causal sequence: Perception causes similar behavior, and the perception of the similar behavior on the part of the other creates shared feelings of empathy and rapport. In short, the widely documented automatic link between perception and behavior exists, at least in pan, as a kind of natural "social glue" that produces empathic understanding and even greater liking between people, without their having to intend or try to have this happen.

As noted above, the studies that showed that the same priming manipulations that influence social perception also influence social behavior are suggestive, but not conclusive, evidence for automatic effects of perception on behavior. What is needed is a demonstration, within a social interaction context, that the perceiver's behavior changes as a function of the behavior of the interaction partner, and that these changes occur without conscious choice or guidance.

Thus, our first goal (Experiment 1) was to provide an experimental test of the existence of nonconsciousmimicry of behavioral mannerisms in a way that (a) determines whether it occurs at greater-than-chance levels, (b) tests whether it occurs among strangers when no affiliation goal is operating, (c) manipulates mannerisms and behaviors of interaction partners (confederates of the experimenter) to determine the direction of causality of the effect, and (d) tests for a chameleon-type change in behavior as a function of the behavior of the current interaction partner. Unlike previous researchers, we did not observe individuals who were already engaged in an interaction; rather, we created dyadic interactions between participants and confederates during which confederates varied their facial expressions and behavioral mannerisms. In Experiments 2 and 3, we sought to verify that these automatic effects of social perception on social interaction produce greater empathy and liking between the interaction partners; in Experiment 3, we examined this issue by testing whether individual differences in empathy covary with individual differences in the chameleon tendency.

EXPERIMENT 1: A TEST OF UNINTENTIONAL MIMICRY BETWEEN STRANGERS

Method

Overview Students participated in two consecutive dyadic sessions. Session 1 consisted of a 10-min interaction with 1 other "participant" (Confederate 1; C1), during which they took turns describing various photographs. Participants then repeated this photograph description task in Session 2 with a 2nd "participant" (Confederate 2; C2).

Confederates varied their mannerisms throughout the interactions. During Session 1, C1 either rubbed his or her face or shook his or her foot. During Session 2, C2 did whichever behavior C1 did not do. Facial expressions varied as well; C1 either smiled or had a neutral expression (i.e., did not smile) throughout Session 1. During Session 2, C2 smiled if C1 had not smiled, and did not smile if C1 had smiled. The order of mannerisms and facial expressions was counterbalanced, and C2 always did the mannerism and facial expression that C1 did not do. A video camera recorded participants during both sessions so that coders could later judge the extent to which participants mimicked the mannerisms and facial expressions of the 2 confederates.

Participants Thirty-nine male and female students enrolled in an introductory psychology course at New York University participated in the experiment in partial fulfillment of a course requirement. Data from 4 of these participants were excluded from subsequent analyses for the following reasons: (a) 3 participants chose to not sign the consent form giving us permission to code and analyze their videotape, and (b) during debriefing, 1 participant expressed suspicion that the other participant was in fact a confederate. However, neither she nor any of the other participants accurately guessed our hypothesis.

Thus, we computed all analyses on responses from a final sample of 35 participants. For 14 participants, C1 smiled and shook his or her foot and C2 did not smile and rubbed his or her face. Because the possibility existed that encountering the smiling confederate first would affect participants' interactions with the nonsmiling C2, it was important to counterbalance the order of facial expressions by having the nonsmiling confederate interact first with some of the participants. Thus, C1 did not smile with 21 participants (of these, C1 rubbed his or her face with 8 and shook his or her foot with 13).

Apparatus and materials Two male and two female assistants served as experimenters and confederates, rotating in the roles of experimenter or confederate. The experiment room had one chair for the experimenter at the front of the room, behind a desk in which the materials and stimuli for the experiment were kept. The room also contained two chairs for the participant and confederate that were placed approximately 1.2 m apart. These two chairs were half-facing each other and half-facing the experimenter's desk. With this arrangement, the participants could see the confederates' mannerisms during the interaction but could not see the experimenter's, whose body was effectively hidden by the desk.

Participants were videotaped throughout both sessions by means of a video camera on a shelf in the corner of the room. The camera was focused on the participant's chair, resulting in a clear view of the participant's entire seated body. To ensure that coders of the videos were blind to condition, we did not videotape the confederates. Thus, when judging a particular participant's responses, the raters did not know the corresponding mannerisms or facial expressions of the 2 confederates.

Color photographs for the experiment were chosen from magazines such as *Newsweek*, *Time*, and *Life*. The photos were cut out of the magazines and mounted on heavy black cardboard. Twelve photos were chosen that ranged somewhat in emotional content, amount of action involved, and ambiguity of what was being portrayed in the photo.[2] These variables were not manipulated systematically, but the photographs were rotated so that participants did not always describe the same type of photo when with the smiling or nonsmiling confederate (e.g., only describing somewhat "happy" photos when with the smiling confederate). Thus, although 6 of the 12 photos were reserved for the confederates (so they could memorize a prepared script for each) and the other 6 were reserved for the participant, the order of the photos within each set varied.

Procedure Each participant completed the experiment individually. Prior to each session, the experimenter turned on the video camera that would record the participant throughout the session. The experimenter then brought the participant into the laboratory room and seated him or her in the participant's chair. The experimenter then left the participant alone in the room for 1 min (ostensibly to retrieve copies of a needed form from another room), during which time the participant was videotaped to obtain a baseline measure. This baseline period was later coded to determine the extent to which the participant was already rubbing his or her face, shaking his or her foot, or smiling before interacting with any confederate.

The experimenter reentered the room and delivered the cover story. It was explained that the purpose of the study was to test a new projective measure being created by some psychologists in the department. (The assumptions underlying the use of projective measures were briefly explained to those participants unfamiliar with them.) The participant was informed that some researchers were trying to develop a revised version of one of the more common measures (the Thematic Apperception Test) that (a) could be administered to more than one person at a time and (b) would use photographs instead of picture drawings.

The participant was told that the researchers were in the initial stage of creating working sets of photographs to serve as the stimuli for the projective test. Toward this end, they were first testing various sets of photos on a "normal" (i.e., nonpatient) population. Specifically, college students were being recruited to describe what they saw in the various photographs. Participants could discuss the visual aspects of the photo, or free associate and say whatever came to mind (including what the people in the photos were thinking or feeling), or both. Importantly, the experimenter emphasized to the participant that responses would not be analyzed by any of the psychologists (or anyone else), so there was no need to be concerned about the content of his or her responses. Instead, the ease with which the students described and generated responses to the photos would ostensibly be taken as the indicator of the usefulness of those particular photos. Accordingly, the participant was told that at the conclusion of the experiment, he or she would be asked about the experience of describing the photographs (e.g., how easy it was to generate responses for them).

The participant was further informed that several sets of photographs had already been gathered and tested on students 1 at a time in individual sessions. The photos were now being tested in group settings, beginning with groups of 2 students at a time. The participant was then given a consent form to sign and told that he or she would be involved in two separate group sessions, each with 1 other participant. It was explained that another session was being conducted concurrently in another room, and that 1 of the participants from a previous session there would be the 1st partner. The experimenter then brought in the 1st other participant (C1) and seated him or her in the confederate's chair. The participant and C1 were each given a set of three photos facing down. The experimenter explained that the two sets of photos were different and reminded them that their task was to take turns describing what they saw in each photograph. They were told to describe each photo in any way they wished for approximately 1 min.

The experimenter suggested that C1 turn over the first photo and begin. C1 described the photograph, following a memorized script to ensure that responses were standardized across different confederates find different experimental sessions. It should be noted that the confederates were trained to deliver the responses with natural hesitation, including pauses, *umms*, and *hmms*. One example of a scripted response refers to a photo of a man holding in his arms a small dog with a leg cast:

> This is a picture of a man holding a small dog—maybe a chihuahua but I'm not sure. The dog's leg is in a cast, so I guess it's broken. I don't know how dogs' legs get broken, but maybe it got stuck somewhere, like in those gutters outside or something. So then it was probably crying or making a lot of noise and this man heard it. The man looks like a pretty nice guy, so he probably felt sorry for the dog and wanted to help it. This picture looks like it's taken at a vet's office, so the man probably brought the dog to the vet and then they put the cast on the leg, And then this picture was taken right after that. The man didn't know who the dog belonged to, so he's having people take pictures of the dog so that the owner can come pick him up.

The experimenter then asked the participant to turn over his or her first photo and begin describing it. After the participant finished, C1 and the participant continued alternating turns until both completed their sets of three photographs. During the interaction, C1 made minimal eye contact with the participant to minimize the possibility that any personal relationship between the two would be established. C1 was either smiling or not smiling and either rubbing his or her face or shaking his or her foot. Behaviors were always performed throughout the interactions.

After all photographs had been described, the experimenter told participants that they would now be switching partners. One of the participants would be brought to the other laboratory room to join another participant, and the other would stay in the current room to meet a new partner. The experimenter escorted C1 out of the laboratory room and approximately 1 min later brought in C2 to join the participant. The experimenter gave the participant and C2 a different set of three photographs each, and once again they alternated taking turns describing them. This time, however, C2 was displaying the mannerism (rubbing his or her face or shaking his or her foot) and facial expression (smiling or not smiling) that C1 had not.

Following the session with C2, the experimenter said that the debriefing would take place individually, and that C2 would be taken to the other laboratory room where he or she would be debriefed by the other experimenter. The experimenter escorted C2 out of the room and returned alone approximately 30 s later. The experimenter then queried the participant in a "funneled" question sequence (i.e., from general to increasingly specific questions about awareness of hypo- theses; see Bargh & Chartrand, in press) to determine if he or she (a) was suspicious that the other participants were in fact confederates, (b) noticed that the confederates each displayed certain mannerisms throughout the session, or (c) thought that the purpose of the experiment was anything other than what the cover story indicated. Finally, the hypotheses and purpose of the study were explained to the participant. The participant was asked to sign a video release form allowing the researchers to examine the data and was thanked for his or her participation in the study.

Results

Interjudge reliability Videotapes were coded by two independent judges blind to the condition of participants. Three time periods were coded for each participant: 1 min of baseline before interacting with confederates (BL), the time spent with C1 (T1), and the time spent with C2 (T2). The coding procedure yielded the following dependent variables: (a) the number of times the participant smiled, (b) the number of times the participant robbed his or her face, and (c) the number of times the participant shook his or her foot.[3]

The following are the interjudge reliabilities: For the number of times smiling, the reliability for the three ratings (BL, TI, and T2) ranged from $r = .79$ to 1.00, with mean $r = .89$. For number of times participants shook their foot, the three ratings ranged from $r = .53$ to $.79$, with mean $r = .68$. For number of times participants robbed their face, the interjudge reliabilities ranged from $r = .33$ to $.60$, mean $r = .50$.[4] All reliabilities were significant at $p < .001$.

The mean of the two judges' ratings was taken to form a single rating for each behavior. Ratings for T1 and T2 were then divided by the number of minutes (to the nearest second) that the interaction lasted to arrive at a rate per minute. (This method had the further advantages of equating T1 and T2 with BL so that the numbers would all be in the same metric and ensuring that any differences would not be artifactually due to somewhat longer or shorter interactions in T1 vs. T2.)

For both the smiling and behavioral measures, a repeated measures analysis of variance (ANOVA) was conducted on the number of times each action occurred per minute. For each analysis, we included the baseline rating as a covariate to adjust for individual differences in performing the key behaviors in the absence of another person. Neither the participant's gender nor the order in which the confederates enacted the various behaviors affected the results, so neither of these variables is discussed further.

Facial expression As predicted, there was a significant effect of confederate expression, $F(1, 34) = 20.31$, $p < .0001$. Participants smiled more times per minute when with the smiling confederate ($M = 1.03$) than with the neutral confederate ($M = 0.36$). This result suggests that participants did indeed mimic the facial expression of the confederates.

Behavioral measures We next conducted a repeated measures ANOVA on the number of times participants engaged in the mannerisms per minute. Confederate behavior (foot shaking vs. face rubbing) and participant behavior (foot shaking vs. face rubbing) were the two within-subject variables. Whereas there were no main effects for confederate behavior ($F < 1$) or participant behavior ($p > .25$), the predicted interaction between the two was, in fact, reliable, $F(1, 34) = 9.36$, $p = .004$ (see Figure 1). Our hypothesized chameleon effect specifically predicts that participants should engage in face rubbing (or foot shaking) more in the presence of the confederate engaging in that behavior than in the presence of the confederate not engaging in that behavior. Consistent with this prediction are our findings that participants rubbed their face more times in the presence of the face-rubbing confederate than when with the foot-shaking confederate, $F(1, 34) = 5.71$, $p < .025$, and shook their foot more times when with the foot-shaking confederate than with the face-rubbing confederate, $F(1, 34) = 3.76$, $p = .06$. These results, in conjunction with the facial expression findings, support our hypothesis that individuals passively take on the mannerisms and facial expressions of those around them without the intention or reason to do so.

Liking as potential mediator If the perception–behavior link is, as we argue, a completely nonconscious, non-goal-dependent mechanism that produces the chameleon effect, mimicry of others should occur even in the absence of a reason to do so, such as pursuing an affiliation goal. In the present study, with one smiling and one nonsmiling confederate, it is reasonable to suppose that participants would be more likely to have an affiliation goal—if they had one at all, which the de sign of the experiment attempted to minimize—with the smiling than with the nonsmiling confederate. Thus, one could conceptualize the smiling and nonsmiling confederates as a likeability manipulation.

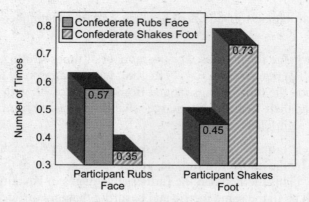

Figure 1. Number of times participants rubbed their face and shook their foot per minute when with a confederate who was rubbing his or her face and a confederate who was shaking his or her foot.

The question becomes, did the participants mimic the foot-shaking and face-rubbing behaviors of the nonsmiling confederate or only those of the smiling confederate? In the following analysis, whichever of the two behaviors the nonsmiling confederate performed was the key behavior for a given participant. We compared how much participants engaged in the key behavior with the nonsmiling confederate with how much they engaged in that same behavior with the smiling confederate (who was doing the other behavior). A repeated measures ANOVA was conducted on the number of times the action occurred per minute. A significant effect of confederate behavior was obtained, $F(1, 34) = 4.16$, $p = .05$. Participants performed the key action more times with the nonsmiling confederate doing that key behavior ($M = .56$) than with the smiling, likable confederate doing the other behavior ($M = .40$). It was not the case that participants only mimicked the behavior of the smiling, apparently friendly confederate and not the nonsmiling, apparently less friendly confederate.

Were the mimicry effects greater in the presence of the smiling confederate? We next compared the extent to which participants mimicked the behavior (either foot shaking or face rubbing) of the smiling confederate more than the behavior of the nonsmiling confederate. Behavior mimicked (face rubbing or foot shaking) when the participant was with the smiling confederate was the between-subjects variable, and confederate expression (smiling versus nonsmiling) was the within-subjects variable. There was no significant main effect for confederate expression across the two behaviors being mimicked, nor was the interaction significant ($Fs < 1$). Thus, there was no evidence in our study that the obtained effects were goal dependent.

Participants' awareness of having engaged in behavioral mimicry For the chameleon effect to be considered passive and automatic, it must be demonstrated that participants were not aware of having mimicked the confederates. Although intuitively it seems unlikely that participants would want to purposefully mimic the confederates' mannerisms, it is possible that participants believed that shaking their foot or rubbing their face simultaneously with the confederate would be beneficial for the interaction in some way, and they mimicked for these conscious, motivated reasons. However, we have evidence that this was not the case. Participants were asked during the funneled debriefing at the conclusion of the experiment whether anything about either of the confederates stood out to them. Participants were then asked whether either of the confederates had any particular mannerisms or ways of speaking that they noticed or that seemed distinctive. One participant (out of 35) mentioned that 1 of the confederates made hand motions while speaking, and 2 others commented on the slouching posture of 1 confederate. However, none of the participants mentioned noticing that the confederates were shaking their foot or rubbing their face. (When asked, most reported that they "hadn't noticed" the mannerisms of the confederate.) Thus, it seems that not only were participants not consciously trying to imitate the mannerisms of the confederates, but they did not even pay attention to these mannerisms in the first place.

Discussion

Researchers have long been interested in nonconscious mimicry, yet there has been little attention given to identifying the mechanism underlying the phenomenon. We have argued that the perception–behavior link can provide such a mechanism. The perception–behavior link posits the existence of a natural and nonconscious connection between the act of perceiving and the act of behaving, such that perceiving an action being done by another makes one more likely to engage in that same behavior. This mechanism can account for the chameleon effect, the tendency of people to take on the postures and mannerisms of those around them.

In Experiment 1, we sought to provide an experimental test of the chameleon effect in which the mannerisms and facial expressions of interaction partners were manipulated and standardized across participants. Analyses revealed that behavioral mimicry did in fact occur at significantly greater than chance levels. Significant mimicry was found for facial expressions and for two different behavioral mannerisms, after controlling for BL measures of each behavior. Furthermore, the design of the experiment, in which the confederates' behavior was predetermined and standardized and so it was clear who was mimicking whom, enables conclusions to be drawn for the first time about the causal direction of the effect. Unlike previous studies, this one showed that the similarity in mannerisms between participants and confederates could not have been due to any third factor.

Moreover, because participants interacted with 2 different partners, each of whom engaged in different facial expressions and behavioral mannerisms, the results demonstrated the true chameleon-like nature of the perception–behavior effect, as the participants' behavior changed as a function of the behavior of their current interaction partner. Thus, they rubbed their face when interacting with the face-rubbing confederate but then reduced face rubbing and increased foot shaking during their interaction with the foot-shaking confederate. No previous study had demonstrated how an individual's behavior naturally adapts to changes in social environmental settings by blending in to each of them successively.

Because the perception–behavior link is preconscious and not goal dependent, for it to be the cause of the chameleon effect, the effect should occur among strangers when no affiliation goal is present. This was found to be the case; participants mimicked the behavior of strangers, even nonsmiling ones who never made eye contact with them. In designing the experiment, we sought to minimize the possibility that participants would choose to pursue an affiliation or other social goal toward the confederates that would cause them, in pursuit of that goal, to engage in behavioral mimicry (even at a nonconscious, goal-dependent, automatic level). Thus, confederates were instructed to not make eye contact with the participants, and when serving as the smiling confederate, to never smile at the participants. Finally, that the obtained behavioral mimicry occurred just as much in the presence of the nonsmiling as the smiling confederate is further evidence against the goal-dependent alternative account.

EXPERIMENT 2: THE ADAPTIVE FUNCTION OF THE CHAMELEON EFFECT

What is the adaptive function served by the chameleon effect, the nonconscious tendency to behave with others as those others are behaving? As reviewed above, there is consensus among researchers that behavior matching is related to greater liking and rapport between the interactants. Our second goal for the present research was to test whether behavior matching does in fact increase liking and create a sense of smoother interactions. Our hypothesis that automatic effects of perception on behavior serve adaptive functions is part of a larger research effort that traces the "downstream" consequences of a variety of immediate, preconscious reactions to the social environment. For example, recent research on the downstream effect of the tendency to automatically evaluate perceived stimuli as either good or bad (e.g., Bargh, Chaiken, Govender, & Pratto, 1992; Bargh, Chaiken, Raymond, & Hymes, 1996; Fazio, Sanbonmatsu, Powell, & Kardes, 1986) has demonstrated direct effects on behavioral predispositions toward those stimuli (Chen & Bargh, 1999), as well as mood effects that reflect the average valence of automatic evaluations made over time in a given environment (Chartrand & Bargh, 1999). The chameleon effect, as another variety of a preconscious automatic process, also likely exists for a useful, adaptive reason.

It is plausible that the chameleon effect serves the basic human need to belong. In a recent review, Baumeister and Leary (1995) argued that according to the existing evidence, the human need to belong is a powerful, fundamental, and extremely pervasive motivation.[5] We desire frequent, nonaversive interactions with others and want to form and maintain strong, stable interpersonal relationships. We try to orient toward fellow human beings in a way that is relatively free from conflict and negative affect. To the extent that two interactants are similar to each other and have things in common (even at the level of behavioral mannerisms), such a smooth, conflict-free interaction will be more likely to occur. Moreover, automatically behaving in a manner similar to other group members—including having similar facial reactions to events—helps prevent an individual member from standing out as different, and so it would help to prevent ostracism and social distance from other group members (see Brewer, 1991).

Researchers of elementary motor mimicry have posited a very specific function served by motor mimicry that is consistent with this analysis. Recall that motor mimicry is a subset of behavior matching that refers to an individual reacting to another person going through a specific, emotion-laden incident (e.g., wincing at the other's pain). The individual reacts as if he or she were experiencing and feeling the same thing as the other person. Bavelas and her colleagues (Bavelas et al., 1988; Bavelas, Black, Lemery, & Mullett, 1986, 1987) take a strong stand that motor mimicry is not an overt manifestation of an intrapersonal process, such as vicarious emotion or cognitive role taking, but rather is an important communication tool that relays the message "I am like you" or "I feel as you do" to the other person.

Over 20 years earlier, Scheflen (1964) similarly suggested that mimicry might serve a communicative function without a person's awareness or intent: "Human behavior can be communicative whether or not it is *intended* to communicate . . . . *The intent of an interactant and the function that a behavior actually has in a group process must be conceptually distinguished* (italics in original; p. 318). We suggest that behavior matching serves this same function, and individuals use behavior mimicry as a communication tool on a completely nonconscious level.

Although behavior-matching researchers have not discussed its use as a communication tool per se, the notion is consistent with the proposed link between behavior matching and rapport. Scheflen (1964) originally posited that people in a group often mirror one another's posture and that this reflects a shared viewpoint. Bernieri and Rosenthal (1991) pointed out that people seem to get along better when their behaviors are well coordinated: "Interpersonal coordination and synchrony may eventually explain how it is that we 'hit it off' immediately with some people and never 'get it together' with others" (p. 429). Tickle-Degnen and Rosenthal (1987) also reviewed the evidence for a link between interpersonal coordination and rapport and suggested that it is quite strong.

Empirical evidence supporting the link between social rapport and interpersonal coordination comes primarily from the work on posture mirroring. In a typical study, La France (1982) found that students frequently displayed the same postural configuration as that of the teacher, and the extent of posture similarity was positively correlated with the students' ratings of rapport, involvement, and togetherness. Interestingly, La France has discovered that posture mirroring (e.g., one person lifting his or her right arm and another person lifting his or her left arm in a "mirror image") is related to rapport, although posture mimicking (e.g., both individuals lifting their right arm) is not (La France & Broadbent, 1976). Additional studies have found a relationship between behavior matching and self-reported rapport and involvement (Charney, 1966; La France, 1979; Trout & Rosenfeld, 1980). Hatfield, Cacioppo, and Rapson (1994) also argued that behavioral mimicry leads to emotional convergence between interaction partners.

Thus, there is consensus among researchers that behavior matching is related to greater liking and rapport. However, there has been disagreement over the causal direction. Some researchers have conceptualized various types of behavioral coordination as by-products or outgrowths of preexisting emotional rapport or liking (Levenson & Ruef, 1997; Scheflen, 1964). However, others have argued for the reverse causal direction. La France (1982), for instance, suggested that posture mirroring may not only reflect shared viewpoints and harmony but may actually be instrumental to achieving them.

Evidence for the mimicry-to-rapport causal direction has been mixed. In a correlational study, La France (1979) used a cross-lag technique to assess causality and found that posture similarity seems to lead to rapport slightly more than vice versa, although there was some evidence that the effect was bidirectional. In a study of the impact of gesture similarity on persuasion and interpersonal influence, Dabbs (1969) manipulated movement similarity by having a confederate "interviewee" mimic the gestures and mannerisms of 1 of 2 participant "interviewers" in the room. Results were equivocal; whereas the participant who was mimicked did not report liking the confederate more than did the participant who was not mimicked, mimicry did cause the confederate to be evaluated more favorably on other dimensions (e.g., he was considered to be well informed and to have sound ideas). In a second experiment, some participants were trained to be confederates 10 min before the start of the experiment and were told to either mimic a 2nd participant or to "antimimic" him (i.e., do the opposite of what he did). Results were again unclear as to the effect of mimicry, but they did suggest that antimimicry could have a negative effect in certain circumstances. Finally, Maurer and Tindall (1983) focused on whether perceptions of a counselor's empathy partially depend on nonverbal cues such as having similar behavioral mannerisms. They found that when counselors mimicked the body positions of their clients, the clients perceived a greater level of expressed empathy on the part of the counselor.

In Experiment 2, we sought to test whether manipulated variations in posture similarity produce variations in liking between interaction partners. We especially wanted to test the extent to which posture similarity affects liking when there is no overarching interpersonal goal held by the interactants toward each other. In both the Dabbs (1969, Experiment 1) and Maurer and Tindall (1983) experiments, there was a role-power differential between the confederate and participant, and so interpersonal goals (e.g., ingratiation) may have affected their results. Our hypothesis, however, is that the chameleon effect operates in a passive, non-goal-dependent manner to create greater liking and ease of interaction. Hence, mimicry of one interaction partner by the other should cause the former to like the partner more and to experience greater ease of interacting, even when the two are strangers or new acquaintances who are not seeking to establish a relationship.

Method

Overview Participants had one 15-min session with another "participant" (a confederate). During this session, the participant and confederate took turns describing what they saw in various photographs. Confederates either mirrored the behavioral mannerisms of the participant throughout the interaction (the experimental condition) or engaged in neutral, nondescript mannerisms (the control condition). When the interaction was over, participants completed a questionnaire on which they were asked to report (a) how much they liked the confederate and (b) how smoothly the interaction had gone.

Participants Seventy-eight male and female students enrolled in an introductory psychology course participated in the experiment in partial fulfillment of a course requirement. Data from 6 of these participants were excluded from analyses for the following reasons: 2 participants in the control condition sat in the same neutral position as the confederates, making it equivalent to the experimental condition in which body language and mannerisms are in synchrony. Four participants suspected that the other participant was in fact a confederate. It should be noted, however, that none of these participants were able to guess our hypothesis. Thus, we computed all analyses on responses from a final sample of 72 participants, with 37 in the mimicking (mirroring) condition and 35 in the control condition.

Apparatus and materials The experiment room was the same as used in Experiment 1. The same color photographs from Experiment 1 were also used for Experiment 2. There were 4 female assistants who served as confederate and experimenter, and they alternated roles. All assistants were trained to mirror the body language and mannerisms of the participants.

Although the confederates were kept blind to the specific hypothesis of the experiment, they were necessarily aware of the manipulation involved and of the participant's assigned experimental condition. It is therefore possible that they could have, intentionally or unintentionally, behaved differently toward the participants who were in the experimental condition (e.g., acted more friendly or likable toward them). To address this possibility, 22 of the sessions (11 of the control condition and 11 of the experimental condition) were videotaped in their entirety to later assess, through the ratings of outside judges, whether the confederates were behaving differently (other than in the mimicry itself) toward participants in the mimicry versus no-mimicry conditions. Both the participant and confederate were visible through the lens of the camera so that judges would be able to see and code the confederate's behavior toward the participant.

The dependent measures were ratings from participants on liking for the confederate and smoothness of the interaction. The key items read, "How likable was the other participant?" and "How smoothly would you say your interaction went with the other participant?" To help camouflage the hypothesis of the study, we embedded these two items among eight other questions that asked about the task itself and the group format (e.g., how easy or difficult it was for them to generate responses to the photos, and whether they thought the various photographs went well together as a single "set"). All items were rated on 9-point scales (for the smoothness item, 1 = *extremely awkward*, 9 = *extremely smooth*; for the likeability item, 1 = *extremely dislikable*, 9 = *extremely likable*).

Procedure The procedure was the same as for Experiment 1, with participants working with confederates to ostensibly help develop the projective measure involving sets of photographs, except that the confederates no longer smiled (or not), shook their foot, or rubbed their face. Instead, during the interaction, the confederate avoided eye contact with the participant and maintained a neutral facial expression. Furthermore, in the mimicry condition, the confederate mirrored the posture, movements, and mannerisms displayed by the participant. In the control condition, the confederate sat in a neutral relaxed position, with both feet on the floor and both hands holding the photos (or resting in the lap).[6]

When the participant and confederate had completed the photograph descriptions, the experimenter explained that they would next complete the questionnaire about the task. Because it was necessary to complete it independently and privately, they would be separated and seated in different rooms. The experimenter asked the confederate to complete the survey in an adjoining room and escorted her there. Then, the experimenter returned to the laboratory room, gave the participant the questionnaire to complete, and told him or her to come to the hallway outside when finished. At this point, the experimenter queried the participant to determine whether he or she was suspicious that (a) the other participant was in fact a confederate, (b) the confederate was mirroring his or her own behaviors, or (c) the purpose of the experiment was anything other than what the cover story indicated. Finally, the purpose and hypotheses of the study were explained to the participant. (Those who were videotaped were asked to sign a video consent form.) The participant was thanked for his or her participation.

Results

Liking and smoothness as a function of being mimicked We predicted that relative to those in the control condition, participants in the experimental condition would report (a) finding the confederate more likable and (b) having smoother interactions with her. To test these hypotheses, a multivariate analysis of variance (MANOVA) was conducted on the liking and smoothness variables, with mimicking of participants by confederates (yes vs. no) as the between-subjects variable. Gender was also included as a between-subjects variable in this and all subsequent analyses, but no reliable main effect for gender or interaction between gender and mimicking emerged, and so the gender variable is not discussed further. In addition, we initially included as an additional between-subjects variable in the

MANOVA whether the experimental session had been videotaped, but this variable also did not interact with any of the effects, Fs < 1. Therefore, the sessions that were videotaped were representative of the larger sample; the liking and smoothness ratings of the participants in these sessions did not differ from the ratings of the participants who were not videotaped.

As predicted, there was an overall effect of mimicking across the two dependent measures, $F(2, 69) = 3.47$, $p = .04$. This effect was not moderated by type of dependent measure, interaction $F < 1$. We also conducted separate univariate tests on the liking and smoothness ratings. Participants in the experimental condition reported liking the confederate more ($M = 6.62$) than did those in the control condition ($M = 5.91$), $F(1, 70) = 5.55$, $p = .02$. Furthermore, they reported that the interaction went more smoothly ($M = 6.76$) than did those in the control condition ($M = 6.02$), $F(1, 70) = 4.08$, $p = .05$. Thus, the results support the hypothesis that mimicry increases liking and fosters smooth, harmonious interactions. Although previous, correlational research showed liking and rapport to be related to posture similarity, this is the fast demonstration that mimicry causes greater liking and smoother interactions.

Confederates' behavior toward participants It is important to consider an alternative explanation for these findings. Although we believe that mimicry by the confederate produced the greater liking and smoothness ratings by participants in that condition, relative to the no-mimicry condition, it is possible that some associated difference in the behavior of the confederates in the two conditions produced the effects. For obvious reasons, it was not possible to keep the confederates blind to the participant's assigned condition (mimicry vs. no-mimicry). Although confederates were kept blind to the specific hypothesis in the study, it remains possible that they unwittingly behaved differently toward the participants in the mimicry versus no-mimicry conditions; for example, they may have behaved in a more friendly manner toward those they mimicked or, more subtly, engaged in greater smiling or made more eye contact with them. If so, this would provide an alternative reason for the participants liking the confederates more in this condition—one having nothing to do with mimicry. Hence, we sought to determine whether there were any such differences in confederate behavior in the two conditions.

As described in the *Method* section, we videotaped a sample ($n = 22$) of the experimental sessions for precisely this reason—to collect evidence germane to this alternative explanation. These videotapes were then independently coded by two judges blind to the experimental hypothesis. For each interaction, the following behaviors were coded: (a) how much eye contact the confederate made

Table 1

Outside Judges' Ratings

(1 = Low, 6 = High) of Confederate's Openness

and Friendliness to Participant as a

Function of Experimental Condition

(Experiment 2)

Measure	No mimicking		Mimicking	
	M	SD	M	SD
Eye contact	1.63	0.52	1.41	0.49
Smiling	1.75	0.53	1.45	0.52
Friendliness	2.94	0.18	3.00	0.00
Liking participant	3.25	0.46	3.23	0.41

with the participant, (b) how much the confederate smiled at the participant, (c) how friendly the confederate acted toward the participant, and (d) how much the confederate appeared to like the participant. All items were rated on a 6-point scale (1 = *low*, 6 = *high*). The reliability between the two judges for the four items combined was quite high, $r = .96$. (The interjudge correlations for each of the individual scale items ranged from $r = .72$ to $r = .91$.) Accordingly, ratings from the two coders were averaged to form a single index for each measure. The means of each of the four ratings are presented in Table 1. No significant differences in eye contact, smiling, friendliness, or liking were observed between the experimental and control conditions (all $ps > .20$). In fact, three of the four measures were actually (but nonsignificantly) lower in the mimicking than the no-mimicking condition. It does not appear that confederates behaved differently toward the participants in the mimicry versus no-mimicry conditions, other than in the mimicry manipulation itself, and so we can more confidently attribute the observed differences in liking for the confederate and for the rated level of smoothness of the interaction to the effects of mimicry.[7]

Participants' awareness of having been mimicked Participants were asked during the funneled debriefing whether they noticed anything in particular about the confederate's behavior or mannerisms and whether anything about the confederate's behavior made them feel awkward or uncomfortable. One participant reported that the confederate kept her head down and did not make eye contact with her. A 2nd participant reported that the confederate was crossing her legs (as was the participant), but she remarked that it "seemed normal and did not make me feel uncomfortable." Thus, only 1 out of 37 participants in the mimicking condition noticed that the confederate had a similar mannerism, but it was not interpreted by that participant as mimicry.

Discussion

After it was demonstrated in Experiment 1 that the perception–behavior link produced chameleon-like passive behavioral mimicry of interaction partners, we sought in Experiment 2 to assess the possible adaptive value of this effect. On the basis of past research linking mimicry to rapport, we hypothesized that the chameleon effect serves the adaptive function of fostering liking between people and creating smooth, harmonious interactions. It follows that if an individual's movements and postures are purposefully mirrored by an interaction partner, that individual should report that the interaction went more smoothly and that the partner was more likable compared with individuals whose movements were not mirrored. The results of Experiment 2 confirmed that, compared with control condition participants, those participants whose movements were mirrored by the confederate both experienced the interaction as having gone more smoothly and liked the confederate significantly more.

It should be noted that this link between mimicking and liking contradicts some previous findings. For instance, La France found that posture similarity and rapport were positively correlated when the interactants were acquainted with each other and involved in an ongoing interaction (La France, 1979, 1982; La France & Broadbent, 1976) but negatively correlated when the interactants were unacquainted (La France & Ickes, 1981; see Bernieri, 1988, for a similar finding). This latter finding implies that the relation between mimicry and rapport should hold only for people involved in an ongoing interaction. The most crucial difference between the La France and Ickes study and ours is that in the former, participants were not interacting at all; rather, they were simply sitting in the same waiting room at the same time. Thus, the positive effects of chameleon-like mimicry for ease of interaction and liking may only accrue within the context of a social interaction and not between strangers who do not interact at all. To us, however, this is an inconsequential constraint that would not diminish the adaptive value of the chameleon effect as a kind of social glue that helps to bind interaction partners together.

EXPERIMENT 3: INDIVIDUAL DIFFERENCES IN NONCONSCIOUS MIMICRY

Although we believe nonconscious behavior mimicry to be a pervasive and ubiquitous phenomenon, we also expect there to be individual differences in the extent to which an individual engages in such behavioral and posture mimicry. Certainly not everyone engages in the chameleon effect to the same degree as did Woody Allen's Zelig. What might determine whether one is more or less likely to nonconsciously mimic others? Surprisingly, no one has thus far posited any personality or individual difference variables as moderators of the chameleon effect, to our knowledge. In Experiment 3, we focused on one such potential moderator.

On the basis of the relation established in Experiment 2 between behavior mimicry on the one hand and liking and interaction smoothness on the other, one individual difference likely to be related to the chameleon effect is empathy. Theoretical distinctions have been made between various components of the empathic response, but research has distilled two major forms. The first is based on cognitive, intellectual reactions, such as the ability to take and understand the other person's perspective. The second is based on visceral, emotional reactions to the others' situation (see Davis, 1983).

We suggest that the cognitive facet of empathy (i.e., perspective taking) is more relevant to the chameleon effect, because, as was demonstrated in Experiment 1, the mechanism that produces the effect is the perception–behavior link. The cause of the chameleon effect is therefore a purely passive, cognitive mechanism that is not associated with or dependent on any particular affective or emotional state. Thus, the most likely candidate for an individual-difference moderator of the chameleon effect would be one concerned with differences in how much attention and thought are paid to one's interaction partners. In other words, a person will be more susceptible to the effects of perception on behavior if he or she engages in greater perceptual activity directed at the other person. Taking the perspective of others is a perceptual, cognitive process that is likely to lead to greater perception of an interaction partner, which in turn leads to more mimicking. Moreover, if it is, as we argue, the passive perception–behavior link that produces the chameleon effect and its consequent benefits for social interaction, then individual differences in the emotional or affective-based form of empathy should not be related to differences in the chameleon effect.

In harmony with this argument is Davis's (1983) finding that perspective taking but not empathic concern (the affective component of empathy) was consistently related to various measures of interpersonal functioning: "Perspective-taking ability should allow an individual to anticipate the behavior and reactions of others, therefore facilitating *smoother* [italics added] and more rewarding interpersonal relationships" (p. 115). Given that (a) we believe social functioning to be one of the adaptive consequences of the chameleon effect, and (b) in Experiment 2 it was demonstrated that mimicry led to smoother interactions, individual differences in perspective taking should be related to individual differences in the extent of the chameleon effect.

We note that many theorists, Mead (1934) and Piaget (1932) among them, have argued that possessing and using an ability to take another's perspective is responsible for much of human social capacity. Among other benefits, well-developed perspective-taking abilities help an individual gain more satisfying interpersonal relations. In a similar vein, Cialdini, Brown, Lewis, Luce, and Neuberg (1997) asserted that the merging of self with other is influenced by perspective taking. It is likely no coincidence that these consequences of frequent perspective taking parallel the consequences of behavioral mimicry we found in Experiment 2. That is, both behavioral mirroring and perspective taking lead to smoother interactions and greater liking. Perhaps, then, one of the reasons why those with a greater tendency to take the perspective of others have greater social functioning and compassion for others is because they engage in more behavioral mimicry; that was our prediction in Experiment 3.

Method

Participants Fifty-five students in an introductory psychology course participated in this study in partial fulfillment of a course requirement. Three of these participants suspected that the confederate was part of the experimental setup, 1 had general suspicions regarding the study, and 1 was not videotaped because of equipment malfunction (again, none of the participants accurately guessed our hypothesis). Data from these 5 participants were excluded from further analysis. Thus, data from 50 participants remained in final analyses.

Apparatus and materials The experiment room was the same as that used in Experiments 1 and 2. Four female assistants alternated serving as confederate and experimenter. Assistants were trained to continually shake their foot and rub their face throughout each interaction as the confederate.

The same color photographs from Experiments 1 and 2 were used. The same video camera setup was used as in Experiment 1, such that only the participants (and not the confederates) were visible through the camera lens.

To measure perspective taking, we used the perspective-taking subscale of Davis's (1980) Interpersonal Reactivity Index (IRI). The IRI also conveniently includes a subscale for empathic concern, which represents the emotional concern-for-others facet of empathy. Thus, administering the IRI allowed us to test our hypothesis that it is the cognitive, perspective-taking component of empathy and not the emotional, empathic-concern facet that moderates the perception–behavior link.

The perspective-taking subscale assesses the tendency to spontaneously adopt the psychological point of view of others. Sample items include "When I'm upset at someone, I usually try to 'put myself in his/her shoes' for a while," "I believe that there are two sides to every question and try to look at them both," and "I sometimes try to understand my friends better by imagining how things look from their perspective." The empathic concern subscale assesses "other-oriented" feelings of sympathy and concern for unfortunate others, and sample items include "I often have tender, concerned feeling for people less fortunate than me"; "I am often quite touched by things that I see happen"; and "Other people's misfortunes do not usually disturb me a great deal." All items are rated on a 5-point scale (A = *does not describe me well*; E = *describes me very well*). There are seven items on each subscale, some of which are reverse-coded. The alpha coefficient for perspective taking is .71 for men and .75 for women; for empathic concern, the alpha is .68 for men and .73 for women.

Procedure Each participant completed the experiment individually. The confederate was always sitting in the waiting area before the participant arrived. The experimenter brought them both into the laboratory room, seating them in the two chairs reserved for them.

The procedure was essentially the same photograph-description task used in Experiments 1 and 2. The major change was that the confederate engaged in two different mannerisms throughout the interaction: rubbing her face and shaking her foot. As in Experiment 2, the confederate avoided eye contact with the participant whenever possible and maintained a neutral facial expression.

As soon as the participant and confederate completed the photograph descriptions, the experimenter asked if they would mind completing a questionnaire that another psychologist in the department was planning to use in a future experiment. All participants agreed to fill out the questionnaire (the IRI). The experimenter explained that because it was necessary to complete the scale independently, they would be separated from each other at this time and seated in separate rooms. The experimenter chose the confederate to complete the survey in an adjoining room and escorted her there. Then the experimenter returned to the laboratory room, gave the participant the IRI scale, and told him or her to come to the hallway outside when the questionnaire was completed. At that point, the experimenter queried the participant as to any suspicions that (a) the other participant was in fact a confederate or (b) the purpose of the experiment was anything other than what the cover story indicated. Next, the purpose and hypotheses of the study were divulged to the participant. The participant was asked to sign a video consent form. Finally, the participant was thanked for his or her participation.

Results

Interjudge reliability Videotapes were coded by a judge for the number of times participants rubbed their face and shook their foot. Approximately half (23) of the videotapes were then coded by a second judge. Reliability between the two judges was very high: for the number of times participants rubbed their face, $r = .97$, and for the number of times they shook their foot, $r = .82$, both significant at $p < .001$. Ratings between the two judges were averaged to form a single rating for face rubbing and foot shaking. Ratings were then divided by the time duration of the interaction (to the nearest second) to arrive at a rate for behavior per minute.

Perspective taking To test the hypothesis that individuals who are high perspective-takers nonconsciously mimic others to a greater extent, we categorized participants into those who scored high and those who scored low on perspective taking. We computed the median on the perspective-taking subscale of the IRI (median = 19) and classified those participants above the median ($n = 28$) into the *high-perspective-taking* category and those below it ($n = 22$) into the *low-perspective-taking* category.

A repeated measures ANOVA was performed with number of times participants rubbed their face and number of times participants shook their foot as a within-subject variable and perspective taking (high vs. low) as a between-subjects variable. Gender was included as an additional between-subjects variable in this and all subsequent analyses, but no significant main effect for gender or interaction between gender and perspective taking was revealed. Thus, the gender variable is not discussed further. As predicted, however, there was a significant main effect of perspective taking across the two types of mimicking, $F(1, 48) = 3.85$, $p = .05$. This main effect was not moderated by an interaction with type of behavior (face rubbing vs. foot shaking), $p > .20$. Specifically, high-perspective takers rubbed their face ($M = 1.30$) and shook their foot ($M = 0.40$) more times per minute than did low-perspective takers ($Ms = 0.85$ and 0.29, respectively). These results support our hypothesis that those individuals who have a greater tendency to take the perspective of others also are more likely to engage in behavioral mimicry.

Empathic concern To test our hypothesis that the emotional facet of empathy would not moderate the chameleon effect, we also performed a median split on the Empathic Concern subscale scores (median = 21). Participants with scores above the median ($n = 28$) were classified into the *high-empathic-concern* category, and those with scores below it ($n = 22$) were placed in the *low-empathic-concern* category.

A repeated measures ANOVA was performed with number of times participants rubbed their face and number of times participants shook their foot as a within-subject variable and empathic concern (high vs. low) as a between-subjects variable. As predicted, there was no main effect of empathic concern across the two types of mimicking, $F < 1$, nor was there an interaction between empathic concern and type of behavior (face rubbing vs. foot shaking), $F < 1$. In fact, the means showed a slight trend for there to be more mimicry of foot shaking and face rubbing among those low in empathic concern than those high on this subscale.

Discussion

Our third goal in this research was to test a personality variable that may moderate the extent to which one engages in behavior mimicry. Because of the link among perspective taking and social skills, empathy with others, and compassion for others, individuals who often take the perspective of others are more likely to have positive, smooth interactions. High-perspective takers may be the ones who are better at nonconsciously guiding social interactions and automatically doing the things that ensure smooth and easy interactions. Part of this may entail mimicking the behavioral mannerisms of interaction partners.

In Experiment 3, we tested whether those who take the perspective of others have more strongly developed this covert mechanism for attaining smooth, positive interactions. Specifically, we predicted that high-perspective takers would be more likely to mimic the mannerisms of another person. We also predicted that the emotional facet of empathy (operationalized as the Empathic Concern subscale of the IRI) would not similarly moderate the cognitive perception–behavior link. As predicted, high-perspective takers mimicked the mannerisms of a confederate more so than did low-perspective takers, and, also as predicted, participants who scored low and participants who scored high on empathic concern did not significantly differ in the extent to which they mimicked the confederate. This supports our prediction that chronic differences in perspective taking would be related to chronic differences in nonconscious mimicking tendencies.

GENERAL DISCUSSION

We have argued that the perception–behavior link, through which merely perceiving an action performed by another can lead one to perform that action, is the mechanism behind the often observed behavior mimicry and consequent empathic understanding within social interactions. In Experiment 1, we tested the existence of the chameleon effect in an experimental demonstration that supported the perception–behavior link as its proximal cause: Changes in a confederate's behavior caused changes in the participant's behavior, in the absence of the participant's awareness of this influence. Experiment 2 provided an explicit test of the commonly held belief that nonconscious mimicry serves the adaptive function of facilitating smooth interactions and fostering liking. In line with this prediction is the finding that individuals whose postures and movements were mirrored by a confederate liked that partner more and thought the interaction went more smoothly compared with those whose behaviors were not mirrored, again without being aware of the true source of this increased empathic understanding and liking. Finally, in Experiment 3, we tested perspective taking as a individual difference that moderates the extent to which one engages in behavior mimicry. As hypothesized, those who frequently take the perspective of interaction partners mimicked the mannerisms of a confederate to a greater extent than did those who less often take the perspective of others, as would be expected if social–perceptual activity mediated the effect.

The present experiments go beyond other recent perception–behavior studies in showing, for the first time, automatic behavioral effects mediated by actual, in-person perception of the partner's behavior (as opposed to priming manipulations that could have influenced behavior directly). They also represent an advance over existing mimicry–empathy research by providing an experimental instead of a correlational demonstration of the effect, by ruling out the need for a purposive interaction goal in order for the effect to occur, and by providing for the first time a mechanism for the effect (viz., the perception–behavior link). Finally, the present investigation shows that two formerly separate effects, previously studied in isolation from one another, are actually outcomes of the same underlying process.

Our conclusion that the effect of perception on behavior is an automatic process that does not depend on conscious choice is consistent with recent neuropsychological findings as well. One telling piece of evidence is the fact that the frequency of direct effects of perception on action is increased in pathological states in which strategic conscious control over behavior is impaired or nonexistent (Prinz, 1990, p. 176). Such "echo-reactions" as the unintentional repetition of the words used by another (*echolalia*) or unintentional imitation of another's actions (*echopraxia*) are commonly observed in patients with aphasia, apraxia, mental retardation, and brain damage whose ability to consciously and intentionally self-regulate is severely impaired. Thus, in the absence of intentional forms of action control, the perception–behavior link remains intact, arguing against the role of conscious choice as a mediator.

Our conclusion is also in harmony with Hilgard's (1965) account of hypnotic suggestion. According to Hilgard, the directives given by the hypnotist are first perceived by the person being hypnotized, and then, because of the suspension of the will that is characteristic of the hypnotic state, passive effects of perception on action are left free to operate. In other words, the suggestions made by the hypnotist have a direct automatic effect on behavior because of the abdication of conscious control by the hypnotized person; in other words, it is an instance of James's (1890) ideomotor action effect in which the ideation is externally induced by the hypnotist (see also Wegner & Wheatley, 1999).

Preconscious Automatic Processes as Adaptive and Beneficial

The perception–behavior link is one of several routes through which the environment can influence behavior without one's awareness, intent, or control. With this particular route, perceptual activity nonconsciously spreads to behavioral representations, increasing the likelihood of behaving similarly to others in the current environment. There has also been research on automatic routes from environment to behavior via the nonconscious activation of motivations and goals (see Bargh, 1990, 1997; Bargh & Gollwitzer, 1994; Chartrand & Bargh, 1996) and via nonconscious evaluation of environmental stimuli (see Bargh, Chaiken, et al., 1996; Chen & Bargh, 1999). Uncovering the adaptive purpose of the perception–behavior link is in harmony with a recent trend in social automaticity research of identifying the adaptive purposes of these various preconscious determinants of behavior; at the same time, it stands in contrast with those theorists who hold that such nonconscious effects are uniformly negative and maladaptive (e.g., Bandura, 1986; Langer, 1989, 1997; Locke & Latham, 1990; Mischel, Cantor, & Feldman, 1996).

For instance, a person's chronic goals within a situation become linked in memory to the representation of that situation, such that entering that environment automatically causes that goal to become active and to operate without the individual's awareness of its activation or guiding role in subsequent behavior (Bargh, 1990; Chartrand & Bargh, 1996). This nonconscious reaction has been conceptualized as an adaptive mechanism because it reflects the individual's history of goal choice within the situation and increases the probability of goal pursuit. It also eliminates the need to consciously choose the goal on each occasion, when attention and thought may be on other matters at the time. Positive, self-actualizing goals, such as achievement, and positive aspects of motivational states, such as persistence and overcoming obstacles to attain the desired goal, have all been shown to occur with nonconscious goal activation and pursuit just as they do with conscious goal pursuit (Bargh & Chartrand, 1999; Bargh, Gollwitzer, Lee Chai, & Barndollar, 1998).

Automatic evaluation research has documented the pervasive tendency for people to classify all environmental stimuli as either positive or negative. This process, too, has been shown to produce adaptive consequences. For one thing, it alerts us to what is beneficial and helpful and what is dangerous in our environment when conscious attention and thought are elsewhere, and it signals the valence of the current environment by automatically affecting the individual's mood (Chartrand & Bargh, 1999). Moreover, approach and avoidance behavioral tendencies are put into motion immediately by positive instead of negative automatic evaluations (Chen & Bargh, 1999), readying the individual to react in an appropriate manner, yet through an entirely nonconscious mechanism.

In the present research we have continued this trend by focusing on the adaptive function of the chameleon effect. Nonconscious behavior mimicry was found to increase liking for the partner and the reported smoothness of the interactions, and individuals who often take the perspective of others engage in it more than do other people.

It should be acknowledged that previous demonstrations of the perception–behavior link did not produce such positive social effects. For instance, in the original Bargh, Chen, et al. (1996) studies, individuals engaged in stereotype-consistent behavior (e.g., hostility) following automatic activation of that stereotype (e.g., for African Americans). Subsequent research has found that such nonconsciously produced stereotype-consistent behavior can produce a self-fulfilling prophecy (Chen & Bargh, 1997), in that one's interaction partner reacts to one's behavior in kind, yet one is not aware of the effect of one's own behavior in causing that stereotype-confirming behavioral response.

That the stereotype version of the perception–behavior effect can produce negative outcomes should come as no surprise, because stereotype effects on perception and judgment are also largely negative. But stereotypes are categories gone awry—they take the perceiver beyond the information actually present in the other person's behavior. This does not mean that categories per se are maladaptive or problematic; to the contrary, they are absolutely essential for normal, moment-to-moment functioning, to simplify the world, to give it meaning, and to furnish anticipations about what is likely to happen next (e.g., Barsalou, 1992; Smith & Medin, 1981). It follows that the typical form of the chameleon effect—behavior tendencies generated nonconsciously from the perceived behavior of one's interaction partner—is, unlike the stereotype version, largely adaptive and of high social utility. This is what we sought to demonstrate in Experiments 2 and 3. The usual form of the chameleon effect, we assert, is to enhance the positivity of social interactions.

Individual Differences in Nonconscious Mimicry

In Experiment 3, we focused on one personality variable that moderated the chameleon effect; however, we do not mean to suggest that no other moderators exist. Further research may well uncover additional individual difference variables that can increase or decrease the extent to which individuals nonconsciously mimic those around them. One such possibility is the *communal/exchange orientation* dimension proposed by Clark and colleagues (Clark & Mills, 1979; Clark, Mills, & Powell, 1986). Individuals with a *communal* orientation towards others might exhibit more nonconscious mimicry than those with an *exchange* orientation, because communally oriented people are, by definition, more perceptually attuned to the needs of others. Moreover, by the same logic, there may be greater frequency of chameleon-like social behavior in collectivistic versus individualistic societies, because the former more than the latter are characterized by interdependence (e.g., Markus & Kitayama, 1991). Therefore, collectivistic cultures are likely to be characterized by a relatively intensified attentional and perceptual focus by individuals on the behavior of others, and in light of the present experimental findings, this increased perception of others' behavior would be expected to produce greater rapport and smoother social interactions.

Implications for Group Processes

At the level of the social group, then, to the extent that members are mimicking each others' facial expressions, postures, mannerisms, and other behaviors, there is likely to be greater cohesion and liking within the group. In Experiment 1, we found that mimicry occurred even in the most minimal circumstances in which the interactants were unacquainted and had no goal to affiliate; thus, it may be that newly formed groups would benefit from nonconscious mimicry and imitation as well as would established groups. We suspect that the chameleon effect contributes to effective behavior coordination among members of a group. The synchrony and immediacy of such behavior coordination in moving schools of fish or flocks of birds, for example, are the result of an automatic, direct effect of perception on behavior (Breder, 1976; Pitcher, 1979; Reynolds, 1987, 1993)—one that clearly does not require conscious choice or reflection to operate. Moreover, the positive effects of empathy, liking, and bonding that occur automatically because of the chameleon effect would likely benefit most newly formed groups in which relationships among the members do not yet exist or are fragile—it would also tend to shape initial feelings among group members in a positive direction.

Such speculations aside, the chameleon effect is clearly a basic and important social psychological phenomenon, one to which all can relate on a personal level. It is our hope that research will continue to elucidate the conditions under which the effect is augmented or diminished. Extending the paradigms into more complex and dynamic group settings seems to us to be an important next step to this end. It seems unlikely to us that such pervasive, nonconscious effects on social behavior as the chameleon effect arose by accident, and such effects are more likely than not to have positive, desirable effects for the individual and for the groups to which he or she belongs.

REFERENCES

Allport, G. W. (1968). The historical background of modern social psychology. In G. Lindzey & E. Aronson (Eds.), *Handbook of social psychology* (2nd ed., Vol. 1, pp. 1–80). Reading, MA: Addison-Wesley.

Anisfeld, M. (1979, July 13). Response to Meltzoff and Moore (1977). *Science, 205*, 214.

Banaji, M. R., Hardin, C., & Rothman, A. J. (1993). Implicit stereotyping in person judgment. *Journal of Personality and Social Psychology, 65*, 272–281.

Bandura, A. (1977). *Social learning theory*. Englewood Cliffs, NJ: Prentice Hall.

Bandura, A. (1986). *Social foundations of thought and action: A social cognitive theory*. Englewood Cliffs, NJ: Prentice Hall.

Bargh, J. A. (1989). Conditional automaticity: Varieties of automatic influence in social perception and cognition. In J. S. Uleman & J. A. Bargh (Eds.), *Unintended thought* (pp. 3–51). New York: Guilford Press.

Bargh, J. A. (1990). Automotives: Preconscious determinants of thought and behavior. In E. T. Higgins & R. M. Sorrentino (Eds.), *Handbook of motivation and cognition* (Vol. 2, pp. 93–130). New York: Guilford Press.

Bargh, J. A. (1994). The four horsemen of automaticity: Awareness, efficiency, intention, and control in social cognition. In R. S. Wyer, Jr., & T. K. Stall (Eds.), *Handbook of social cognition* (2nd ed., pp. 1–40). Hillsdale, NJ: Erlbaum.

Bargh, J. A. (1997). The automaticity of everyday life. In R. S. Wyer, Jr. (Ed.), *Advances in social cognition* (Vol. 10, pp. 1–61). Mahwah, NJ: Erlbaum.

Bargh, J. A. (1999). The cognitive monster. In S. Chaiken & Y. Trope (Eds.), *Dual process theories in social psychology* (pp. 361–382). New York: Guilford Press.

Bargh, J. A., Chaiken, S., Govender, R., & Pratto, F. (1992). The generality of the automatic attitude activation effect. *Journal of Personality and Social Psychology, 62*, 893–912.

Bargh, J. A., Chaiken, S., Raymond, P., & Hymes, C. (1996). The automatic evaluation effect: Unconditionally automatic attitude activation with a pronunciation task. *Journal of Experimental Social Psychology, 32*, 104–128.

Bargh, J. A., & Chartrand, T. L. (1999). The unbearable automaticity of being. *American Psychologist, 54*, 462–479.

Bargh, J. A., & Chartrand, T. L. (in press). Studying the mind in the middle: A practical guide to priming and automaticity research. In H. Reis & C. Judd (Eds.), *Research methods for the social sciences*. New York: Cambridge University Press.

Bargh, J. A., Chen, M., & Burrows, L. (1996). Automaticity of social behavior: Direct effects of trait construct and stereotype activation on action. *Journal of Personality and Social Psychology, 71*, 230–244.

Bargh, J. A., & Gollwitzer, P. (1994). Environmental control of goal-directed action: Automatic and strategic contingencies between situations and behavior. In W. D. Spaulding (Ed.), *Nebraska Symposium on Motivation* (Vol. 41, pp. 71–124). Lincoln: University of Nebraska Press.

Bargh, J. A., Gollwitzer, P., Lee Chai, A., & Barndollar, K. (1998). *Bypassing the will: Nonconscious self-regulation through automatic goal pursuit*. Manuscript submitted for publication, New York University.

Bargh, J. A., & Thein, R. D. (1985). Individual construct accessibility, person memory, and the recall–judgment link: The case of information overload. *Journal of Personality and Social Psychology, 46*, 1129–1146.

Barsalou, L. W. (1992). Cognitive psychology: *An overview for cognitive scientists*. Hillsdale, NJ: Erlbaum.

Baumeister, R. F., & Leary, M. R. (1995). The need to belong: Desire for interpersonal attachments as a fundamental human motivation. *Psychological Bulletin, 117*, 497–529.

Bavelas, J. B., Black, A., Chovil, N., Lemery, C. R., & Mullett, J. (1988). Form and function in motor mimicry: Topographic evidence that the primary function is communication. *Human Communication Research, 14*, 275–299.

Bavelas, J. B., Black, A., Lemery, C. R., & Mullett, J. (1986). "I show how you feel": Motor mimicry as a communicative act. *Journal of Personality and Social Psychology, 50*, 322–329.

Bavelas, J. B., Black, A., Lemery, C. R., & Mullett, J. (1987). Motor mimicry as primitive empathy. In N. Eisenberg & J. Strayer (Eds.), *Empathy and its development* (pp. 317–338). Cambridge, England: Cambridge University Press.

Berkowitz, L. (1984). Some effects of thoughts on anti- and prosocial influences of media events: A cognitive–neoassociation analysis. *Psychological Bulletin, 95*, 410–427.

Bernieri, F. J. (1988). Coordinated movement and rapport in teacher-student interactions. *Journal of Nonverbal Behavior, 12*, 120–138.

Bernieri, F. J., & Rosenthal, R. (1991). Interpersonal coordination: Behavior matching and interactional synchrony. In R. S. Feldman & B. Rimé, (Eds.), *Fundamentals of nonverbal behavior* (pp. 401–432). Cambridge, England: Cambridge University Press.

Breder, C. M. (1976). Fish schools as operational structures. *Fishery Bulletin, 74*, 471–502.

Brewer, M. B. (1988). A dual process model of impression formation. In R. S. Wyer, Jr., and T. K. Srull (Eds.), *Advances in social cognition* (Vol. 1, pp. 1–36). Hillsdale, NJ: Erlbaum.

Brewer, M. B. (1991). The social self: On being the same and different at the same time. *Personality and Social Psychology Bulletin, 17*, 475–482.

Carlston, D. E., & Skowronski, J. J. (1994). Savings in the relearning of trait information as evidence for spontaneous inference generation. *Journal of Personality and Social Psychology, 66*, 840–856.

Carver, C. S., Ganellen, R. J., Froming, W. J., & Chambers, W. (1983). Modeling: An analysis in terms of category accessibility. *Journal of Experimental Social Psychology, 19*, 403–421.

Charney, E. J. (1966). Psychosomatic manifestations of rapport in psychotherapy. *Psychosomatic Medicine, 28*, 305–315.

Chartrand, T. L., & Bargh, J. A. (1996). Automatic activation of impression formation and memorization goals: Nonconscious goal priming reproduces effects of explicit task instructions. *Journal of Personality and Social Psychology, 71*, 464–478.

Chartrand, T. L., & Bargh, J. A. (1999). *Consequences of automatic evaluation for mood.* Manuscript in preparation, New York University.

Chen, M., & Bargh, J. A. (1997). Nonconscious behavioral confirmation processes: The self-fulfilling consequences of automatic stereotype activation. *Journal of Experimental Social Psychology, 33*, 541–560.

Chen, M., & Bargh, J. A. (1999). Consequences of automatic evaluation: Immediate behavioral predispositions to approach or avoid the stimulus. *Personality and Social Psychology Bulletin, 25*, 215–224.

Chen, M., Chartrand, T. L., Lee Chai, A., & Bargh, J. A. (1998). Priming primates: Human and otherwise. *Behavioral and Brain Sciences, 21*, 685–686.

Cialdini, R. B., Brown, S. L., Lewis, B. P., Luce, C., & Neuberg, S. L. (1997). Reinterpreting the empathy–altruism relationship: When one into one equals oneness. *Journal of Personality and Social Psychology, 73*, 481–494.

Clark, M. S., & Mills, J. (1979). Interpersonal attraction in exchange and communal relationships. *Journal of Personality and Social Psychology, 37*, 12–24.

Clark, M. S., Mills, J., & Powell, M. C. (1986). Keeping track of needs in communal and exchange relationships. *Journal of Personality and Social Psychology, 51*, 333–338.

Condon, W. S., & Ogston, W. D. (1966). Sound film analysis of normal and pathological behavior patterns. *Journal of Nervous and Mental Disease, 143*, 338–347.

Condon, W. S., & Sander, L. W. (1974). Synchrony demonstrated between movements of the neonate and adult speech. *Child Development, 45*, 456–462.

Dabbs, J. M. (1969). Similarity of gestures and interpersonal influence. *Proceedings of the 77th Annual Convention of the American Psychological Association, 4*, 337–339.

Darwin, C. (1965). *The expression of the emotions in man and animals*. Chicago: University of Chicago Press. (Original work published 1872)

Davis, M. H. (1980). A multidimensional approach to individual differences in empathy. *Catalog of Selected Documents in Psychology, 10*, 85.

Davis, M. H. (1983). Measuring individual differences in empathy: Evidence for a multidimensional approach. *Journal of Personality and Social Psychology, 44*, 113–126.

Devine, P. G. (1989). Stereotypes and prejudice: Their automatic and controlled components. *Journal of Personality and Social Psychology, 56*, 5–18.

Dijksterhuis, A., Aarts, H., Bargh, J. A., & van Knippenberg, A. (1998). *Intergroup contact and automatic behavior*. Manuscript submitted for publication, University of Nijmegen, the Netherlands.

Dijksterhuis, A., Spears, R., Postmes, T., Stapel, D. A., Koomen, W., van Knippenberg, A., & Scheepers, D. (1998). Seeing one thing and doing another: Contrast effects in automatic behavior. *Journal of Personality and Social Psychology, 75*, 862–871.

Dijksterhuis, A., & van Knippenberg, A. (1998). The relation between perception and behavior, or how to win a game of Trivial Pursuit. *Journal of Personality and Social Psychology, 74*, 865–877.

Dimberg, U. (1982). Facial reactions to facial expressions. *Psychophysiology, 19*, 643–647.

Dittmann, A. T., & Llewellyn, L. G. (1968). Relationship between vocalizations and head nods as listener responses. *Journal of Personality and Social Psychology, 9*, 79–84.

Dittmann, A. T., & Llewellyn, L. G. (1969). Body movement and speech rhythm in social conversation. *Journal of Personality and Social Psychology, 11*, 98–106.

Fazio, R. H., Sanbonmatsu, D. M., Powell, M. C., & Kardes, F. R. (1986). On the automatic activation of attitudes. *Journal of Personality and Social Psychology, 50*, 229–238.

Galef, B. G. (1988). Imitation in animals: History, definition and interpretation of data from the psychological laboratory. In T. Zentall & B. G. Galef (Eds.), *Comparative social learning* (pp. 3–28). Hillsdale, NJ: Erlbaum.

Hatfield, E., Cacioppo, J. T., & Rapson, R. L. (1994). *Emotional contagion*. Cambridge, England: Cambridge University Press.

Herr, P. M., Sherman, S. J., & Fazio, R. H. (1984). On the consequences of priming: Assimilation and contrast effects. *Journal of Experimental Social Psychology, 19*, 323–340.

Heyes, C. M. (1993). Imitation, culture and cognition. *Animal Behaviour, 46*, 999–1010.

Higgins, E. T. (1989). Knowledge accessibility and activation: Subjectivity and suffering from unconscious sources. In J. S. Uleman & J. A. Bargh (Eds.), *Unintended thought* (pp. 75–123). New York: Guilford Press.

Higgins, E. T. (1996). Knowledge activation: Accessibility, applicability, and salience. In E. T. Higgins & A. W. Kruglanski (Eds.), *Social psychology: Handbook of basic principles* (pp. 133–168). New York: Guilford Press.

Higgins, E. T., Rholes, W. S., & Jones, C. R. (1977). Category accessibility and impression formation. *Journal of Experimental Social Psychology, 13*, 141–154.

Hilgard, E. R. (1965). *Hypnotic susceptibility*. New York: Harcourt, Brace & World.

Jacobson, S. W., & Kagan, J. (1979, July 13). Response to Meltzoff and Moore (1977). *Science, 205*, 215.

James, W. (1890). *Principles of psychology*. New York: Holt.

Kaitz, M., Meschulach-Sarfaty, O., Auerbach, J., & Eidelman, A. (1988). A reexamination of newborns' ability to imitate facial expressions. *Developmental Psychology, 24*, 3–7.

Kendon, A. (1970). Movement coordination in social interaction: Some examples described. *Acta Psychologica, 32*, 1–25.

Koffka, K. (1925). *Die grundlagen der psychischen entwicklung* [The foundations of psychological development]. Osterwieck, Germany: Zickfeldt.

La France, M. (1979). Nonverbal synchrony and rapport: Analysis by the cross-lag panel technique. *Social Psychology Quarterly, 42*, 66–70.

La France, M. (1982). Posture mirroring and rapport. In M. Davis (Ed.), *Interaction rhythms: Periodicity in communicative behavior* (pp. 279–298). New York: Human Sciences Press.

La France, M., & Broadbent, M. (1976). Group rapport: Posture sharing as a nonverbal indicator. *Group and Organization Studies, 1*, 328–333.

La France, M., & Ickes, W. (1981). Posture mirroring and interactional involvement: Sex and sex typing effects. *Journal of Nonverbal Behavior, 5*, 139–154.

Langer, E. (1989). *Mindfulness*. Reading, MA: Addison-Wesley.

Langer, E. (1997). *The power of mindful learning*. Reading, MA: Addison-Wesley.

Lashley, K. S. (1951). The problem of serial order in behavior. In L. A. Jeffress (Ed.), *Cerebral mechanisms in behavior: The Hixon Symposium* (pp. 112–136). New York: Wiley & Sons.

Levenson, R. W., & Ruef, A. M. (1997). Physiological aspects of emotional knowledge and rapport. In W. Ickes (Ed.), *Empathic accuracy* (pp. 44–73). New York: Guilford Press.

Locke, E. A., & Latham, G. P. (1990). *A theory of goal setting and task performance*. Englewood Cliffs, NJ: Prentice Hall.

Macrae, C. N., Bodenhausen, G. V., Milne, A. B., Castelli, L., Schloerscheidt, A. M., & Greco, S. (1998). On activating exemplars. *Journal of Experimental Social Psychology, 34*, 330–354.

Markus, H. R., & Kitayama, S. (1991). Culture and the self: Implications for cognition, emotion, and motivation. *Psychological Review, 98*, 224–253.

Masters, J. C. (1979, July 13). Response to Meltzoff and Moore (1977). *Science, 205*, 215.

Maurer, R. E., & Tindall, J. H. (1983). Effect of pastural congruence on client's perception of counselor empathy. *Journal of Counseling Psychology, 30*, 158–163.

McDowall, J. J. (1978). Interactional synchrony: A reappraisal. *Journal of Personality and Social Psychology, 36*, 963–975.

Mead, G. H. (1934). *Mind, self, and society*. Chicago: University of Chicago Press.

Meltzoff, A. N., & Moore, M. K. (1977, October 7). Imitation of facial and manual gestures by human neonates. *Science, 198*, 75–78.

Meltzoff, A. N., & Moore, M. K. (1979, July 13). Note responding to Anisfeld, Masters, and Jacobson and Kagan's comments on Meltzoff and Moore (1977). *Science, 205*, 217–219.

Meltzoff, A. N., & Moore, M. K. (1983). Newborn infants imitate adult facial gestures. *Child Development, 54*, 702–709.

Mischel, W., Cantor, N., & Feldman, S. (1996). Principles of self-regulation: The nature of willpower and self-control. In E. T. Higgins & A. W. Kruglanski (Eds.), *Social psychology: Handbook of basic principles* (pp. 329–360). New York: Guilford Press.

Muesseler, J., & Hommel, B. (1997). Blindness to response-compatible stimuli. *Journal of Experimental Psychology: Human Perception and Performance, 23*, 861–872.

Mussweiler, T., & Foerster, J. (1998). *The sex→aggression link: A perception–behavior dissociation.* Manuscript submitted for publication, Universitat Wurzburg.

Piaget, J. (1932). *The moral judgment of the child.* London: Kegan, Paul, Trench, Trubner.

Piaget, J. (1946). *La formation du symbole chez l'enfant* [Symbol formation in the child]. Paris: Delachaux & Niestlé.

Pitcher, T. J. (1979). Sensory information and the organization of behavior in a shoaling cyprinid fish. *Animal Behavior, 27*, 126–149.

Prinz, W. (1990). A common coding approach to perception and action. In O. Neumann & W. Prinz (Eds.), *Relationships between perception and action* (pp. 167–201). Berlin: Springer-Verlag.

Reynolds, C. W. (1987). Flocks, herds, and schools: A distributed behavioral model. *Computer Graphics, 21*, 25–34.

Reynolds, C. W. (1993). An evolved, vision-based behavioral model of coordinated group motion. In J.-A. Meyer, H. L. Roitblat, & S. W. Wilson (Eds.), *From animals to animats 2* (pp. 384–392). Cambridge, MA: MIT Press.

Scheflen, A. E. (1964). The significance of posture in communication systems. *Psychiatry, 27*, 316–331.

Smith, A. (1966). *The theory of moral sentiments.* New York: Augustus M. Kelley. (Original work published 1759.)

Smith, E. R., & Medin, D. L. (1981). *Categories and concepts.* Cambridge, MA: Harvard University Press.

Smith, E. R., & Zarate, M. A. (1992). Exemplar-based model of social judgment. *Psychological Review, 99*, 3–21.

Srull, T. K., & Wyer, R. S., Jr. (1979). The role of category accessibility in the interpretation of information about persons: Some determinants and implications. *Journal of Personality and Social Psychology, 37*, 1660–1672.

Srull, T. K., & Wyer, R. S., Jr. (1980), Category accessibility and social perception: Some implications for the study of person memory and interpersonal judgment. *Journal of Personality and Social Psychology, 38*, 841–856.

Stapel, D. A., Koomen, W., & van der Pligt, J. (1997). Categories of category accessibility: The impact of trait versus exemplar priming on person judgments. *Journal of Personality and Social Psychology, 74*, 878–893.

Tickle-Degnen, L., & Rosenthal, R. (1987). Group rapport and nonverbal behavior. *Review of Personality and Social Psychology, 9*, 113–136.

Tomasello, M., Savage-Rumbaugh, E. S., & Kruger, A. C. (1993). Imitative learning of actions on objects by children, chimpanzees, and enculturated chimpanzees. *Child Development, 64*, 1688–1705.

Trout, D., & Rosenfeld, H. M. (1980). The effect of postural lean and body congruence on the judgment of psychotherapeutic rapport. *Journal of Nonverbal Communication, 4*, 176–190.

Uleman, J. S., Newman, L. S., & Moskowitz, G. B. (1996). People as flexible interpreters: Evidence and issues from spontaneous trait inference. In M. P. Zanna (Ed.), *Advances in experimental social psychology* (Vol. 28, pp. 211–279). New York: Academic Press.

Vaughan, K. B., & Lanzetta, J. T. (1980). Vicarious instigation and conditioning of facial expressive and autonomic responses to a model's expressive display of pain. *Journal of Personality and Social Psychology, 38*, 909–923.

Wegner, D. M., & Wheatley, T. P. (1999). Apparent mental causation: Sources of the experience of will. *American Psychologist, 54*, 480–492.

Winter, L., & Uleman, J. S. (1984). When are social judgments made? Evidence for the spontaneousness of trait inferences. *Journal of Personality and Social Psychology, 47*, 237–252.

Wyer, R. S., Jr., & Stall, T. K. (1989). *Memory and cognition in its social context.* Hillsdale, NJ: Erlbaum.

Zajonc, R. B., Adelmann, K. A., Murphy, S. T., & Niedenthal, P. M. (1987). Convergence in the physical appearance of spouses. *Motivation and Emotion, 11*, 335–346.

Received April 30, 1998

Revision received December 17, 1998

Accepted December 17, 1998

NOTES

1. Although motor-mimicry researchers have manipulated confederates' behaviors, they were not interested in (and therefore did not manipulate) general postures or behavioral mannerisms. Instead, the experimenters created situations in which participants observed a confederate experiencing a specific event and emotion and then tested whether participants reacted as if the experience were happening to them (e.g., Bavelas et al., 1988; Bavelas, Black, Lemery, & Mullett, 1987).

2. Although an effort was made to avoid photographs with strong emotional content, at the same time we needed to choose photos that would (a) be convincing as stimuli for a projective measure and (b) be able to stimulate 1–2 min of description as well as conjecture as to what was being thought or felt by the people in the photographs.

3. We also coded number of seconds participants spent smiling, rubbing their face, and shaking their foot. The correlations between these seconds measures and the number of times measures was high (for smiling, $r = .92$; for face rubbing, $r = .88$; for foot shaking, $r = .94$). Because of this redundancy, we report only the number of times analyses in the text. However, we computed all analyses on the number of seconds as well, and the results showed the identical pattern and significance level as the number of times analyses.

4. Reliability between judges was higher for the foot-shaking than for the face-rubbing measures. Because there are many physical gestures that can be made in the facial area (e.g., scratching an itch, playing with an earring, fixing hair), a detailed coding key was created and used by both raters. However, judgment calls had to be made, which reduced reliability. It should be noted that in Experiment 2 the reliability for this measure was substantially higher.

5. Brewer's (1991) model of optimal distinctiveness is consistent with this argument and puts it in a larger framework by bringing in a second, opposing need. In this model, social identity is viewed as a reconciliation between the two needs: On the one hand, we have a need for validation, similarity to others, and a sense of belonging, and on the other, we have a need for uniqueness, individuation, and a sense of distinctiveness.

6. It was important that the confederates in the nonmimicking condition not come across as stiff and awkward, while the mimicking confederates came across as relaxed, mobile, and animated. This potential confounded difference in behavior might provide an alternative explanation for our results: The participants liked the confederate in the mimicking condition more not because they were being mimicked by her, but rather because she seemed more relaxed, at ease, animated, and interesting than the confederate in the neutral condition. Consequently, we instructed all confederates to sit in a relaxed (i.e., not stiff and upright) position in both the mimicking and nonmimicking conditions; the only difference was that in the mimicking condition the relaxed position happened to mirror the participant's position, whereas in the nonmimicking condition it did not.

7. Ideally, one would obtain the judges' blind ratings of the likeability of the confederates per se—that is, how likeable a person who is not being mimicked considers the confederate to be. Such a rating would correspond more directly to the liking ratings made by the participants. However, the same confederate interacted with many different participants—sometimes mimicking them and sometimes not. Thus, an overall likeability rating for a given confederate would necessarily include both mimicking and nonmimicking sessions. To avoid this problem and to obtain separate ratings for the mimicking versus nonmimicking conditions, we opted instead to have judges rate the confederates' likeableness toward each individual participant.

READING 8

Behavioral Study of Obedience

Milgram's research on obedience to authority is the best known, most dramatic, and most controversial in the history of social psychology. Inspired by the events of World War II Nazi Germany, Milgram constructed a laboratory setting that called upon ordinary people, in response to commands issued by a psychology experimenter, to inflict increasing amounts of pain against an innocent man. Would anyone do it? If so, under what conditions? And what could be done to empower individuals to resist? The following article is Milgram's account of the first of many experiments he would go on to conduct on this subject. Read it, try to put yourself into the shoes of those who took part, and consider what it says about human nature and the way in which each of us can be overwhelmed by powerful situations. Then read in Chapter 7 (Conformity) about the numerous variations on this study that Milgram performed and ask yourself why some factors made little or no difference on the rates of obedience and why other factors did have a significant impact on these results.

BEHAVIORAL STUDY OF OBEDIENCE*

Stanley Milgram

Yale University

This article describes a procedure for the study of destructive obedience in the laboratory. It consists of ordering a naive S to administer increasingly more severe punishment to a victim in the context of a learning experiment. Punishment is administered by means of a shock generator with 30 graded switches ranging from Slight Shock to Danger: Severe Shock. The victim is a confederate of the E. The primary dependent variable is the maximum shock the S is willing to administer before he refuses to continue further. 26 Ss obeyed the experimental commands fully, and administered the highest shock on the generator. 14 Ss broke off the experiment at some point after the victim protested and refused to provide further answers. The procedure created extreme levels of nervous tension in some Ss. Profuse sweating, trembling, and stuttering were typical expressions of this emotional disturbance. One unexpected sign of tension—yet to be explained—was the regular occurrence of nervous laughter, which in some Ss developed into uncontrollable seizures. The variety of interesting behavioral dynamics observed in the experiment, the reality of the situation for the S, and the possibility of parametric variation within the framework of the procedure, point to the fruitfulness of further study.

Obedience is as basic an element in the structure of social life as one can point to. Some system of authority is a requirement of all communal living, and it is only the man dwelling in isolation who is not forced to respond, through defiance or submission, to the commands of others.

Obedience, as a determinant of behavior, is of particular relevance to our time. It has been reliably established that from 1933–45 millions of innocent persons were systematically slaughtered on command. Gas chambers were built, death camps were guarded, daily quotas of corpses were produced with the same

---

* SOURCE; Milgram, Stanley, "Behavioral Study of Obedience," *Journal of Abnormal and Social Psychology*, 1963, Vol. 67, No. 4, 371–378. Copyright © renewed 1991 by Alexandra Milgram. Permission granted by Alexandra Milgram.

efficiency as the manufacture of appliances. These inhumane policies may have originated in the mind of a single person, but they could only be carried out on a massive scale if a very large number of persons obeyed orders.

Obedience is the psychological mechanism that links individual action to political purpose. It is the dispositional cement that binds men to systems of authority. Facts of recent history and observation in daily life suggest that for many persons obedience may be a deeply ingrained behavior tendency, indeed, a prepotent impulse overriding training in ethics, sympathy, and moral conduct. C. P. Snow (1961) points to its importance when he writes:

> When you think of the long and gloomy history of man, you will find more hideous crimes have been committed in the name of obedience than have ever been committed in the name of rebellion. If you doubt that, read William Shirer's "Rise and Fall of the Third Reich." The German Officer Corps were brought up in the most rigorous code of obedience . . . in the name of obedience they were party to, and assisted in, the most wicked large scale actions in the history of the world [p. 24].

While the particular form of obedience dealt with in the present study has its antecedents in these episodes, it must not be thought all obedience entails acts of aggression against others. Obedience serves numerous productive functions. Indeed, the very life of society is predicated on its existence. Obedience may be ennobling and educative and refer to acts of charity and kindness, as well as to destruction.

General Procedure

A procedure was devised which seems useful as a tool for studying obedience (Milgram, 1961). It consists of ordering a naïve subject to administer electric shock to a victim. A simulated shock generator used, with 30 clearly marked voltage levels that range from 15 to 450 volts. The instrument bears verbal designations that range from Slight Shock to Danger: Severe Shock. The responses of the victim, who is a trained confederate of the experimenter, are standardized. The orders to administer shocks are given to the naïve subject in the context of a "learning experiment" ostensibly set up to study the effects of punishment on memory. As the experiment proceeds the naïve subject is commanded to administer increasingly more intense shocks to the victim, even to the point of reaching the level marked Danger: Severe Shock. Internal resistances become stronger, and at a certain point the subject refuses to go on with the experiment. Behavior prior to this rupture is considered "obedience," in that the subject complies with the commands of the experimenter. The point of rupture is the act of disobedience. A quantitative value is assigned to the subject's performance based on the maximum intensity shock he is willing to administer before he refuses to participate further. Thus for any particular subject and for any particular experimental condition the degree of obedience may be specified with a numerical value. The crux of the study is to systematically vary the factors believed to alter the degree of obedience to the experimental commands.

The technique allows important variables to be manipulated at several points in the experiment. One may vary aspects of the source of command, content and form of command, instrumentalities for its execution, target object, general social setting, etc. The problem, therefore, is not one of designing increasingly more numerous experimental conditions, but of selecting those that best illuminate the *process* of obedience from the sociopsychological standpoint.

Related Studies

The inquiry bears an important relation to philosophic analyses of obedience and authority (Arendt, 1958; Friedrich, 1958; Weber, 1947), an early experimental study of obedience by Frank (1944), studies in "authoritarianism" (Adorno, Frenkel-Brunswik, Levinson, & Stanford, 1950; Rokeach, 1961), and a recent series of analytic and empirical studies in social power (Cartwright, 1959). It owes much to the long concern with *suggestion* in social psychology, both in its normal forms (e.g., Binet,

1900) and in its clinical manifestations (Charcot, 1881). But it derives, in the first instance, from direct observation of a social fact; the individual who is commanded by a legitimate authority ordinarily obeys. Obedience comes easily and often. It is a ubiquitous and indispensable feature of social life.

METHOD

Subjects

The subjects were 40 males between the ages of 20 and 50, drawn from New Haven and the surrounding communities. Subjects were obtained by a newspaper advertisement and direct mail solicitation. Those who responded to the appeal believed they were to participate in a study of memory and learning at Yale University. A wide range of occupations is represented in the sample. Typical subjects were postal clerks, high school teachers, salesmen, engineers, and laborers. Subjects ranged in educational level from one who had not finished elementary school, to those who had doctorate and other professional degrees. They were paid $4.50 for their participation in the experiment. However, subjects were told that payment was simply for coming to the laboratory, and that the money was theirs no matter what happened after they arrived. Table 1 shows the proportion of age and occupational types assigned to the experimental condition.

Personnel and Locale

The experiment was conducted on the grounds of Yale University in the elegant interaction laboratory. (This detail is relevant to the perceived legitimacy of the experiment.

TABLE 1

Distribution of Age and Occupational Types

in the Experiment

Occupations	20–29 years n	30–39 years n	40–50 years n	Percentage of total (occupations)
Workers, skilled and unskilled	4	5	6	37.5
Sales, business, and white collar	3	6	7	40.0
Professional	1	5	3	22.5
Percentage of total (Age)	20	40	40	

Note: Total $N = 40$

In further variations, the experiment was dissociated from the university with consequences for performance.) The role of experimenter was played by a 31-year-old high school teacher of biology. His manner was impassive, and his appearance somewhat stern throughout the experiment. He was dressed in a gray technician's coat. The victim was played by a 47-year-old accountant, trained for the role; he was of Irish-American stock, whom most observers found mild-mannered and likable.

Procedure

One naive subject and one victim (an accomplice) performed in each experiment. A pretext had to be devised that would justify the administration of electric shock by the naive subject. This was effectively accomplished by the cover story. After a general introduction on the presumed relation between punishment and learning, subjects were told:

But actually, we know *very little* about the effect of punishment on learning, because almost no truly scientific studies have been made of it in human beings.

For instance, we don't know *how much* punishment is best for learning—and we don't know how much difference it makes as to who is giving the punishment, whether an adult learns best from a younger or an older person than himself—or many things of that sort.

So in this study we are bringing together a number of adults of different occupations and ages. And we're asking some of them to be teachers and some of them to be learners. We want to find out just what effect different people have on each other as teachers and learners, and also what effect *punishment* will have on learning in this situation.

Therefore, I'm going to ask one of you to be the teacher here tonight and the other one to be the learner.

Does either of you have a preference?

Subjects then drew slips of paper from a hat to determine who would be the teacher and who would be the learner in the experiment. The drawing was rigged so that the naive subject was always the teacher and the accomplice always the learner. (Both slips contained the word "Teacher.") Immediately after the drawing, the teacher and learner were taken to an adjacent room and the learner was strapped into an "electric chair" apparatus.

The experimenter explained that the straps were to prevent excessive movement while the learner was being shocked. The effect was to make it impossible for him to escape from the situation. An electrode was attached to the learner's wrist, and electrode paste was applied "to avoid blisters and burns." Subjects were told that the electrode was attached to the shock generator in the adjoining room.

In order to improve credibility the experimenter declared, in response to a question by the learner: "Although the shocks can be extremely painful, they cause no permanent tissue damage."

Learning task The lesson administered by the subject was a paired-associate learning task. The subject read a series of word pairs to the learner, and then read the first word of the pair along with four terms. The learner was to indicate which of the four terms had originally been paired with the first word. He communicated his answer by pressing one of four switches in front of him, which in turn lit up one of four numbered quadrants in an answerbox located atop the shock generator.

Shock generator The instrument panel consists of 30 lever switches set in a horizontal line. Each switch is clearly labeled with a voltage designation that ranges from 15 to 450 volts. There is a 15-volt increment from one switch to the next going from left to right. In addition, the following verbal designations are clearly indicated for groups of four switches going from left to right: Slight Shock, Moderate Shock, Strong Shock, Very Strong Shock, Intense Shock, Extreme Intensity Shock, Danger: Severe Shock. (Two switches after this last designation are simply marked XXX.)

Upon depressing a switch: a pilot light corresponding to each switch is illuminated in bright red; an electric buzzing is heard; an electric blue light, labeled "voltage energizer," flashes; the dial on the voltage meter swings to the right; various relay clicks are sounded.

The upper left-hand corner of the generator is labeled Shock Generator, Type ZLB, Dyson Instrument Company, Waltham, Mass. Output 15 Volts–450 Volts.

Details of the instrument were carefully handled to insure an appearance of authenticity. The panel was engraved by precision industrial engravers, and all components were of high quality. No subject in the experiment suspected that the instrument was merely a simulated shock generator.[1]

Sample shock Each naive subject is given a sample shock on the shock generator, prior to beginning his run as teacher. This shock is always 45 volts, and is applied by pressing the third switch of the generator. The shock is applied to the wrist of the naive subject, and has its source in a 45-volt battery wired into the generator. This further convinces the subject of the authenticity of the generator.

Shock instructions The subject is told to administer a shock to the learner each time he gives a wrong response. Moreover—and this is the key command—the subject is instructed to "move one level higher on the shock generator each time the learner flashes a wrong answer." He is also instructed to announce the voltage level before administering a shock. This serves to continually remind subjects of the increasing intensity of shocks administered to the learner.

Preliminary and regular run Pretests revealed that the procedure of reading words and administering shocks requires some practice before it can be handled smoothly. Therefore, immediately preceding the regular run," the teacher is given a preliminary series of 10 words to read to the learner. There are 3 neutral words in the practice series (i.e., words that the learner answers correctly), so that shocks are administered for 7 of the words, with the maximum shock at 105 volts (moderate shock). Almost all subjects master the procedure by the time the preliminary run is over.

Subjects are then presented with a second list, and are told that the procedure is the same as for the first list; the experimenter adds, however:

> When you get to the bottom of the list, repeat it over again, and continue giving shocks, until the learner has learned all the pairs correctly.

The experimenter instructs the subject to,

> start from 15 volts and increase the shock level one step each time the learner gives a wrong answer.

Feedback from the victim In all conditions the learner gives a predetermined set of responses to the word pair test, based on a schedule of approximately three wrong answers to one correct answer. In the present experimental condition no vocal response or other sign of protest is heard from the learner until Shock Level 300 is reached. When the 300-volt shock is administered, the learner pounds on the wall of the room in which he is bound to the electric chair. The pounding can be heard by the subject. From this point on, the learner's answers no longer appear on the four-way panel.

At this juncture, subjects ordinarily turn to the experimenter for guidance. The experimenter instructs the subject to treat the absence of a response as a wrong answer, and to shock the subject according to the usual schedule. He advises the subjects to allow 5–10 seconds before considering no response as a wrong answer, and to increase the shock level one step each time the learner fails to respond correctly. The learner's pounding is repeated after the 315-volt shock is administered; afterwards he is not heard from, nor do his answers reappear on the four-way signal box.

Experimenter feedback At various points in the experiment the subject may turn to the experimenter for advice on whether he should continue to administer shocks. Or he may indicate that he does not wish to go on. It was important to standardize the experimenter's responses to these inquiries and reactions.

If the subject indicated his unwillingness to go on, the experimenter responded with a sequence of "prods," using as many as necessary to bring the subject into line.

> Prod 1: Please continue, *or* Please go on.

> Prod 2: The experiment requires that you continue.

> Prod 3: It is absolutely essential that you continue.

> Prod 4: You have no other choice, you *must* go on.

The prods were always made in sequence; Only if Prod 1 had been unsuccessful, could Prod 2 be used. If the subject refused to obey the experimenter after Prod 4, the experiment was terminated. The experimenter's tone of voice was at all times firm, but not impolite. The sequence was begun anew on each occasion that the subject balked or showed reluctance to follow orders.

Special prods. If the subject asked if the learner was liable to suffer permanent physical injury, the experimenter said:

> Although the shocks may be painful, there is no permanent tissue damage, so please go on. [Followed by Prods 2, 3, and 4 if necessary.]

If the subject said that the learner did not want to go on, the experimenter replied:

> Whether the learner likes it or not, you must go on until he has learned all the word pairs correctly. So please go on, [Followed by Prods 2, 3, and 4 if necessary.)

Dependent Measures

The primary dependent measure for any subject is the maximum shock he administers before he refuses to go any further. In principle this may vary from 0 (for a subject who refuses to administer even the first shock) to 30 (for a subject who administers the highest shock on the generator). A subject who breaks off the experiment at any point prior to administering the thirtieth shock level is termed a *defiant* subject. One who complies with experimental commands fully, and proceeds to administer all shock levels commanded, is termed an *obedient* subject.

Further records With few exceptions, experimental sessions were recorded on magnetic tape. Occasional photographs were taken through one-way mirrors. Notes were kept on any unusual behavior occurring during the course of the experiments. On occasion, additional observers were directed to write objective descriptions of the subjects' behavior. The latency and duration of shocks were measured by accurate timing devices.

Interview and dehoax Following the experiment, subjects were interviewed; open-ended questions, projective measures, and attitude scales were employed. After the interview, procedures were undertaken to assure that the subject would leave the laboratory in a state of well being. A friendly reconciliation was arranged between the subject and the victim, and an effort was made to reduce any tensions that arose as a result of the experiment.

RESULTS

Preliminary Notions

Before giving an account of the experimental results, it is instructive to consider how persons predict others will perform when commanded to administer powerful shocks to another person. Fourteen Yale seniors, all psychology majors, were provided with a detailed description of the experimental situation. They were asked to reflect carefully on it, and to predict the behavior of 100 hypothetical subjects. More specifically, they were instructed to plot the distribution of obedience of "100 Americans of diverse occupations, and ranging in age from 20 to 50 years," who were placed in the experimental situation.

There was considerable agreement among the respondents on the expected behavior of hypothetical subjects. All respondents predicted that only an insignificant minority would go through to the end of the shock series. (The estimates ranged from 0 to 3%; i.e., the most "pessimistic" member of the class predicted that of 100 persons, 3 would continue through to the most potent shock available on the shock generator—450 volts.) The class mean was 1.2%. The question was also posed informally to colleagues of the author, and the most general feeling was that few if any subjects would go beyond the designation Very Strong Shock.

Results of Experiment I

Subjects accept situation With few exceptions subjects were convinced of the reality of the experimental situation, that they were administering shocks to another person, and the most potent shocks were extremely painful. In the post-experimental interview subjects were asked: "How painful to the learner were the last few shocks that you administered to him?" Subjects were instructed to indicate their answers on a printed 14-point scale ranging from "Not at all painful" to "Extremely painful." The modal response was 14 (Extremely painful) with the mean at 13.42.

Signs of extreme tension Many subjects showed signs of nervousness in the experimental situation, and especially upon administering the more powerful shocks. In a large number of cases the degree of tension reached extremes that are rarely seen in sociopsychological laboratory studies. Subjects were observed to sweat, tremble, stutter, bite their lips, groan, and dig their fingernails into their flesh. These were characteristic rather than exceptional responses to the experiment.

One sign of tension was the regular occurrence of nervous laughing fits. Fourteen of the 40 subjects showed definite signs of nervous laughter and smiling. The laughter seemed entirely out of place, even bizarre. Full-blown, uncontrollable seizures were observed for 3 subjects. On one occasion we observed a seizure so violently convulsive that it was necessary to call a halt to the experiment. The subject, a 46-year-old encyclopedia salesman, was seriously embarrassed by his untoward and uncontrollable behavior. In the post-experimental interviews subjects took pains to point out that they were not sadistic types, and that the laughter did not mean they enjoyed shocking the victim.

Distribution of scores It had been conjectured that persons would not, in general, agree to administer shocks beyond the level designated as Very Strong Shock. The distribution of maximum shocks for this experiment is shown in Table 2. The obtained distribution of scores deviates radically from the prediction.

Upon command of the experimenter, each of the 40 subjects went beyond the expected breakoff point. No subject stopped prior to administering Shock Level 20. (At this level—300 volts—the victim kicks on the wall and no longer provides answers to the teacher's multiple-choice questions.)

Of the 40 subjects, 5 refused to obey the experimental commands beyond the 300-volt level. Four more subjects administered one further shock, and then refused to go on. Two broke off at the 330-volt level, and 1 each at 345, 360, and 375 volts. Thus a total of 14 subjects defied the experimenter. It is instructive to reprint their remarks at the point of defiance, as transcribed from the tape recordings:

> [0124] I think he's trying to communicate, he's knocking. . . . Well it's not fair to shock the guy . . . these are terrific volts. I don't think this is very humane. . . . Oh, I can't go on with this; no, this isn't right. It's a hell of an experiment. The guy is suffering in there. No, I don't want to go on. This is crazy. [Subject refused to administer more shocks.]

> [0123] He's banging in there. I'm gonna chicken out. I'd like to continue, but I can't do that to a man. . . .I'm sorry I can't do that to a man. I'll hurt his heart. You take your check. . . . No really, I couldn't do it.

TABLE 2

Distribution of Breakoff Points

Verbal designation and voltage indication	Number of subjects for whom this was maximum shock
Slight Shock	
15	0
30	0
45	0
60	0
Moderate Shock	
75	0
90	0
105	0
120	0
Strong Shock	
135	0
150	0
165	0
180	0
Very Strong Shock	
195	0
210	0
225	0
240	0
Intense Shock	
255	0
270	0
285	0
300	5
Extreme Intensity Shock	
315	4
330	2
345	1
360	1
Danger: Severe Shock	
375	1
390	0
405	0
420	0
XXX	
435	0
450	26

These subjects were frequently in a highly agitated and even angered state. Sometimes, verbal protest was at a minimum, and the subject simply got up from his chair in front of the shock generator, and indicated that he wished to leave the laboratory.

Of the 40 subjects, 26 obeyed the orders of the experimenter to the end, proceeding to punish the victim until they reached the most potent shock available on the shock generator. At that point, the experimenter called a halt to the session. (The maximum shock is labeled 450 volts, and is two steps beyond the designation: Danger: Severe Shock.) Although obedient subjects continued to administer shocks, they often did so under extreme stress. Some expressed reluctance to administer shocks beyond the 300-volt level, and displayed fears similar to those who defied the experimenter; yet they obeyed.

After the maximum shocks had been delivered, and the experimenter called a halt to the proceedings, many obedient subjects heaved sighs of relief, mopped their brows, rubbed their fingers over their eyes, or nervously fumbled cigarettes. Some shook their heads, apparently in regret. Some subjects had remained calm throughout the experiment, and displayed only minimal signs of tension from beginning to end.

DISCUSSION

The experiment yielded two findings that were surprising. The first finding concerns the sheer strength of obedient tendencies manifested in this situation. Subjects have learned from childhood that it is a fundamental breach of moral conduct to hurt another person against his will. Yet, 26 subjects abandon this tenet in following the instructions of an authority who has no special powers to enforce his commands. To disobey would bring no material loss to the subject; no punishment would ensue. It is clear from the remarks and outward behavior of many participants that in punishing the victim they are often acting against their own values. Subjects often expressed deep disapproval of shocking a man in the face of his objections, and others denounced it as stupid and senseless. Yet the majority complied with the experimental commands. This outcome was surprising from two perspectives: first, from the standpoint of predictions made in the questionnaire described earlier. (Here, however, it is possible that the remoteness of the respondents from the actual situation, and the difficulty of conveying to them the concrete details of the experiment, could account for the serious underestimation of obedience.)

But the results were also unexpected to persons who observed the experiment in progress, through one-way mirrors. Observers often uttered expressions of disbelief upon seeing a subject administer more powerful shocks to the victim. These persons had a full acquaintance with the details of the situation, and yet systematically underestimated the amount of obedience that subjects would display.

The second unanticipated effect was the extraordinary tension generated by the procedures. One might suppose that a subject would simply break off or continue as his conscience dictated. Yet, this is very far from what happened. There were striking reactions of tension and emotional strain. One observer related:

> I observed a mature and initially poised businessman enter the laboratory smiling and confident. Within 20 minutes he was reduced to a twitching, stuttering wreck, who was rapidly approaching a point of nervous collapse. He constantly pulled on his earlobe, and twisted his hands. At one point he pushed his fist into his forehead and muttered: "Oh God, let's stop it." And yet he continued to respond to every word of the experimenter, and obeyed to the end.

Any understanding of the phenomenon of obedience must rest on an analysis of the particular conditions in which it occurs. The following features of the experiment go some distance in explaining the high amount of obedience observed in the situation.

1. The experiment is sponsored by and takes place on the grounds of an institution of unimpeachable reputation, Yale University. It may be reasonably presumed that the personnel are competent and reputable. The importance of this background authority is now being studied by conducting a series of experiments outside of New Haven, and without any visible ties to the university.

2. The experiment is, on the face of it, designed to attain a worthy purpose—advancement of knowledge about learning and memory. Obedience occurs not as an end in itself, but as an instrumental element in a situation that the subject construes as significant, and meaningful. He may not be able to see its full significance, but he may properly assume that the experimenter does.

3.   The subject perceives that the victim has voluntarily submitted to the authority system of the experimenter. He is not (at first) an unwilling captive impressed for involuntary service. He has taken the trouble to come to the laboratory presumably to aid the experimental research. That he later becomes an involuntary subject does not alter the fact that, initially, he consented to participate without qualification. Thus he has in some degree incurred an obligation toward the experimenter.

4.   The subject, too, has entered the experiment voluntarily, and perceives himself under obligation to aid the experimenter. He has made a commitment, and to disrupt the experiment is a repudiation of this initial promise of aid.

5.   Certain features of the procedure strengthen the subject's sense of obligation to the experimenter. For one, he has been paid for coming to the laboratory. In part this is canceled out by the experimenter's statement that:

      Of course, as in all experiments, the money is yours simply for coming to the laboratory. From this point on, no matter what happens, the money is yours.[2]

6.   From the subject's standpoint, the fact that he is the teacher and the other man the learner is purely a chance consequence (it is determined by drawing lots) and he, the subject, ran the same risk as the other man in being assigned the role of learner. Since the assignment of positions in the experiment was achieved by fair means, the learner is deprived of any basis of complaint on this count. (A similar situation obtains in Army units, in which—in the absence of volunteers—a particularly dangerous mission may be assigned by drawing lots, and the unlucky soldier is expected to bear his misfortune with sportsmanship.)

7.   There is, at best, ambiguity with regard to the prerogatives of a psychologist and the corresponding rights of his subject. There is a vagueness of expectation concerning what a psychologist may require of his subject, and when he is overstepping acceptable limits. Moreover, the experiment occurs in a closed setting, and thus provides no opportunity for the subject to remove these ambiguities by discussion with others. There are few standards that seem directly applicable to the situation, which is a novel one for most subjects.

8.   The subjects are assured that the shocks administered to the subject are "painful but not dangerous." Thus they assume that the discomfort caused the victim is momentary, while the scientific gains resulting from the experiment are enduring.

9.   Through Shock Level 20 the victim continues to provide answers on the signal box. The subject may construe this as a sign that the victim is still willing to "play the game." It is only after Shock Level 20 that the victim repudiates the rules completely, refusing to answer further.

      These features help to explain the high amount of obedience obtained in this experiment. Many of the arguments raised need not remain matters of speculation, but can be reduced to testable propositions to be confirmed or disproved by further experiments.[3]

      The following features of the experiment concern the nature of the conflict which the subject faces.

10.   The subject is placed in a position in which he must respond to the competing demands of two persons: the experimenter and the victim. The conflict must be resolved by meeting the demands of one or the other; satisfaction of the victim and the experimenter are mutually exclusive. Moreover, the resolution must take the form of a highly visible action, that of continuing to shock the victim or breaking off the experiment. Thus the subject is forced into a public conflict that does not permit any completely satisfactory solution.

11. While the demands of the experimenter carry the weight of scientific authority, the demands of the victim spring from his personal experience of pain and suffering. The two claims need not be regarded as equally pressing and legitimate. The experimenter seeks an abstract scientific datum; the victim cries out for relief from physical suffering caused by the subject's actions.

12. The experiment gives the subject little time for reflection. The conflict comes on rapidly. It is only minutes after the subject has been seated before the shock generator that the victim begins his protests. Moreover, the subject perceives that he has gone through but two-thirds of the shock levels at the time the subject's first protests are heard. Thus he understands that the conflict will have a persistent aspect to it, and may well become more intense as increasingly more powerful shocks are required. The rapidity with which the conflict descends on the subject, and his realization that it is predictably recurrent may well be sources of tension to him.

13. At a more general level, the conflict stems from the opposition of two deeply ingrained behavior dispositions: first, the disposition not to harm other people, and second, the tendency to obey those whom we perceived to be legitimate authorities.

REFERENCES

Adorno, T., Frenkel-Brunswik, Else, Levinson, D. J., & Sanford, R. N. *The authoritarian personality*. New York: Harper, 1950.

Arendt, H. What was authority? In C. J. Friedrich (Ed.), *Authority*. Cambridge: Harvard Univer. Press, 1958. Pp. 81–112.Binet, A. *La suggestibilité*. Paris: Schleicher, 1900.

Buss, A. H. *The psychology of aggression*. New York: Wiley, 1961.

Cartwright, S. (Ed.) *Studies in social power*. Ann Arbor; University of Michigan Institute for Social Research, 1959.

Charcot, J. M. *Oeuvres complètes*. Paris: Bureaux du Progrès Médical, 1881.

Frank, J. D. Experimental studies of personal pressure and resistance. *J. Gen. Psychol.*, 1944, 30, 23–64.

Friedrich, C. J. (Ed.). *Authority*. Cambridge; Harvard Univer. Press, 1958.

Milgram, S. Dynamics of obedience, Washington: National Science Foundation, 25 January 1961. (Mimeo)

Milgram, S. Some conditions of obedience and disobedience to authority. *Hum. Relat.*, 1964, in press.

Rokeach, M. Authority, authoritarianism, and conformity. In I. A. Berg & B. M. Bass (Eds.), *Conformity and deviation*. New York; Harper, 1961. Pp. 230–257.

Snow, C. P. Either-or, *Progressive,* 1961 (Feb.), 24.

Weber, M. The theory of social and economic organization. Oxford: Oxford Univer. Press, 1947.

NOTES

1. A related technique, making use of a shock generator, was reported by Buss (1961) for the study of aggression in the laboratory. Despite the considerable similarity of technical detail in the experimental procedures, both investigators proceeded in ignorance of the other's work. Milgram provided plans and photographs of his shock generator, experimental procedure, and first results in a report to the National Science Foundation in January 1961. This report received only limited circulation. Buss reported his procedure 6 months later, but to a wider audience. Subsequently, technical information and reports were exchanged. The present article was first received in the Editor's office on December 27, 1961; it was resubmitted with deletions on July 27, 1962.

2. Forty-three subjects, undergraduates at Yale University, were run in the experiment without payment. The results are very similar to those obtained with paid subjects.

3. A series of recently completed experiments employing the obedience paradigm is reported in Milgram (1964).

(Received July 27, 1962)

READING 9

Bringing in the Experts: How Team Composition and Collaborative Planning Jointly Shape Analytic Effectiveness

As discussed in Chapter 8 (Group Processes), there are a variety of factors that contribute to successful group dynamics. The chapter section on "Strategies for Improvement," and especially Figure 8.8, specifically addresses this 2008 study, by Woolley, et al., which examined how analytic team performance is affected by the inclusion of experts and collaborative planning. Forty-one four-person groups were assembled to solve a terrorist plot. They had 45 minutes to correctly identify three guilty individuals from a pool of ten suspects, one target from a group of five, and the terrorists' plans. All groups had the same four types of evidence, but some had experts and some did not, and some had collaborative planning intervention (20 teams total, 10 with special abilities and 10 with average abilities) while others did not (21 teams total, 10 with special abilities and 11 with average abilities). The results showed that teams with special abilities (experts) as well as those with planning intervention but no special abilities did no better than groups without planning intervention. It was only the groups that had experts *and* planning intervention that did relatively well. The combination was necessary to improve success.

BRINGING IN THE EXPERTS: HOW TEAM COMPOSITION AND COLLABORATIVE PLANNING JOINTLY SHAPE ANALYTIC EFFECTIVENESS

Anita Williams Woolley

Harvard University

Margaret E. Gerbasi

Princeton University

Christopher F. Chabris

Union College

Stephen M. Kosslyn

J. Richard Hackman

Harvard University

Anita Williams Woolley, Margaret E. Gerbasi, Christopher F. Chabris, Stephen M. Kosslyn and J. Richard Hackman, "Bringing in the Experts: How Team Composition and Collaborative Planning Jointly Shape Analytic Effectiveness," *Small Group Research*, Vol 39, No. 3, June 2008, http://sgr.sagepub.com/cgi/content/abstract/39/3/352.

ABSTRACT— *This study investigates the separate and joint effects of the inclusion of experts and collaborative planning on the performance of analytic teams. Teams either did or did not include members with expert-level task-relevant cognitive abilities, and either did or did not receive an intervention that fostered collaborative planning. Results support the authors' hypothesis that analytic performance requires both task-appropriate expertise and collaborative planning to identify strategies for optimally using that expertise. Indeed, high expertise in the absence of collaborative planning actually decreased team performance. Teams engaging in collaborative planning were more likely to effectively integrate their information on key aspects of the analytic problem, which significantly enhanced their analytic performance. Furthermore, information integration mediated the effects of the interaction of expertise and collaboration on performance. The implications of the findings for the optimal use of team member skills and the development of team performance strategies are discussed.*

KEYWORDS: team performance; experts; collaboration; information integration.

Many prominent organizational failures are rooted in flawed analysis of data that are used to guide action. Flawed medical diagnoses, misinterpretation of financial indicators, and biased interpretations of intelligence data can result in ill-advised actions that have unfortunate consequences. In many of these situations, team members from different specialties are asked to work together to integrate multiple sources of information and draw conclusions. In this article, we explore the conditions under which teams whose members are specialists can collaborate effectively to analyze incomplete or unreliable data and use those data to generate trustworthy conclusions about unknown states of affairs.

Analytic work invariably involves both cognitive and social processes. At core, analysis is a cognitive activity. Although analysts often draw on both technological aids and input from others, it ultimately is the human brain that organizes and interprets data to generate an assessment of an event that has happened, is happening, or is likely to happen. But analytic work also is inherently a social process. The lone analyst working in isolation to extract the meaning from a set of data is the exception rather than the rule. Instead, analysts typically draw heavily on the expertise, experience, and insights of their colleagues in developing and testing their conclusions (Hackman & O'Connor, 2004).

Previous research on the cognitive and social aspects of the analytic process has been carried out as if the two factors are independent. This research explores the possibility that a robust understanding of the factors that shape analytic performance can be obtained only by examining the interaction of member expertise and collaborative planning on analytic performance.

Not Expertise Alone

Considerable evidence documents that cognitive abilities shape team performance. The general intelligence of members, for example, has been shown to predict a number of team effectiveness criteria (LePine, 2005; Neuman, Wagner, & Christiansen, 1999), as well as team learning (Ellis et al., 2003). The relationship between cognitive ability and performance is particularly strong for tasks that are unfamiliar (Devine, 1999). Composing teams to include content experts therefore should raise the quality of the Authors' Note: An earlier version of this article was presented at the 2007 meeting of the Interdisciplinary Network for Group Research, Lansing, Michigan. This investigation was supported by National Science Foundation (NSF) Research Grant REC-0106070, CFDA No. 47.076, with support from Fred Ambrose and the Intelligence Technology Innovation Center at the Central Intelligence Agency. We gratefully acknowledge the research assistance of Jonathon Schuldt, Benjamin Bibler, Abigail Donahue, and Benjamin White. Address correspondence to Anita Williams Woolley, 33 Kirkland St., Cambridge MA 02138; e-mail: anita@post.harvard.edu team's product by expanding and deepening the level of knowledge and skill available to the team.

Experts are individuals who possess an appreciably higher level of knowledge or skill than the average person (Ericsson & Lehmann, 1996; Patel, Groen, & Arocha, 1990). An individual's expertise can be the result of training and experience or may be a function of his or her cognitive or physical abilities (Ericsson, 2005; Volmer, 2006). Because a person's cognitive abilities are particularly germane to analytic work, we focus on them in this research. Specifically, we take advantage of recent advances in cognitive neuroscience that offer the possibility of using brain-based measures to assess members' cognitive abilities (Cabeza & Nyberg, 2000; Kosslyn, 1994; Kozhevnikov, Kosslyn, & Shephard, 2005). Analytic teams that include members with strong task-relevant abilities have greater potential to perform well than teams composed entirely of average-ability members.

Integrating experts into a team can create social dynamics that compromise team performance. Research on team diversity shows that bringing together teams of members from different social categories can create significant difficulties in collaborative work (Bunderson & Sutcliffe, 2002; Caruso & Woolley, in press; Dahlin, Weingart, & Hinds, 2005; Jehn, Northcraft, & Neale, 1999; Thomas-Hunt, Ogden, & Neale, 2003). Even in the absence of social categories, designating particular team members experts can evoke status dynamics that override benefits that can be obtained from the higher overall ability of the team. High-status experts may be disinclined to take seriously the views of others, and lower status members may be tempted to give more credence to higher status members than is warranted by their actual expertise (Beersma et al., 2003; Hackman & Morris, 1983; Littlepage, Robison, & Reddington, 1997). Merely including high-expertise members in teams that perform analytic work, therefore, may be insufficient to foster effective team performance. Members also must be aware of the full complement of their teammates' abilities and, important to note, must have the opportunity to develop a performance strategy that enables them to optimally use those capabilities.

These dysfunctions can be overcome when members of well-designed teams collaborate to formulate and implement a performance strategy that is uniquely suited to task and situational requirements (Hackman, Brousseau, & Weiss, 1976; Okhuysen, 2001; Okhuysen & Eisenhardt, 2002; Woolley, 1998). Explicit coordination processes are necessary for tasks that are highly interdependent (Wittenbaum, Vaughan, & Stasser, 1998), but competent team collaboration about work strategy rarely occurs spontaneously (Gurtner, Tschan, Semmer, & Nagele, 2007; Hackman & Wageman, 2005). Therefore, an intervention usually is required to induce members to engage in explicit discussions about how they will carry out their collaborative work and, important to note, how they will capture and use well the contributions of individual members who have special task expertise. We hypothesize, therefore, that both ability composition and an intervention to help members engage in collaborative planning are required for effective performance. Specifically, position alone.

> *Hypothesis 1*: **The interaction of team ability composition and collaborative planning more strongly predicts team performance than does team composition.**

Not Collaboration Alone

Analytic work involves multiple steps, about which considerable research has been done: recognition of the situation in need of assessment (Bazerman, 2006; Chugh & Bazerman, 2007; Moreland & Levine, 1992), definition of the problem (Fiore & Schooler, 2004), creation or selection of the information to be considered (Heuer, 1999), pooling of knowledge and coordination of members' inputs (Faraj & Sproull, 2000), and decision making about analytic conclusions (Davis, 1996; Kerr & Tindale, 2004). The research literature on team analytic performance is pessimistic about how well teams accomplish these functions. For example, teams tend to combine information ineffectively, omitting pieces of critical information (Henry, 1995); they focus too much on shared information (Stasser, Stewart, & Wittenbaum, 1995); and they do not coordinate expertise well, often giving specific members' contributions more or less weight than is warranted by their actual abilities (Bottger & Yetton, 1988; Hackman & Morris, 1983; Hackman & Wageman, 2005).

Even well-designed and competently administered strategy-planning interventions cannot compensate for the absence of task-critical member capabilities, however. Only teams whose membership includes individuals with ample task-relevant expertise will be helped by them, as is illustrated by a recent study in which dyads were required to navigate a virtual maze and identify repeated instances of complex objects (Woolley et al., 2007). The task required two specific abilities: skill at navigation (spatial ability) and skill at storing images of complex forms (object memory ability). Both of these abilities reflect the operation of distinct neural systems (Kozhevnikov et al., 2005). One member of each team was assigned to navigate and one to tag repetitions of forms. Teams were composed of members who were either strong or weak on each of the two abilities and, after completing work on the first maze, were given the opportunity to converse about how they were working together. These conversations about work strategy enhanced team performance only when members had been assigned to roles that were incongruent with their abilities (i.e., the person with high spatial ability was assigned to memorize shapes, or the person with high object ability was assigned to the navigation task). Conversation did not help when role assignments were consistent with members' abilities—and actually impaired performance when both members were high on the same ability. Therefore, planning more strongly predicts team performance than does collaborative planning alone.

> **Hypothesis 2**: The interaction of team ability composition and collaborative planning more strongly predicts team performance than does collaborative planning alone.

Team Information Integration

A critical challenge for teams performing analytic work is to find ways to extract, organize, and integrate all information that can inform the team's assessment that is known to some, but not all, team members. Research evidence affirms that coordinating member knowledge and expertise is critical to success for knowledge tasks (Faraj & Sproull, 2000), but teams frequently fail to do this effectively (Bunderson, 2003; Cronin & Weingart, 2007), particularly if they lack members with the intrapersonal diversity, or breadth of personal skills and experience, to help bridge among others with more narrow expertise (Bunderson & Sutcliffe, 2002). Absent an effective strategy for dealing with this challenge, team members may either become so overwhelmed with data that they cannot make sense of what the data mean (e.g., Mintzberg, Raisinghani, & Theoret, 1976; Yen, Fan, Sun, Hanratty, & Dumer, 2006), or they may fail to detect links or associations among independent facts that could provoke original ideas or stimulate fresh thinking (Okhuysen & Eisenhardt, 2002).

To overcome these problems, an analytic team requires some systematic means of structuring its search for data and for evaluating the evidence the team unearths. In analytic work, certain variables usually can be assessed sooner and more reliably than others and then used to structure follow-on searches for other evidence. A murder investigation team, for example, needs to identify the weapon used, the perpetrator, and the motive. In many cases, the weapon can be determined more readily than the other elements, both because there are fewer possibilities and because information obtained about it is likely to be reasonably trustworthy. Because certain people and certain motives will fit better with some weapons than with others, identification of the weapon can inform and constrain subsequent data gathering about possible perpetrators and motives. This iterative process can continue until a coherent story emerges, at which point additional analytic strategies, such as testing alternative hypotheses and trying out structured analogies, can be used to protect against confirmation biases and to explore the merits of various alternative story lines.

The same logic holds for analytic teams. Analytic teams that engage in effective collaborative planning should devise better performance strategies and exhibit better information integration, which in turn improves performance. Specifically,

Hypothesis 3: Information integration mediates the effects of the interaction of expertise and collaborative planning on team analytic performance.

Method

We tested the research hypotheses in an experimental study of four-person teams that performed a partial analog intelligence analysis task. The task required members to assess and integrate diverse kinds of data to determine what suspected terrorists were planning. Two factors were experimentally manipulated: (a) team composition (experts vs. no experts) and (b) collaborative planning intervention (presence vs. absence of guidance about ways to use member resources well). Performance measures included both the objective accuracy of each team's analysis and independent assessments of the quality of their reasoning.

Participants

A sample of 1,692 Boston-area students and residents were recruited on an Internet bulletin board for preliminary screening of cognitive abilities and were given a $10 gift certificate from an online retailer as compensation. Of these participants, 164 (41 four-person groups) were selected to take part in the experiment, based on their scores on the screening tests (described in more detail below). Those selected for the experiment were paid an additional $25 for participating. Sixty-three percent of the participants were women; participant age ranged from 18 to 59 ($M = 27$, $SD = 8.7$), and all were college students or graduates.

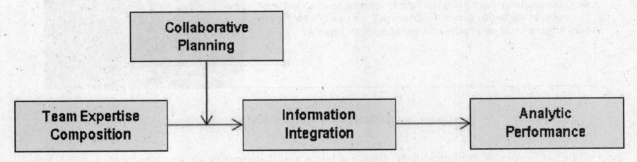

Figure 1 depicts the hypothesized relationships among the variables investigated in this study and their impact on performance.

Task

The task required four-person teams to solve a terrorist plot within 45 min by correctly identifying three guilty individuals from a pool of 10 suspects, one target building from five potential locations, and the terrorists' planned activities. Four types of evidence were provided, as described below. The evidence was available to the teams on four eMac computers placed together in the room, each of which was loaded with brief biographical sketches of all the suspects and one of the four types of evidence.

The task was structured so that obtaining the correct answer required both accurate analysis of each set of evidence and integration across the four different kinds of evidence. Both the setup of the experimental room and the large quantity of available evidence encouraged groups to spend some time working on their individual computers to analyze a single type of evidence before coming together to discuss and draw conclusions about what they had learned.

Materials

Four types of evidence were supplied to help the teams determine the terrorists' plans: (a) degraded security camera photos, (b) surveillance video footage without audio, (c) a codeword-based e-mail set, and (d) reconnaissance photos and building plans. Figure 2 contains examples of each type of evidence. The degraded security camera photos were supplied from each of the five suspected plot locations. Photos of 5 of the 10 suspects were mixed in with 10 distracter photos from each location, and participants were instructed to determine which of the 10 suspects appeared at each of the five locations, with the implication that the guilty suspects would have all visited the targeted building. Surveillance video footage of each suspect leaving a hazardous materials laboratory where critical chemicals were stolen provided additional information for participants to use to determine who seemed nervous as they departed. Codeword-based e-mails exchanged between the suspects were supplied to provide details of the plot itself. Finally, reconnaissance photos, found on a personal digital assistant (PDA) suspects purportedly had lost, could be matched up to building plans to reveal the probable location of the plot.

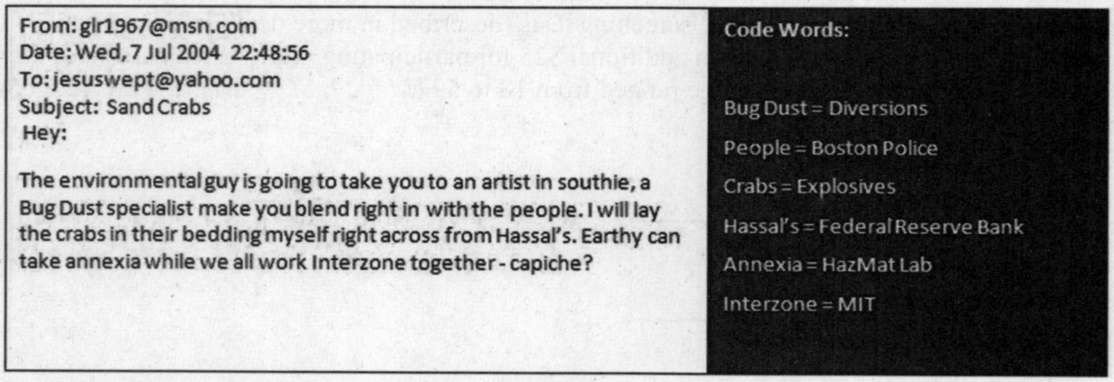

From: glr1967@msn.com
Date: Wed, 7 Jul 2004 22:48:56
To: jesuswept@yahoo.com
Subject: Sand Crabs
 Hey:

The environmental guy is going to take you to an artist in southie, a Bug Dust specialist make you blend right in with the people. I will lay the crabs in their bedding myself right across from Hassal's. Earthy can take annexia while we all work Interzone together - capiche?

Code Words:

Bug Dust = Diversions

People = Boston Police

Crabs = Explosives

Hassal's = Federal Reserve Bank

Annexia = HazMat Lab

Interzone = MIT

Figure 2a
Sample of Encrypted E-Mail

Two of the four types of evidence, the e-mail evidence and the security camera photo evidence, were designed to require specific cognitive abilities for successful analysis. Analysis of the e-mails was constrained by limiting participants to a single viewing of numerous code words used in the e-mails. Furthermore, they were not permitted to write down the codes. These restrictions increased the degree to which strong verbal memory was required to analyze the e-mail evidence. Analysis of the security camera photos was made difficult by degrading the quality of the photos and increasing their graininess. This increased the degree to which face-recognition ability was required to analyze the security camera data. Pretest data affirmed that participants' verbal memory (assessed by a paired-associates memory test, described below) and their ability to recognize faces were significantly correlated with their ability to correctly analyze the e-mail and security camera photo evidence ($r = .48$, $p < .001$ and $r = .47$, $p = .013$, respectively). The video surveillance footage and building plan layouts did not require special abilities and were shown in a pretest to be challenging but achievable by most participants.

Figure 2b
Sample Degraded Security Camera Photos

Figure 2c
Screen Shot of Security Camera Footage of Suspect

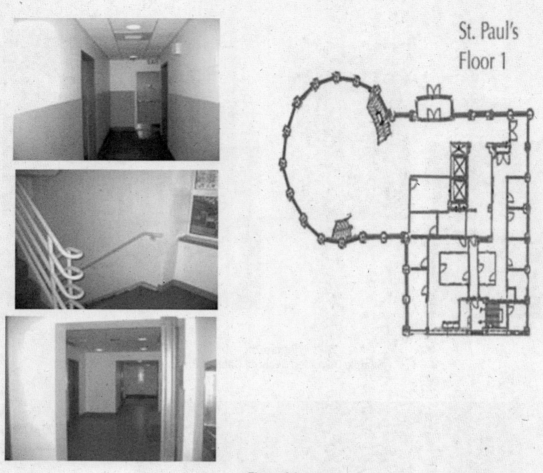

Figure 2d
Sample Photographs and Blueprints Used to Determine
Route Through Building

Measures of Cognitive Abilities

The two cognitive abilities used in selecting experts—verbal memory (VM) and face recognition (FR) ability—were assessed using a paired-associates memory task and the Cambridge Face Memory Test (CFMT; Duchaine & Nakayama, 2006), respectively.

VM. The paired-associates task required respondents to remember the pairings of nouns from a list of 25 pairs. The test was constructed using Paivio, Yuille, and Madigan's (1968) norms for concreteness and imagery of nouns. One hundred nouns were tested, each of which had a concreteness rating less than 2.5 on a scale from 1 (most abstract) to 7 (most concrete).

All nouns tested had frequency ratings higher than 3 per million. We used these words to create two 25-item lists of pairs, and also used latent semantic analysis matrices to minimize the semantic relatedness of cues and targets in each list (Howard & Kahana, 2002). The average latent semantic association in List 1 was .078; for List 2 it was .086.

The paired-associates lists were pretested online by 127 participants. Performance on the two lists was significantly correlated ($r = .67$, $p < .001$). List 1, which was slightly more difficult than List 2 ($M = .49$, $SD = .22$; and $M = .58$, $SD = .26$, respectively), was chosen for use in screening participants.

FR. The CFMT requires respondents to examine a set of target faces and then to recognize the targets among sets of distracter faces of increasing graininess. Although the present implementation of the test was adapted for online use using Psyscope-FL, all stimuli and timings were identical to those used by Duchaine and Nakayama (2006). The scores of the 127 pretest participants ($M = .77$, $SD = .14$) were comparable to those previously obtained by Duchaine and Nakayama.

Screening and selection. We developed eligibility criteria for participation in the experimental study based on the performance of the 127 pretest participants and applied them to the 1,692 individuals who were screened. Excellent performance was set at the 90th percentile (FR score > .93, VM score > .76); good performance was set as between the 66th and the 33rd percentiles (.71 < FR score < .85, .32 < VM score < .52); and fair performance was set as below the 33rd percentile (FR score < .71, VM score < .32). Performance falling between the 66th and 90th percentiles was considered null, and those participants were not invited to the laboratory for the team portion of the study.

Respondents were eligible for the experimental portion of the study as nonexperts if they received either a fair or good score on both tasks. Participants falling between the 66th and 90th percentiles were considered null and excluded in order to maximize the ability distinction between experts and nonexperts. Those who received an excellent score on one task and a fair or good score on the other task were considered experts in the domain in which they received the excellent score. Of the 1,692 people completing the screening, 112 (6.6%) qualified as FR experts, 120 (7%) as VM experts, and 789 (47%) as nonexperts. Among the remaining 671 respondents, 37 (2%) received excellent scores on both tasks, and the rest (37%) had a score on either or both tasks that fell between good and excellent and were not invited to participate in the experiment.

Experimental Conditions and Procedure

The experiment was conducted using a 2 × 2 design, with expertise composition (special ability or average ability) crossed by collaborative planning (planning intervention or no planning intervention). We manipulated team expertise composition by constructing either (a) special ability teams consisting of one VM expert, one FR expert, and two nonexperts, or (b) average-ability teams consisting of four nonexperts.

Collaborative planning was manipulated by either (a) requiring teams to discuss explicitly who would be responsible for which type of evidence, and to plan how they would integrate the various types of evidence to determine who the terrorists were and what they were planning, or (b) allowing members to launch immediately into their work on the task. Specifically, teams receiving the collaborative planning intervention were given a worksheet that delineated the steps of the planning exercise, and the investigator started a 10-min QuickTime presentation that guided the teams through those steps. The exercise required members to collectively review the types of evidence they were provided, relate the evidence to components of the problem solution (e.g., suspects, location, or plot), review member abilities and their relationship to the types of analyses that were involved, and then plan their approach to their analysis. Completion of the exercise occurred during the team's work time; thus, these teams had 10 min less than others to spend on the task itself.

Forty-one teams were assigned to the four experimental conditions as follows: 20 teams received the collaborative planning intervention (10 special ability, 10 average ability), and 21 teams received no intervention (10 special ability, 11 average ability).

Once all team members had arrived at the laboratory, they were shown a 6-min QuickTime presentation describing the terrorist scenario, the evidence that was available, and suggestions about how they might use their time (specifically, 30 min for organization and individual evidence analysis followed by 15 min for discussion and integration). The investigator then gave each member of the team his or her personal ability report based on the online screening. Participants learned whether they were fair, good, or excellent for each of the two key abilities—word-pair memory and FR ability. Teams were encouraged to share their scores with each other in determining how to divide up their work, at which time the expert members (when present) were revealed. All teams correctly assigned expert members to the appropriate roles.

Teams were given time warnings when 15 min and 5 min remained. When time had elapsed, the investigator collected the answer sheet from the team and gave them a postsession questionnaire to complete. They then were debriefed, thanked, and dismissed.

Outcome Measures

Performance. Each team was given a single score for its final solution to the plot. This score combined a suspect score, a building score, and a plot score. The suspect score was the number of suspects the team correctly identified as terrorists. The building score was whether the team correctly identified the building that was the suspects' target. Teams were given full credit for selecting the target building and half credit for selecting the building that suspects visited and discussed in the e-mails but were using as a decoy for the real target. The plot score was a weighted total of the correct plot elements the team identified. Pretests indicated that the plot elements varied in difficulty due to the number of times they were mentioned in the e-mail and the number of code words needing translation in discerning their details. In analysis, these plot elements were weighted for the difficulty of their determination as follows. Three easy-to-detect elements were assigned a weight of 1.0, three moderately difficult plot elements were assigned a weight of 2.0, three hard-to-detect plot elements were assigned a weight of 3.0, and four commonly but incorrectly identified plot elements were given a weight of $-.75$. Two judges independently read and scored the plot descriptions for each team; the interrater reliability of the judges' ratings was .98. The few discrepancies in their evaluations were discussed and resolved. The suspect, building, and plot scores were then z scored and summed to form the overall correctness score.

Table 1 Mean Performance Scores by Condition

Condition		Performance	Information Integration
No experts/no planning	M	-0.02_b	4.91_a
	SD	2.37	2.43
No experts/planning	M	0.04_b	$5.20_{a,b}$
	SD	2.13	1.93
Experts/no planning	M	-0.80_a	$4.40a$
	SD	2.03	1.26
Experts/planning	M	1.04_c	6.60_b
	SD	2.47	2.12
Total	M	0.00	5.14
	SD	2.18	2.06

Note: Means in the same column that do not share subscripts differ at *p* <.05, one-tailed.

Information integration. The information integration score assessed whether a team's answer was internally consistent. Teams were given credit for integration by selecting suspects that had appeared in the security camera photos at the building the team selected as the target, regardless of whether the suspects or target selected were part of the correct solution. Similarly, they were given credit for the number of plot elements they listed that were consistent with their selected building target. Because these elements of the solution were typically determined by different team members, integration of these solutions indicates integration of the work of the team. The suspect and plot-consistency scores were standardized and combined to form the information integration measure.

Results

Hypothesis 1 states that the interaction of team expertise composition and collaborative planning would jointly control more variance in performance than expertise composition alone. Table 1 displays standard deviations and comparisons of means by condition, and Table 2 displays the results of regression analyses. The results support Hypothesis 1. The difference between the effect sizes for team composition and those for the interaction of composition and collaborative planning on performance is statistically significant ($\beta = -.57$ for team composition vs. $\beta = .87$ for the interaction); $t(38) = 11.68$, $p <.0001$, $d = 3.79$.

Hypothesis 2, which predicts that the interaction of team expertise composition and collaborative planning would control more variance in performance than collaborative planning alone, was also supported. The effects of collaborative planning and the effects of the interaction of expertise and planning are significantly different ($\beta = -.38$ for collaborative planning vs. $\beta = .87$ for the interaction); $t(38) = 10.84$, $p <.0001$, $d = 3.52$.

Table 2 Results of Regression Analyses for Team Performance

| | Team Performance | | | |
| | Step 1 | | Step 2 | |
	β	t	β	t
Expertise composition	−.38	−0.77	−.10	−0.28
Collaboration	−.57	−1.15	−.15	−0.40
Expertise × Collaboration	.87	1.78*	.14	.27
Information Integration			.72	5.69***
R^2	.08		.52	
F	1.12		9.64	
ΔR^2			.44***	

*$p <.10$. ***$p <.01$.

Finally, there is support for the third hypothesis, which predicts that information integration will mediate the effects of the interaction of expertise and planning on performance. As discussed above, the interaction of composition and collaborative planning significantly predicts performance. Information integration also significantly predicts performance ($\beta = .72$), and when the two together are used to predict performance, the effect of the interaction of composition and collaborative planning decreases significantly ($\beta = .14$). A Sobel test indicates that the change in β is significant with the addition of the mediator ($Z = 2.05$, $p = .04$), confirming the presence of a mediated effect. Examination of team social interaction further suggests how teams went about effectively integrating information. Teams that structured their search by solving the plot location first (the lowest variability, highest reliability element) performed significantly better than those that did not, $t(38) = 3.35$, $p = .002$, and those receiving a collaborative planning intervention were significantly more likely to structure their search in this way: 40% of intervention (confidence interval [CI]: 19%, 64%) versus 14% of nonintervention (CI: 3%, 36%), $\chi2(df = 1, n = 41) = 3.45$, $p = .03$, one-tailed.

Conclusion and Discussion

These findings suggest that team analytic work is accomplished most effectively when teams include task-relevant experts and the team explicitly explores strategies for coordinating and integrating members' work.

Prior work has examined the importance of team composition. We know that functional diversity is important, and that teams with relevant functional diversity generally outperform teams that lack such diversity (Dahlin et al., 2005; Thomas-Hunt et al., 2003). We also know that teams of specialists can fail to share information effectively when they lack individuals with sufficient personal breadth to translate between members (Bunderson & Sutcliffe, 2002). Because it is not always possible to include members with the necessary intrapersonal diversity, we must also consider ways that teams can help themselves to create the right bridges through collaborative planning. However, existing research has shown that such planning rarely happens in the absence of a leadership or instructional intervention (Hackman et al., 1976; Wittenbaum et al., 1998). The present findings affirm that conclusion and further suggest that such interventions are especially important for teams including expert members. Teams including experts that did not receive the collaborative planning intervention performed worse than other teams, raising the perverse possibility that the presence of expert members may actually decrease team effectiveness if members are not helped to use the experts' special talents. Because analytic teams almost always consist of members who bring a diversity of expertise and experience to the work, further research on the factors that can increase such teams' ability to recognize and use well these resources is needed.

One of the benefits of collaborative planning, we found, was that it resulted in members more effectively integrating information. For many analytic tasks, resolution of uncertainty about certain questions early in the analytic process radically constrains the scope of what must be dealt with subsequently—and thereby reduces considerably analysts' data processing load. If, for example, antiterrorism analysts can determine the specific geographical area in which a terrorist activity is being planned, then they can focus mainly on data relevant to that area and not spread their analytic resources across all possible areas. Structuring analysis in this way is particularly valuable for analyses conducted by teams, because team analytic tasks almost always are broader in scope than those assigned to individuals, and therefore pose a greater risk that analysts will be overwhelmed by the sheer quantity of the information to be processed. We found that teams that conducted a structured search through the available evidence, which in almost all cases were those that had received the collaborative planning intervention, did indeed perform better than those that gave the same priority to all aspects of the overall task in the early stages of their work. This finding is significant for the current task, as the piece of information that the analyses needed to be structured around and subordinated to was held by a nonexpert member of the team. We found that expert teams not receiving a collaborative planning intervention helping them to weight member inputs appropriately were less likely to integrate their information effectively in this kind of situation.

In summary, there appear to be two important benefits of the collaborative planning intervention. The first benefit of the intervention is to increase members' awareness of their teammates' task-relevant expertise and experience, and thereby to increase the team's chances of fully using members' contributions. The second benefit is to increase the degree to which all members, as a consequence of working through the steps in the intervention together, come to appropriately structure their work and weight their expertise such that all members can contribute to the team's collective task. Further research on these secondary effects of strategy-planning interventions could both increase basic understanding of work team processes and be of considerable practical use in guiding those who create and lead task-performing teams.

Notes

1. The lists were shown for 6 s first in a learning phase, followed by a 10-min distracter task, followed by the four alternative multiple-choice recognition trials for the words. List 1 was always completed first so that any interference would not vary across participants. Word pairs were shown in a random order that was fixed across participants. Each target word appeared four times—once as the correct choice and three times as a distracter. Thus, the task was very difficult; chance performance was 25%.

2. The weight for incorrect elements was devised so that it perfectly balanced with the score that teams could receive for the three easiest plot elements, which made it possible to distinguish between teams that were indiscriminately writing down everything they could think of from those who were carefully filtering all of the information.

REFERENCES

Bazerman, M. (2006). Climate change as a predictable surprise. *Climate Change, 77*, 170-193.

Beersma, B., Hollenbeck, J. R., Humphrey, S. E., Moon, H., Conlon, D. E., & Ilgen, D. R. (2003). Cooperation, competition, and team performance: Toward a contingency approach. *Academy of Management Journal, 46*, 572-590.

Bottger, P. C., & Yetton, P. W. (1988). An integration of process and decision scheme explanations of group problem solving performance. *Organizational Behavior and Human Decision Processes, 42*, 234-249.

Bunderson, J. S. (2003). Recognizing and utilizing expertise in work groups: A status characteristics perspective. *Administrative Science Quarterly, 48*, 557-591.

Bunderson, J. S., & Sutcliffe, K. M. (2002). Comparing alternative conceptualizations of functional diversity in management teams: Process and performance effects. *Academy of Management Journal, 45*, 875-893.

Cabeza, R., & Nyberg, L. (2000). Imaging cognition II: An empirical review of 275 PET and FMRI studies. *Journal of Cognitive Neuroscience, 12*, 1-47.

Caruso, H. M., & Woolley, A. W. (in press). Manifesting the value of cognitive diversity in teams: The critical role of emergent interdependence. In M. A. Neale, E. Mannix, & K. Phillips (Eds.), *Research on managing groups and teams: Groups & diversity* (Vol. 9) Oxford, UK: Elsevier Science Press.

Chugh, D., & Bazerman, M. H. (2007). Bounded awareness: What you fail to see can hurt you. *Mind and Society, 6*, 1-18.

Cronin, M. A., & Weingart, L. R. (2007). Representational gaps, information processing, and conflict in functionally diverse teams. *Academy of Management Review, 32*, 761-773.

Dahlin, K. B., Weingart, L. R., & Hinds, P. J. (2005). Team diversity and information use. *Academy of Management Journal, 48*, 1107-1123.

Davis, J. H. (1996). Group decision making and quantitative judgments: A consensus model. In E. Witte & J. H. Davis (Eds.), *Understanding group behavior: Consensual action by small groups* (Vol. 1, pp. 35-59). Mahwah, NJ: Lawrence Erlbaum.

Devine, D. J. (1999). Effects of cognitive ability, task knowledge, information sharing, and conflict on group decision-making effectiveness. *Small Group Research, 30*, 608-634.

Duchaine, B., & Nakayama, K. (2006). The Cambridge Face Memory Test: Results for neurologically intact individuals and an investigation of its validity using inverted face stimuli and prosopagnosic participants. *Neuropsychologia, 44*, 576-585.

Ellis, A. P. J., Hollenbeck, J. R., Ilgen, D. R., Porter, C. O., West, B. J., & Moon, H. (2003). Team learning: Collectively connecting the dots. *Journal of Applied Psychology, 88*, 821-835.

Ericsson, K. A. (2005). Recent advances in expertise research: A commentary on the contributions to the special issue. *Applied Cognitive Psychology, 19*, 233-241.

Ericsson, K. A., & Lehmann, A. C. (1996). Expert and exceptional performance: Evidence of maximal adaptation to task constraints. *Annual Review of Psychology, 47*, 273-305.

Faraj, S., & Sproull, L. (2000). Coordinating expertise in software development teams. *Management Science, 46*, 1554-1568.

Fiore, S. M., & Schooler, J. W. (2004). Process mapping and shared cognition: Teamwork and the development of shared problem models. In E. Salas & S. M. Fiore (Eds.), *Team cognition: Understanding the factors that drive process and performance* (pp. 133-152). Washington, DC: American Psychological Association.

Gurtner, A., Tschan, F., Semmer, N. K., & Nagele, C. (2007). Getting groups to develop good strategies: Effects of reflexivity interventions on team process, team performance, and shared mental models. *Organizational Behavior and Human Decision Processes, 102*, 127-142.

Hackman, J. R., Brousseau, K. R., & Weiss, J. A. (1976). The interaction of task design and group performance strategies in determining group effectiveness. *Organizational Behavior and Human Decision Processes, 16*, 350-365.

Hackman, J. R., & Morris, C. G. (1983). Group tasks, group interaction process, and group performance effectiveness. In H. H. Blumberg, A. P. Hare, V. Kent, & M. Davies (Eds.), *Small groups and social interaction* (Vol. 1, pp. 331-345. Chichester, UK: Wiley.

Hackman, J. R., & O'Connor, M. (2004). *What makes for a great analytic team? Individual vs. Team approaches to intelligence analysis*. Washington, DC: Intelligence Science Board, Office of the Director of Central Intelligence.

Hackman, J. R., & Wageman, R. (2005). A theory of team coaching. *Academy of Management Review, 30*, 269-287.

Henry, R. A. (1995). Improving group judgment accuracy: Information sharing and determining the best member. *Organizational Behavior and Human Decision Processes, 62*, 190-197.

Heuer, R. J., Jr. (1999). *Psychology of intelligence analysis*. Washington, DC: Government Printing Office.

Howard, M. W., & Kahana, M. J. (2002). When does semantic similarity help episodic retrieval? *Journal of Memory and Language, 46*, 85-98.

Jehn, K. A., Northcraft, G. B., & Neale, M. A. (1999). Why differences make a difference: A field study of diversity, conflict, and performance in workgroups. *Administrative Science Quarterly, 44*, 741-763.

Kerr, N. L., & Tindale, S. R. (2004). Group performance and decision making. *Annual Review of Psychology, 55*, 623-655.

Kosslyn, S. M. (1994). *Image and brain: The resolution of the imagery debate*. Cambridge, MA: MIT Press.

Kozhevnikov, M., Kosslyn, S. M., & Shephard, J. (2005). Spatial versus object visualizers: A new characterization of visual cognitive style. *Memory & Cognition, 33*, 710-726.

LePine, J. A. (2005). Adaptation of teams in response to unforeseen change: Effects of goal difficulty and team composition in terms of cognitive ability and goal orientation. *Journal of Applied Psychology, 90*, 1153-1167.

Littlepage, G., Robison, W., & Reddington, K. (1997). Effects of task experience and group experience on group performance, member ability, and recognition of expertise. *Organizational Behavior and Human Decision Processes, 69*, 133-147.

Mintzberg, H., Raisinghani, D., & Theoret, A. (1976). The structure of "unstructured" Decision processes. *Administrative Science Quarterly, 21*, 246-275.

Moreland, R. L., & Levine, J. M. (1992). Problem identification by groups. In S. Worchel, W. Wood, & J. A. Simpson (Eds.), *Group process and productivity* (pp. 17-47). Newbury Park, CA: Sage.

Neuman, G. A., Wagner, S. H., & Christiansen, N. D. (1999). The relationship between work-team personality composition and the job performance of teams. *Group & Organization Management, 24*, 28-45.

Okhuysen, G. A. (2001). Structuring change: Familiarity and formal interventions in problem-solving groups. *Academy of Management Journal, 40*, 794-808.

Okhuysen, G. A., & Eisenhardt, K. M. (2002). Integrating knowledge in groups: How formal interventions enable flexibility. *Organization Science, 13*, 370-386.

Paivio, A., Yuille, J. C., & Madigan, S. A. (1968). Concreteness, imagery, and meaningfulness values for 925 nouns. *Journal of Experimental Psychology Monograph Supplement, 76*(No. 1, Part 2), 1-25.

Patel, V. L., Groen, G. J., & Arocha, J. F. (1990). Medical expertise as a function of task difficulty. *Memory & Cognition, 18*, 394-406.

Stasser, G., Stewart, D. D., & Wittenbaum, G. M. (1995). Expert roles and information exchange during discussion: The importance of knowing who knows what. *Journal of Experimental Social Psychology, 31*, 244-265.

Thomas-Hunt, M. C., Ogden, T. Y., & Neale, M. A. (2003). Who's really sharing? Effects of social and expert status on knowledge exchange within groups. *Management Science, 49*, 464-477.

Volmer, J. (2006). *Individual expertise and team performance: Results of three empirical studies.* Unpublished doctoral dissertation, Technischen Universität Carolo-Wilhelmina in Braunschweig, Braunschweig, Germany.

Wittenbaum, G. M., Vaughan, S. I., & Stasser, G. (1998). Coordination in task-performing groups. In R. S. Tindale, L. Heath, J. Edwards, E. J. Posavac, F. B. Bryant, Y. Suarez-Balcazar, E. Henderson-King, & J. Myers (Eds.), *Theory and research on small groups* (pp. 177-205). New York: Plenum.

Woolley, A. W. (1998). Effects of intervention type and timing on group task performance. Journal of *Applied Behavioral Science, 34*, 30-46.

Woolley, A. W., Hackman, J. R., Jerde, T. J., Chabris, C. F., Bennett, S. L., & Kosslyn, S. M. (2007). Using brain-based measures to compose teams: How individual capabilities and team collaboration strategies jointly shape performance. *Social Neuroscience, 2*, 96-105.

Yen, J., Fan, X., Sun, S., Hanratty, T., & Dumer, J. (2006). Agents with shared mental models for enhanced team decision making. *Decision Support Systems, 41*, 634-653.

Anita Williams Woolley is a postdoctoral fellow at Harvard University. She received her PhD in organizational behavior from Harvard University. Her research focuses on issues that affect collaborative analysis and task performance in teams.

Margaret E. Gerbasi is a graduate student in social psychology at Princeton University. She received her AB in psychology from Princeton University in 2004. Her research interests include the relationship between self-interest and other-interest and the interaction of norms and power structures.

Christopher F. Chabris is an assistant professor of psychology at Union College. He received his PhD in psychology and his AB in computer science, both from Harvard University. His research focuses on the mechanisms, causes, and consequences of individual differences in cognition and decision making.

Stephen M. Kosslyn is chair and John Lindsley Professor of Psychology at Harvard University and an associate psychologist in the Department of Neurology at the Massachusetts General Hospital. He received his PhD in psychology from Stanford University. His research focuses primarily on the nature of visual mental imagery, visual perception, and visual communication.

J. Richard Hackman is Edgar Pierce Professor of Social and Organizational Psychology at Harvard University. He conducts research on a variety of topics in social and organizational psychology, including team dynamics and performance, leadership effectiveness, and the design of self-managing organizational units.

The Nature and Predictors of the Trajectory of Change in Marital Quality for Husbands and Wives Over the First 10 Years of Marriage

At some point in their lives, most people enjoy an intimate romantic relationship, many get married, and some get divorced. How do intimate relationships progress over time? Is there a typical developmental pattern? Clearly, all marriages are different and cannot be squeezed into single mold. But recent studies show that some general patterns do emerge when large numbers of marital partners are periodically surveyed about their satisfaction. Recently, Kurdek (1999) reported on a longitudinal study of married couples in which he measured each partner's level of satisfaction every year for ten years. How did he measure satisfaction and what did he find? Is marriage an extended honeymoon? Do married couples in general become more satisfied over time, or less satisfied, or is there an uneven pattern of change? In the following article, Kurdek sought to answer these questions while, at the same time, noting that everyone is different and that no two marriages are alike.

THE NATURE AND PREDICTORS OF THE TRAJECTORY OF CHANGE IN MARITAL QUALITY FOR HUSBANDS AND WIVES OVER THE FIRST 10 YEARS OF MARRIAGE[*]

Lawrence A. Kurdek

Wright State University

Four parameters of the trajectory of change in marital quality (initial status as well as linear, quadratic, and cubic patterns of change) were estimated for husbands and wives over the first 10 years of marriage (n = 522 couples at Year 1 and 93 couples at Year 10). Both husbands and wives started their trajectories of change at fairly high levels of marital quality and showed a cubic pattern of change such that marital quality declined fairly rapidly in the early years of marriage, stabilized, and then declined again. Whereas individual-differences variables predicted the initial status of the trajectory, husbands and wives living with only their biological children showed a steeper decline in marital quality than husbands and wives living without children or stepchildren.

I thank the couples who participated in this study and Steve Raudenbush for answering questions about hierarchical linear modeling.

Marriage is usually described in developmental literature as a normative personal life event that occurs in early adulthood (e.g., Gould, 1978; Levinson, Darrow, Klein, Levinson, & McKee, 1978; G. E.

[*] Lawrence A. Kurdek, "The Nature and Predictors of the Trajectory of Change in Marital Quality for Husbands and Wives Over the First 10 Years of Marriage," Developmental Psychology, Vol. 35, No. 5, pp. 1283-1296. Copyright (c) 1999 by the American Psychological Association. Reproduced with permission.
 Correspondence concerning this article should be addressed to Lawrence A. Kurdek, Department of Psychology, Wright State University, Dayton, Ohio 45435-0001. Electronic mail may be sent to larry.kurdek@wright.edu.

Vaillant, 1977) and influences the nature of subsequent developmental tasks (e.g., Havighurst, 1972). The present study focuses on the complementary view that marriage itself can be viewed from a developmental perspective. For example, Kovacs (1983) regarded marriage not as a single life event but as a set of stages in which spouses attempt to achieve a balance between dependence and autonomy as they negotiate issues of control, power, and authority.

Despite evidence that approximately 90% of both men and women in the United States are married by the age of 45 (United States Bureau of the Census, 1997), that marital happiness is centrally important for adults' overall well-being (Glenn & Weaver, 1981), that there is substantial variability in the happiness of those who are in durable marriages (Heaton & Albrecht, 1991), and that nearly half of all marriages end in divorce (National Center for Health Statistics, 1991), there is currently a lack of descriptive information regarding both how marital quality changes and the variables that affect the pattern of this change.

Karney and Bradbury (1995) noted that one reason for the lack of this information is that few researchers have recruited both spouses from newly wed couples and repeatedly assessed their appraisals of marital quality over time with the same measure. These authors further noted that in the few studies that met these criteria, researchers usually studied change in marital quality by assessing differences in the means of each spouse's marital quality score over time. For example, MacDermid, Huston, and McHale (1990) found that husbands and wives reported equivalent declines in mean quality of satisfaction and love over three assessments spanning the first 2.5 years of marriage.

Karney and Bradbury (1997) argued that more precise information about the nature of change in marital quality can be obtained by focusing not on average levels of marital quality over time but rather on the *trajectory of change* in marital quality over time. Derived from growth curve analyses of longitudinal data collected over more than two time points, this trajectory includes information regarding the level of marital quality at the start of the marriage (e.g., high) and—depending on how many assessments are available—the number of bends or changes in the curve over time (see Cohen & Cohen, 1983, p. 233).

If data are available from at least four assessments, then one can determine whether the growth function that best describes the pattern of change in marital quality is linear, quadratic, or cubic. For a linear function, the rate of change is the same from assessment to assessment, and there are no bends in the growth curve. For a quadratic function, there is one phase of accelerated change resulting in one bend in the growth curve (e.g., marital quality may decline over the early years of marriage and then level off). Finally, for a cubic function, there are two phases of accelerated change resulting in two bends in the growth curve (e.g., marital quality may decline over the early years of marriage, level off, and then decline again).

In what appears to be the only report of findings from growth curve analyses of longitudinal data from newly wed couples, Karney and Bradbury (1997) obtained global assessments of marital quality from 54 pairs of first-married spouses up to eight times over the first 4 years of marriage. They found that a linear rather than a quadratic growth function fit the pattern of change in marital quality for both husbands and wives, that husbands and wives showed equivalent rates of linear decline in marital quality, and that husbands' rate of linear decline and wives' rate of linear decline were positively related. The finding that change in marital quality was not accelerated (i.e., that the quadratic growth function was not significant) is noteworthy because it is at odds with accounts that feelings of closeness and passion decline at a fairly rapid pace in the early stages of the relationship (Kovacs, 1983; Sternberg, 1986).

The first purpose of this study was to build on Karney and Bradbury's (1997) evidence regarding the normative pattern of change in marital quality for newlywed couples in two ways. First, newly wed spouses in remarriages after divorce as well as newly wed spouses in first marriages were assessed. The inclusion of remarried spouses is important because reports have shown that only 54% of all current marriages involve both spouses in first marriages (Clarke, 1995b). Second, spouses were assessed over the first 10 years of marriage rather than over only the first 4 years of marriage. The longer time span provided an opportunity to explore whether the growth curve of marital quality for spouses in fairly durable marriages had multiple bends (i.e., conformed to a cubic growth function).

In the current study, marital quality was assessed with Spanier's (1976) Dyadic Adjustment Scale, one of the most widely used measures in the literature on marital quality. Although this measure includes subscores regarding the level of agreement between partners on important issues, amount of shared activity, degree of expressed affection, and level of satisfaction with the relationship, these four subscores tend to be so highly intercorrelated that they conform to a single second-order factor (Sabourin, Lussier, Laplante, & Wright, 1991). Consequently, only the total score was used.

For each spouse, two questions regarding the growth curve for marital quality were of interest: (a) At what level of marital quality does the growth curve start, and (b) what is the growth function—linear (equal rates of change), quadratic (one bend or phase of accelerated change), or cubic (two bends or phases of accelerated change)—that best describes the pattern of change? On the basis of Karney and Bradbury's (1997) findings as well as the commonly held view that marriages begin at peak levels of positivity, the trajectory of change in marital quality for each spouse was expected to start at a high level of marital quality. Despite Karney and Bradbury's failure to obtain evidence of accelerated change, there was reason to expect one or even two phases of accelerated change. Consonant with a "honeymoon-is-over" effect (Kovacs, 1983; Sternberg, 1986), the decline in marital quality might be especially steep over the early years of the marriage and then stabilize. Further, consonant with a "7-year-itch" effect (Kovacs, 1983) as well as evidence that the median duration of marriage for divorcing couples is about 7 years (Clarke, 1995a), one might also expect that a second phase of accelerated change follows the period of stabilization.

In addition to determining which growth function best describes the pattern of change in marital quality, a growth curve analysis of longitudinal data on marital quality also provides a way to assess whether a variable that is a risk factor for marital distress exerts its deleterious effect on marital quality by being linked to low levels of marital quality at the start of the marriage or to a pattern of deterioration in marital quality over time. In their study of newly wed couples, Karney and Bradbury (1997) found that two risk factors assessed at the beginning of the marriage—psychological distress (neuroticism) and problematic conflict resolution styles—were related differently to the parameters of the growth trajectory. High levels of psychological distress predicted that spouses would begin the trajectory at low levels of marital quality, whereas frequent negative conflict resolution styles predicted declines in marital quality.

The second purpose of this study was to build on Karney and Bradbury's (1997) evidence regarding the factors that explained variability in each spouse's trajectory of change in marital quality. Of particular interest was whether three sets of variables predicted any of the four parameters of the trajectory of interest here—initial status as well as a linear, quadratic, or cubic pattern of change. The first set of predictor variables included information about each spouse's divorce history. This information was of interest because the probability of marital distress is high for spouses who have experienced multiple divorces (Clarke, 1995a; Wilson & Clarke, 1992). Consequently, spouses were categorized as having experienced no divorce (the reference group), one divorce, or multiple divorces. If people who remarry after multiple divorces are at risk for marital distress because they are quick to identify marital problems and have low thresholds for dealing with marital distress (Brody, Neubaum, & Forehand, 1988), then, compared with people who have not been divorced, they (as well as their spouses) may be especially likely to show early accelerated declines in marital quality rather than merely low levels of marital quality at the start of the marriage.

The second set of predictor variables included information regarding either the presence of residential stepchildren at the start of the marriage or the presence of any children born during the course of the marriage. The presence of residential stepchildren was relevant because spouses in stepfamilies have been thought to have unique sources of stress related to ill-defined social and legal roles for stepparents, the prevalence of myths holding the stepfamily to unachievable standards, and difficulties related to interacting with complex family systems that include former spouses and their kin (Ganong & Coleman, 1994).

The presence of biological children born during the course of the marriage was of interest because there is conflicting evidence regarding how marital quality changes over the course of the family life cycle. Data from retrospective reports (e.g., Burr, 1970) support the view that marital quality follows a U-shaped pattern such that marital quality is lowest when children are present, whereas data from prospective reports show that parents and nonparents do not differ in how marital quality changes over time (Karney & Bradbury, 1997; MacDermid et al., 1990; C. O. Vaillant & Vaillant, 1993).

In the present study, couples were divided into three child-related groups: couples in which husbands and wives never lived with either children or stepchildren over the course of the study (the reference group); couples in which husbands lived with only the children of their wives from a previous marriage (i.e., residential stepfather families); and couples in which husbands and wives lived with only their own biological offspring at some point during the study. Other child-status groups (e.g., couples with residential stepmothers and couples in which spouses lived with stepchildren and their own biological children) were too few in number to be included.

It seemed plausible that husbands with stepchildren might report lower initial levels of marital quality than those without children or stepchildren because the cost of having stepchildren is likely to be known at the beginning of the marriage (Ganong & Coleman, 1994). Alternatively, if interactions with stepchildren become increasingly negative as the stepchildren grow older and negotiate issues regarding personal autonomy (Hetherington & Clingempeel, 1992), then husbands who live with stepchildren may be especially likely to show declines in marital quality over time. Because previous findings regarding how a couple's own biological children affect marital quality are inconsistent, no hypotheses on this issue were advanced.

The final set of predictor variables included individual-differences variables known to be linked, either concurrently or prospectively, to marital quality. Studies of concurrent linkages have shown that partners with low evaluations of their spouses' dependability (Rempel, Holmes, & Zanna, 1985), strong dysfunctional beliefs about relationships (e.g., disagreements are destructive; Eidelson & Epstein, 1982), low expressiveness (or "femininity"; Kurdek & Schmitt, 1986a), or high levels of psychological distress (Karney, Bradbury, Fincham, & Sullivan, 1994) tend to report low marital quality. Longitudinal studies indicate that wives with high levels of instrumentality (or "masculinity") tend to report decreases in marital satisfaction (Bradbury, Campbell, & Fincham, 1995).

Of interest here was whether values for these five individual-differences variables assessed at the beginning of the marriage showed intraspouse as well as cross-spouse relations to the four elements of each spouse's own trajectory of change in marital quality. That is, were husbands' own individual-differences variables as well as those of their wives linked to where each one began the trajectory as well as to each one's rate of linear, curvilinear, and cubic change? Although researchers have rarely examined intraspouse and cross-spouse effects, two studies are relevant here.

In the first study, Karney and Bradbury (1997) found that high levels of psychological distress (neuroticism) at the start of the marriage for both husbands and wives were linked to husbands' beginning the trajectory at low levels of marital quality. However, no such links were obtained for wives, and psychological distress was not related to the rate of linear change for either spouse. In the second study, Bradbury et al. (1995) found that wives' marital satisfaction tended to decline to the extent that they were high in instrumentality and that their husbands were low in both instrumentality and expressiveness. Because there was no compelling reason for these linkages to have occurred for only one spouse and because of the scarcity of information regarding what personality variables at the start of the marriage predict change in marital quality, only a general hypothesis was advanced. This was that husbands' and wives' problematic levels of the individual-differences variables assessed at the start of the marriage (i.e., low dependability of spouse, strong dysfunctional beliefs, high instrumentality, low expressiveness, and high psychological distress) would be linked to the low initial status of each one's own trajectory of change in marital quality.

METHOD

Participants

Participants were recruited from the lists of marriage licenses published in the *Dayton Daily News* from May 1986 through January 1988. Generally, licenses appeared 1 month after the marriage. Each couple was sent a letter that described the focus of the study as the identification of factors contributing to marital happiness. Although the initial letter indicated that the study would involve the completion of five annual mail surveys, there was sufficient interest in the study to extend it another 5 years. If both spouses were interested in participating in the study, they returned information regarding names and address in a postage-paid envelope. Of the 7,899 couples who received the letter, 1,407 indicated an interest in the study. This response rate of 18% is similar to those obtained from other studies that recruited participants from public records (e.g., 18% by Davila, Bradbury, Cohan, & Tochluk, 1997; and 17% by Spanier, 1976).

Completed surveys were returned by 538 couples at Year 1. This return rate of 38% is similar to the rate of 33% obtained by Kurdek and Schmitt (1986b) in a study that involved a survey of similar length but that required the anonymous participation of both partners. Because of their small numbers, couples in which a spouse was remarried after the death of a previous spouse and couples in which a spouse died in the course of the study were not included, leaving the base sample at Year 1 at 522 couples.

For these couples, the mean age at Year 1 was 29.09 years ($SD = 7.54$) for husbands and 27.05 years ($SD = 6.72$) for wives, and the mean length of cohabitation was 0.74 years ($SD = 1.06$). Nearly all of the husbands (95%) and wives (95%) were White. The modal level of education for each spouse was the completion of a baccalaureate degree (32% of husbands and 33% of wives), and most husbands (92%) and wives (79%) were employed. There were two modal levels of personal annual income for husbands: 15% earned between \$15,000 and \$19,999, and another 15% earned between \$25,000 and \$29,999. Twenty-three percent of the wives earned less than \$5,000. The numbers of husbands with 0, 1, and multiple divorces were 339, 132, and 51, respectively, whereas the corresponding numbers for wives were 334, 131, and 57. The numbers of couples with no children, only biological children born after the marriage, and only residential stepchildren in stepfather families were 215, 140, and 77, respectively. Ninety couples did not belong to any of these child-status categories because they were members of fairly small subgroups (e.g., couples who experienced a premarital pregnancy or couples who had both biological children and stepchildren).

Procedure

At each annual assessment (Year 1 through Year 10), couples were mailed two identical surveys. The Year 1 survey included measures of background information, divorce history, child-related status, individual-differences variables, and marital quality. Follow-up surveys included measures of child-related status and marital quality. Spouses were directed to complete their surveys privately and not to discuss their answers until the surveys had been completed and returned in separate postage-paid envelopes. However, no checks were made to ensure that these directions were followed.

For the follow-up surveys, if completed surveys were not returned by both spouses within a 1-month period after they were mailed, a letter prompting a response was sent. In this letter, spouses also were given an opportunity to indicate whether they had separated or divorced (not distinguished) or to withdraw from the study. Three prompt letters were sent. If no response was received after the third letter, participants were notified that they would not be contacted further (i.e., they were dropped from the study), but they were asked to provide information on couple status (i.e., still living together or separated or divorced). The number of couples at each assessment is presented for each of the four outcome status categories (completed all assessments, separated, withdrew, and dropped) in Table 1. Bias in the sample of couples who completed all 10 assessments is addressed later.

Measure of Background Information at Year 1

Spouses provided information regarding age, gender, race, education (represented by eight intervals ranging from completion of less than seventh grade to the award of a doctorate), annual personal income (represented by 12 intervals ranging from $5,000 or less to $50,000 or more), and the number of months they had lived with their husbands or wives.

Measure of Divorce History at Year 1

Spouses provided information about their divorce history by selecting one of four options: (a) "This is my first marriage," (b) "I have been divorced, and this is my first remarriage," (c) "I have been divorced twice, and this is my second remarriage," or (d) "I have been divorced more than twice, and this is my third or more remarriage." Because only a few of the respondents selected option (d), they were combined with the respondents who selected option (c) to form a single multiple-divorce group.

Table 1

Number of Couples in Each Follow-Up Status

Category by Year of Assessment

Year	Completed all Assessments	Separated	Withdrew	Dropped
1	522	–	–	–
2	392	–	–	–
3	307	21	16	48
4	262	13	6	26
5	230	7	6	19
6	197	6	15	12
7	150	7	29	11
8	130	3	9	8
9	113	1	11	5
10	93	1	7	12

Note. Dashes indicate that values were not computed.

Measure of Child-Related Status at Each Assessment

Spouses were asked to list the first name, the age, and the gender of each child living with them as well as their relationship to each child (e.g., mother or stepfather). From this information, three child-status groups were formed. These included couples in which husbands and wives never lived with either children or stepchildren, couples in which husbands lived with only the children of their wives from a previous marriage, and couples in which husbands and wives lived with only their biological children. Of the 140 couples who lived with only their biological children, the numbers making the transition to parenthood during the course of the first through the ninth assessment were 32, 31, 26, 23, 6, 11, 4, 5, and 2, respectively. The mean number and the mean age of children and stepchildren are presented in Table 2 by year of assessment. It is noteworthy that, on the average, biological children (53% of whom were female) were preschoolers and stepchildren (51% of whom were female) were adolescents.

Measures of Individual-Differences Variables at Year 1

Dependability of spouse Respondents used a 7-point scale ranging from 1 (*strongly disagree*) to 7 (*strongly agree*) to indicate how strongly they agreed with six items from the Dependability subscale of Rempel et al.'s (1985) Trust Scale (e.g., "I have found that my partner is a thoroughly dependable person, especially when it comes to things that are important"). High scores reflected high levels of spousal dependability. Cronbach's alpha for the summed composite score was .70 for husbands and .76 for wives.

Means were 36.81 (SD = 5.07) for husbands and 36.28 (SD = 5.84) for wives. Additional psychometric properties of this score are described by Rempel et al.

Dysfunctional beliefs about relationships Respondents used a 6-point scale ranging from 0 (*very false*) to 5 (*very true*) to indicate how strongly they endorsed 32 beliefs from Eidelson and Epstein's (1982) Relationship Beliefs Inventory that included "disagreement is destructive" (e.g., "I take it as a personal insult when my partner disagrees with an important idea of mine"), "mindreading is expected" (e.g., "I get very upset if my partner does not recognize how I am feeling and I have to tell him/her"), "partners cannot change" (e.g., "My partner does not seem capable of behaving other than he/she does now"), and "sexual perfection is expected" (e.g., "I get upset if I think I have not completely satisfied my partner sexually"). High scores indicated strong dysfunctional beliefs. Cronbach's alpha for the summed composite score was .83 for husbands and .82 for wives. Means were 51.81 (*SD* = 13.51) for husbands and 50.59 (*SD* = 13.73) for wives. Additional psychometric properties of this score are presented by Bradbury and Fincham (1993).

Instrumentality and expressiveness Respondents used a 7-point scale ranging from 1 (*never or almost never true*) to 7 (*always or almost always true*) to describe themselves in terms of instrumentality (11 items; e.g., "assertive, strong personality, dominant") and expressiveness (12 items; e.g., "affectionate, compassionate, eager to soothe hurt feelings"). Items were based on Kurdek's (1987) factor analysis of items from Bem's (1974) Sex Role Inventory (BSRI). High scores indicated high levels of instrumentality and expressiveness. Cronbach's alphas for the summed composite instrumentality and expressiveness scores were .86 and .88, respectively, for husbands and .86 and .87, respectively, for wives. For instrumentality, means were 55.77 (*SD* = 9.46) for husbands and 50.82 (*SD* = 9.98) for wives. For expressiveness, means were 67.46 (*SD* = 8.40) for husbands and 71.67 (*SD* = 7.28) for wives. Relevant information on the psychometric properties of scores derived from the BSRI is provided by Kurdek (1987) as well as by Brems and Johnson (1990).

Psychological distress Respondents used a 5-point scale ranging from 0 (*not at all*) to 4 (*extremely*) to indicate how much discomfort 90 problems from Derogatis's (1983) Symptom Checklist–90–Revised caused them during the past 7 days. Symptoms covered the areas of somatization, obsessions and compulsions, interpersonal sensitivity, depression, anxiety, hostility, phobic anxiety, paranoid ideation, and psychoticism. High scores indicated severe symptoms. Cronbach's alpha for the summed composite score was .97 for husbands and .97 for wives. Means were 41.28 (*SD* = 36.84) for husbands and 45.97 (*SD* = 38.29) for wives. Additional psychometric properties of this score are presented by Derogatis (1983) as well as by Schwarzwald, Weisenberg, and Solomon (1991). For descriptive purposes, correlations between all of the individual-differences scores for husbands and wives are presented in Table 3. Because correlations within spouses and between spouses were not high, each score was retained.

Measure of Marital Quality

At each assessment, marital quality was assessed by the total score from Spanier's (1976) 32-item Dyadic Adjustment Scale, for which high scores reflect high marital quality. Over the 10 assessments, Cronbach's alpha for the summed composite score (maximum value = 151) ranged from .90 to .96 for husbands and from .91 to .95 for wives. Additional psychometric properties of this score are reported by Kurdek (1992).

RESULTS

Bias in the Longitudinal Sample

Although the growth curve analyses used in this study included data from all 522 couples (see later), bias in the sample of couples who completed all 10 assessments was evaluated with a one-way (couple status) multivariate analysis of variance in which the 93 couples with all 10 assessments were compared with the 429 couples with fewer than 10 assessments on three sets of variables from Year 1. The first set included the following 11 demo- graphic variables: husband's age, education, employment status (0 = *unemployed*, 1 = *employed*), income, and number of divorces; wife's age, education, employment status (0 = *unemployed*, 1 = *employed*), income, and number of divorces; and years of cohabitation. The second set included the following 10 individual-differences variables: husband and wife versions of dependability of spouse, relationship beliefs, instrumentality, expressiveness, and psychological distress. Finally, the third set included husband and wife versions of the marital quality score.

The multivariate effect was significant for the set of demographic variables, $F(11, 510) = 5.91, p < .001$. Univariate analyses indicated that relative to husbands who did not complete all assessments, husbands who did had higher levels of education and higher personal annual incomes, $Fs(1, 520) = 39.05$ and 7.34, respectively, $ps < .01$. In addition, relative to wives who did not complete all assessments, wives who did had higher levels of education, $F(1, 520) = 43.14, p < .01$.

Table 2

Mean Number of Children and Stepchildren, Mean Age (in Years) of Children and Stepchildren, and Sample Size (n) by Year of Assessment

	Children			Stepchildren		
Year	Number	Age	n	Number	Age	n
1	–	–	–	1.56	8.84	72
2	1.16	1.03	32	1.55	10.60	40
3	1.10	1.05	52	1.57	13.20	23
4	1.20	1.30	69	1.67	14.33	15
5	1.31	1.23	86	1.73	15.29	11
6	1.51	1.88	81	1.60	15.75	10
7	1.60	2.07	67	1.60	18.13	10
8	1.80	2.42	59	1.71	18.00	7
9	1.81	2.93	57	1.25	17.63	4
10	1.96	3.84	52	1.50	20.75	2

Note. Dashes indicate that values were not computed.

Table 3

Pearson Correlations Between Husband (H) and Wife (W) Year 1 Scores

Score	1	2	3	4	5	6	7	8	9	10
1. H dependability	–									
2. H beliefs	−.33**	–								
3. H instrumentality	.05	−.04	–							
4. H expressiveness	.24**	−.24**	.23**	–						
5. H distress	−.28**	.35**	−.02	−.14**	–					
6. W dependability	.21**	−.19*	−.04	.07	−.19**	–				
7. W beliefs	−.20**	.28**	−.01	−.12**	.12**	−.39**	–			
8. W instrumentality	.00	−.02	.13**	.19**	−.03	.02	−.10*	–		
9. W expressiveness	.11*	−.04	.13**	.10*	.03	.12	−.11*	.11*	–	
10. W distress	−.22**	.16**	.03	−.01	.20**	−.31**	.40**	−.06	−.03	–

Note. $N = 522$; *$p < .05$; ** $p < .01$.

TABLE 4

An Example of the Level 1 Data Setup for One Couple With Scores From the

Dyadic Adjustment Scale (DAS) at Each Year of Assessment

		Husband				Wife			
Code	DAS	Intercept	Linear	Quadratic	Cubic	Intercept	Linear	Quadratic	Cubic
001	110	1	−9	6	−42	0	0	0	0
001	108	1	−7	2	14	0	0	0	0
001	109	1	−5	−1	35	0	0	0	0
001	118	1	−3	−3	31	0	0	0	0
001	117	1	−1	−4	12	0	0	0	0
001	116	1	1	−4	−12	0	0	0	0
001	130	1	3	−3	−31	0	0	0	0
001	118	1	5	−1	−35	0	0	0	0
001	124	1	7	2	−14	0	0	0	0
001	119	1	9	6	42	0	0	0	0
001	111	0	0	0	0	1	−9	6	−42
001	106	0	0	0	0	1	−7	2	14
001	101	0	0	0	0	1	−5	−1	35
001	109	0	0	0	0	1	−3	−3	31
001	104	0	0	0	0	1	−1	−4	12
001	112	0	0	0	0	1	1	−4	−12
001	106	0	0	0	0	1	3	−3	−31
001	113	0	0	0	0	1	5	−1	−35
001	116	0	0	0	0	1	7	2	−14
001	107	0	0	0	0	1	9	6	42

Note. The first 10 DAS scores are from the husband at Year 1 through Year 10, respectively, whereas the second 10 scores are from the wife.

The multivariate effect was also significant for the set of individual-differences variables, $F(10, 511) = 3.77, p < .01$. Univariate analyses indicated that relative to husbands who did not complete all assessments, husbands who did had lower scores regarding dysfunctional beliefs and instrumentality, $Fs(1, 520) = 4.20$ and 5.41, respectively, $ps < .05$, and that relative to wives who did not complete all assessments, wives who did had higher scores for dependability and lower scores for dysfunctional beliefs, expressiveness, and psychological distress, $Fs(1, 500) = 6.39, 15.82, 6.36$, and 5.68, respectively, $ps < .05$. Finally, the multivariate effect for the two marital quality scores was not significant, indicating that the two groups of couples were equivalent on spouses' reports of relationship quality at the beginning of the marriage. Nonetheless, because of the other differences found, the current sample cannot be regarded as representative.

Statistical Issues

Determining where husbands and wives began their trajectory of change in marital quality and assessing whether the pattern of change in marital quality for each spouse was best captured by a linear, quadratic, or cubic growth function posed two problems regarding statistical analyses. First, because Pearson correlations between husbands' and wives' marital quality scores ranged from .56 to .64 over the 10 assessments, separate analyses could not be conducted for each spouse without biased tests of statistical significance (Kenny, 1996). Instead, one analysis needed to be done in which the four effects for one spouse (i.e., initial status as well as linear, quadratic, and cubic patterns of change) were estimated and tested for statistical significance with controls for the four effects of the other spouse. Second, because over the course of the study, couples separated, withdrew from the study, or were dropped from the study, sample size decreased from Year 1 to Year 10. To prevent the loss of information for couples without complete data, I needed to conduct analyses so that information from all couples could be used.

Both statistical problems were solved by conducting two-level hierarchical linear modeling analyses with version 4.04 of Bryk, Raudenbush, and Congdon's (1996) Hierarchical Linear Modeling (HLM) program. Raudenbush, Brennan, and Barnett's (1995) guidelines for analyzing data from marital dyads were followed (see Willett, Singer, & Martin, 1998, for a general discussion of growth modeling). In all two-level analyses, the model at Level 1 captured aspects of within-couple variability in marital quality, whereas the model at Level 2 captured facets of between-couples variability in each aspect of within-couple variability. Specifically, the model at Level 1 treated the couple as the unit of analysis and used a set of coded vectors (see Pedhazur, 1982, chap. 14) to define the four parameters of the trajectory of growth in marital quality for each spouse within each couple. An example of the Level 1 record of one couple with marital quality scores from the Dyadic Adjustment Scale at all 10 assessments is presented in Table 4.

As shown in this table, for each spouse, intercepts (i.e., estimates of initial status) were identified by dummy variables, and linear, quadratic, and cubic components of each spouse's growth curve were identified by sets of orthogonal polynomial contrasts that provided unique weights for the marital quality score at each of the 10 assessments (see Cohen & Cohen, 1983, p. 243). For example, the weights for the linear component were –9, –7, –5, –3, –1, 1, 3, 5, 7, and 9 for scores from Year 1 through Year 10, respectively. For couples with incomplete data, as many of the 10 assessment weights were assigned as there were assessments available.

In equation form (see Equation 1 below, where H = husband and W = wife), it can be seen that the Level 1 model simultaneously defined a cubic growth model for each spouse (four parameters for husbands and four parameters for wives), thereby controlling for the problem of partner interdependence:

$$\text{Marital quality} = H (\text{intercept} + \text{linear component}$$
$$+ \text{quadratic component} + \text{cubic component})$$
$$+ W (\text{intercept} + \text{linear component}$$
$$+ \text{quadratic component} + \text{cubic component}). \quad (1)$$

Because the HLM program (Bryk et al., 1996) first uses ordinary least-squares methods to estimate the eight parameters on an individual couple-by-couple basis, the problem of having couples with differing numbers of assessments in the same analysis was handled such that each couple had its own growth curve. These initial least-squares values were used to obtain more precise estimates of Level 1 effects using empirical Bayes methods such that Level 1 estimates were optimally derived so as to borrow strength from the information provided by the full sample (see Bryk et al., 1996, pp. 4–5).[1] Thus, the estimates reported here were based on data from the entire sample of 522 couples, resulting in a total of 4,792 assessments of marital quality for each spouse.

Estimating the growth curve for each spouse required that each of the eight parameters of the Level 1 model in Equation 1 become an outcome variable to be explained by variables in the Level 2 model, plus a random couple effect. Length of cohabitation was included in the Level 2 model as a control variable. Thus, the growth curve model that included the intercept (or initial status) and the linear, quadratic, and cubic components of change comprised Equation 1 at Level 1 and the following eight equations at Level 2:

H intercept = grand mean + length of cohabitation

$$+ \text{random couple effect. (2)}$$

H linear component = grand mean + length of cohabitation

$$+ \text{random couple effect. (3)}$$

H quadratic component = grand mean

$$+ \text{length of cohabitation} + \text{random couple effect. (4)}$$

H cubic component = grand mean + length of cohabitation

$$+ \text{random couple effect. (5)}$$

W intercept = grand mean + length of cohabitation

$$+ \text{random couple effect. (6)}$$

W linear component = grand mean + length of cohabitation

$$+ \text{random couple effect. (7)}$$

W quadratic component = grand mean

$$+ \text{length of cohabitation} + \text{random couple effect. (8)}$$

W cubic component = grand mean + length of cohabitation

$$+ \text{random couple effect. (9)}$$

Estimates of the Level 2 coefficients (fixed effects) as well as both the variance associated with each fixed effect and the covariation among the fixed effects (random effects) were accomplished through full maximum-likelihood methods which, in the present case, allowed the fit of nested models to be compared.

The Nature of the Trajectory of Change in Marital Quality

Four nested models were estimated to determine where spouses started the trajectory of change in marital quality and whether the growth curve for each spouse was best characterized as linear, quadratic, or cubic in nature. The first model (intercept) estimated only husband and wife intercepts. The second model (linear) estimated spousal intercepts and linear components of the growth curve. The third model (quadratic) estimated spousal intercepts and linear and quadratic components of the growth curve. Finally, the fourth model (cubic) estimated spousal intercepts and linear, quadratic, and cubic components of the growth curve. Thus, "higher order" models were tested with controls for "lower order" effects. Findings regarding the fixed effects (estimates of the parameters of the "best" growth curve) are presented before those relevant to the random effects (the amount of variability within each parameter and the correlations between those parameters).

Fixed effects The fit of a hierarchical linear model is assessed within the HLM program (Bryk et al., 1996) by a deviance statistic. Low values of this statistic reflect good fit. In the present study, the improved fit of increasingly more complex growth models was assessed by testing whether the decrease in the deviance statistic associated with going from the more simple to the more complex model was statistically significant. (The sample size for these tests changes because the relevant statistic is based on the number of cases with complete data.) These tests indicated that the linear model provided a better fit to the data than did the intercept model, $\chi^2(11, N = 392) = 1,357.81, p < .01$; that the quadratic model provided a better fit to the data than did the linear model, $\chi^2(15, N = 307) = 203.33, p < .01$; and that the cubic model provided a better fit to the data than did the quadratic model, $\chi^2(19, N = 197) = 118.83, p < .01$. Thus, of the four models, the cubic growth model provided the best fit to the pattern of change in marital quality.

The unstandardized coefficients for each of the four parameters of each spouse's cubic growth model are presented for husbands and wives in the top panel (Model 1) of Table 5. In the HLM program, these coefficients are tested for statistical significance with a t ratio. Following Karney and Bradbury (1997), I converted t ratios to effect-size rs to facilitate the interpretation of the coefficients.[2] Small, medium, and large effects were designated by rs of .10, .30, and .50, respectively (per Cohen, 1988). As shown in Table 5, the level of marital quality at the beginning of the trajectory was fairly high for both spouses. (Because the total Dyadic Adjustment Scale score was always greater than 0, both initial status effects had to be significant, so the relevant effect sizes are not presented.) As also shown in Table 5, the significant cubic effect for each spouse was medium in size. For descriptive purposes, a graphical estimate of the nature of the growth curve for each spouse was derived by plotting the observed means of the marital quality scores obtained at each of the 10 assessments for the 93 couples who provided data for all years. The resulting graph is only an estimate, however, because—as noted earlier—the actual parameter estimates were based on information provided by the full sample of 522 couples. As shown in Figure 1, a cubic growth function best represented the pattern of change for each spouse because there were two bends in the growth curve. For each spouse, marital quality declined fairly rapidly over the first 4 years of marriage (the first phase of accelerated change), stabilized, and then declined again at about the 8th year of marriage (the second phase of accelerated change).[3]

Random effects The random effects associated with the cubic growth model addressed two issues. First, was there sufficient variability within each parameter of the cubic growth model to warrant retaining each parameter in later analyses that were designed to account for such variability? The standard deviations for each of the eight random effects from the cubic model are presented in the diagonal of Table 6. The HLM program provides a chi-square test regarding the heterogeneity of the variance of each random effect. Because each of the eight resulting chi-square values was significant— $\chi^2(195, N = 197)$ ranged from 224.38 (for wife's cubic change) to 4,295.80 (for wife's initial status), ps < .01—the eight-parameter model was used in later analyses designed to explain the variability within each parameter.

TABLE 5

Fixed Effects Estimates for Two Models of the Trajectory of Change in Marital Quality

Parameter	Husband			Wife		
	Coefficient	t	r	Coefficient	t	r
Model 1: Controlling for length of cohabitation						
Initial status	111.48	124.85**	–	111.04	117.56**	–
Growth curve						
Linear component	−0.69	−8.61**	−.52	−0.89	−9.98**	−.58
Quadratic component	0.37	4.79**	.32	0.28	3.67**	.25
Cubic component	−0.03	−4.75**	−.32	−0.03	−4.60**	−.31
Model 2: Controlling for length of cohabitation and follow-up status						
Initial status	115.45	79.32**	–	116.86	77.35**	–
Growth curve						
Linear component	−0.44	−4.47**	−.30	−0.54	−5.06**	−.34
Quadratic component	0.27	2.64**	.18	0.18	1.78	.13
Cubic component	−0.03	−3.24**	−.23	−0.03	−2.50**	−.18

Note. Dashes indicate that no value was calculated because the estimate for initial status had to be different from 0.

** $p < .01$.

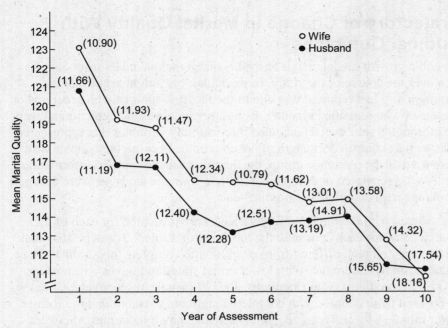

Figure 1. Mean marital quality scores (and standard deviations) by spouse and year of assessment for couples completing all 10 assessments (*n* = 93).

TABLE 6

Standard Deviations for Random Effects and Correlations Between Random Effects

Random effect	1	2	3	4	5	6	7	8
1. Husband initial	13.93							
2. Wife initial	.79	14.60						
3. Husband linear	.64	.51	0.81					
4. Wife linear	.56	.59	.88	0.97				
5. Husband quadratic	−.10	−.06	−.20	−.24	0.68			
6. Wife quadratic	.00	−.13	.00	−.02	.82	0.70		
7. Husband cubic	−.05	.10	−.16	−.27	−.06	−.24	0.05	
8. Wife cubic	.35	.42	.19	.02	−.44	−.57	.79	0.06

Note. Standard deviations are presented in the diagonal, and correlations are presented below the diagonal.

The second issue was the extent to which husbands' trajectory of change in marital quality was related to that of their wives. Correlations among all of the random effects are presented below the diagonal of the data matrix in Table 6, from which cross-spouse correlations can be obtained. As shown in this table, because the husband-wife correlations were highly positive for initial status, linear change, quadratic change, and cubic change, spouses' trajectories of change in marital quality were very similar to one another. A multivariate test within the HLM program was run to determine whether the four parameters for husbands differed from the corresponding four parameters for wives. This test was significant, $\chi^2(4, N = 197) = 9.99$, $p < .05$. Subsequent univariate comparisons indicated that husbands and wives differed on only one of the four parameters: Relative to husbands, wives showed a steeper rate of linear change, $\chi^2(1, N = 197) = 8.68$, $p < .01$.

The Nature of the Trajectory of Change in Marital Quality With Controls for Longitudinal Outcomes

One possible concern with the cubic growth model just described is that it included data from couples with different outcome statuses over the course of the study. In particular, one might argue that the pattern of deterioration in marital quality just reported was due to the fact that spouses who separated or divorced were included with spouses who remained together. Consequently, a second cubic model was estimated in which Equations 2 through 9 (at Level 2) included three dummy variables that represented variability in outcome status (as well as controls for length of cohabitation). Because the couples with complete longitudinal data were used as the reference group, the dummy variables carried information about the extent to which couples who separated or divorced, withdrew from the study, or were dropped from the study differed from couples with complete longitudinal data.

The unstandardized weights associated with the three dummy variables are presented for each of the four parameters of the growth trajectory for each spouse in the top panel of Table 7. It can be seen that couples in which spouses separated or divorced differed from couples with complete longitudinal data in that the former group included husbands and wives with lower initial status and wives with steeper linear decreases: effect-size $rs = -.30$ (medium), $-.46$ (medium), and $.29$ (small), respectively. Couples who withdrew from the study differed from couples with complete longitudinal data in that the former group included wives with lower initial status: effect-size $r = -.17$ (small). Finally, couples who were dropped from the study differed from couples with complete longitudinal data in that the former group included husbands and wives with lower initial status and husbands and wives with steeper linear change: effect-size $rs = -.18$ (small), $-.25$ (small), $-.14$ (small), and $-.18$ (small), respectively.

With regard to the estimates of the parameters of the growth trajectory with controls for outcome status (as well as length of cohabitation), the degree to which increasingly more complex growth models improved the fit of the model to the data again was assessed. As in the previous analysis, the linear model provided a better fit to the data than did the intercept model, $\chi^2(17, N = 392) = 1{,}451.28, p < .01$; the quadratic model provided a better fit to the data than did the linear model, $\chi^2(21, N = 307) = 187.15, p < .01$; and the cubic model provided a better fit to the data than did the quadratic model, $\chi^2(25, N = 197) = 114.91, p < .01$. Thus, even with additional controls for outcome status, the cubic growth model still provided the best fit to the pattern of change in marital quality. However, as shown in the bottom portion of Table 5, the strength of the cubic effect was reduced from medium to small for both husbands and wives. Because the effects associated with outcome status were significant, following Karney and Bradbury (1997), I used the dummy variables representing these effects, along with length of cohabitation, as control variables in all subsequent analyses.

Explaining Variability in Each Parameter of the Trajectory of Change

Attention is now directed to whether spouses' divorce history, the presence of residential children or step-children, and spouses' individual-differences variables predicted any of the parameters that defined the cubic pattern of change in marital quality.

Divorce history For husbands and wives, the link between both their own divorce history and that of their spouse and each of the four parameters relevant to their own trajectory of change in marital quality was examined with a two-level model. The Level 1 model included husbands' own initial status, linear change, quadratic change, and cubic change as well as the four parallel terms for wives. At Level 2, each of these terms was explained by two sets of variables. These included the set of four control variables (length of cohabitation and the three dummy variables capturing information about outcome status) and a set of four dummy variables that carried information regarding the husband's own divorce history and that of the wife (no divorce, one divorce, or multiple divorces). Within this second set, two of the dummy variables represented variability in one spouse's own divorce history (with no divorce as the reference group), and the other two dummy variables represented variability in the divorce history of the other spouse (again, with no divorce as the reference group). Thus, eight equations with eight terms were specified at Level 2, four for each spouse.

The resulting unstandardized coefficients are presented in the second panel of Table 7. Although 2 of the 32 coefficients associated with comparisons between spouses with a history of one divorce and those with a history of no divorce were significant, they might best be regarded as chance findings. Of more substantive interest is the finding that none of the coefficients associated with comparisons between spouses with a history of multiple divorce and those with a history of no divorces was significant. Analyses not reported here indicated that Husband Divorce History × Wife Divorce History interactions also were not significant and that main effects for divorce history were still nonsignificant even when outcome status was not controlled.

The resulting unstandardized coefficients are presented in the second panel of Table 7. Although 2 of the 32 coefficients associated with comparisons between spouses with a history of one divorce and those with a history of no divorce were significant, they might best be regarded as chance findings. Of more substantive interest is the finding that none of the coefficients associated with comparisons between spouses with a history of multiple divorce and those with a history of no divorces was significant. Analyses not reported here indicated that Husband Divorce History × Wife Divorce History interactions also were not significant and that main effects for divorce history were still nonsignificant even when outcome status was not controlled.

Presence of residential children or stepchildren The link between whether the couple lived with children or stepchildren and each of the four parameters of the growth trajectory at Level 1 for each spouse was examined by including seven terms in each of the eight equations at Level 2. These included the set of four control variables (length of cohabitation and three dummy variables representing outcome status) and three dummy variables in which couples with no children were contrasted with each of three other groups: couples living with only their own biological children at some point in the study, couples in which the husband lived with only his stepchildren, and an "other" category that included the remaining couples. As can be seen from the unstandardized coefficients presented in the third panel of Table 7, relative to couples who did not live with any children, those who lived with only their biological children included husbands and wives with lower initial status for marital quality as well as stronger linear declines in marital quality: effect-size $rs = -.19$ (small), $-.13$ (small), $-.21$ (small), and $-.14$ (small), respectively.

In order to explore this linear effect in more detail, I tested a two-level model using data from only the 140 couples living with their biological children. The Level 1 model included four terms such that marital quality was defined in terms of the husband intercept, the husband linear component, the wife intercept, and the wife linear component. In turn, at Level 2, these four terms became outcome scores, each to be explained by five terms that captured much of the heterogeneity within this subsample of couples: years of cohabitation (as a control variable), year during which the transition to parenthood was made (ranging from 1 to 9), total number of children at last assessment (ranging from 1 to 4), total number of male children (ranging from 0 to 3), and mean age of all children (ranging from 1 to 8 years).

TABLE 7

Unstandardized Coefficients Associated With Predictors of Each Parameter of the Trajectory of Change in Marital Quality

Predictor	Initial status		Linear change		Quadratic change		Cubic change	
	Husband	Wife	Husband	Wife	Husband	Wife	Husband	Wife
Outcome status (with controls for length of cohabitation)								
Separated vs. complete	−14.82**	−25.93**	−0.68	−2.60**	0.80	−0.51	0.03	−0.02
Withdrew vs. complete	−2.64	−5.32*	−0.27	−0.45	−0.06	−0.05	−0.01	0.00
Dropped vs. complete	−5.06**	−7.66**	−0.43*	−0.62**	0.18	−0.10	0.00	−0.02
Divorce history (with controls for length of cohabitation and outcome status)								
1 vs. none								
Husband	3.73	5.55**	0.10	0.18	0.12	0.26	0.01	0.00
Wife	−2.52	−1.88	−0.35*	−0.16	0.10	0.19	0.00	−0.01
Multiple vs. none								
Husband	0.82	1.89	−0.02	0.08	0.10	0.18	−0.05	0.00
Wife	−1.49	−0.52	−0.42	−0.46	−0.37	−0.46	−0.02	−0.02
Child status (with controls for length of cohabitation and outcome status)								
Biological vs. none	−4.87**	−3.46*	−0.48**	−0.35*	−0.24	−0.27	0.00	0.00
Step vs. none	−0.49	−2.10	−0.24	−0.36	−0.12	−0.19	0.00	−0.02
Other vs. none	−2.53	−1.03	−0.38	−0.21	−0.32	−0.20	−0.03	−0.02
Individual-differences variables (with controls for length of cohabitation and outcome status)								
Dependability								
Husband	0.95**	0.69**	−0.44	0.01	0.02	0.00	0.00	0.00
Wife	0.71**	1.17**	0.00	0.02	0.01	0.01	0.00	0.00
Dysfunctional beliefs								
Husband	−0.25**	−0.18**	−0.01	−0.01	0.00	0.00	0.00	0.00
Wife	−0.12**	−0.23**	0.00	0.00	0.00	0.00	0.00	0.00
Sex role self-concept								
Instrumentality								
Husband	0.05	−0.01	0.00	0.01	0.00	0.00	0.00	0.00
Wife	−0.03	−0.08	0.00	.00	0.00	0.00	0.00	0.00
Expressiveness								
Husband	0.38**	0.26**	−0.02*	−0.01	−0.01	0.00	0.00	0.00
Wife	0.32**	0.43**	0.00	0.00	0.00	0.01	0.00	0.00
Psychological distress								
Husband	−0.12**	−0.08**	−0.01**	−0.01*	0.00	0.00	0.00	0.00
Wife	−0.05**	−0.07**	0.00	0.00	0.00	0.00	0.00	0.00

*$p < .05$.

**$p < .01$.

As can be seen from the unstandardized coefficients presented in Table 8, with controls for the other predictors at Level 2, year of transition and total number of children independently explained variability in each of the four parameters. Specifically, fathers and mothers who made the transition to parenthood relatively early started their respective trajectories of change at fairly low levels of marital quality, rs = .30 (medium) and .40 (medium), respectively, and they experienced relatively steep declines in marital quality, rs = .25 (small) and .35 (medium), respectively. In addition, fathers and mothers who had a relatively large number of children started their respective trajectories of change at fairly low levels of marital quality, rs = .18 (small) and .17 (small), respectively, and they experienced relatively steep declines in marital quality, rs = .24 (small) and .20 (small), respectively. In analyses not reported here, effects associated with the interaction between the timing of the transition to parenthood and total number of children, total number of male children, and mean age of all children were also examined. None of these effects was significant.

TABLE 8

Unstandardized Coefficients Associated with

Predictors of Each Parameter of the Trajectory of Change in Marital Quality for Couples Living with Only Their Biological Children

Predictor	Initial status		Linear change	
	Husband	Wife	Husband	Wife
Year of transition to parenthood	2.33**	3.00**	0.16**	0.25**
No. of total children	4.10*	3.54*	0.44**	0.36*
No. of total male children	−2.48	−1.15	−0.16	−0.01
Mean age of all children	0.39	1.26	0.01	0.09

Note. Years of cohabitation was used as a control variable.

*$p < .05$.

**$p < .01$.

Individual-differences variables Because with two exceptions—instrumentality and expressiveness—the individual-differences variables did not form a coherent conceptual package, separate analyses were conducted for each variable. Instrumentality and expressiveness were considered together because they represented two dimensions of sex role self-concept. Thus, for dependability, dysfunctional beliefs, and psychological distress, each of the four parameters of a spouse's own trajectory of change in marital quality at Level 1 was explained for each spouse by the set of four control variables (length of cohabitation and three dummy variables carrying information about outcome status) and the self-version and spouse version of the individual-differences variable of interest, resulting in eight equations (four for each spouse) with six terms at Level 2. For the analyses involving sex role self-concept, self-versions of instrumentality and expressiveness and spouse versions of instrumentality and expressiveness were considered together, for a total of eight equations with seven terms at Level 2.

The resulting unstandardized coefficients are presented in the last panel of Table 7 and reveal one striking pattern: Independent intraspouse and cross-spouse effects were obtained for dependability of spouse, dysfunctional beliefs, expressivity, and psychological distress, but almost exclusively for the initial status of the trajectory of change. Specifically, husbands who began their trajectory of change at fairly low levels of marital quality at the start of their marriages regarded their wives as low in dependability (effect-size r = .42, medium), endorsed many dysfunctional beliefs about relationships (r = −.31, medium), saw themselves as low in expressiveness (r = .29, small), and reported high psychological distress (r = .38, medium). In addition, they also had wives who, at the start of the marriage, regarded them as low in dependability (effect-size r = .37, medium), endorsed many dysfunctional beliefs about relationships (r = −.16, small), saw themselves as low in expressiveness (r = .23, small), and reported high psychological distress (r = −.20, small).

In parallel fashion, wives who started their trajectory at fairly low levels of marital quality at the beginning of the marriage regarded their husbands as low in dependability (effect-size $r = .54$, large), endorsed many dysfunctional beliefs about relationships ($r = -.29$, small), saw themselves as low in expressiveness ($r = .30$, medium), and reported high psychological distress ($r = .25$, small). In addition, they also had husbands who, at the beginning of the marriage, regarded them as low in dependability (effect-size $r = .32$, medium), endorsed many dysfunctional beliefs about relationships ($r = -.21$, small), saw themselves as low in expressiveness ($r = .20$, small), and reported high psychological distress ($r = .24$, small).

DISCUSSION

The Nature of the Trajectory of Change in Marital Quality

The focus of this study was not on marriage as a static life event but on marital quality as a developmental phenomenon. Accordingly, the first purpose of this study was to describe the nature of change in marital quality over the first 10 years of marriage. Growth curve analyses were conducted on reports of marital quality from a sample of both spouses that is among the largest ever recruited and among the longest ever continuously assessed in this area of study. In order to explore rather complex patterns of change, a cubic growth curve was fitted for each spouse. This curve consisted of the level of marital quality with which the curve began and whether the pattern of change was characterized as changing at the same rate from assessment to assessment (linear), as having one phase of accelerated change (quadratic), or as having two phases of accelerated change (cubic).

Similar to the findings of Karney and Bradbury (1997), who used growth curve analyses to characterize the nature of change in marital quality for 54 first-married couples over the first 4 years of marriage, the growth curves of husbands and wives in the current study over the first 10 years of marriage were positively related to each other. In an extension of Karney and Bradbury's findings, husbands and wives in the present study (with controls for the length of time they had been living together) showed a similar pattern of cubic change such that marital quality declined fairly rapidly over the first 4 years of marriage (the first phase of accelerated change), stabilized, and then declined again at about the 8th year of marriage (the second phase of accelerated change). Although reduced in strength, the cubic growth effect remained significant for each spouse even when additional controls for the outcome status of couples over the course of this investigation (e.g., separated or divorced, withdrew from the study, were dropped from the study, or provided all 10 assessments) were introduced. Further, with these controls, the parameters of husbands' trajectories were equivalent to those of their wives.

As a normative account of how marital quality changes over time, the present findings have implications for how adult development is conceptualized. In his classic description of the developmental tasks of adulthood, Havighurst (1972) characterized early adulthood as a time of selecting a mate and adjusting to marriage and portrayed middle adulthood as a time of revitalizing marriage. The findings regarding change in marital quality over time suggest that early adulthood—a developmental period when most people still marry for the first time (United States Bureau of the Census, 1997)—might also be described as a time when one needs to be prepared for two sets of normative declines in marital quality. The first decline occurs over the early years of marriage, consistent with the common notion of a "honeymoon is over" effect (Kovacs, 1983; Sternberg, 1986). The second decline occurs at about the 8th year of marriage, consistent with the common notion of a 7-year-itch effect (Kovacs, 1983). Given evidence that evaluations of outcomes depend on the standards of evaluations used (see review by Higgins, Strauman, & Klein, 1986), the severity of some instances of marital distress might be mitigated by spouses' expecting and being prepared for "normal" periods of decline in marital quality.

One issue that merits further investigation is whether any specific dimensions of marital quality are most likely to decline over time. Addressing this issue is problematic for at least two reasons. First, there is as yet no well-articulated and empirically defended multidimensional model of marital quality (Fincham, 1998). Second, current measures that assess multiple dimensions of marital quality, such as Spanier's (1976) Dyadic Adjustment Scale, which was used in the present study, have the unfortunate psychometric property of highly intercorrelated subscores with attendant statistical problems of multicollinearity. Perhaps Sternberg's (1986) argument that love can be conceptualized in terms of intimacy, passion, and commitment is one starting point for further investigation into the structure of marital quality. It is possible, for example, that different components of marital quality change in different ways. For example, passion, because of its initial high extremes, may decline most quickly, whereas commitment, especially when viewed as barriers to leaving the marriage, may actually increase over time (Adams & Jones, 1997).

Accounting for Variability in the Trajectory of Change in Marital Quality

The second purpose of this study was to determine whether variability in any of the four parameters of the growth trajectory was accounted for by three sets of factors: spouses' divorce history, whether couples had children or stepchildren over the course of the study, and spouses' individual-differences variables assessed at the start of the marriage. The findings regarding divorce history were remarkable in that intrapartner and cross-partner effects were largely nonsignificant even when no controls were made for outcome status. This unexpected pattern of findings might be due to the fact that the group of multiply divorced spouses collapsed spouses that were divorced twice with those divorced more than twice.

In their discussion of "serial marriers," Brody et al. (1988) speculated that persons who have been divorced more than twice are at risk for psychological problems because of dysfunctional personality characteristics, unrealistic expectations of marriage, poorly developed negotiation and compromise skills, and cumulative negative stresses associated with living in a society in which serial marriers are regarded negatively. Unfortunately, the risk status of serial marriers could not be evaluated in this study because their number was too small to warrant including them as a distinct group.

The effects regarding having children or stepchildren are noteworthy because they indicate that relative to husbands and wives with no children or stepchildren, those who lived with only their biological children during the course of the study not only started their trajectories at lower levels of marital quality but also showed steeper linear declines in marital quality over time. Both of these effects are somewhat difficult to interpret because no information was available regarding the reasons why couples did not have children. For example, couples could want children eventually but postpone having them, deliberately choose not to have children, or not be able to have children for medical reasons (Houseknecht, 1987).

It is possible that spouses who eventually lived with only their biological children started their trajectories at lower levels of marital quality than those who never lived with any children or stepchildren because they were less motivated to maintain positive illusions about their relationships (Murray, Holmes, & Griffin, 1996). The perception that one's marital relationship is less than perfect may, in time, fuel one's desire to experience a parental relationship, perhaps as one way to compensate for emotional deficiencies within the marital relationship (Belsky, Youngblade, Rovine, & Volling, 1991). Alternatively, spouses who are highly invested in having children may regard their marriages as missing some critical element until children actually arrive.

The finding that relative to husbands and wives with no children or stepchildren, those who lived with only their biological children showed steeper linear declines in marital quality over time may be explained by the fact that in the present sample, most biological children were infants or preschoolers. It is possible that the presence of very young children acts as a barrier to ending even a marriage that is deteriorating (Cherlin, 1977). Consistent with the findings from this study that the decline in marital quality was especially likely for spouses who made the transition to parenthood fairly early in their marital careers and had many children, it is also plausible that the decline in marital quality is linked to an increase in the stressors of parenting that occur as young children develop (e.g., Belsky, Woodworth, & Crnic, 1996) and that leave parents with little time and energy to nurture their marital relationship. It would be of interest to determine whether marital quality stabilizes or even increases as children become more autonomous.

In light of discussions of the special stressors associated with living with stepchildren (see summary by Ganong & Coleman, 1994), the finding that the trajectory of change in marital quality for couples with no children or stepchildren was the same as that for spouses in stepfather families is consistent with Martin and Bumpass's (1989) finding that wives' bringing children into a remarriage does not affect the odds of marital success. It is possible that one of the factors that protected the marital quality of spouses in stepfather families was that the stepchildren in these families tended to be adolescents. Although raising adolescents in stepfather families has its own set of issues regarding discipline and control (Hetherington & Clingempeel, 1992), the relative autonomy of adolescents need not interfere with, and may even facilitate, the development of positive marital quality between mothers and stepfathers.

Finally, the effects associated with the individual-differences variables are of note in that they involved both intrapartner and cross-partner links for both husbands and wives only to the initial status of the trajectory of change in marital quality. Consistent with the findings of earlier studies assessing concurrent linkages between individual-differences variables and marital quality, spouses who started their trajectories at relatively low levels of marital quality also reported at the beginning of their marriages low dependability of spouse (Rempel et al., 1985), strong dysfunctional beliefs regarding relationships (Eidelson & Epstein, 1982), low expressiveness (Kurdek & Schmitt, 1986a), and high psychological distress (Karney et al., 1994). The present findings extend these earlier reports by also showing that these individual-differences variables have independent, parallel cross-spouse effects for both husbands and wives.

The findings that having children or stepchildren was linked to linear change in marital quality whereas individual-differences variables assessed at the start of the marriage were linked to the initial status of the trajectory of marital quality are reminiscent of Karney and Bradbury's (1997) findings that spousal interactional patterns (such as one might expect to occur in family systems with children) forecast linear declines in marital quality whereas spouses' individual-differences variables measured at the beginning of the marriage were linked only to the initial status of the trajectory. To the extent that identifying characteristics of persons predisposed to marital distress is deemed important (e.g., Holman, Larson, & Harmer, 1994), the inability of individual-differences variables to predict change in marital quality is sobering. However, given that this change may need to be understood in terms of dynamic tensions between spouses' developing needs and desires rather than in terms of their fairly stable intrapersonal predispositions (Montgomery, 1993), the inability of the individual-differences variables to predict change in marital quality is, in hindsight, not too surprising.

Limitations and Conclusions

The findings from this study need to be viewed with its limitations in mind, four of which are noted here. First, no claim can be made that the couples studied were representative of all newly wed couples because couples at the beginning of the study were disproportionately White and college educated. Second, although the growth curve analyses used all of the available data and controlled for outcome status, the rate of attrition was fairly high, and couples who provided data at all 10 assessments were biased with regard to demographic and individual-differences variables. Third, all of the data collected in this study were self-reported, with attending biases of self-presentation. Fourth, although the notion that marital quality changes in terms of two phases of accelerated change is a plausible interpretation of the cubic growth model, no analyses were conducted that tested precisely when the discontinuities in change occurred (Willett, 1997).

Despite these limitations, this study included a fairly large sample of newlyweds with diverse divorce histories who were studied annually for a longer period of time than in most other comparable studies. Overall, the findings (a) validate Karney and Bradbury's (1997) exhortation that marital researchers attend to the trajectory of change in marital quality; (b) suggest that a pattern of two phases of decline in marital quality is normative: and (c) document that whereas individual-differences variables at the start of the marriage are linked in an intraspouse and cross-spouse manner to the initial status of the trajectory of change in marital quality, only variables that tap some aspect of spousal interactions (such as whether they have children) are linked to the level of change in marital quality.

REFERENCES

Adams, J. M., & Jones, W. H. (1997). The conceptualization of marital commitment: An integrative analysis. *Journal of Personality and Social Psychology, 72*, 1177–1196.

Belsky, J., Woodworth, S., & Crnic, K. (1996). Trouble in the second year: Three questions about family interaction. *Child Development, 67*, 556–578.

Belsky, J., Youngblade, L., Rovine, M., & Volling, B. (1991). Patterns of marital change and parent-child interaction. *Journal of Marriage and the Family, 53*, 487–498.

Bem, S. L. (1974). The measurement of psychological androgyny. *Journal of Consulting and Clinical Psychology, 46*, 1053–1070.

Bradbury, T. N., Campbell, S. M., & Fincham, F. D. (1995). Longitudinal and behavioral analysis of masculinity and femininity in marriage. *Journal of Personality and Social Psychology, 68*, 328–341.

Bradbury, T. N., & Fincham, F. D. (1993). Assessing dysfunctional cognition in marriage: A reconsideration of the Relationship Belief Inventory. *Psychological Assessment, 5*, 92–101.

Brems, C., & Johnson, M. E. (1990). Reexamination of the Bem Sex-Role Inventory: The Interpersonal BSRI. *Journal of Personality Assessment, 55*, 484–498.

Brody, G. H., Neubaum, E., & Forehand, R. (1988). Serial marriage: A heuristic analysis of an emerging family form. *Psychological Bulletin, 103*, 211–222.

Bryk, A. S., & Raudenbush, S. W. (1992). *Hierarchical linear models: Applications and data analysis methods*. Newbury Park, CA: Sage.

Bryk, A. S., Raudenbush, S. W., & Congdon, R. T. (1996). *Hierarchical linear and nonlinear modeling with the HLM/2L and HLM/3L programs*. Chicago: Scientific Software International.

Burr, W. R. (1970). Satisfaction with various aspects of marriage over the life cycle: A random middle class sample. *Journal of Marriage and the Family, 32*, 29–37.

Cherlin, A. (1977). The effect of children on marital dissolution. *Demography, 14*, 265–272.

Clarke, S. C. (1995a). Advance report of final divorce statistics, 1989 and 1990. *Monthly Vital Statistics Report* (Vol. 43, No. 9, Supplement). Hyattsville, MD: National Center for Health Statistics.

Clarke, S. C. (1995b). Advance report of final marriage statistics, 1989 and 1990. *Monthly Vital Statistics Report* (Vol. 43, No. 12, Supplement). Hyattsville, MD: National Center for Health Statistics.

Cohen, J. (1988). *Statistical power analysis for the behavioral sciences*. Hillsdale, NJ: Erlbaum.

Cohen, J., & Cohen, P. (1983). *Applied multiple regression/correlation analysis for the behavioral sciences.* Hillsdale, NJ: Erlbaum.

Davila, J., Bradbury, T. N., Cohan, C. L., & Tochluk, S. (1997). Marital functioning and depressive symptoms: Evidence for the stress generation model. *Journal of Personality and Social Psychology, 73,* 849–861.

Derogatis, L. (1983). *SCL-90-R: Administration, scoring, and procedures manual.* Towson, MD: Clinical Psychometric Research.

Eidelson, R. J., & Epstein, N. (1982). Cognition and relationship maladjustment: Development of a measure of relationship beliefs. *Journal of Consulting and Clinical Psychology, 50,* 715–720.

Fincham, F. D. (1998). Child development and marital relations. *Child Development, 69,* 543–574.

Ganong, L. H., & Coleman, M. (1994). *Remarried family relationships.* Thousand Oaks, CA: Sage.

Glenn, N. D., & Weaver, C. N. (1981). The contribution of marital happiness to global happiness. *Journal of Marriage and the Family, 43,* 161–168.

Gould, R. L. (1978). *Transformations: Growth and change in adult life.* New York: Simon & Schuster.

Havighurst, R. J. (1972). *Developmental tasks and education.* New York: McKay.

Heaton, T. B., & Albrecht, S. L. (1991). Stable unhappy marriages. *Journal of Marriage and the Family, 53,* 747–758.

Hetherington, E. M., & Clingempeel, W. G. (1992). Coping with marital transitions. *Monographs of the Society for Research in Child Development. 57* (2–3, Serial No. 227).

Higgins, E. T., Strauman, T., & Klein, R. (1986). Standards and the process of self-evaluation: Multiple affects from multiple stages. In R. M. Sorrentino & E. T. Higgins (Eds.), *Handbook of motivation and cognition* (pp. 23–63). New York: Guilford Press.

Holman, T. B., Larson, J. H., & Harmer, S. L. (1994). The development and predictive validity of a new premarital assessment instrument. *Family Relations, 43,* 46–52.

Houseknecht, S. K. (1987). Voluntary childlessness. In M. B. Sussman & S. K. Steinmetz (Eds.), *Handbook of marriage and the family* (pp. 369–396). New York: Plenum.

Karney, B. R., & Bradbury, T. N. (1995). The longitudinal course of marital quality and stability: A review of theory, method, and research. *Psychological Bulletin, 118,* 3–34.

Karney, B. R., & Bradbury, T. N. (1997). Neuroticism, marital interaction, and the trajectory of marital satisfaction. *Journal of Personality and Social Psychology, 72,* 1075–1092.

Karney, B. R., Bradbury, T. N., Fincham, F. D., & Sullivan, K. T. (1994). The role of negative affectivity in the association between attributions and marital satisfaction. *Journal of Personality and Social Psychology, 66,* 413–424.

Kenny, D. A. (1996). Modes of nonindependence in dyadic research. *Journal of Social and Personal Relationships, 13,* 279–294.

Kovacs, L. (1983). A conceptualization of marital development. *Family Therapy, 3,* 183–210.

Kurdek, L. A. (1987). Sex role self scheme and psychological adjustment in coupled homosexual and heterosexual men and women. *Sex Roles, 17,* 549–562.

Kurdek, L. A. (1992). Dimensionality of the Dyadic Adjustment Scale: Evidence from heterosexual and homosexual couples. *Journal of Family Psychology, 6,* 22–35.

Kurdek, L. A., & Schmitt, J. P. (1986a). Interaction of sex role self-concept with relationship quality and relationship beliefs in married, heterosexual cohabiting, gay, and lesbian couples. *Journal of Personality and Social Psychology, 51*, 365–370.

Kurdek, L. A., & Schmitt, J. P. (1986b). Relationship quality of partners in heterosexual married, heterosexual cohabiting, gay, and lesbian relationships. *Journal of Personality and Social Psychology, 51*, 711–720.

Levinson, D. J., Darrow, C. N., Klein, E. B., Levinson, M. H., & McKee, B. (1978). *The seasons of a man's life*. New York: Knopf.

MacDermid, S. M., Huston, T. L., & McHale, S. M. (1990). Changes in marriage associated with the transition to parenthood: Individual differences as a function of sex-role attitudes and changes in division of household labor. *Journal of Marriage and the Family, 52*, 475–486.

Martin, T. C., & Bumpass, L. (1989). Trends in marital disruption. *Demography, 26*, 37–52.

Montgomery, B. M. (1993). Relationship maintenance versus relationship change: A dialectical dilemma. *Journal of Social and Personal Relationships, 10*, 205–223.

Murray, S. L., Holmes, J. G., & Griffin, D. W. (1996). The self-fulfilling nature of positive illusions in romantic relationships: Love is not blind, but prescient. *Journal of Personality and Social Psychology, 71*, 1155–1180.

National Center for Health Statistics. (1991). Advance report of final marriage statistics, 1988. *Monthly Vital Statistics Report* (Vol. 39, No. 12, Supplement 2). Hyattsville, MD: U.S. Public Health Service.

Pedhazur, E. J. (1982). *Multiple regression in behavioral research*. New York: Holt, Rinehart & Winston.

Raudenbush, S. W., Brennan, R. T., & Barnett, R. C. (1995). A multivariate hierarchical model for studying psychological change within married couples. *Journal of Family Psychology, 9*, 161–174.

Rempel, J. K., Holmes, J. G., & Zanna, M. P. (1985). Trust in close relationships. *Journal of Personality and Social Psychology, 49*, 95–112.

Rosenthal, R., & Rosnow, R. L. (1984). *Essentials of behavioral research: Methods and data analysis*. New York: McGraw-Hill.

Sabourin, S., Lussier, Y., Laplante, B., & Wright, J. (1991). Unidimensional and multidimensional models of dydadic adjustment: A hierarchical integration. *Psychological Assessment, 2*, 219–230.

Schwarzwald, J., Weisenberg, M., & Solomon, Z. (1991). Factor invariance of SCL-90-R: The case of combat stress reaction. *Psychological Assessment. 3*, 385–390.

Spanier, G. B. (1976). Measuring dyadic adjustment. *Journal of Marriage and the Family, 38*, 15–28.

Sternberg, R. J. (1986). A triangular theory of love. *Psychological Review, 93*, 119–135.

U.S. Bureau of the Census. (1997). *Statistical abstract of the United States: 1997*. Washington, DC: U.S. Government Printing Office.

Vaillant, C. O., & Vaillant, G. E. (1993). Is the U-curve of marital satisfaction an illusion? A 40-year study of marriage. *Journal of Marriage and the Family, 55*, 230–239.

Vaillant, G. E. (1977). *Adaptation to life*. Boston: Little, Brown.

Willett, J. B. (1997). Measuring change: What individual growth modeling buys you. In E. Amsel & K. A. Renninger (Eds.), *Change and development: Issues of theory, method, and application* (pp. 213–243). Mahwah, NJ: Erlbaum.

Willett, J. B., Singer, J. D., & Martin, N. C. (1998). The design and analysis of longitudinal studies of development and psychopathology in context: Statistical models and methodological recommendations. *Development and Psychopathology, 10*, 395–426.

Wilson, B. F., & Clarke, S. C. (1992). Remarriages: A demographic profile. *Journal of Family Issues, 13*, 123–141.

Received July 13, 1998

Revision received March 8, 1999

Accepted March 9, 1999

NOTES

1. The HLM program also provided information regarding whether the ordinary least-squares estimates of change were reliable. The reliability of each parameter is defined as the ratio of the variance of the true means to the variance of the estimates and depends on the number of observations per spouse, the magnitude of the variance associated with the true means, and the magnitude of the variance associated with measurement error. Generally, the reliability of the least-squares estimate of the mean increases with the number of observations per spouse, the amount of variance among spouses in their true means, and the number of items in the scale. In the current study, the reliabilities vary from couple to couple because the number of observations varies with the number of completed assessments. The HLM program calculated the average of these reliabilities with data from the 197 couples that had sufficient data for computation. The reliability values for intercept (initial status), linear change, quadratic change, and cubic change were .71, .50, .33, and .20 for husbands, respectively, and .72, .53, .34, and .26 for wives, respectively. Bryk and Raudenbush (1992, p. 202) recommended that average reliabilities should exceed .05 in order to avoid computational difficulties with the iterative computing routines. The current reliabilities exceeded this cutoff value and ensured that it was possible to use each spouse-specific change parameter to discriminate between couples.

2. According to Rosenthal and Rosnow (1984, p. 217), $r = \sqrt{[t^2/(t^2 + df)]}$. In HLM analyses, df = the number of Level 2 units (e.g., couples) − the number of Level 2 predictors − 1. By convention, r (which is always positive in sign) was assigned a positive or negative sign that matched the corresponding t ratio.

3. The two-level baseline model was also estimated with data from only the 93 couples with complete data. Estimates were similar to those obtained for the total sample. For husbands, respective unstandardized estimates for initial status the linear component, the quadratic component, and the cubic component were 114.65, −0.40, 0.19, and −0.03, with corresponding t ratios of 96.02, −4.83, 2.80, and −3.43, $ps < .01$. For wives, respective unstandardized estimates for initial status, the linear component, the quadratic component, and the cubic component were 116.23, −0.54, 0.12, and −0.03, with corresponding t ratios of 103.39, −6.73, 1.99, and −3.72, $ps < .05$. There was significant variability within each of the eight parameters, $\chi^2(92, N = 93)$ ranging from 115.17 (wife's cubic component) to 3,782.60 (husband's initial status), $ps < .05$.

Group Inhibition of Bystander Intervention In Emergencies

If you were in an emergency and needed help, would you rather there be one witness to your situation or several? Although common sense would suggest the latter, Latané and Darley's classic research on bystander intervention suggests that the answer may not be so obvious. Their research was inspired by the tragic death of a woman in New York City whose murder most likely could have been prevented had any of 38 witnesses to her attack intervened on her behalf. How could these bystanders have been so callous as to not even call the police until it was too late? Latané and Darley speculated that the presence of multiple bystanders may inhibit any one bystander from taking action. In this article they articulate some of the reasons why this may be, and report an ingeniously designed experiment that illustrates how the presence of multiple bystanders can even inhibit individuals from taking action in a potential emergency even when their *own* lives might be in danger! Consider how this experiment fits within the context of the discussion of bystander intervention in Chapter 10 (Helping), as well as how social comparison (Chapter **) and social influence (Chapter 9) processes are implicated in this research.

GROUP INHIBITION OF BYSTANDER INTERVENTION IN EMERGENCIES[1]*

Bibb Latané[2]

Columbia University

John M. Darley[3]

New York University

Male undergraduates found themselves in a smoke-filling room either alone, with 2 nonreacting others, or in groups of 3. As predicted, Ss were less likely to report the smoke when in the presence of passive others (10%) or in groups of 3 (38% of groups) than when alone (75%). This result seemed to have been mediated by the way Ss interpreted the ambiguous situation; seeing other people remain passive led Ss to decide the smoke was not dangerous.

Emergencies, fortunately, are uncommon events. Although the average person may read about them in newspapers or watch fictionalized versions on television, he probably will encounter fewer than half a dozen in his lifetime. Unfortunately, when he does encounter one, he will have had little direct personal experience in dealing with it. And he must deal with it under conditions of urgency, uncertainty, stress, and fear. About all the individual has to guide him is the secondhand wisdom of the late movie, which is often as useful as "Be brave" or as applicable as "Quick, get lots of hot water and towels!"

---

* Bibb Latane and John M. Darley, "Group Inhibition of Bystander Intervention," Journal of Personality and Social Psychology, 1968, Vol. 10, No. 3, pp. 215-221 Copyright (c) 1968 by the American Psychological Association. Reproduced with permission.

Under the circumstances, it may seem surprising that anybody ever intervenes in an emergency in which he is not directly involved. Yet there is a strongly held cultural norm that individuals should act to relieve the distress of others. As the Old Parson puts it, "In this life of froth and bubble, two things stand like stone—kindness in another's trouble, courage in your own." Given the conflict between the norm to act and an individual's fears and uncertainties about getting involved, what factors will determine whether a bystander to an emergency will intervene?

We have found (Darley & Latané, 1968) that the mere perception that other people are also witnessing the event will markedly decrease the likelihood that an individual will intervene in an emergency. Individuals heard a person undergoing a severe epileptic-like fit in another room. In one experimental condition, the subject thought that he was the only person who heard the emergency; in another condition, he thought four other persons were also aware of the seizure. Subjects alone with the victim were much more likely to intervene on his behalf, and, on the average, reacted in less than one-third the time required by subjects who thought there were other bystanders present.

"Diffusion of responsibility" seems the most likely explanation for this result. If an individual is alone when he notices an emergency, he is solely responsible for coping with it. If he believes others are also present, he may feel that his own responsibility for taking action is lessened, making him less likely to help.

To demonstrate that responsibility diffusion rather than any of a variety of social influence processes caused this result, the experiment was designed so that the onlookers to the seizure were isolated one from another and could not discuss how to deal with the emergency effectively. They knew the others could not see what they did, nor could they see whether somebody else had already started to help. Although this state of affairs is characteristic of many actual emergencies (such as the Kitty Genovese murder in which 38 people witnessed a killing from their individual apartments without acting), in many other emergencies several bystanders are in contact with and can influence each other. In these situations, processes other than responsibility diffusion will also operate.

Given the opportunity to interact, a group can talk over the situation and divide up the helping action in an efficient way. Also, since responding to emergencies is a socially prescribed norm, individuals might be expected to adhere to it more when in the presence of other people. These reasons suggest that interacting groups should be better at coping with emergencies than single individuals. We suspect, however, that the opposite is true. Even when allowed to communicate, groups may still be worse than individuals.

Most emergencies are, or at least begin as, ambiguous events. A quarrel in the street may erupt into violence, but it may be simply a family argument. A man staggering about may be suffering a coronary or an onset of diabetes; he may be simply drunk. Smoke pouring from a building may signal a fire; on the other hand, it may be simply steam or air-conditioning vapor. Before a bystander is likely to take action in such ambiguous situations, he must first define the event as an emergency and decide that intervention is the proper course of action.

In the course of making these decisions, it is likely that an individual bystander will be considerably influenced by the decisions he perceives other bystanders to be taking. If everyone else in a group of onlookers seems to regard an event as nonserious and the proper course of action as nonintervention, this consensus may strongly affect the perceptions of any single individual and inhibit his potential intervention.

The definitions that other people hold may be discovered by discussing the situation with them, but they may also be inferred from their facial expressions or their behavior. A whistling man with his hands in his pockets obviously does not believe he is in the midst of a crisis. A bystander who does not respond to smoke obviously does not attribute it to fire. An individual, seeing the inaction of others, will judge the situation as less serious than he would if he were alone.

In the present experiment, this line of thought will be tested by presenting an emergency situation to individuals either alone or in the presence of two passive others, confederates of the experimenter who have been instructed to notice the emergency but remain indifferent to it. It is our expectation that this passive behavior will signal the individual that the other bystanders do not consider the situation to be dangerous. We predict that an individual faced with the passive reactions of other people will be influenced by them, and will thus be less likely to take action than if he were alone.

This, however, is a prediction about individuals; it says nothing about the original question of the behavior of freely interacting groups. Most groups do not have preinstructed confederates among their members, and the kind of social influence process described above would, by itself, only lead to a convergence of attitudes within a group. Even if each member of the group is entirely guided by the reactions of others, then the group should still respond with a likelihood equal to the average of the individuals.

An additional factor is involved, however. Each member of a group may watch the others, but he is also aware that the others are watching him. They are an audience to his own reactions. Among American males it is considered desirable to appear poised and collected in times of stress. Being exposed to public view may constrain an individual's actions as he attempts to avoid possible ridicule and embarrassment.

The constraints involved with being in public might in themselves tend to inhibit action by individuals in a group, but in conjunction with the social influence process described above, they may be expected to have even more powerful effects. If each member of a group is, at the same time, trying to appear calm and also looking around at the other members to gauge their reactions, all members may be led (or misled) by each other to define the situation as less critical than they would if alone. Until someone acts, each person only sees other nonresponding bystanders, and, as with the passive confederates, is likely to be influenced not to act himself.

This leads to a second prediction. Compared to the performance of individuals, if we expose groups of naive subjects to an emergency, the constraints on behavior in public coupled with the social influence process will lessen the likelihood that the members of the group will act to cope with the emergency.

It has often been recognized (Brown, 1954, 1965) that a crowd can cause contagion of panic, leading each person in the crowd to overreact to an emergency to the detriment of everyone's welfare. What is implied here is that a crowd can also force inaction on its members. It can suggest, implicitly but strongly, by its passive behavior, that an event is not to be reacted to as an emergency, and it can make any individual uncomfortably aware of what a fool he will look for behaving as if it is.

METHOD

The subject, seated in a small waiting room, faced an ambiguous but potentially dangerous situation as a stream of smoke began to puff into the room through a wall vent. His response to this situation was observed through a one-way glass. The length of time the subject remained in the room before leaving to report the smoke was the main dependent variable of the study.

Recruitment of subjects

Male Columbia students living in campus residences were invited to an interview to discuss "some of the problems involved in life at an urban university." The subject sample included graduate and professional students as well as undergraduates. Individuals were contacted by telephone and most willingly volunteered and actually showed up for the interview. At this point, they were directed either by signs or by the secretary to a "waiting room" where a sign asked them to fill out a preliminary questionnaire.

Experimental manipulation

Some subjects filled out the questionnaire and were exposed to the potentially critical situation while alone. Others were part of three-person groups consisting of one subject and two confederates acting the part of naive subjects. The confederates attempted to avoid conversation as much as possible. Once the smoke had been introduced, they stared at it briefly, made no comment, but simply shrugged their shoulders, returned to the questionnaires and continued to fill them out, occasionally waving away the smoke to do so. If addressed, they attempted to be as uncommunicative as possible and to show apparent indifference to the smoke. "I dunno," they said, and no subject persisted in talking.

In a final condition, three naive subjects were tested together. In general, these subjects did not know each other, although in two groups, subjects reported a nodding acquaintanceship with another subject. Since subjects arrived at slightly different times and since they each had individual questionnaires to work on, they did not introduce themselves to each other, or attempt anything but the most rudimentary conversation.

Critical situation

As soon as the subjects had completed two pages of their questionnaires, the experimenter began to introduce the smoke through a small vent in the wall. The "smoke" was finely divided titanium dioxide produced in a stoppered bottle and delivered under slight air pressure through the vent.[4] It formed a moderately fine-textured but clearly visible stream of whitish smoke. For the entire experimental period, the smoke continued to jet into the room in irregular puffs. By the end of the experimental period, vision was obscured by the amount of smoke present.

All behavior and conversation was observed and coded from behind a one-way window (largely disguised on the subject's side by a large sign giving preliminary instructions). If the subject left the experimental room and reported the smoke, he was told that the situation "would be taken care of." If the subject had not reported the presence of smoke by 6 minutes from the time he first noticed it, the experiment was terminated.

RESULTS

Alone condition

The typical subject, when tested alone, behaved very reasonably. Usually, shortly after the smoke appeared, he would glance up from his questionnaire, notice the smoke, show a slight but distinct startle reaction, and then undergo a brief period of indecision, perhaps returning briefly to his questionnaire before again staring at the smoke. Soon, most subjects would get up from their chairs, walk over to the vent, and investigate it closely, sniffing the smoke, waving their hands in it, feeling its temperature, etc. The usual alone subject would hesitate again, but finally walk out of the room, look around outside, and, finding somebody there, calmly report the presence of the smoke. No subject showed any sign of panic; most simply said, "There's something strange going on in there, there seems to be some sort of smoke coming through the wall . . . ."

The median subject in the alone condition had reported the smoke within 2 minutes of first noticing it. Three-quarters of the 24 people who were run in this condition reported the smoke before the experimental period was terminated.

Two passive confederates condition

The behavior of subjects run with two passive confederates was dramatically different; of 10 people run in this condition, only 1 reported the smoke. The other 9 stayed in the waiting room as it filled up with smoke, doggedly working on their questionnaire and waving the fumes away from their faces. They coughed, rubbed their eyes, and opened the window—but they did not report the smoke. The difference between the response rate of 75% in the alone condition and 10% in the two passive confederates condition is highly significant ($p < .002$ by Fisher's exact test, two-tailed).

Three naive bystanders

Because there are three subjects present and available to report the smoke in the three naive bystander condition as compared to only one subject at a time in the alone condition, a simple comparison between the two conditions is not appropriate. On the one hand, we cannot compare speeds in the alone condition with the average speed of the three subjects in a group, since, once one subject in a group had reported the smoke, the pressures on the other two disappeared. They legitimately could (and did) feel that the emergency had been handled, and any action on their part would be redundant and potentially confusing. Therefore the speed of the *first* subject in a group to report the smoke was used as the dependent variable. However, since there were three times as many people available to respond in this condition as in the alone condition, we would expect an increased likelihood that at least one person would report the smoke even if the subjects had no influence whatsoever on each other. Therefore we mathematically created "groups" of three scores from the alone condition to serve as a base line.[5]

In contrast to the complexity of this procedure, the results were quite simple. Subjects in the three naive bystander condition were markedly inhibited from reporting the smoke. Since 75% of the alone subjects reported the smoke, we would expect over 98% of the three-person groups to contain at least one reporter. In fact, in only 38% of the eight groups in this condition did even 1 subject report ($p < .01$). Of the 24 people run in these eight groups, only 1 person reported the smoke within the first 4 minutes before the room got noticeably unpleasant. Only 3 people reported the smoke within the entire experimental period.

Cumulative distribution of report times

Figure 1 presents the cumulative frequency distributions of report times for all three conditions. The figure shows the proportion of subjects in each condition who had reported the smoke by any point in the time following the introduction of the smoke. For example, 55% of the subjects in the alone condition had reported the smoke within 2 minutes, but the smoke had been reported in only 12% of the three-person groups by that time. After 4 minutes, 75% of the subjects in the alone condition had reported the smoke; no additional subjects in the group condition had done so. The curve in Figure 1 labeled "Hypothetical Three-Person Groups" is based upon the mathematical combination of scores obtained from subjects in the alone condition. It is the expected report times for groups in the three-person condition if the members of the groups had no influence upon each other.

It can be seen in Figure 1 that for every point in time following the introduction of the smoke, a considerably higher proportion of subjects in the alone condition had reported the smoke than had subjects in either the two passive confederates condition or in the three naive subjects condition. The curve for the latter condition, although considerably below the alone curve, is even more substantially inhibited with respect to its proper comparison, the curve of hypothetical three-person sets. Social inhibition of response was so great that the time elapsing before the smoke was reported was greater when there were more people available to report it (alone versus group $p < .05$ by Mann-Whitney U test).

Superficially, it appears that there is a somewhat higher likelihood of response from groups of three naive subjects than from subjects in the passive confederates condition. Again this comparison is not justified; there are three people free to act in one condition instead of just one. If we mathematically combine scores for subjects in the two passive confederates condition in a similar manner to that described above for the alone condition, we would obtain an expected likelihood of response of .27 as the hypothetical base line. This is not significantly different from the .37 obtained in the actual three-subject groups.

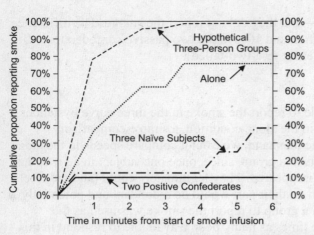

Figure 1. Cumulative proportion of subjects reporting the smoke over time.

Noticing the smoke

In observing the subject's reaction to the introduction of smoke, careful note was taken of the exact moment when he first saw the smoke (all report latencies were computed from this time). This was a relatively easy observation to make, for the subjects invariably showed a distinct, if slight, startle reaction. Unexpectedly, the presence of other persons delayed, slightly but very significantly, noticing the smoke. Sixty-three percent of subjects in the alone condition and only 26% of subjects in the combined together conditions noticed the smoke within the first 5 seconds after its introduction ($p < .01$ by chi-square). The median latency of noticing the smoke was under 5 seconds in the alone condition; the median time at which the first (or only) subject in each of the combined together conditions noticed the smoke was 20 seconds (this difference does not account for group-induced inhibition of reporting since the report latencies were computed from the time the smoke was first noticed).

This interesting finding can probably be explained in terms of the constraints which people feel in public places (Goffman, 1963). Unlike solitary subjects, who often glanced idly about the room while filling out their questionnaires, subjects in groups usually kept their eyes closely on their work, probably to avoid appearing rudely inquisitive.

Postexperimental interview

After 6 minutes, whether or not the subjects had reported the smoke, the interviewer stuck his head in the waiting room and asked the subject to come with him to the interview. After seating the subject in his office, the interviewer made some general apologies about keeping the subject waiting for so long, hoped the subject hadn't become too bored and asked if he "had experienced any difficulty while filling out the questionnaire." By this point most subjects mentioned the smoke. The interviewer expressed mild surprise and asked the subject to tell him what had happened. Thus each subject gave an account of what had gone through his mind during the smoke infusion.

Subjects who had reported the smoke were relatively consistent in later describing their reactions to it. They thought the smoke looked somewhat "strange," they were not sure exactly what it was or whether it was dangerous, but they felt it was unusual enough to justify some examination. "I wasn't sure whether it was a fire but it looked like something was wrong." "I thought it might be steam, but it seemed like a good idea to check it out."

Subjects who had not reported the smoke also were unsure about exactly what it was, but they uniformly said that they had rejected the idea that it was a fire. Instead, they hit upon an astonishing variety of alternative explanations, all sharing the common characteristic of interpreting the smoke as a nondangerous event. Many thought the smoke was either steam or air-conditioning vapors, several thought it was smog, purposely introduced to simulate an urban environment, and two (from different groups) actually suggested that the smoke was a "truth gas" filtered into the room to induce them to answer the questionnaire accurately. (Surprisingly, they were not disturbed by this conviction.) Predictably, some decided that "it must be some sort of experiment" and stoically endured the discomfort of the room rather than overreact.

Despite the obvious and powerful report-inhibiting effect of other bystanders, subjects almost invariably claimed that they had paid little or no attention to the reactions of the other people in the room. Although the presence of other people actually had a strong and pervasive effect on the subjects' reactions, they were either unaware of this or unwilling to admit it.

DISCUSSION

Before an individual can decide to intervene in an emergency, he must, implicitly or explicitly, take several preliminary steps. If he is to intervene, he must first *notice* the event, he must then *interpret* it as an emergency, and he must decide that it is his personal *responsibility* to act. At each of these preliminary steps, the bystander to an emergency can remove himself from the decision process and thus fail to help. He can fail to notice the event, he can fail to interpret it as an emergency, or he can fail to assume the responsibility to take action.

In the present experiment we are primarily interested in the second step of this decision process, interpreting an ambiguous event. When faced with such an event, we suggest, the individual bystander is likely to look at the reactions of people around him and be powerfully influenced by them. It was predicted that the sight of other, nonresponsive bystanders would lead the individual to interpret the emergency as not serious, and consequently lead him not to act. Further, it was predicted that the dynamics of the interaction process would lead each of a group of naive onlookers to be misled by the apparent inaction of the others into adopting a nonemergency interpretation of the event and a passive role.

The results of this study clearly support our predictions. Individuals exposed to a room filling with smoke in the presence of passive others themselves remained passive, and groups of three naive subjects were less likely to report the smoke than solitary bystanders. Our predictions were confirmed—but this does not necessarily mean that our explanation for these results is the correct one. As a matter of fact, several alternatives are available.

Two of these alternative explanations stem from the fact that the smoke represented a possible danger to the subject himself as well as to others in the building. Subjects' behavior might have reflected their fear of fire, with subjects in groups feeling less threatened by the fire than single subjects and thus being less concerned to act. It has been demonstrated in studies with humans (Schachter, 1959) and with rats (Latané, 1968; Latané & Glass, 1968) that togetherness reduces fear, even in situations where it does not reduce danger. In addition, subjects may have felt that the presence of others increased their ability to cope with fire. For both of these reasons, subjects in groups may have been less afraid of fire and thus less likely to report the smoke than solitary subjects.

A similar explanation might emphasize not fearfulness, but the desire to hide fear. To the extent that bravery or stoicism in the face of danger or discomfort is a socially desirable trait (as it appears to be for American male undergraduates), one might expect individuals to attempt to appear more brave or more stoic when others are watching than when they are alone. It is possible that subjects in the group condition saw themselves as engaged in a game of "Chicken," and thus did not react.

Although both of these explanations are plausible, we do not think that they provide an accurate account of subjects' thinking. In the postexperimental interviews, subjects claimed, *not* that they were unworried by the fire or that they were unwilling to endure the danger; but rather that they decided that there was no fire at all and the smoke was caused by something else. They failed to act because they thought there was no reason to act. Their "apathetic" behavior was reasonable—given their interpretation of the circumstances.

The fact that smoke signals potential danger to the subject himself weakens another alternative explanation, "diffusion of responsibility." Regardless of social influence processes, an individual may feel less personal responsibility for helping if he shares the responsibility with others (Darley & Latané, 1968). But this diffusion explanation does not fit the present situation. It is hard to see how an individual's responsibility for saving himself is diffused by the presence of other people. The diffusion explanation does not account for the pattern of interpretations reported by the subjects or for their variety of nonemergency explanations.

On the other hand, the social influence processes which we believe account for the results of our present study obviously do not explain our previous experiment in which subjects could not see or be seen by each other. Taken together, these two studies suggest that the presence of bystanders may affect an individual in several ways; including both "social influence" and "diffusion of responsibility."

Both studies, however, find, for two quite different kinds of emergencies and under two quite different conditions of social contact, that individuals are less likely to engage in socially responsible action if they think other bystanders are present. This presents us with the paradoxical conclusion that a victim may be more likely to get help, or an emergency may be more likely to be reported, the fewer people there are available to take action. It also may help us begin to understand a number of frightening incidents where crowds have listened to but not answered a call for help. Newspapers have tagged these incidents with the label "apathy." We have become indifferent, they say, callous to the fate of suffering others. The results of our studies lead to a different conclusion. The failure to intervene may be better understood by knowing the relationship among bystanders rather than that between a bystander and the victim.

REFERENCES

Brown, R. W. Mass phenomena. In G. Lindzey (Ed.), *Handbook of social psychology*. Vol. 2. Cambridge: Addison-Wesley, 1954.

Brown, R. *Social psychology*. New York: Free Press of Glencoe, 1965.

Darley, J. M., & Latané, B. Bystander intervention in emergencies: Diffusion of responsibility. *Journal of Personality and Social Psychology*, 1968, 8, 377–383.

Goffman, E. *Behavior in public places*. New York: Free Press of Glencoe, 1963.

Latané, B. Gregariousness and fear in laboratory rats. *Journal of Experimental Social Psychology*, 1968, in press.

Latané, B., & Glass, D. C. Social and nonsocial attraction in rats. *Journal of Personality and Social Psychology*, 1968, 9, 142–146.

Schachter, S. *The psychology of affiliation*. Stanford: Stanford University Press, 1959.

(Received December 11, 1967)

NOTES

1. We thank Lee Ross and Keith Gerritz for their thoughtful efforts. This research was supported by National Science Foundation Grants GS 1238 and GS 1239. The experiment was conducted at Columbia University.

2. Now at the Ohio State University.

3. Now at Princeton University.

4. Smoke was produced by passing moisturized air, under pressure, through a container of titanium tetrachloride, which, in reaction with the water vapor, creates a suspension of tantium dioxide in air.

5. The formula for calculating the expected proportion of groups in which at least one person will have acted by a given time is $1 - (1 - p)^n$ where p is the proportion of single individuals who act by that time and n is the number of persons in the group.

READING 12

Effects of songs with prosocial lyrics on prosocial thoughts, affect, and behavior

As discussed in Chapter 2 (Doing Social Psychology Research) and Chapter 11 (Aggression), much research has focused on the harmful effects of exposure to violent media in various forms. Tobias Greitemeyer, however, took his experiment in the opposite direction and conducted a set of experiments designed to determine if exposure to prosocial (socially positive) media promoted prosocial outcomes. Through three experiments, Greitemeyer,tested his hypothesis that "listening to prosocial (relative to neutral) songs increased the accessibility of prosocial thoughts (Experiment 1) and led to more interpersonal empathy (Experiment 2)…Experiment 3 addressed behavioral outcomes from listening to songs with prosocial content in that actual helping behavior was addressed." A varying number of German college students were the participants in the three experiments; the results confirmed the hypothesis and led Greitemeyer to determine that "media exposure affects social behavior and related variables not only negatively, but may also do so positively."

Note: Chapter 2 includes a somewhat detailed discussion of this particular experiment, while Chapter 11 more generally deals with media influence and aggression.

EFFECTS OF SONGS WITH PROSOCIAL LYRICS ON PROSOCIAL THOUGHTS, AFFECT, AND BEHAVIOR

Tobias Greitemeyer

University of Sussex

ABSTRACT—*Previous research has shown that exposure to violent media increased aggression-related affect and thoughts, physiological arousal, and aggressive behavior as well as decreased prosocial tendencies. The present research examined the hypothesis that exposure to prosocial media promotes prosocial outcomes. Three studies revealed that listening to songs with prosocial (relative to neutral) lyrics increased the accessibility of prosocial thoughts, led to more interpersonal empathy, and fostered helping behavior. These results provide first evidence for the predictive validity of the General Learning Model [Buckley, K. E., & Anderson, C. A. (2006). A theoretical model of the effects and consequences of playing video games. In P. Vorderer, & J. Bryant, (Eds.), Playing video games: Motives responses and consequences (pp. 363–378). Mahwah, NJ: Lawrence Erlbaum Associates] for the effects of media with prosocial content on prosocial thought, feeling, and behavior.*

KEYWORDS: prosocial behavior, music, media effects

Tobias Greitemeyer, "Effects of songs with prosocial lyrics on prosocial thoughts, affect, and behavior," *Journal of Experimental Social Psychology*, Vol. 45, pp. 186-190
Address correspondence to Tobias Greitemeyer, Department of Psychology, University of Sussex, BNI 9Q, Brighton, England, UK; E-mail address: t.greitemeyer@sussex.ac.uk.

Exposure to media is omnipresent in people's daily life. For instance, listening to music—the topic of the present paper—is of substantial importance to many people: In Europe, according to Nielsen Interactive Entertainment, people spend an average of 10.55 hours per week listening to music. Similarly, the average American youth listens to music 1.5–2.5 hours per day, not including the time they are exposed to music via music videos (Roberts, Foehr, & Rideout, 2003). Other research (Rentfrow & Gosling, 2003) also revealed that people consider music an important aspect of their lives, which is at least as important as most other leisure activities. This has led to the suggestion that media exposure could be an important determinant of pro- (Mares & Woodard, 2005) and antisocial behavior Robinson, Wilde, Navracruz, Haydel, & Varady (2001). However, whereas negative effects of exposure to media with violent content on aggressive behavior are well-documented, research on the effects of media with prosocial content on prosocial tendencies has been relatively sparse. Thus, in the present research, the hypothesis is examined that exposure to songs with prosocial lyrics increases prosocial thoughts, affect, and behavior. So far, this has not been tested.

Research on media violence

It is well-documented that exposure to violent media promotes aggressive thoughts, feelings, and behavior, and decreases prosocial behavior (for an overview, see Bushman & Huesmann, 2006). For instance, correlational evidence indicated that consumers of rap and heavy metal music reported more hostile attitudes (Rubin, West, & Mitchell, 2001). Experimental studies corroborated this finding: Listening to aggressive (relative to neutral) song lyrics increased aggressive thoughts, hostile feelings (Anderson, Carnagey, & Eubanks, 2003), and aggressive action (Fischer & Greitemeyer, 2006; Hansen & Hansen, 1990). Past research has also addressed the impact of violent video games on aggressive cognitions, affect, and behavior. For instance, playing a violent (relative to a neutral) video game increases the hostile expectation bias (Bushman & Anderson, 2002), state hostility and anxiety levels (Anderson & Ford, 1986), desensitization to violence (Bartholow, Bushman, & Sestir, 2006; Carnagey, Anderson, & Bushman, 2007), punitive behavior (Bartholow & Anderson, 2002), physical violence (Gentile et al., 2004), and criminal actions (Anderson & Dill, 2000), and decreases donations to a charity (Chambers & Ascione, 1987) and cooperative behavior (Sheese & Graziano, 2005). Recent longitudinal evidence (Anderson, Gentile, & Buckley, 2007) further revealed that exposure to violent video games had not only short-term effects, but also long-term consequences in that aggressive tendencies were significantly predicted by video game violence exposure five months earlier (even after controlling for Time 1 aggressive tendencies). In sum, the detrimental effects of exposure to violent media on aggression-related variables are well-documented.

Research on the effects of television on prosocial behavior

There is some indirect evidence for the possibility that exposure to prosocial songs increases prosocial tendencies: it has been shown that exposure to television with prosocial content has some positive effects. In an early study (Sprafkin, Liebert, & Poulos, 1975), children were exposed to a film about the dog Lassie. In the prosocial condition, Lassie saved her puppies by barking for help. In the control condition, no prosocial behavior was exhibited. Results revealed that children in the prosocial condition were more likely to help a puppy in need of help than children in the control condition. Two meta-analyses (Hearold, 1986; Mares & Woodard, 2005) corroborated this finding: Exposure to prosocial television content has beneficial effects on prosocial behavior.

Theoretical perspectives

The effects of violent media on aggression-related variables have been mainly explained by the General Aggression Model (GAM) proposed by Anderson and colleagues (e.g., Anderson & Bushman, 2002). This model integrates various theories, including social learning theory and related social-cognitive research, affective aggression model, social information-processing model, script theory, and excitation transfer model. According to the GAM, exposure to violent media activates an individual's internal states (cognition, affect, and arousal), which in turn change the interpretation of a potential conflict situation that results in aggressive behavior. The initial impulse to violent media is based on an automatic appraisal of the situation. However, when sufficient resources (e.g., cognitive capacity, motivation) are available a more thoughtful behavioral reaction could also occur. In addition, the model does not only account for short term effects of violent media exposure on aggression, but also for long term changes as a results of repeated encounters with violent media (i.e., each media exposure episode constitutes a learning trial).

Recently, this model has been expanded into a General Learning Model (GLM) to explain the effects of both violent and non-violent media on social behavior (Buckley & Anderson, 2006). As with the GAM, the GLM assumes that media exposure affects internal variables, consisting of cognition, affect, and arousal, which lead to behavior. However, rather than focusing only on the negative consequences of exposure to antisocial media, the GLM suggests that positive media can have positive effects. Thus, depending on the content of the media, either negative or positive effects of media exposure on social behavior are to be expected. That is, whereas antisocial media instigate aggression and aggression-related variables, prosocial media should foster prosocial outcomes. However, whereas many studies have documented the influence of violent media exposure on aggression and aggression-related variables, the effects of media with prosocial content on prosocial outcomes has not been examined. Thus, the predictive validity of the GLM for prosocial effects of media has not been tested.

The present research

For this reason, the present research examined positive effects of exposure to prosocial songs. The first two studies measured prosocial thoughts and affects, which are possible precursors, as outlined by GLM, of prosocial action. Specifically, the hypothesis was tested that listening to prosocial (relative to neutral) songs increased the accessibility of prosocial thoughts (Experiment 1) and led to more interpersonal empathy (Experiment 2). Finally, Experiment 3 addressed behavioral outcomes from listening to songs with prosocial content in that actual helping behavior was assessed.

Pilot testing

In all experiments, participants listened to two songs. To increase the ecological validity of the experimental manipulation, one song with English lyrics and one song with German lyrics were used. Artists and genres were matched across experimental conditions. Participants in the prosocial condition were exposed to: "Love generation" (Bob Sinclair) and "Kommt zusammen" (2raumwohnung). Participants in the neutral condition were exposed to: "Rock this party" (Bob Sinclair) and "Lachen und Weinen" (2raumwohnung). These songs were pretested in two pilot studies. Participants were from the same participant pool as in the three main experiments. In both pilot studies, participants listened to either the two prosocial or the two neutral songs. In the first pretest, there were 40 participants (28 women, 12 men). After listening of each song, they rated to what extent the song lyrics were prosocial, how much they liked the song, and to what extent the song was arousing. All items were assessed on scales from 0 = *not at all* to 7 = *definitely*. As intended, the content of the prosocial songs was perceived as being more prosocial (English song: $M = 4.85$, $SD = 1.46$; German song: $M = 4.20$, $SD = 1.88$) than the content of the neutral songs (English song: $M = 2.55$, $SD = 1.73$; German song: $M = 0.65$, $SD = 0.81$), $t(38) = 4.54$, $p < .001$, $d = 1.44$; $t(38) = 7.75$, $p < .001$, $d = 2.45$, respectively. In contrast, there were no significant differences with regard to liking (prosocial English song: $M = 3.00$, $SD = 2.18$; neutral English song: $M = 3.10$, $SD = 1.80$; $t(38) = 0.16$, $p = .88$, $d = 0.05$; prosocial German song: $M = 2.40$, $SD = 2.35$; neutral German song: $M = 3.15$, $SD = 1.84$; $t(38) = 1.12$, $p = .27$, $d = 0.36$) and arousal (prosocial English song: $M = 3.20$, $SD = 1.74$; neutral English song: $M = 3.00$, $SD = 1.86$; $t(38) = 0.35$, $p = .73$, $d = 0.11$; prosocial German song: $M = 1.60$, $SD = 2.21$; neutral German song: $M = 2.75$, $SD = 1.89$; $t(38) = 1.77$, $p = .09$, $d = 0.56$). In the second pretest (39 women, 11 men), perceived arousal and mood were assessed. The Perceived Arousal Scale (Anderson, Deuser, & DeNeve, 1995) contains 31 adjectives describing feelings of arousal (e.g., aroused) or lack of arousal (e.g., drowsy). Lack of arousal items were reverse scored. Positive and negative emotions were assessed by employing the PANAS (Watson, Clark, & Tellegen, 1988). Arousal properties of the prosocial ($M = 2.88$, $SD = 0.74$) and neutral songs ($M = 3.03$, $SD = 0.79$) were relatively similar, $t(48) = 0.71$, $p = .48$, $d = 0.20$. In addition, there were no significant effects for mood, neither on the positive affect scale (prosocial: $M = 2.36$, $SD = 0.75$, neutral: $M = 2.12$, $SD = 0.77$), $t(48) = 1.08$, $p = .29$, $d = 0.32$, nor on the negative affect scale (prosocial: $M = 1.40$, $SD = 0.38$, neutral: $M = 1.48$, $SD = 0.50$), $t(48) = 0.60$, $p = .55$, $d = 0.18$. Thus, because the arousal and mood properties of the songs used were relatively similar, effects of the songs on prosocial thoughts, feelings, and behavior cannot be attributed to mood and arousal differences. (With was aimed for: inasmuch as both prosocial and neutral songs can affect arousal, the arousal route is scientifically less interesting than the cognitive and the affective route, respectively.)

Experiment 1

The aim of Experiment 1 was to test the effect of prosocial songs on prosocial thoughts. It was expected that listening to prosocial (relative to neutral) songs would increase the accessibility of prosocial thoughts.

Methods

Participants and Design. Participants were 34 students (19 women, 11 men, four participants did not indicate their sex) of the Ludwig-Maximilians University (LMU) in Munich, Germany, who were randomly assigned to one of the two song conditions (prosocial vs. neutral). There were 18 participants in the prosocial condition and 16 participants in the neutral condition.

Procedure and Materials. Participants were welcomed by one female experimenter and learned that the purpose of the present study was to examine the impact of songs on thinking. To assess prosocial thought accessibility, a word completion task was used. Such a task has been successfully employed in previous research into the effects of violent media on aggressive thoughts (e.g., Anderson et al., 2003; Barlett, Harris, & Bruey, 2008).[1] Participants received a list of 18 word fragments. Their task was to fill in the missing letters to form a word. For instance, ''hi____'' can become the prosocial word ''hilfe'' (''help'') or the neutral word ''hier'' (''here''). Accessibility of prosocial thoughts was the proportion of word completions that were prosocial (that is, number of prosocial thoughts divided by the total number of word fragments completed).

Then, participants responded to two control questions to verify that the prosocial and the neutral songs differed in content. For each song, participants rated to what extent the song lyrics were about helping and cooperation, respectively. These ratings were highly correlated and thus combined to a prosocial index (English song: $\alpha = .75$; German song: $\alpha = .82$). Finally, participants answered demographic questions, were thanked, and fully debriefed. Participants were tested in small groups of three to four people.

---

[1] The use of the word completion task may raise concerns about suspicion and demand characteristics. Thus, although during debriefing none of the participants indicated awareness of the true purpose of the experiment, future research using thought accessibility tasks that do not require conscious expression of remembering (such as a reading reaction time task or a lexical decision task) and are thus not as easily affected by demand characteristics as direct memory tasks would be of interest.

Results and discussion

As intended, the content of the prosocial and the neutral songs clearly differed. The content of the prosocial songs was perceived as being more prosocial (English song: $M = 4.94$, $SD = 1.47$; German song: $M = 4.50$, $SD = 1.29$) than the content of the neutral songs (English song: $M = 2.56$, $SD = 1.54$; German song: $M = 2.00$, $SD = 1.57$), $t(32) = 4.61$, $p < .001$, $d = 1.58$; $t(32) = 5.09$, $p < .001$, $d = 1.74$, respectively.

The effect of type of song on prosocial thought accessibility was reliable: Participants who had listened to the prosocial songs ($M = 0.21$, $SD = 0.11$) had higher prosocial word completion scores than those who had listened to the neutral songs ($M = 0.14$, $SD = 0.08$), $t(32) = 2.05$, $p < .05$, $d = 0.73$. Participant sex had no significant effect on prosocial thought accessibility, $t(28) = 0.49$, $p = .63$, $d = 0.19$.

As expected, listening to songs with prosocial content increased the accessibility of prosocial thoughts. Thus, these results provide first evidence for the hypothesis that exposure to prosocial media affects an individual's internal state that, as outlined by GLM, may instigate behavioral reactions. Before data on the effects of exposure to prosocial songs on helping behavior are presented, I first address a second main route on how media exposure may affect behavior: empathy as an indicator of affect. This was done in Experiment 2.

Experiment 2

Experiment 2 tested an important contributor to prosocial behavior, namely, empathy (Batson, 1991). It was expected that listening to prosocial (relative to neutral) songs would increase empathy toward others in need.

Methods

Participants and Design. Participants were 38 students (27 women, 11 men) of the LMU. There were 18 participants in the prosocial condition and 20 participants in the neutral condition.

Procedure and Materials. As in Experiment 1, participants were welcomed by a female experimenter. They learned that they would take part in a marketing survey. After listening to each song, participants indicated their liking of the song. Participants then learned that another study was being conducted in which participants were asked to read essays from other participants. Because the participant who was supposed to read the essays did not show up for the study, the participant was asked to read and respond to two essays (adapted from DeWall & Baumeister, 2006). The first essay stated that the author broke up with his girlfriend, although they had been together for quite a long time and had been very close. Recently, however, things had changed and she told him that she did not want to be tied down to just one person. The author stated that he was suffering severely. In the second essay, the author noted that he broke his leg during an intramural game. He had played for this team for three years, but now this season is over for him. In addition to this mental pain, his injury physically hurts. Life on campus is very difficult because of his crutches. He is really down and this is all he thinks about. Directly after each essay, participants indicated how sympathetic, compassionate, and soft-hearted they felt toward the author of the essay (see Maner & Gailliot, 2007). These items were highly correlated and thus pooled in an empathy scale (romantic relationship: $\alpha = .75$; broken leg: $\alpha = .72$).

As in Experiment 1, participants rated to what extent the song lyrics were about helping and cooperation, respectively. These ratings were moderately correlated and thus combined to a prosocial index (English song: $\alpha = .55$; German song: $\alpha = .68$). Finally, participants answered demographic questions, were thanked, and fully debriefed. All participants were tested individually.

Results and discussion

As in Experiment 1, the content of the prosocial songs was perceived as being more prosocial (English song: $M = 4.22$, $SD = 1.32$; German song: $M = 4.28$, $SD = 1.77$) than the content of the neutral songs (English song: $M = 2.70$, $SD = 1.51$; German song: $M = 1.70$, $SD = 1.37$), $t(36) = 3.30$, $p < .01$, $d = 1.07$; $t(36) = 5.05$, $p < .001$, $d = 1.63$, respectively.

As expected, listening to prosocial songs increased empathy toward others in need. A 2 (type of song) × 2 (essay: romantic vs. broken leg) ANOVA with repeated measures on the latter factor revealed a significant main effect for type of song, $F(1,36) = 6.51$, $p < .05$, $\eta^2 = .15$. Participants who had listened to the prosocial songs (weighted $M = 7.05$) felt more empathy than those who had listened to the neutral songs (weighted $M = 5.78$). The interaction was not significant, $F(1,36) = 0.22$, $p = .64$, $\eta^2 = .01$. Finally, participant sex had no significant effect on empathy, $F(1,36) = 1.11$, $p = .30$, $\eta^2 = .03$. Liking of songs did not differ among experimental conditions. In addition, when controlling for liking, the effect for type of song on empathy remained significant, $F(1, 34) = 6.14$, $p < .05$, $\eta^2 = .15$.

To summarize, Experiment 2 revealed that exposure to songs with prosocial lyrics fostered interpersonal empathy. In concert with Experiment 1, findings of Experiment 2 suggest that exposure to prosocial media activates two of the main routes (cognition and affect) proposed by GLM on how media exposure influences behavior.

Experiment 3

After Experiments 1 and 2 have shown that exposure to songs with prosocial content affects cognition and affect that, as outlined by GLM, may instigate behavioral reactions, Experiment 3 examines whether listening to prosocial songs indeed affects prosocial action. It was expected that listening to prosocial (relative to neutral) songs would foster prosocial behavior.

Methods

Participants and Design. Participants were 90 students (55 women, 35 men) of the LMU. They received 2 € (approximately $3.20) for their participation. There were 45 participants in the prosocial condition and 45 participants in the neutral condition.

Procedure and Materials. At the onset, participants were welcomed by two female experimenters and learned that they would participate in a marketing survey on music preferences. Then, the second experimenter left the room, and the participants listened to the songs. After listening to the songs, the first experimenter left the room, and the second experimenter, who was unaware of the participant's experimental condition, reentered the room. She gave the participants the 2 €, and explained that the university was collecting donations for a non-profit organization. Participants were told that it would be great if they would donate these 2 € but that it would be also fine if they did not donate. Upon saying this, the experimenter pointed at a box on which the non-profit organization's information was printed. The experimenter left the room for 2 min and then returned. Finally, participants were probed for suspicion, debriefed, and thanked. None of the participants indicated any relatedness among listening to the songs and the donation to the non-profit organization. The money was indeed donated to the non-profit organization.

Note that—because measurement of the possible mediators may prime the concept for all participants and thus change subsequent measures of pro- and antisocial action—prosocial behavior was assessed, but no possible mediators (see Spencer, Zanna, & Fong, 2005). In fact, previous research into the effects of violent video games (e.g., Lindsay & Anderson, 2000) has shown that measuring aggressive cognitions changes subsequent measures of aggressive behavior.

Results and discussion

As predicted, participants who had listened to the prosocial songs were more likely to donate money than participants who had listened to the neutral songs, $\chi^2(1, N = 90) = 4.56, p < .05, w = .27$. Of the 45 participants who had listened to the prosocial songs, 24 donated. Of the 45 participants who had listened to the neutral songs, 14 donated. That is, 53% of the prosocial song condition helped, whereas 31% in the neutral song game condition did so. Participant sex had no significant effect on donating, $\chi^2(1, N = 90) = 0.12, p = .73$.

In summary, listening to songs with prosocial lyrics increased helping behavior. Thus, after Experiments 1 and 2 have shown that prosocial songs influence cognition and affect, which—according to GLM—are two of the main routes on how media exposure leads to behavior, Experiment 3 in fact revealed that exposure to prosocial media promoted prosocial reactions. However, because prosocial behavior and the possible mediators were assessed in different studies, it remains unclear whether accessibility of prosocial thoughts and/or interpersonal empathy indeed constitute the mediating path from media exposure to action. In the present research, I wanted to provide first evidence for the effects of listening to prosocial songs on prosocial cognitions, affects, and behaviors. Clarifying the exact causal mechanisms awaits future research.

General discussion

The aim of the present research was to examine the hypothesis that exposure to prosocial media fosters prosocial tendencies. In fact, listening to prosocial (relative to neutral) songs increased the accessibility of prosocial thoughts, led to more empathy, and instigated prosocial action. Whereas previous research has demonstrated that violent media increased aggression-related thoughts, feeling, and behavior (Bushman & Huesmann, 2006), the present research shows that media with prosocial content result in prosocial tendencies. Thus, media exposure affects social behavior and related variables not only negatively, but may also do so positively (see Greitemeyer & Osswald, 2007, for the effects of prosocial video games on prosocial behavior). Note also that across studies the effect for song exposure on thoughts, feeling, and behavior was medium to large.

Theoretical Implications, limitations, and future research

As noted above, using the GAM as a framework, there has been abundant research demonstrating detrimental consequences of exposure to violent media on aggression-related variables. To also account for positive effects of media exposure, this model has been expanded into the GLM (Buckley & Anderson, 2006), but, as yet, the predictive validity of the GLM for the effects of exposure to prosocial media on prosocial tendencies has not been tested. Thus, the present studies constitute the first empirical evidence that the effects of media exposure on social tendencies indeed depend to a great extent on the content of the media being consumed.

As proposed by GLM, the present set of studies showed that listening to songs with prosocial lyrics affected behavioral reactions as well as an individual's internal states (cognition and affect) that are assumed to elicit behavior. However, as noted above, the present research did not address whether exposure to prosocial media indeed led to behavioral reactions through these internal states. Thus, future research assessing internal states as well as behavioral reactions in one study would be informative in this regard. Nevertheless, based on the present results, it appears that the aim of GLM to bring the effects of media exposure on pro- and antisocial tendencies together within a common theoretical framework is not only a valuable endeavor, but is also supported by empirical evidence.

Previous research has demonstrated that violent media increased aggression and decreased prosocial behavior (Anderson & Bushman, 2001). Here, evidence was presented that listening to prosocial songs increased prosocial behavior. Thus, future research may examine whether exposure to prosocial songs does not only increase prosocial tendencies, but also decreases aggression and aggression-related variables.

The reader should be well aware that the present results are limited to the short-term: the effects of listening to prosocial songs on immediate thoughts, affects, and behaviors were examined. However, repeated exposure to media may affect long-term behavior (Huesmann & Miller, 1994). According to GLM, repeated encounters with prosocial media may yield long term changes in personality through the development and construction of knowledge structures. In addition, the present results materialized even though participants listened to only two songs. In real life, when people may repeatedly listen to prosocial songs, the positive effects on prosocial behavior might be even more pronounced. Thus, the media does not only increase the likelihood of aggressive and violent behavior, but could be also effectively used to improve social interactions.

Acknowledgment

I am grateful to Colin Wayne Leach for suggestions on a previous draft of this manuscript.

REFERENCES

Anderson, C. A., & Bushman, B. J. (2001). Effects of violent video games on aggressive behavior, aggressive cognition, aggressive affect, physiological arousal, and prosocial behavior: A meta-analytic review of the scientific literature. *Psychological Science, 12*, 353–359.

Anderson, C. A., & Bushman, B. J. (2002). Human aggression. *Annual Review of Psychology, 53*, 27–51.

Anderson, C. A., Carnagey, N. L., & Eubanks, J. (2003). Exposure to violent media: The effects of songs with violent lyrics on aggressive thoughts and feelings. *Journal of Personality and Social Psychology, 84*, 960–971.

Anderson, C. A., & Dill, K. E. (2000). Video games and aggressive thoughts, feelings, and behavior in the laboratory and in life. *Journal of Personality and Social Psychology, 78*, 772–790.

Anderson, C. A., & Ford, C. M. (1986). Affect of the game player: Short term effects of highly and mildly aggressive video games. *Personality and Social Psychology Bulletin, 12*, 390–402.

Anderson, C. A., Gentile, D. A., & Buckley, K. E. (2007). *Violent video game effects on children and adolescents: Theory, research, and public policy.* New York: Oxford University Press.

Anderson, C. A., Deuser, W. E., & DeNeve, K. (1995). Hot temperatures, hostile affect, hostile cognition, and arousal: Tests of a general model of affective aggression. *Personality and Social Psychology Bulletin, 21*, 434–448.

Bartholow, B. D., & Anderson, C. A. (2002). Effects of violent video games on aggressive behavior. *Journal of Experimental Social Psychology, 38*, 283–290.

Bartholow, B. D., Bushman, B. J., & Sestir, M. A. (2006). Chronic violent video game exposure and desensitization to violence: Behavioral and event-related brain potential data. *Journal of Experimental Social Psychology, 42*, 532–539.

Barlett, C. P., Harris, R. J., & Bruey, C. (2008). The effect of the amount of blood in a violent video game on aggression, hostility, and arousal. *Journal of Experimental Social Psychology, 44*, 539–546.

Batson, C. D. (1991). *The altruism question: Towards a social-psychological answer.* Hillsdale, NJ: Erlbaum.

Buckley, K. E., & Anderson, C. A. (2006). A theoretical model of the effects and consequences of playing video games. In P. Vorderer & J. Bryant (Eds.), *Playing video games: Motives, responses, and consequences* (pp. 363–378). Mahwah NJ: Lawrence Erlbaum.

Bushman, B. J., & Anderson, C. A. (2002). Violent video games and hostile expectations: A test of the general aggression model. *Personality and Social Psychology Bulletin, 28*, 1679–1686.

Bushman, B. J., & Huesmann, L. R. (2006). Short-term and long-term effects of violent media on aggression in children and adults. *Archives of Pediatrics and Adolescent Medicine, 160*, 348–352.

Carnagey, N. L., Anderson, C. A., & Bushman, B. J. (2007). The effect of video game violence on physiological desensitization to real-life violence. *Journal of Experimental Social Psychology, 43*, 489–496.

Chambers, J. H., & Ascione, F. R. (1987). The effects of prosocial and aggressive video games on children's donating and helping. *Journal of Genetic Psychology, 148*, 499–505.

DeWall, C. N., & Baumeister, R. F. (2006). Alone but feeling no pain: Effects of social exclusion on physical pain tolerance and pain threshold, affective forecasting, and interpersonal empathy. *Journal of Personality and Social Psychology, 91*, 1–15.

Fischer, P., & Greitemeyer, T. (2006). Music and aggression. The impact of sexualaggressive song lyrics on aggression-related thoughts, emotions and behavior toward the same and the opposite sex. *Personality and Social Psychology Bulletin, 32*, 1165–1176.

Gentile, D. A., Lynch, P. J., Linder, J. R., & Walsh, D. A. (2004). The effects of violent video game habits on adolescent hostility, aggressive behaviors, and school peformance. *Journal of Adolescence, 27*, 5–22.

Greitemeyer, T., & Osswald, S. (submitted for publication). *Effects of prosocial video games on prosocial behavior.*

Hansen, C. H., & Hansen, R. D. (1990). The influence of sex and violence on the appeal of rock music videos. *Communication Research, 17*, 212–234.

Hearold, S. (1986). A synthesis of 1043 effects of television on social behavior. In G. Comstock (Ed.), *Public communication of behavior* (pp. 65–133). San Diego, CA: Academic Press.

Huesmann, L. R., & Miller, L. S. (1994). Long-term effects of repeated exposure to media violence in childhood. In L. R. Huesmann (Ed.), *Aggressive behavior: Current perspectives* (pp. 153–186). New York: Plenum Press.

Lindsay, J. L., & Anderson, C. A. (2000). From antecedent conditions to violent actions: A general affective aggression model. *Personality and Social Psychology Bulletin, 26*, 533–547.

Maner, J. K., & Gailliot, M. (2007). Altruism and egoism: Prosocial motivations for helping depend on relationship context. *European Journal of Social Psychology, 37*, 347–358.

Mares, M. L., & Woodard, E. (2005). Positive effects of television on children's social interactions: A meta-analysis. *Media Psychology, 7*, 301–322.

Rentfrow, P. J., & Gosling, S. D. (2003). The do re mi's of everyday life: The structure and personality correlates of music preferences. *Journal of Personality and Social Psychology, 84*, 1236–1256.

Roberts, D. F., Foehr, U. G., & Rideout, V. (2003). *Generation M: Media in the lives of 8–18 year-olds.* Menlo Park, CA: Henry J. Kaiser Foundation.

Robinson, T. N., Wilde, M. L., Navracruz, L. C., Haydel, K. F., & Varady, A. (2001). Effects of reducing children's television and video game use on aggressive behavior: A randomized controlled trial. *Archives Pediatrics and Adolescent Medicine, 155*, 17–23.

Rubin, A. M., West, D. V., & Mitchell, W. S. (2001). Differences in aggression attitudes toward women and distrust as reflected in popular music preferences. *Media Psychology, 3*, 25–42.

Sheese, B. E., & Graziano, W. G. (2005). Deciding to defect. The effects of video-game violence on cooperative behavior. *Psychological Science, 16*, 354–357.

Spencer, S. J., Zanna, M. P., & Fong, G. T. (2005). Establishing a causal chain: Why experiments are often more effective than mediational analyses in examining psychological processes. *Journal of Personality and Social Psychology, 89*, 845–851.

Sprafkin, J. N., Liebert, R. M., & Poulos, R. W. (1975). Effects of a prosocial televised example on children's helping. *Journal of Experimental Child Psychology, 20*, 119–126.

Watson, D., Clark, L. A., & Tellegen, A. (1988). Development and validation of brief measures of positive and negative affect: The PANAS scales. *Journal of Personality and Social Psychology, 54*, 1063–1070.

READING 13

Weapons as Aggression-Eliciting Stimuli

Understanding the causes of human aggression is an important mission for social psychology in this increasingly violent world. As is discussed in Chapter 11 of your textbook, the frustration-aggression hypothesis generated a great deal of attention when it was introduced in 1939, and the research it inspired caused it to be revised and modified in a variety of ways. Inspired by this research but also recognizing its limitations, Leonard Berkowitz offered an important contribution to our understanding of the situational determinants of aggression by emphasizing the roles of anger and thought on aggression. Berkowitz argued that when people are angry, they are in a state of readiness to aggress. Frustration is but one cause of anger. Whether or not an angered person will behave aggressively depends, in part, on whether aggression-enhancing cues are present in the situation. Berkowitz proposed that the presence of such a cue in a situation can automatically increase the likelihood of aggression. The aggression-enhancing cue examined in the study reported in this reading was the presence of weapons. Berkowitz and LePage addressed the question of "whether weapons can serve as aggression-eliciting stimuli, causing an angered individual to display stronger violence than he would have shown in the absence of such weapons." Note that Berkowitz and LePage did not investigate whether the presence of weapons would prompt people to *use* the weapons to aggress; rather, they examined the more subtle point of whether the presence of weapons would increase the underlying likelihood of responding aggressively that is, even if the weapons are not used in the actual aggression. As you read this article, consider the implications of this research for understanding aggression in general, but also for the ongoing debates about gun control and the prevalence of violence depicted in the media.

WEAPONS AS AGGRESSION-ELICITING STIMULI[*]

Leonard Berkowitz and Anthony LePage

University of Wisconsin

An experiment was conducted to test the hypothesis that stimuli commonly associated with aggression can elicit aggressive responses from people ready to act aggressively. One hundred male university students received either 1 or 7 shocks, supposedly from a peer, and were then given an opportunity to shock this person. In some cases a rifle and revolver were on the table near the shock key. These weapons were said to belong, or not to belong, to the available target person. In other instances there was nothing on the table near the shock key, while for a control group 2 badminton racquets were on the table near the key. The greatest number of shocks was given by the strongly aroused Ss (who had received 7 shocks) when they were in the presence of the weapons. The guns had evidently elicited strong aggressive responses from the aroused men.

---

[*] Leonard Berkowitz and Anthony LePage, "Weapons as Aggression-Eliciting Stimuli," Journal of Personality and Social Psychology, 1967, Vol. 7, No. 2, pp. 202-207. Copyright (c) 1967 by the American Psychological Association. Reproduced with permission.

Human behavior is often goal directed, guided by strategies and influenced by ego defenses and strivings for cognitive consistency. There clearly are situations, however, in which these purposive considerations are relatively unimportant regulators of action. Habitual behavior patterns become dominant on these occasions, and the person responds relatively automatically to the stimuli impinging upon him. Any really complete psychological system must deal with these stimulus-elicited, impulsive reactions as well as with more complex behavior patterns. More than this, we should also be able to specify the conditions under which the various behavior determinants increase or decrease in importance.

The senior author has long contended that many aggressive actions are controlled by the stimulus properties of the available targets rather than by anticipations of ends that might be served (Berkowitz, 1962, 1964, 1965). Perhaps because strong emotion results in an increased utilization of only the central cues in the immediate situation (Easterbrook, 1959; Walters & Parke, 1964), anger arousal can lead to impulsive aggressive responses which, for a short time at least, may be relatively free of cognitively mediated inhibitions against aggression or, for that matter, purposes and strategic considerations.[1] This impulsive action is not necessarily pushed out by the anger, however. Berkowitz has suggested that appropriate cues must be present in the situation if aggressive responses are actually to occur. While there is still considerable uncertainty as to just what characteristics define aggressive cue properties, the association of a stimulus with aggression evidently can enhance the aggressive cue value of this stimulus. But whatever its exact genesis, the cue (which may be either in the external environment or represented internally) presumably elicits the aggressive response. Anger (or any other conjectured aggressive "drive") increases the person's reactivity to the cue, possibly energizes the response, and may lower the likelihood of competing reactions, but is not necessary for the production of aggressive behavior.[2]

A variety of observations can be cited in support of this reasoning (cf. Berkowitz, 1965). Thus, the senior author has proposed that some of the effects of observed violence can readily be understood in terms of stimulus-elicited aggression. According to several Wisconsin experiments, observed aggression is particularly likely to produce strong attacks against anger instigators who are associated with the victim of the witnessed violence (Berkowitz & Geen, 1966, 1967; Geen & Berkowitz, 1966). The frustrater's association with the observed victim presumably enhances his cue value for aggression, causing him to evoke stronger attacks from the person who is ready to act aggressively.

More direct evidence for the present formulation can be found in a study conducted by Loew (1965). His subjects, in being required to learn a concept, either aggressive or nature words, spoke either 20 aggressive or 20 neutral words aloud. Following this "learning task," each subject was to give a peer in an adjacent room an electric shock whenever this person made a mistake in his learning problem. Allowed to vary the intensity of the shocks they administered over a 10-point continuum, the subjects who had uttered the aggressive words gave shocks of significantly greater intensity than did the subjects who had spoken the neutral words. The aggressive words had evidently evoked implicit aggressive responses from the subjects, even though they had not been angered beforehand, which then led to the stronger attacks upon the target person in the next room when he supposedly made errors.

Cultural learning shared by many members of a society can also associate external objects with aggression and thus affect the objects' aggressive cue value. weapons are a prime example. For many men (and probably women as well) in our society, these objects are closely associated with aggression. Assuming that the weapons do not produce inhibitions that are stronger than the evoked aggressive reactions (as would be the case, e.g., if the weapons were labeled as morally "bad"), the presence of the aggressive objects should generally lead to more intense attacks upon an available target than would occur in the presence of a neutral object.

The present experiment was designed to test this latter hypothesis. At one level, of course, the findings contribute to the current debate as to the desirability of restricting sales of firearms. Many arguments have been raised for such a restriction. Thus, according to recent statistics, Texas communities having virtually no prohibitions against firearms have a much higher homicide rate than other American cities possessing stringent firearm regulations, and J. Edgar Hoover has maintained in *Time* magazine that the availability of firearms is an important factor in murders (Anonymous, 1966). The experiment reported here seeks to determine how this influence may come about. The availability of weapons obviously makes it easier for a person who wants to commit murder to do so. But, in addition, we ask whether weapons can serve as aggression-eliciting stimuli, causing an angered individual to display stronger violence than he would have shown in the absence of such weapons. Social significance aside, and at a more general theoretical level, this research also attempts to demonstrate that situational stimuli can exert "automatic" control over socially relevant human actions.

METHOD

Subjects

The subjects were 100 male undergraduates enrolled in the introductory psychology course at the University of Wisconsin who volunteered for the experiment (without knowing its nature) in order to earn points counting toward their final grade. Thirty-nine other subjects had also been run, but were discarded because they suspected the experimenter's confederate (21), reported receiving fewer electric shocks than was actually given them (7), had not attended to information given them about the procedure (9), or were run while there was equipment malfunctioning (2).

Procedure

General design Seven experimental conditions were established, six organized in a 2×3 factorial design, with the seventh group serving essentially as a control. Of the men in the factorial design, half were made to be angry with the confederate, while the other subjects received a friendlier treatment from him. All of the subjects were then given an opportunity to administer electric shocks to the confederate, but for two-thirds of the men there were weapons lying on the table near the shock apparatus. Half of these people were informed the weapons belonged to the confederate in order to test the hypothesis that aggressive stimuli which also were associated with the anger instigator would evoke the strongest aggressive reaction from the subjects. The other people seeing the weapons were told the weapons had been left there by a previous experimenter. There was nothing on the table except the shock key when the last third of the subjects in both the angered and nonangered conditions gave the shocks. Finally, the seventh group consisted of angered men who gave shocks with two badminton racquets and shuttlecocks lying near the shock key. This condition sought to determine whether the presence of *any* object near the shock apparatus would reduce inhibitions against aggression, even if the object were not connected with aggressive behavior.

Experimental manipulations When each subject arrived in the laboratory, he was informed that two men were required for the experiment and that they would have to wait for the second subject to appear. After a 5-minute wait, the experimenter, acting annoyed, indicated that they had to begin because of his other commitments. He said he would have to look around outside to see if he could find another person who might serve as a substitute for the missing subject. In a few minutes the experimenter returned with the confederate. Depending upon the condition, this person was introduced as either a psychology student who had been about to sign up for another experiment or as a student who had been running another study.

The subject and confederate were told the experiment was a study of physiological reactions to stress. The stress would be created by mild electric shocks, and the subjects could withdraw, the experimenter said, if they objected to these shocks. (No subjects left.) Each person would have to solve a problem knowing that his performance would be evaluated by his partner. The "evaluations" would be in the form of electric shocks, with one shock signifying a very good rating and 10 shocks meaning the performance was judged as very bad. The men were then told what their problems were, the subject's task was to list ideas a publicity agent might employ in order to better a popular singer's record sales and public image. The other person (the confederate) had to think of things a used-car dealer might do in order to increase sales. The two were given 5 minutes to write their answers, and the papers were then collected by the experimenter who supposedly would exchange them.

Following this, the two were placed in separate rooms, supposedly so that they would not influence each other's galvanic skin response (GSR) reactions. The shock electrodes were placed on the subject's right forearm, and GSR electrodes were attached to fingers on his left hand, with wires trailing from the electrodes to the next room. The subject was told he would be the first to receive electric shocks as the evaluation of his problem solution. The experimenter left the subject's room saying he was going to turn on the GSR apparatus, went to the room containing the shock machine and the waiting confederate, and only then looked at the schedule indicating whether the subject was to be angered or not. He informed the confederate how many shocks the subject was to receive, and 30 seconds later the subject was given seven shocks (angered condition) or one shock (nonangered group). The experimenter then went back to the subject, while the confederate quickly arranged the table holding the shock key in the manner appropriate for the subject's condition. Upon entering the subject's room, the experimenter asked him how many shocks he had received and provided the subject with a brief questionnaire on which he was to rate his mood. As soon as this was completed, the subject was taken to the room holding the shock machine. Here the experimenter told the subject it was his turn to evaluate his partner's work. For one group in both the angered and nonangered conditions the shock key was alone on the table (no-object groups). For two other groups in each of these angered and nonangered conditions, however, a 12-gauge shotgun and a .38-caliber revolver were lying on the table near the key (aggressive-weapon conditions). One group in both the angered and nonangered conditions was informed the weapons belonged to the subject's partner. The subjects given this treatment had been told earlier that their partner was a student who had been conducting an experiment.[3] They now were reminded of this, and the experimenter said the weapons were being used in some way by this person in his research (associated-weapons condition); the guns were to be disregarded. The other men were told simply the weapons "belong to someone else" who "must have been doing an experiment in here" (unassociated-weapons group), and they too were asked to disregard the guns. For the last treatment, one group of angered men found two badminton racquets and shuttlecocks lying on the table near the shock key, and these people were also told the equipment belonged to someone else (badminton-racquets group).

Immediately after this information was provided, the experimenter showed the subject what was supposedly his partner's answer to his assigned problem. The subject was reminded that he was to give the partner shocks as his evaluation and was informed that this was the last time shocks would be administered in the study. A second copy of the mood questionnaire was then completed by the subject after he had delivered the shocks. Following this, the subject was asked a number of oral questions about the experiment, including what, if any, suspicions he had. (No doubts were voiced about the presence of the weapons.) At the conclusion of this interview the experiment was explained, and the subject was asked not to talk about the study.

Dependent Variables

As in nearly all the experiments conducted in the senior author's program, the number of shocks given by the subjects serves as the primary aggression measure. However, we also report here findings obtained with the total duration of each subject's shocks, recorded in thousandths of a minute. Attention is also given to each subject's rating of his mood, first immediately after receiving the partner's evaluation, and again immediately after administering shocks to the partner. These ratings were made on a series of 10 13-point bipolar scales with an adjective at each end, such as "calm-tense" and "angry-not angry."

RESULTS

Effectiveness of Arousal Treatment

Analyses of variance of the responses to each of the mood scales following the receipt of the partner's evaluation indicate the prior-shock treatment succeeded in creating differences in anger arousal. The subjects getting seven shocks rated themselves as being significantly angrier than the subjects receiving only one shock ($F = 20.65, p < .01$). There were no reliable differences among the groups within any one arousal level. Interestingly enough, the only other mood scale to yield a significant effect was the scale "sad-happy." The aroused-seven-shocks men reported a significantly stronger felt sadness than the men getting one shock ($F = 4.63, p > .05$).

Aggression Toward Partner

A preliminary analysis of variance of the shock data for the six groups in the 3×2 factorial design yielded the findings shown in Table 1. As is indicated by the significant interaction, the presence of the weapons significantly affected the number of shocks given by the subject when the subject had received seven shocks. A Duncan multiple-range test was then made of the differences among the seven conditions means, using the error variance from a seven-group one-way analysis of variance in the error term. The mean number of shocks administered in each experimental condition and the Duncan test results are given in Table 2. The hypothesis guiding the present study receives good support. The strongly provoked men delivered more frequent electrical attacks upon their tormentor in the presence of a weapon than when nonaggressive objects (the badminton racquet and shuttlecocks) were present or when only the shock key was on the table. The angered subjects gave the greatest number of shocks in the presence of the weapons associated with the anger instigator, as predicted, but this group was not reliably different from the angered-unassociated-weapons conditions. Both of these groups expressing aggression in the presence of weapons were significantly more aggressive than the angered-neutral-object condition, but only the associated-weapons condition differed significantly from the angered-no-object group.

Some support for the present reasoning is also provided by the shock-duration data summarized in Table 3. (We might note here, before beginning, that the results with duration scores—and this has been a consistent finding in the present research program—are less clear-cut than the findings with number of shocks given.) The results indicate that the presence of weapons resulted in a decreased number of attacks upon the partner, although not significantly so, when the subjects had received only one shock beforehand. The condition differences are in the opposite direction, however, for the men given the stronger provocation. Consequently, even though there

TABLE 1

Analysis of Variance Results for Number

of Shocks Given by Subjects in Factorial Design

Source	df	MS	F
No. Shocks received (A)	1	182.04	104.62[*]
Weapons association (B)	2	1.90	1.09
A × B	2	8.73	5.02[*]
Error	84	1.74	

[*]$p < .01$

TABLE 2

Mean Number of Shocks Given in

Each Condition

Condition	Shocks received	
	1	7
Associated weapons	2.60_a	6.07_d
Unassociated weapons	2.20_a	5.67_{cd}
No object	3.07_a	4.67_{bc}
Badminton racquets	–	4.60_b

Note: Cells having a common subscript are not significantly different at the .05 level by Duncan multiple-range test. There were 10 subjects in the seven-shocks-received-badminton-racquets group and 15 subjects in each of the other conditions.

TABLE 3

Mean Total Duration of Shocks Given in

Each Condition

Condition	Shocks received	
	1	7
Associated weapons	17.93_c	46.93_a
Unassociated weapons	17.33_c	39.47_{ab}
No object	24.47_{bc}	34.80_{ab}
Badminton racquets	–	34.90_{ab}

Note: The duration scores are in thousandths of a minute. Cells having a common subscript are not significantly different at the .05 level by Duncan multiple-range test. There were 10 subjects in the seven-shocks-received-badminton-racquet group and 15 subjects in each of the other conditions.

are no reliable differences among the groups in this angered condition, the angered men administering shocks in the presence of weapons gave significantly longer shocks than the nonangered men also giving shocks with guns lying on the table. The angered-neutral-object and angered-no-object groups, on the other hand, did not differ from the nonangered-no-object condition.

Mood Changes

Analyses of covariance were conducted on each of the mood scales, with the mood ratings made immediately after the subjects received their partners' evaluation held constant in order to determine if there were condition differences in mood changes following the giving of shocks to the partner. Duncan range tests of the adjusted condition means yielded negative results, suggesting that the attacks on the partner did not produce any systematic condition differences. In the case of the felt anger ratings, there were very high correlations between the ratings given before and after the shock administration, with the Pearson *rs* ranging from .89 in the angered-unassociated-weapons group to .99 in each of the three unangered conditions. The subjects could have felt constrained to repeat their initial responses.

DISCUSSION

Common sense, as well as a good deal of personality theorizing both influenced to some extent by an egocentric view of human behavior as being caused almost exclusively by motives within the individual, generally neglect the type of weapons effect demonstrated in the present study. If a person holding a gun fires it, we are told either that he wanted to do so (consciously or unconsciously) or that he pulled the trigger "accidentally." The findings summarized here suggest yet another possibility: The presence of the weapon might have elicited an intense aggressive reaction from the person with the gun, assuming his inhibitions against aggression were relatively weak at the moment. Indeed, it is altogether conceivable that many hostile acts which supposedly stem from unconscious motivation really arise because of the operation of aggressive cues. Not realizing how these situational stimuli might elicit aggressive behavior, and not detecting the presence of these cues, the observer tends to locate the source of the action in some conjectured underlying, perhaps repressed, motive. Similarly, if he is a Skinnerian rather than a dynamically oriented clinician, he might also neglect the operation of aggression-eliciting stimuli by invoking the concept of operant behavior, and thus sidestep the issue altogether. The sources of the hostile action, for him, too, rest within the individual, with the behavior only steered or permitted by discriminative stimuli.

Alternative explanations must be ruled out, however, before the present thesis can be regarded as confirmed. One obvious possibility is that the subjects in the weapons condition reacted to the demand characteristics of the situation as they saw them and exhibited the kind of behavior they thought was required of them. ("These guns on the table mean I'm supposed to be aggressive, so I'll give many shocks.") Several considerations appear to negate this explanation. First, there are the subjects' own verbal reports. None of the subjects voiced any suspicions of the weapons and, furthermore, when they were queried generally denied that the weapons had any effect on them. But even those subjects who did express any doubts about the experiment typically acted like the other subjects. Thus, the eight nonangered-weapons subjects who had been rejected gave only 2.50 shocks on the average, while the 18 angered-no-object or neutral-object men who had been discarded had a mean of 4.50 shocks. The 12 angered-weapon subjects who had been rejected, by contrast, delivered an average of 5.83 shocks to their partner. These latter people were evidently also influenced by the presence of weapons.

Setting all this aside, moreover, it is not altogether certain from the notion of demand characteristics that only the angered subjects would be inclined to act in conformity with the experimenter's supposed demands. The non-angered men in the weapons group did not display a heightened number of attacks on their partner. Would this have been predicted beforehand by researchers interested in demand characteristics? The last finding raises one final observation. Recent unpublished research by Allen and Bragg indicates that awareness of the experimenter's purpose does not necessarily result in an increased display of the behavior the experimenter supposedly desires. Dealing with one kind of socially disapproved action (conformity), Allen and Bragg demonstrated that high levels of experimentally induced awareness of the experimenter's interests generally produced a decreased level of the relevant behavior. Thus, if the subjects in our study had known the experimenter was interested in observing their *aggressive* behavior, they might well have given less, rather than more, shocks, since giving shocks is also socially disapproved. This type of phenomenon was also not observed in the weapons conditions.

Nevertheless, any one experiment cannot possibly definitely exclude all of the alternative explanations. Scientific hypotheses are only probability statements, and further research is needed to heighten the likelihood that the present reasoning is correct.

REFERENCES

Anonymous. A gun-toting nation. *Time*, August 12, 1966.

Berkowitz, L. *Aggression: A social psychological analysis*. New York: McGraw-Hill, 1962.

Berkowitz, L. Aggressive cues in aggressive behavior and hostility catharsis. *Psychological Review*, 1964, 71, 104–122.

Berkowitz, L. The concept of aggressive drive: Some additional considerations. In L. Berkowitz (Ed.), *Advances in experimental social psychology*. Vol. 2. New York: Academic Press, 1965. Pp. 301–329.

Berkowitz, L., & Geen, R. G. Film violence and the cue properties of available targets. *Journal of Personality and Social Psychology*, 1966, 3, 525–530.

Berkowitz, L., & Geen, R. G. Stimulus qualities of the target of aggression: A further study. *Journal of Personality and Social Psychology*, 1967, 5, 364–368.

Buss, A. *The psychology of aggression*. New York: Wiley, 1961.

Easterbrook, J. A. The effect of emotion on cue utilization and the organization of behavior. *Psychological Review*, 1959, 66, 183–201.

Geen, R. G., & Berkowitz, L. Name-mediated aggressive cue properties. *Journal of Personality*, 1966, 34, 456–465.

Loew, C. A. Acquisition of a hostile attitude and its relationship to aggressive behavior. Unpublished doctoral dissertation, State University of Iowa, 1965.

Walters, R. H., & Parke, R. D. Social motivation, depen-dency, and susceptibility to social influence. In L. Berkowitz (Ed.), *Advances in experimental social psychology*. Vol. 1. New York: Academic Press, 1964. Pp. 231–276.

NOTES

1. Cognitive processes can play a part even in impulsive behavior, most notably by influencing the stimulus qualities (or meaning) of the objects in the situation. As only one illustration, in several experiments by the senior author (cf. Berkowitz, 1965) the name applied to the available target person affected the magnitude of the attacks directed against this individual by angered subjects.

2. Buss (1961) has advanced a somewhat similar conception of the functioning of anger.

3. This information evidently was the major source of suspicion; some of the subjects doubted that a student running an experiment would be used as a subject in an other study, even if he were only an undergraduate. This information was provided only in the associated-weapons conditions, in order to connect the guns with the partner, and, consequently, this ground for suspicion was not present in the unassociated-weapons groups.

(Received October 5, 1966)

READING 14

Stand by Your Man: Indirect Prescriptions for Honorable Violence and Feminine Loyalty in Canada, Chile, and the United States

As discussed in Chapter 11 (Aggression), socialization of aggression varies by culture. In their discussion of what anthropologists call a "culture of honor," Kassin and Fein point out that such cultures emphasize honor and social status, particularly for males. Through a series of studies, researchers (including Dov Cohen, Richard Nisbett, Joseph Vandello, and their colleagues) examined such divergent cultures as those found in the American South, Brazil, Chile, and Canada. In the reading presented here, Vandello, Cohen, Grandon, and Franiuk compared the culture of honor in two studies. In the first, the participants were northern U.S. Anglos (a subculture without a strong honor tradition) and Latinos and southern Anglos (subcultures emphasizing honor). In the second, the participants were Anglo-Canadians (without strong honor tradition) and Chileans (strong honor tradition). Study one had participants view a video of a woman describing an abusive relationship. Comparatively, those from honor subcultures were more favorable to the woman if she stayed in the relationship. Study two had participants listen to audiotapes of a husband describing a violent conflict with his wife. When the conflict was related to jealousy, an honor issue, those from honor-tradition subcultures rated the husband's actions more positively. When the conflict was related to spending too much money, not an honor issue, there was no difference in the way participants from the varied cultures viewed the conflict.

STAND BY YOUR MAN: INDIRECT PRESCRIPTIONS FOR HONORABLE VIOLENCE AND FEMININE LOYALTY IN CANADA, CHILE, AND THE UNITED STATES

Joseph A. Vandello

University of South Florida

Dov Cohen

University of Illinois at Urbana–Champaign

Ruth Grandon

University of Waterloo

Renae Franiuk

Aurora University

Joseph A. Vandello, Dov Cohen, Ruth Grandon and Renae Franiuk, "Stand by Your Man: Indirect Prescriptions for Honorable Violence and Feminine Loyalty in Canada, Chile, and the United States," *Journal of Cross-Cultural Psychology*, Vol. 40, No. 81, 2009, < http://jcc.sagepub.com/cgi/content/abstract/40/1/81 > Correspondence concerning this article may be addressed to Joseph Vandello, Department of Psychology, PCD 4118G, University of South Florida, Tampa, Florida 33620-7200; e-mail: vandello@cas.usf.edu.

ABSTRACT—*Cultural values emphasizing female loyalty, sacrifice, and male honor may indirectly sanction relationship violence and reward women who remain in abusive relationships. Two studies compare participants from subcultures emphasizing honor (Latinos and southern Anglos in Study 1, Chileans in Study 2) and subcultures without strong honor traditions (northern U.S. Anglos in Study 1, Anglo-Canadians in Study 2). In Study 1, participants watch a videotape of a woman describing an abusive relationship. Participants from honor cultures are relatively more favorable to the woman if she stays in the relationship, compared to northerners. In Study 2, Chilean and Canadian students listen to audiotapes of a husband describing a violent conflict with his wife. Chileans rate the husband and his actions more positively than Canadians do when the conflict is jealousy related (perceived flirting), but no cultural differences are found when the conflict is unrelated to jealousy (spending too much money).*

KEYWORDS: domestic violence; honor; culture; aggression; partner violence; jealousy

Despite increased attention over the past generation, domestic violence remains disturbingly common in the United States and other Western hemisphere nations (Vandello & Cohen, unpublished document). Roughly a quarter of women in the United States will experience physical violence from an intimate partner at some point in their adult lives (Straus & Gelles, 1986; Tjaden & Thoennes, 1998; Wilt & Olson, 1996), with similar rates reported among Canadian women (Haskell & Randall, 1993; Smith, 1987). Across Latin America, the problem may be even worse, with estimates from some surveys of over half of all adult women reporting physical violence from a partner (Archer, 2006; Heise, Pitanguy, & Germain, 1994; Vandello & Cohen, unpublished document).

It would be a mistake, however, to assume that cultural norms or attitudes directly support domestic violence. On the contrary, survey evidence suggests that people are quite opposed to male violence against women. In fact, under most circumstances, people see violence against women as much worse than violence against men, in part because of norms of chivalry that oblige protecting women from harm (see Felson, 2002, p. 67; Glick & Fiske, 2001). People inhibit violence against women, particularly when an audience is present (Felson, 1982), and people tend to be much less aggressive toward women than men, both in laboratory and real-world settings (Daly & Wilson, 1988; Eagly & Steffen, 1986). More generally, groups usually develop strong norms prohibiting violence by stronger entities against weaker entities (Thibaut & Kelley, 1959).

If attitudes are largely opposed to harming women, how can we account for the prevalence of domestic violence? Is domestic violence simply a deviant act that occurs occasionally despite cultural prohibitions about violence against women? Certainly, individual pathology can be a contributing factor (Dutton, 1998; Dutton, Starzomski, & Ryan, 1996; also see Yost & Zurbriggen, 2006; Zurbriggen, 2000), but we believe that a full understanding requires going beyond individual personality factors. The present studies consider how male violence in relationships may be indirectly sanctioned or condoned because of certain cultural ideals about gender and certain cultural scripts regarding expectations in romantic relationships. Specifically, we explore two complementary notions of masculinity and femininity that might indirectly excuse or minimize violence (also see Best, 2001). First, cultural ideals of femininity might indirectly sanction, excuse, or minimize violence by rewarding women in abusive situations for being loyal. A woman might be seen as strong, sacrificing, and honorable for "standing by her man," even in the face of conflict and violence. Second, in certain cultural contexts, emphases on honor might dictate that men protect their manly reputations against events that would shame them, and these expectations might justify or excuse the use of violence in response to jealousy-related conflicts in romantic relationships.

In previous research (Vandello & Cohen, 2003), we have shown how these gender expectations may be especially salient in more traditional cultures where male honor, female loyalty, and sexual modesty are stressed. For instance, in one study (Vandello & Cohen, 2003, Study 1), we found that Brazilians, belonging to a culture with strong norms about honor, were more likely than Americans to view a cuckolded man as less honorable and manly; Brazilians were also more likely to accept a man's violence against his wife in response to her infidelity. In a second study, we demonstrated that American cultural groups with relatively strong traditions of honor (southern Anglos and Latinos) sent more messages condoning aggression against a woman and encouraging her to remain loyal to her partner after witnessing an abusive encounter, compared to a group of northern Anglos.

In the present research, we sought to replicate and extend this research in several ways. First, our previous research suggests a good deal of ambivalence about domestic violence. On one hand, people across cultures tend to acknowledge that violence is wrong or undesirable and that women should not have to be victims. At the same time, people (particularly from honor cultures) may more implicitly or indirectly credit women for staying in abusive relationships by expressing more positive feelings about a woman's character if she stays. We test this idea directly in the first study of this article, using a far more innocuous jealousy provocation than used previously. In the present study, the man in the story goes into a jealous rage after his fiancée merely gets a ride home from a male coworker. The incident suggests a rather pathological jealousy on the part of the husband, and the question is how respondents evaluate a woman who either leaves or stays in such circumstances. Second, our past research involved scenarios describing violence that involved a prototypical honor concern (i.e., real or suspected infidelity). We used such scenarios in the expectation that they would elicit the biggest cultural differences. However, because we did not vary the sort of provocation, one question left unanswered is whether members of honor cultures are simply more condoning in general of male violence against women. To rule out this possibility, in the second study of this article, we manipulated the type of conflict (honor related vs. nonhonor related) to demonstrate that violence is only condoned in honor cultures in limited culturally prescribed circumstances. Third, we extended our samples to explore the generalizability of honor norms: In our first study, we considered subcultures within the United States with honor traditions (Latinos and southern Anglos; also see Vandello & Cohen, 2003); in our second study, we compared Chileans, who belong to a culture with strong historical traditions of honor and high rates of domestic violence (Caufield, Chambers, & Putnam, 2005; Ceballo, Ramirez, Castillo, Caballero, & Lozoff, 2004; Johnson & Lipsett-Rivera, 1998; McWhirter, 1999), to Anglo-Canadians, who do not have a strong honor tradition. Fourth, in our past research on honor and violence, we have assumed but not directly tested that cultural differences in the importance of honor mediate cultural differences in attitudes about violence. In our second study, we tested mediation by measuring cultural concerns with honor.

Notions of Femininity and Masculinity

Honorable Feminine Loyalty and Sacrifice

Sacrifice, altruism, and loyalty in romantic relationships have been common themes in Western mythologies about women for some time (Walker & Goldner, 1995; Wood, 2001). Common stereotypes portray women as relatively refined and morally superior to men. Applied to romantic relationships, this moral refinement and superiority implies both accepting or at least tolerating males' less refined (e.g., aggressive) manners and celebrating women's ability to nurse, tame, or civilize these men, even in the face of abuse (Wood, 2001). For example, a letter from Victorian America gave this advice on marriage: "Few women understand at the outset that in marrying, they have simply captured a wild animal, and staked their chances for future happiness on their capacity to tame him . . . at the core of his nature he cherishes still his original savagery, the taming of which is to be the lifework of the woman who has taken him in charge. It is a task which will require her utmost of Christian patience, fidelity, and love" (as cited in Haller & Haller, 1984, p. 110).

Rosen (1996) notes the connection between the belief in women's altruistic power to reform men and the psychological chains that keep women in abusive relationships, calling this cultural script the "Beauty and the Beast fantasy." As an example, she quotes an abused woman she interviewed describing her husband, "He was a bully that I was willing to tame . . . He had been hurt somewhere along the way and I knew that. And I thought that if I gave him everything that I had we could live in bliss forever" (p. 163).

Although stereotypes of men as unrefined and women as moral and taming may be eroding across the West, we believe that these themes still hold some power as relationship scripts, particularly in cultures of honor. Pulitzer Prize–winning Alabaman author Rick Bragg describes his own subculture in this way: "The men in the South, we just ain't much good. A big part of the time we are just not worth killin.' And if it were not for those women who keep us upright, we would never make it" (Chesser Aspell, 1998, p. 90).

One particularly pervasive symbol of the ideal of feminine sacrifice in Latin American cultures is the Virgin Mary. This powerful gender symbol forms the basis of the Latin concept of "marianismo," which is a counterpart to the male concept of machismo (Stevens, 1973). According to the ideals of marianismo, women are morally and spiritually superior to men. However, women are also expected to accept male dominance and subvert their own individual interests to those of the family. Self-sacrifice and suffering for one's family are celebrated feminine ideals (McLoyd, Cauce, Takeuchi, & Wilson, 2000; Sugihara & Warner, 2002). Gender roles are changing in Latin American cultures as women take on a more direct role as providers in families and as many women reject some of the traditional prescriptions of femininity. However, even as a Latina feminist movement has emerged, high value is still placed on sacrifice in women's roles as wives and mothers (Espin, 1997; Stevens, 1994).

In short, we argue that although contemporary attitudes toward male violence against women have become increasingly negative, cultural themes celebrating feminine sacrifice and loyalty still remain strong, particularly in more traditional, honor-based cultures that stress family integrity over individualism. So although violence itself may be repudiated, the expectation for female sacrifice and loyalty may lead to people rewarding women for remaining in abusive relationships. We tested this ambivalence about female victims of domestic violence in Experiment 1.

Aggression as Masculine Honor

Certain cultural scripts about male behavior may also contribute indirectly to a degree of tolerance for domestic violence. Toughness and a perceived willingness to use violence are key components of masculinity in honor cultures (Cohen & Vandello, 2001; Nisbett & Cohen, 1996; Vandello, Cohen, & Ransom, 2008). Masculine honor is never assured but must be earned and continually defended on a public stage (Gilmore, 1990). With respect to romantic relationship scripts, a man's ability to exert control over his partner is an important component of masculine identity, and her betrayal represents the ultimate act of shame for him. Thus, a woman's infidelity, or the threat of infidelity, is an especially sensitive matter for a man, not simply because it violates his personal trust but also because of the public threat of shame and the loss of masculine honor it entails. Because of this, we might expect hypersensitivity to relationship trust issues and jealousy-related conflict. It is possible that a certain degree of violence may even be excused, provided that the man's violence is seen as legitimately used to protect his honor (Vandello & Cohen, 2003). So whereas violence against women in general is seen as unacceptable, violence under certain prescribed circumstances (e.g., perceived threats of infidelity) may be excused or at least minimized in cultures that stress the importance of masculine honor. We examine this hypothesis in our second experiment, comparing evaluations of a man who hit his wife over a jealousy-related (vs. a nonjealousy-related) incident.

Experiment 1

Experiment 1 was designed to explore whether women might be rewarded indirectly for loyalty in the face of abuse, by measuring people's evaluations of a woman who was in a relationship in which violence had occurred. We predicted that although people would not be favorable to domestic violence, they might still show indirect support for a loyal woman. Specifically, we predicted that individuals from cultures with honor traditions (Latinos and southern Anglos; see Vandello & Cohen, 2003) would evaluate a woman who remained loyal in an abusive relationship more positively than would individuals from a cultural background where honor was less of a salient theme (northern Anglos); conversely, the honor groups would evaluate a woman who left a relationship more negatively than would the nonhonor group.

Participants watched a videotape of a woman in an interview session discussing a relationship in which physical abuse had occurred. The tapes were manipulated such that in some cases, the woman decided to leave the relationship and in other cases she stayed. After watching the video, participants rated the woman on a number of characteristics, and they rated their reaction to the woman's decision to leave or stay.

Method

Participants and Cultural Classification. Participants were 163 students (82 males and 81 females) drawn from introductory psychology classes at the University of Illinois, selected from three cultural groups: northern Anglos ($n = 61$), southern Anglos ($n = 41$), and Latinos ($n = 61$). Recruitment and classification of southern and northern participants was based on permanent residence and follows similar procedures of our other work (see Cohen, Vandello, Puente, & Rantilla, 1999; Leung & Cohen, 2006; Vandello & Cohen, 2003; Vandello et al., 2008). Participants who had spent at least a third of their life in the South were considered southern; all others were considered northern.[1] Following U.S. Census classification, the South was defined as Alabama, Arkansas, Delaware, Florida, Georgia, Kentucky, Louisiana, Maryland, Mississippi, Missouri, North Carolina, Oklahoma, South Carolina, Tennessee, Texas, Virginia, and West Virginia. In addition, we recruited students from the southern half of Illinois (counties south of Springfield) and classified them as southern, consistent with evidence from other research we have conducted (Cohen et al., 1999; Leung & Cohen, 2007; Vandello & Cohen, 2003; Vandello et al., 2008). According to historians, ethnographers, demographers, economists, and sociologists, the south of Illinois is culturally part of the South, being settled primarily by people from Tennessee, Kentucky, and the Carolinas. In fact, of the approximately 50 counties below Springfield, all but 2 were primarily settled by people from these four southern states (Adams, 1993; Atack, 1989; Wirt, 1989; see Cohen et al., 1999, for a discussion of southern classification issues).

Procedure. Upon entering the lab, participants were given a brief cover story explaining that the purpose of the study was to explore people's perceptions of relationships and relationship conflicts. They were told that the counseling department had earlier recruited people who were engaged to be married to come in and discuss their relationships. These people (who were supposedly all from a different community) agreed to be videotaped. The researchers reinterviewed these same people several months later to check on the development of the relationship. The participants were told that they would be watching excerpts from one of these videotapes and then making some judgments about the person and the relationship.

All participants received a short written profile of the woman in the video. To control for possible differences in rating an in-group versus out-group member, Latino participants were told that the woman was Mexican American, and Anglo participants were told that she was White (the woman had dark hair and features such that either ethnic categorization was plausible).

The videotape segments were approximately 7 minutes in length. The video included some short introductory information about how the woman met her fiancé, how long they had been dating, and so on. Early on in the video, she noted that the fiancé had an aggressive history (he got into a fight at a bar the first time she saw him). At one point in the video, the woman was asked to recall a conflict situation she had been in with her fiancé and how she handled it. She then described a time in which she had been driven home from work by a male coworker. Upon discovering this, her fiancé became jealous and an argument ensued, escalated, and ended with him striking her in the face.

Up until this point, all participants watched the same video segment. The counselor on the video then asked the woman what she did in response to the violence, and participants saw one of three different endings to the video. The endings were scripted to reflect differing cultural notions for appropriate female roles in relationships. In the first version, the woman left the man, and in the other two versions, she remained in the relationship:

Version 1. The woman said that she ended the relationship immediately after he hit her and had since ended all communication with the man: "I'm sure he's a good guy at heart, but I'm not going to be someone's punching bag. So I ended the relationship right then and there."

Version 2. The woman said that she got angry and didn't talk to him for a few days, but then she nurtured and supported him, portraying herself as one who tried to "love away" his wild edge. When asked if he had ever hit her again, she replied, "no."

Version 3. This scenario was exactly the same as version 2, except that the last question revealed that he had continued to be abusive. When asked if he had ever hit her again, she replied, "Yeah, a couple of times."

We decided to include two different versions of the woman who stayed in the relationship to distinguish between violence as a seemingly isolated, single event, versus violence that had recurred. Results revealed that there were no interactions between culture and the two versions (2 and 3) of the video in which the woman stayed in the relationship. Thus, for all analyses, results of the two "stay" video versions were collapsed, creating a general comparison of the videos in which the woman stayed versus the video in which she left.

Dependent Variables

After watching the video, participants completed a questionnaire probing reactions to how the woman handled the specific conflict, as well as more general impressions of the woman.

Ratings of the conflict response. Participants were asked to assess how the woman handled the relationship conflict by answering two questions: "How well do you think she handled the conflict described on the tape?" and "Do you believe that she will be happy with how she handled the conflict described on the tape?" Both questions were answered on 5-point scales, and the items were averaged to form a composite Conflict Response dimension ($\alpha = .87$).

Ratings of the woman. Participants also completed a questionnaire asking about their general impressions of the woman. They were first asked about their overall feelings of warmth toward the woman. Seven items tapped this Warmth dimension: "How similar are you to the woman on the video?"; How likely is it that you would be friends with her?"; "How much do you share the same values with the woman?"; "How easily do you feel you could relate to the woman?"; "How much would you enjoy interacting with this woman?"; "How much did you like the woman?"; "How sympathetic did you feel toward the woman?" Items were answered on 5-point scales. We aggregated these seven items to yield a composite Warmth dimension ($\alpha = .86$).

Two items asked participants to rate how smart the woman was: "How smart do you think she is?"; "How foolish do you think she is?" Participants used a scale of 1 to 5 to respond to these items. After reverse-scoring the foolish item, these questions were averaged to form a Smart dimension ($\alpha = .69$).

Participants then rated the woman on how well she would fit seven female roles: romantic partner, marital partner, friend, best friend, sister, mother, and adoptive parent, from 1 (*not very good*) to 5 (*excellent*). These items were aggregated to form an overall Feminine Roles dimension (α = .91).

After filling out the questionnaires, participants completed an extensive demographics questionnaire and were fully debriefed. The experimenter discussed the problem of domestic abuse, distributing information about local domestic violence resources. Training measures were taken to make sure that the experimenters were sensitive to issues of domestic violence as well as the validity of cultural differences in relationship styles.

Results

The pattern of responses of participants from the two honor groups (Latinos and southern Anglos) were extremely similar, as expected. Thus, the responses of these two groups were combined into one "honor" culture grouping.2 For all analyses, the main comparison was a Culture (Latino and southern Anglo vs. northern Anglo) × Woman's Response (woman left vs. woman stayed) interaction. There were almost no gender interactions, so the data were collapsed across gender except where noted.

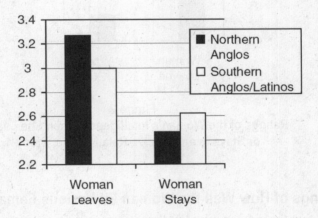

Figure 1
Ratings of Warmth Toward a Woman who Leaves or
Stays in an Abusive Relationship, Study 1

Ratings of the Conflict Resolution

On average, participants believed that the woman responded to the relationship conflict better when she ended the relationship (M = 4.00, SD = .80) as compared to when she stayed (M = 2.16, SD = .83), $F(1, 159)$ = 213.69, (p < .001), d = 2.44. There was no Culture × Video interaction, $F(1, 159)$ = .17, *ns*.

Participants' Warmth Toward the Woman

In general, participants expressed slightly more warmth toward the woman who ended the relationship (M = 3.09, SD = .54) than the woman who stayed (M = 2.56, SD = .63), $F(1, 159)$ = 27.98 (p < .001, d = .84). However, this effect was qualified by a significant Culture Video interaction, $F(1, 159)$ = 4.08, p < .05, effect size f = .16 (see Figure 1). As expected, northern Anglos, relative to southern Anglos and Latinos, expressed more warmth toward the woman who ended the relationship, Ms = 3.27 (.38) versus 3.00 (.58); southern Anglos and Latinos (relative to northern Anglos) expressed more warmth toward (or at least expressed less negativity about) the woman who stayed in the relationship, Ms = 2.62 (.68) versus 2.47 (.55).

Participants' Rating of the Woman's Smartness

The same pattern emerged for the Smartness dimension as the Warmth dimension. On average, participants thought that the woman who ended the relationship was smarter ($M = 3.58$, $SD = .72$) than the woman who stayed ($M = 2.50$, $SD = .65$), $F(1, 159) = 93.96$, $p < .001$, $d = 1.54$. Northern Anglos, relatives to southern Anglos and Latinos, believed that the woman who ended the relationship was smarter, $Ms = 3.75$ (.69) versus 3.50 (.73), whereas southern Anglos and Latinos (relative to northern Anglos) believed that the woman who stayed in the relationship was smarter (or at least less foolish), $Ms = 2.60$ (.66) versus 2.36 (61); Culture × Video = $F(1, 159) = 4.41$, $p < .05$, $f = .16$ (see Figure 2).

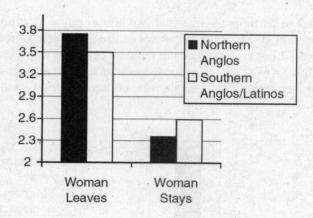

Figure 2
Ratings of the Woman's Intelligence When She Leaves
or Stays in an Abusive Relationship, Study 1

Participants' Ratings of How Well the Woman Fit Various Female Roles

Participants believed that the woman who left the relationship fit various feminine roles better than the woman who stayed, $Ms = 3.16$ (.82) versus 2.89 (.86), $F(1, 159) = 3.92$, $p = .05$, $d = .31$. There was no Culture × Video interaction ($F < 1$). Apparently, although individuals from cultures of honor attributed more warmth and intelligence to the woman who stayed in the relationship than did northern Anglos, this did not generalize to a belief that she fit various female roles better. There was a Gender × Video interaction such that women believed that the woman who left was more fit for the various roles than the woman who stayed, $Ms = 3.36$ (.83) versus 2.78 (.84), whereas men thought the woman who left and the woman who stayed were equally fit for the roles, $Ms = 2.96$ (.78) versus 2.99 (.88), interaction $F(1, 159) = 4.57$, $p < .05$, $f = .17$.

Demographics

All participants completed an extensive demographic questionnaire. To examine whether our Latino/southern versus northern effects were confounded with other demographic variables, we examined whether the groups differed on several potentially relevant characteristics. Analysis showed that the two groups (Latinos and southern Anglos vs. northern Anglos) were quite similar. The groups did not differ ($ps > .10$) in terms of school curriculum, year in school, age, percentage of life in a rural area, religious service attendance, number of brothers or sisters, fraternity and sorority membership, father's and mother's military service, participation in sports in high school and college, SAT scores, parents' marital status, and living arrangements while growing up. Significant or marginal differences were found with respect to their religious preference ($p = .06$), ACT scores ($p < .05$), high school GPA

($p = .06$), and parents' socioeconomic status ($p = .085$). However, none of the four variables on which the groups differed correlated with the main dependent variables for which significant cultural effects were found (participants' warmth toward the female and ratings of her smartness; all $rs < .12$, $ps > .13$). In summary, there were few demographic differences between the two groups, and the demographic differences that did emerge were unrelated to variables in which culture effects were found.

Summary

Two patterns stand out. First, participants were much more positive about a woman who left the abusive man compared to the woman who stayed, and they rated the specific conflict resolution strategy of leaving more positively than staying. The second pattern was a Culture × Conflict Response interaction in evaluations of the woman. The Culture × Response interactions were between small and medium in terms of effect size; however, they were significant and in the expected direction. Thus, members of honor cultures were relatively more positive toward a woman who stayed (expressed more warmth toward her and rated her as smarter) and were relatively less positive toward a woman who left, as compared to their northern counterparts.

In sum, the results of Experiment 1 were moderately supportive of the hypotheses. However, they were qualified by (a) the overall tendency to evaluate the woman who stayed more negatively than the woman who left and (b) the absence of a Culture × Video interaction on two of our dependent variables. We return to these qualifications in the General Discussion section of the article.

Experiment 2: Chilean Versus Anglo-Canadian Evaluations of Abusive Men

With some qualifications, Experiment 1 showed that members of honor cultures were more positive— or at least less negative—toward women who stayed in abusive relationships, as compared to members of a nonhonor culture. In our second experiment, we looked at a complementary set of expectations for men, examining cultural differences in evaluations of men who engage in relationship abuse.

Despite normal constraints against harming women, these constraints may be lifted if women violate certain cultural prescriptions. This may be particularly the case in cultures where honor and public reputation are central concerns to a man and where a woman's betrayal puts him in a position of deep shame. Thus, we would predict that although people will be generally negative toward a man who uses physical violence against his partner, people from honor cultures will be less negative if the violence is precipitated by some action of the woman that may deeply threaten a man's honor (e.g., when the violence occurs in the context of a jealousy-inducing situation). We predicted that the sanctioning of violence in honor cultures would be limited to situations in which the triggering event was related to jealousy (a clear honor-relevant situation), and we expected no cultural differences in acceptability of violence unrelated to honor (in this case, a conflict over spending money).3 To explore the generalizability of our honor predictions, we chose two different cultural groups to compare: Chileans, from a culture with strong honor roots; and Anglo-Canadians from Ontario, who do not have a strong honor tradition. We also directly measured our two cultural groups' endorsement of abstract principles about honor.

Method

Participants. Participants were 153 students (68 females and 85 males) from the University of Santiago in Santiago, Chile; and 177 students (89 females and 88 males) from the University of Waterloo in Waterloo, Canada. Participants in Canada received either credit toward introductory psychology classes or $8 for their participation. Participants in Chile were recruited through classes by requesting their participation. Canadian and Chilean participants did not differ in their marital status ($p > .10$). The Canadian sample (mean age = 19.7 years) was slightly older than the Chilean sample (mean age = 18.8

years; $p < .001$), and Canadians were more likely to have no religious denomination ($p < .05$), more likely to be Protestant ($p < .002$), and less likely to be Catholic ($p < .001$). Canadian respondents also went to church less frequently and considered their religious faith less important to them, as compared to Chilean respondents ($p < .001$). However, controlling for age and the religion variables does not alter the study's results or the conclusions that we describe.

Procedure. Participants from both samples were run in small groups. To prevent participants from influencing each other's evaluations, they were either seated one behind the other facing the tape recorder (in Chile) or in separate cubicles (in Canada). Participants were told that the experiment would examine people's perceptions of marital conflict. Therefore, they would listen to audiotaped excerpts from interviews with husbands who participated in a previous study at the university. Participants were told that the men had agreed to provide their first names (John for the Canadian sample and Juan for the Chilean sample), their pictures, and their city of residence (Toronto for the Canadian sample, Santiago for the Chilean sample).

All participants listened to interviews in which a husband described a past marital conflict that ended in violence with the husband pulling his wife by her hair and punching her in the face. Two audiotaped scenarios were created, manipulating the incident that triggered the conflict. One scenario described abuse over a jealousy-related incident: the husband believes his wife is flirting with another man at a party. The other scenario described abuse over a nonjealousy-related incident: the husband is upset about his wife spending money budgeted for the expenses of the week on personal items such as makeup and clothing. The actor portraying the husband spoke both English and Spanish, and the same actor read the script in English and Spanish. Scripts were written in English and translated to Spanish by one of the researchers and back-translated by an independent translator. Individuals from both Chile and Canada reviewed and made suggestions regarding culturally appropriate use of language and presentation of the scenarios.

Dependent Measures.

After listening to the interview, participants completed a questionnaire asking about their perceptions of the husband and his actions.

Acceptability of violence. Five questions asked about the appropriateness of the husband's reaction during the conflict, with higher scores indicating greater appropriateness (on a scale of 1 to 6). The items asked participants to rate the husband's reactions on the dimensions of (a) necessary or unnecessary, (b) good or bad, (c) justified or unjustified, (d) understandable or not understandable, and (d) acceptable or not acceptable. These five items were combined to form an overall Acceptability of Violence dimension ($\alpha = .82$).

Warmth toward the husband. Five questions asked participants to provide their general impression of the husband in terms of their warmth toward him, with higher scores indicating greater warmth (on a scale of 1 to 5): "How similar are you to John (Juan)?"; How likely is it that you would be friends with John (Juan)?"; "Do you share the same values with John (Juan)?"; "How easy is it for you to identify with John (Juan)?"; "How much would you enjoy interacting with John (Juan)?" We aggregated these five items to yield a composite Warmth dimension ($\alpha = .77$).

Ratings of husband's character as a good partner. Cross-culturally, the two characteristics that people rate as most important in a mating partner are kindness and intelligence (Buss, 1989; Figueredo et al., 2005; Miller, 1998). Thus, we created an index of 11 items that would tap into these qualities of being a good mate. Participants were asked to rate the husband in terms of the characteristics: kind or unkind, good person or bad person, warm or cold, good friend or bad friend, affectionate or not affectionate, intelligent or unintelligent, inquisitive or uninquisitive, foolish or not foolish, wise or unwise, practical or impractical, and simple or ingenious (these 11 items were rated on 5-point scales and were essentially the same as the goodness and wisdom items used to rate a female confederate in Vandello and Cohen, 2003, $\alpha = .73$).

Husband's love toward partner. We also asked several questions about the husband's love for his wife. Within intimate relationships, extreme jealousy and even violence are sometimes considered manifestations of love (McWhirter, 1999; Puente & Cohen, 2003), and we suspected this might be especially the case in honor cultures. Of course, one may see jealousy as a sign of love but still disapprove of violence. We included this variable not as a direct measure of approval but rather as a measure of a factor that might mitigate or even serve as an excuse for the violent act. Following Puente and Cohen (2003), we asked about the husband's companionate love for his wife and his passionate or romantic love for her. The companionate love questions asked, "How much does John love Rose?"; "How much concern does John feel for Rose?"; and "How much respect does John have for Rose?" ($\alpha = .62$). The passionate love questions asked, "How much passion does John feel for Rose?"; "How much does John need Rose?"; and "How much does John want to be with Rose?" ($\alpha = .73$).4 Both scales used 1 to 5 response options.

Secondary measures: Honor endorsement, honor prized, and ambivalent sexism. To confirm our expectation that honor was a more salient and prized value in Chile compared to Canada, we also included two measures to assess cultural differences in honor-related attitudes. As a part of a separate questionnaire, nine items asked participants about their agreement (1 to 7) with gender-specific honor values. Five items were specific to male honor, such as: "A man must defend his honor at any cost," "A real man must be capable of defending himself against an insult," and so on. Four items were specific to female honor: "A woman must protect the family's good reputation," "A woman's honor must be defended by the men in the family," and so on. We called this 9-item measure the Honor Endorsement Index ($\alpha = .86$). Also part of this questionnaire was a slightly more disguised measure of honor. The respondents were asked to indicate the qualities they thought were most important in a son or a daughter (on a scale from 0 to 100, with higher numbers indicating that the quality was more desirable). Among the list, the ones most directly relevant to the present concerns were those asking about the importance of being honorable, pure, respected by others, having a spirit of sacrifice (for the daughters), and being masculine (for the sons). The participant's ratings for these items were averaged together to create an Honor Prized Index ($\alpha = .89$).

Participants also completed Glick and Fiske's (1996) Ambivalent Sexism Inventory. Although not directly a measure of honor, the scale does include items that tap into related notions, particularly benevolent sexism items that address chivalrous beliefs about women's refinement. This scale has also proved useful in predicting attitudes toward domestic violence in other cultures of honor (Brazil and Turkey, see Glick, Sakalli-Ugurlu, Ferreira, & Aguiar de Souza, 2002). Finally, participants completed a brief demographics questionnaire, were debriefed, thanked, and dismissed.

Results

Acceptability of Violence

We predicted that although people would in general have a fairly negative reaction to the husband's violence, Chileans would be more forgiving of this violence than would Canadians, but only when it came from the jealousy-related conflict. As expected, in the jealousy condition, Chileans were more accepting of the violence as compared to Canadians, $M = 2.24$ (.88) for Chileans, $M = 1.61$ (.66) for Canadians, $t(144) = 5.73$, $p < .001$, $d = .96$. In the nonjealousy condition, Chileans and Canadians were equally unfavorable to the husband's violence, $M = 1.68$ (.74) for Chileans and $M = 1.61$ (.66) for Canadians, $t < 1$. The predicted Culture × Type of Incident interaction was significant, $F(1, 302) = 14.10$, $p < .001$, $f = .22$ (see Table 1 for a summary of the main findings for Study 2).

Warmth Toward the Husband

We predicted the same Culture × Type of Incident interaction on the Warmth dimension. That is, we hypothesized that Chileans would feel warmer toward the husband than would Canadians when his violence was jealousy related but not when it was unrelated to jealousy. Consistent with this hypothesis, Chileans, $M = 1.82$ (.55), were significantly warmer toward the husband than Canadians were, $M = 1.52$ (.53), in the jealous condition, $t(145) = 3.53$, $p < .001$, $d = .59$; but participants from the two cultures did not differ in the nonjealous condition, $M = 1.66$ (.64) for Chileans and $M = 1.56$ (.57) for Canadians, $t < 1$. The predicted Culture × Type of Incident interaction was significant, $F(1, 303) = 4.05$, $p < .05$, $f = .12$.

Table 1

Chileans' and Canadians' Ratings of the Husband on Various Dimensions When His Violence is the Result of Jealousy-Versus Nonjealousy-Related Conflicts, Study 2

	Nonjealousy	Jealousy
Acceptability of the violence		
Chile	1.68 (.74)	2.24 (.88)
Canada	1.61 (.66)	1.61 (.66)
Warmth toward the husband		
Chile	1.66 (.64)	1.82 (.55)
Canada	1.56 (.57)	1.52 (.53)
Husband's character as a good partner		
Chile	2.54 (.46)	2.65 (.46)
Canada	2.45 (.51)	2.35 (.45)
Husband's companionate love		
Chile	2.07 (.60)	2.44 (.76)
Canada	2.27 (.66)	2.24 (.65)

Note: All Country × Type of Incident interactions are significant, $p < .05$. Numbers in parentheses refer to standard deviations.

Ratings of the Husband's Character as a Good Partner

Again, we predicted a Culture × Type of Incident interaction on the ratings of the husband's character as a good partner. Specifically, we hypothesized that Chileans would rate the husband's general traits more positively than would Canadians when his violence was jealousy related but not when it was unrelated to jealousy. Consistent with this hypothesis, Chileans, $M = 2.65$ (.46), rated the husband more positively than Canadians did, $M = 2.35$ (.45), in the jealous condition, $t(145) = 3.90$, $p < .001$, $d = .65$; but the two countries did not differ in the nonjealous condition, $M = 2.54$ (.46) for Chileans and $M = 2.45$ (.51) for Canadians, $t < 1$. The predicted Culture × Type of Incident interaction was significant, $F(1, 302) = 3.87$, $p < .05$, $f = .11$.

Husband's Love for His Wife

Companionate love. Chileans believed that the husband felt more love, respect, and concern when he hit his wife over the jealousy incident, $M = 2.44$ (.76), as compared to when he hit her over the nonjealousy incident, $M = 2.07$ (.60), t(150) = 3.36, $p < .001$, $d = .55$. For Canadians, the type of incident did not make any difference, jealous $M = 2.24$ (.65), nonjealous $M = 2.27$ (.66). The predicted Country × Type of Incident interaction was significant, $F(1, 303) = 7.62$, $p < .01$, $f = .16$.

Passionate love. Puente and Cohen (2003) found that men who hit or raped their wives over an incident of jealousy were rated as having more passionate love for their wives, as compared to when they hit or raped over a nonjealous incident. Both Chileans and Canadians showed this effect, M for jealousy related incident = 4.02 (.66), M for nonjealousy = 3.08 (.79), $F(1, 302) = 125.52$, $p < .001$, $d = 1.29$; and they did so to equal degrees, Country × Type of Incident interaction, $F = .26$, ns. Finally, Canadians rated the husband as showing more passionate love overall, M for Canadians = 3.70 (.79), M for Chile = 3.35 (.90), $F = 18.64$, $p < .001$, $d = .49$.

Measures of honor endorsed, honor prized. As expected, Chilean students scored higher than Canadian students on the abstract attitudes measure of Honor Endorsed, $M = 4.16$

(1.09) versus 2.96 (1.04), $F(1, 304) = 110.99$, $p < .001$, $d = 1.21$. For the items that asked about the qualities important for a son or daughter, Chileans also thought the Honor Prized items were more important than Canadians did, $Ms = 83$ (18) versus 72 (18), $F(1, 304) = 33.99$, $p < .001$, $d = .66$. Chileans also rated nearly all the qualities (including Nonhonor qualities) as more important than Canadians did, suggesting there may have been response bias issues. However, when we controlled for response bias by regressing out ratings of the Nonhonor qualities, Chileans still rated the items in the Honor Prized index as more important than Canadians did, $t(307) = 2.54$, $p < .01$, $\beta = .09$.

Ambivalent sexism. Chileans scored higher than Anglo-Canadians on both the hostile sexism, $Ms = 2.42$ (.60) versus 1.93 (.54), and benevolent sexism portions, $Ms = 3.05$ (.65) versus 2.11 (.66) of the Ambivalent Sexism Inventory, $F(1, 304) = 18.93$, $p < .001$, $d = .50$ and $F(1, 304) = 79.81$, $p < .001$, $d = 1.02$, respectively.

Mediation Analyses

Traditional mediational analysis. We next examined whether these two honor indices mediated the cultural differences that were observed in the jealousy condition. First, we standardized and combined the acceptability of violence, warmth toward John, ratings of John's character, and ratings of his companionate love into one mega-dependent variable representing the effects we observed in the jealousy condition ($\alpha = .73$ for this aggregate variable, with higher numbers indicating more approval of violence). Next, we performed a traditional mediation analysis (Baron & Kenny, 1986), using Honor Endorsed as our mediating variable. Culture was significantly correlated with both the mediating variable and the outcome variable ($\beta s = .49$ and .36, respectively; both $ps < .001$). And when the mega-dependent variable was regressed simultaneously on Culture and Honor Endorsed, the effect of culture decreased significantly to $\beta = .25$, $p < .01$. The Sobel test indicating that the drop was significant was $Z = 2.79$, $p < .01$. (The Honor Endorsed variable remained a significant predictor of our dependent variable in the regression [$\beta = .22$, $p < .01$]). We thus seemed to find that Honor Endorsed partially mediated our cultural effect. A second set of analyses, using Honor Prized as the mediating variable, did not find that Honor Prized mediated the cultural difference.

Emic mediational analysis. Using traditional mediation analyses, there seems to be some support (but not overwhelming support) for the construct of honor mediating at least some of the between-culture differences we found for approval of violence in the jealousy condition. However, the traditional mediation analysis ignores one very important issue that arises in cross-cultural research—namely, measurement equivalence (see Van de Vijver & Leung, 2001). We have two measures of valuing honor (Honor Endorsed and Honor Prized), both appear face valid, and both show the expected mean difference across cultures; but the measures differ in their predictive validity within cultures. More specifically, each measure predicts the mega-dependent variable within one culture but not within the other. Thus, the 9-item Honor Endorsed index predicts more approval of the jealous, violent husband among Canadians ($\beta = .38$, $b = .27$, $p < .001$) but not among Chileans ($\beta = .10$, $b = .07$, $p < .45$). And the Honor Prized index predicts more approval of the jealous, violent husband among Chileans ($\beta = .53$, $b = .03$, $p < .03$) but not among Canadians, when response bias is controlled for. In fact, for Canadians, higher scores on the Honor Prized index predicted less approval for the jealous, violent husband

($\beta = -.31$, $b = -.01$, $p < .04$). Thus, neither the Honor Endorsed index nor the Honor Prized index alone completely mediated the between-culture difference in the traditional analysis, because the indices work differently within each culture (despite the indices showing the expected mean differences between cultures). However, if Anglo-Canadians had scores on the Honor Endorsed index that were as high as those of Chileans and if Chileans had scores on the Honor Prized index that were as low as those of Anglo-Canadians, the between-culture difference on the dependent variable would have been completely wiped out. In other words, if for each culture, one predicts approval of jealousy-related violence from the honor index that was predictively valid within that culture, then one would find that between-culture differences would be eliminated. To spell this out concretely, the mega-dependent variable mean for the Anglo-Canadians in the jealousy condition was $-.17$ and the regression predicting it from the honor variables was $y = -.35 + (.27063 \times \text{Honor Endorsed}) - (.01197 \times \text{Honor Prized qualities}) + (.00286 \times \text{Nonhonor qualities})$, the last term being included to control for response bias. If the mean for the Anglo Canadians on the Honor Endorsed variable had been as high as 4.02 (the Chilean value in the jealousy condition) instead of 2.87 (the actual Anglo-Canadian value), the predicted mega-dependent variable mean for the Anglo-Canadians would have been .14 instead of $-.17$. For the Chileans, the mega-dependent variable mean was .41 and the regression predicting it from the honor variables was $y = 3.15 + (.07363 \times \text{Honor Endorsed}) + (.0254 \times \text{Honor Prized qualities}) - (.05858 \times \text{Nonhonor qualities})$. If the mean for the Chileans on the Honor Prized variable had been as low as 69.21 (the Anglo-Canadian value in the jealousy condition) instead of 81.21 (the actual Chilean value), the predicted mega-dependent variable mean for the Chileans would have been .10 instead of .41. The predicted scores of .10 versus .14 indicate that the cultural difference of .41 versus $-.17$ would be completely eliminated if one predicted the dependent variable from the Honor index that was predictively valid within each culture. Conceptually, honor mediates the between-culture difference, but only if one allows honor to be operationally defined differently within each culture so that it has predictive validity within each (see Triandis, 1994, for a discussion of emic and etic measures).

Predictive and discriminant validity. The Honor Prized measure had discriminant as well as predictive validity for our Chilean sample. That is, for our Chilean sample, using the model above, Honor Prized predicted approval of jealousy-related violence ($b = .44$, $\beta = .53$, $t = 2.18$, $p = .03$), but it did not predict approval for nonjealousy-related violence ($b = .10$, $\beta = .13$, $t = .67$, $p = .50$). The Honor Endorsed variable did not fare as well among the Canadians, predicting jealousy-related violence ($b = .33$, $\beta = .38$, $t = 3.69$, $p < .001$) and nonjealousy-related violence ($b = .27$, $\beta = .33$, $t = 3.10$, $p = .003$). Thus, even though the Honor Endorsed measure generated the expected cross-cultural difference, was significant in the traditional mediational analysis, and performed well in the emic mediation analysis by showing predictive validity within the Canadian sample, the measure still needs some work if it is to be used as an emic measure of honor, capable of differentially predicting greater aggression in response to blatant threats to male honor, among Anglo-Canadian respondents.

Effects of Gender

For most of the dependent variables, there were also gender effects. Men were more likely than women to believe the violence was acceptable, $M = 1.91$ (.84) versus 1.59 (.63), $F(1, 302) = 18.07$, $p < .001$, $d = .49$; to feel greater warmth toward the husband, $M = 1.79$ (.65) versus 1.45 (.42), $F(1, 303) = 32.09$, $p < .001$, $d = .65$; to rate his character more positively, $M = 2.55$ (.50) versus 2.41 (.45), $F(1, 302) = 7.17$, $p < .01$, $d = .31$; to believe he showed more companionate love, $M = 2.37$ (.62) versus 2.15 (.70), $F(1, 303) = 8.65$, $p < .004$, $d = .34$; and to score higher on the Honor Endorsed index, $M = 3.97$ (1.10) versus 3.14 (1.16), $F(1, 304) = 55.69$, $p < .001$, $d = .86$. There were also two Country $\times$ Gender Effects, with the gender gap being bigger among Canadians than among Chileans for the Warmth and Character items. Finally, there was a Gender $\times$ Country $\times$ Type of Incident interaction for the passionate love variable. Whereas both Chileans and Canadians believed that the husband passionately loved his wife more in the jealousy as compared to nonjealousy condition, Canadian women showed this effect to a greater extent than Canadian men, whereas Chilean men and women showed this effect to a similar degree, $F(1, 302) = 3.74$, $p < .05$, $f = .11$.

Summary

In sum, Chileans were more positive about the violent husband and his actions than Canadians were—but only when his violence was in response to a jealousy-inducing scenario in which his wife was flirting with another man. Thus, when the violence was in response to a nonjealousy-related scenario (i.e., a financial disagreement), there were no cultural differences in evaluations. However, for the jealousy scenario, Chileans were significantly more likely than Canadians to feel warmly toward the husband, believe that his reaction was acceptable, believe that he showed the characteristics of a good partner, and believe that he showed more companionate love toward his wife. These differences between Canadians and Chileans in the jealousy condition tended to be in the moderate to large range, according to conventional criteria. There was also evidence that this cultural difference in response to the jealousy scenario was mediated by honor values. Traditional methods suggested honor as a partial mediator. However, what might be called an "emic mediation analysis" suggested that honor fully mediated the culture effect. The latter type of analysis is more complicated than a traditional mediation analysis, because in the emic mediation analysis, honor was operationally defined differently within each culture so that the honor variable would have predictive validity within each.

Although the differential predictive validity of our two honor measures was not expected, we can speculate on why this pattern emerged. One possibility is that the Honor Endorsed measure is an explicit measure and this type of measure may be most effective in cultures where the construct is less salient (i.e., Canada). In contrast, where honor is a salient theme (i.e., Chile), a more subtle, indirect measure such as the Honor Prized Index might predict more variance. Relatedly, because honor is less approved of in Canada, questions that ask directly about its approval will capture important variance. Where honor is more widely approved of (Chile), honor may need to be contrasted with other valued traits to understand how much relative importance it has for people within a culture.

The amount of variance on the Honor Endorsed and Honor Prized measure was similar for both Anglo-Canadians and Chileans, so a simple "ceiling effect" explanation is not particularly plausible. A more complicated account about the sources of variation on these variables and what these might usefully predict within a given culture is needed. (And again, as noted, further work on the discriminant validity of the Honor Endorsed measure among Anglo-Canadians should be part of this future research.) These accounts offer possible explanations for which sorts of measures might work better in different cultures and may suggest interesting methodological considerations for further cross-cultural work. More generally, further theoretical and empirical work on the possibilities and pitfalls of emic mediational analysis is also needed.

General Discussion

The primary goal of the present studies was to explore cultural differences in reactions to couples in abusive relationships. Despite widespread norms condemning violence against women, in the abstract, we predicted that cultural traditions that emphasize the importance of honor might create ambivalence about the use of violence. Although not directly approving of violence, honor norms might provide indirect support for violent scripts by (a) approving of women who express loyalty in the face of abuse and (b) excusing or downplaying male violence that is perceived to be in defense of masculine honor.

Experiment 1 served as a preliminary investigation into whether people would indirectly reward a woman in an abusive relationship by seeing her in a more positive light for remaining loyal. Latinos and southern Anglos, two cultural groups within the United States that emphasize honor, rated an abused woman who remained loyal more positively (or at least less negatively) in terms of her warmth and intelligence than did northern Anglos. Although remaining in an abusive relationship might be seen as foolish, passive, or weak in cultures that stress individualism and egalitarianism, in the context of more traditional, honor-based cultures, loyalty and sacrifice may be sometimes credited as signs of strength and integrity (Vandello & Cohen, 2003). So although the violence itself may be seen as undesirable, a "good" woman will remain loyal in the face of conflict.

Indeed, many stereotypical images of the ideal U.S. southern woman portray her as having a tough core hidden under a more delicate, refined veneer. "Steel magnolias" and "Mack trucks disguised as powder puffs," for example, are southern colloquialisms describing the ideal woman's balance between inner strength and outward femininity (Johnson, 1999; Wilson & Ferris, 1989). Part of this inner strength may be demonstrated through

honoring her commitment to her man, even in tough times. As the lyrics to the country music standard by singer (and Mississippi native) Tammy Wynette advise: "But if you love him you'll forgive him, even though he's hard to understand. And if you love him, be proud of him, cuz after all he's just a man . . . Stand by your man." Consistent with this image, Vandello and Cohen (2003) found that Southerners and Latinos (but not northern Anglos) rated a woman as stronger and more agentic when she remained loyal in an abusive relationship, compared to a woman who threatened to leave it.

In our second experiment, we turned to perceptions of men who use violence in romantic relationships. Just as romantic scripts may indirectly favor women who sacrifice their own well-being by remaining loyal in abusive relationships, scripts for romantic relationships may dictate that a certain amount of violence by the man is acceptable if it is perceived to be in the defense of his masculine honor and reputation. To test this, we had Chilean and Anglo-Canadian students listen to a husband talk about a past violent encounter with his wife. Although attitudes toward the husband's violence were negative overall, Chileans were more excusing than Canadians of the man when his violence was perceived to be jealousy related and thus involved a potentially deep threat to his masculine honor. Similarly, Chileans (as compared to Anglo-Canadians) had a warmer overall impression of the violent husband, were more likely to think he had the qualities of a good relationship partner, and believed that he showed more companionate love for his wife— but only when his violence was jealousy related.

These complementary expectations for female loyalty and male defense of honor in jealousy-threatening situations may help explain why domestic violence rates are relatively high in the southern United States and in Latin American cultures (see Vandello & Cohen, 2006). They may also help explain why Latinas tend to remain in abusive relationships longer than Anglo-Americans do. Torres (1987), for instance, found that Hispanic-American women tend to remain in abusive relationships longer than Anglo-American women before leaving their men and tend to go back to these relationships more frequently after the abuse. Some portion of these tendencies are probably explained by differences in economic resources that empower women to leave bad relationships. However, it also seems plausible that cultural norms and scripts (such as those illustrated in the experiments of this article) may exert influence over and above resource effects. We believe that further work that examines norms and scripts and economic opportunities together will be useful, in part because the economic or structural reasons for behavior are not independent of the cultural ones. In other (nonexperimental) work, we are examining how cultural ideals of purity are so tightly bound up with the economic and structural arrangements of a society. In these nonexperimental data, we find that norms for female purity are very negatively related to women's economic and structural power in a society (Vandello & Cohen, 2008). Studying norms and scripts at a micro level of analysis and studying how cultural ideas get realized in institutions and social structures at a more macro level should give a fuller, complementary understanding of the forces that influence women to stay or leave abusive relationships. More generally, we believe that there are bidirectional feedback loops between phenomena that are more structural and those that are more cultural, and studying such loops is an important direction for future research (Cohen, 2007; Schooler, 2007; Vandello & Cohen, 2003, in press).

Some Limitations

One obvious limitation of the present studies is our reliance on college student samples. Although this was helpful in giving us some comparability for our cross-cultural samples, there are, of course, still problems. One issue is that Chilean college students are a more elite segment of the population than Canadian college students are. (Approximately 7% of Chilean adults, age 25 to 64, have a university degree, whereas the rate is 2 to 3 times that number in Canada; UNESCO, 1999; U.S. Census Bureau, 1999). All other things equal, this probably biases the data against finding the expected cross-cultural differences, though this cannot be said with certainty (Vandello & Cohen, 2003). More important, the selection of college students gives us samples in both countries that are elite, young, and generally inexperienced in long-term relationships. The attitudes of this proportion of the population may not generalize to attitudes of people who are married or more experienced in relationships. Further work can examine the attitudes of populations that are both older and less elite.

Another limitation of the present work involves the limited number of scenarios explored. For example, in Experiment 2, we attributed the difference in the way Chileans and Canadians responded to the jealousy versus overspending scenarios in terms of their concern about honor. However, there are other possibilities: Perhaps Chilean students were less tolerant of the violence in the overspending scenario because they care less about money matters. Perhaps Chileans and Canadians differed in how they assigned fault for this conflict. Perhaps Chileans regard all infidelity (rather than just female infidelity and its consequent threat to male honor) as a more serious offense than Canadians do, and so on. (To the extent that one may generalize from one Latin American sample to another, this last possibility may be rendered less plausible. Thus, in Vandello and Cohen [2003], both Brazilians and residents of the United States were condemning of a man who had an affair, relative to a man who remained loyal to his wife. However, it was the U.S. respondents [Anglo-Americans from Illinois] who condemned the male infidelity more than the Brazilians did. This finding of the Brazilians is suggestive, but clearly, Brazilians may be quite different than Chileans, and one generalizes across samples at one's peril [Cohen, 2007]). In the present study, we focused on just a few scenarios so that we could create vivid, compelling stimuli that would involve the participant. Questionnaires that ask about a greater variety of situations would help us nail down the very specific factors in a situation that participants are responding to.

Concluding Comments

An additional important issue has to do with the size of the effects. Between-culture effects in Experiment 2 were in the medium to large range; however, effects in Experiment 1 were in the small to medium range, as defined by conventional criteria. Relatedly and more critically, effects in Experiment 1 were small in comparison to the overwhelming tendency of most Experiment 1 participants to favor leaving the boyfriend rather than staying. Does this imply that "yes, there are cultural differences but they are relatively small in size when one looks at the broader cross-cultural consensus within the United States?" We are of two minds on this question. On one hand, we think that there is a good deal of consensus within the United States about intimate violence, and not always in the direction of condemning it. That is, we believe that there are streams of thought in mainstream American culture that are relatively accepting of certain forms of relationship violence. In an earlier study (Puente & Cohen, 2003), people judged that a man who hit or raped his wife after a jealousy-related argument loved his wife more than a man who hit or raped his wife after another type of incident. In addition, people also judged that a man who hit or raped his wife after a jealousy-related argument loved his wife just as much as a man who did not commit any violence after a jealousy-related argument. There is a stream of thought in American culture that regards jealousy as a sign of love and is thus ready to excuse or mitigate jealousy-related violence. People may not articulate and may not even realize that they hold such attitudes, but experimental designs (presenting compelling scenarios where people do vs. do not respond with aggression after a particular incident) can help uncover such attitudes (Vandello & Cohen, 2003, Study 1; Puente & Cohen, 2003, Studies 2 and 3).

Given that Study 1 elicited such an overwhelmingly negative response from participants, we doubt that our materials were subtle enough to capture some of these attitudes that people do not admit or do not realize they have. If the provocation in Study 1 was not so trivial (getting a ride home from a male coworker), if the boyfriend in the story didn't have such an aggressive history, and if the materials had focused on some of the boyfriend's positive qualities, perhaps results would be different. That is, perhaps we would have seen

(a) more tolerance for the boyfriend's actions from all groups of participants, (b) a larger cultural effect because there would be something about the boyfriend to sympathize with, or (c) both of the above. Again, research with a greater range of stimuli (and a greater range of subject populations) can help map out the scope of both the similarities and differences within American culture.

In sum, the present experimental results sketched out some of the factors that can contribute to differences in rates of domestic violence between cultures. In particular, cultures of honor tend to have relatively high rates of spousal abuse. Experiment 1 showed how honor cultures may enable this violence through expectations for female loyalty in the face of male aggression. Experiment 2 showed how such cultures may support (or at least not condemn) violence by legitimating its use in defense of male honor. Understanding norms for both male and female behavior is important for understanding how high rates of violence may arise. Domestic violence may not be explicitly endorsed, but it does not have to be. Values that permit such violence are embedded in our norms about what a good woman should do and what a good husband may do in the name of his honor.

Notes

1. The western of the United States shares certain cultural similarities to the South in terms of honor. Only one of our participants had spent a substantial portion of his life in the West, and we classified him with the honor group. Dropping this individual or putting him in with the nonhonor group does not change the results.

2. The interaction of Latino versus Southerner × Stay versus Leave was not significant for any dependent variable, all $ps > .10$.

3. This is not to say that honor-related conflicts can only be about infidelity. Honor is threatened when status and reputation are threatened. Honor cultures differ from nonhonor cultures in (a) how likely they are to construe a given situation as threatening honor and (b) what one is expected to do in response to honor-threatening situations (Cohen, Nisbett, Bowdle, & Schwarz, 1996). We intended the nonjealousy scenario in this study to not be blatantly honor threatening. (To the extent that it is perceived to be honor threatening, the data would go against our predictions by lessening the chance of finding the expected Culture × Type of Incident interactions.)

4. The item, "How much does John love Rose?" improved the reliability of the Companionate Love scale but not the Passionate Love scale. In addition, it showed a slightly higher correlation with the Companionate Love items. Thus, we grouped this item with the Companionate Love index. If it is removed from the Companionate Love index and is instead part of the Passionate Love index (as in Puente & Cohen, 2003), the Country × Type of Incident interaction for Companionate Love becomes stronger, $F(1, 311) = 10.13$, $p < .002$.

REFERENCES

Adams, J. (1993). Resistance to "modernity": Southern Illinois farm women and the cult of domesticity. *American Ethnologist, 20*, 89–113.

Archer, J. (2006). Cross-cultural differences in physical aggression between partners: A social-role analysis. *Personality and Social Psychology Review, 10*, 133–153.

Atack, J. (1989). The evolution of regional economic differences within Illinois, 1818-1850. In P. Nardulli (Ed.), *Diversity, conflict, and state politics* (pp. 61–94). Urbana: University of Illinois Press.

Baron, R. M., & Kenny, D. A. (1986). The moderator-mediator variable distinction in social psychological research: Conceptual, strategic and statistical considerations. *Journal of Personality and Social Psychology, 51*, 1173–1182.

Best, D. L. (2001). Gender concepts: Convergence in cross-cultural research and methodologies. *Cross-Cultural Research, 35*, 23–43.

Buss, D. M. (1989). Sex differences in human mate preferences. *Behavioral and Brain Sciences, 12*, 1–49.

Caufield, S., Chambers, S. C., & Putnam, L. (Eds.). (2005). *Honor, status, and law in modern Latin America*. Durham, NC: Duke University Press.

Ceballo, R., Ramirez, C., Castillo, M., Caballero, G. A., & Lozoff, B. (2004). Domestic violence and women's mental health in Chile. *Psychology of Women Quarterly, 28*, 298–308.

Aspell, M.C. (May, 1998). Mama's boy. *American Way*, p. 90.

Cohen, D. (1999). Methods in cultural psychology. In S. Kitayama & D. Cohen (Eds.), *Handbook of cultural psychology* (pp. 196–236). New York: Guilford.

Cohen, D., Nisbett, R. E., Bowdle, B., & Schwarz, N. (1996). Insult, aggression, and the southern culture of honor. *Journal of Personality and Social Psychology, 70*, 945–960.

Cohen, D., & Vandello, J. A. (2001). Honor and "faking" honorability. In R. Nesse (Ed.), *Evolution and the capacity for commitment* (pp. 163–185). New York: Russell Sage.

Cohen, D., Vandello, J. A., Puente, S., & Rantilla, A. K. (1999). "When you call me that, smile!" How norms for politeness, interaction styles, and aggression work together in southern culture. *Social Psychology Quarterly, 62,* 257–275.

Daly, M., & Wilson, M. (1988). *Homicide*. New York: de Gruyter.

Dutton, D. G. (1998). *The abusive personality: Violence and control in intimate relationships*. New York: Guilford.

Dutton, D. G., Starzomski, A. J., & Ryan, L. (1996). Antecedents of borderline personality organization in wife assaulters. *Journal of Family Violence, 11*, 113–132.

Eagly, A. H., & Steffen, V. J. (1986). Gender and aggressive behavior: A meta-analytic review of the social psychological literature. *Psychological Bulletin, 100*, 309–330.

Espin, O. M. (1997). *Latina realities: Essays on healing, migration, and sexuality*. Boulder, CO: Westview.

Felson, R. B. (1982). Impression management and the escalation of aggression and violence. *Social Psychology Quarterly, 45*, 245–254.

Felson, R. B. (2002). *Violence and gender reexamined*. Washington, DC: American Psychological Association.

Figueredo, A., Sefcek, J., Vasquez, G., Brumbach, B., King, J., & Jacobs, W. (2005). Evolutionary personality psychology. In D. Buss (Ed.), *Handbook of evolutionary psychology* (pp. 851–877). Hoboken, NJ: Wiley.

Gilmore, D. D. (1990). *Manhood in the making: Cultural conceptions of masculinity.* New Haven, CT: Yale University Press.

Glick, P., & Fiske, S. T. (1996). The ambivalent sexism inventory: Differentiating hostile and benevolent sexism. *Journal of Personality and Social Psychology, 70,* 491–512.

Glick, P., & Fiske, S. T. (2001). An ambivalent alliance: Hostile and benevolent sexism as complementary justifications of gender inequality. *American Psychologist, 56,* 109–118.

Glick, P., Sakalli-Ugurlu, N., Ferreira, M. C., & Aguiar de Souza, M. (2002). Ambivalent sexism and attitudes toward wife abuse in Turkey and Brazil. *Psychology of Women Quarterly, 26,* 292–297.

Haller, J. S., & Haller, R. M. (1984). Sex in Victorian America. In J. H. Cary & J. Weinberg (Eds.), *The social fabric* (pp. 109–124). Boston: Little, Brown.

Haskell, L., & Randall, M. (1993). *The women's safety project: Summary of key statistical findings.* Ottawa, Ontario: Canadian Panel on Violence Against Women.

Heise, L. L., Pitanguy, A., & Germain, A. (1994). *Violence against women: The hidden health burden.* Washington DC: World Bank.

Johnson, M. (1999). *The seven signs of southernness: Famous southerners on being southern.* Birmingham, AL: Southernness.

Johnson, L. L., & Lipsett-Rivera, S. (1998). *The faces of honor: Sex, shame, and violence in colonial Latin America.* Albuquerque: University of New Mexico Press.

Leung, A. K-Y., & Cohen D. (2006). *Within and between-culture variation: Individual differences and the cultural logics of honor, face, and dignity cultures.* Unpublished manuscript, University of Illinois at Urbana–Champaign.

McLoyd, V. C., Cauce, A. M., Takeuchi, D., & Wilson, L. (2000). Marital processes and parental socialization in families of color: A decade review of research. *Journal of Marriage and the Family, 62,* 1070–1093.

McWhirter, P. T. (1999). La violencia privada: Domestic violence in Chile. *American Psychologist, 54,* 37–40.

Miller, G. (1998). *Sexual selection and the mind.* Retrieved August 7, 2006, from http://www.edge.org/documents/archive/edge41.html.

Nisbett, R. E., & Cohen, D. (1996). *Culture of honor: The psychology of violence in the South.* Boulder, CO: Westview.

Puente, S., & Cohen, D. (2003). Jealousy and the meaning (or nonmeaning) of violence. *Personality and Social Psychology Bulletin, 29,* 449–460.

Rosen, K. H. (1996). The ties that bind women to violent premarital relationships: Processes of seduction and entrapment. In D. D. Cahn & S. A. Lloyd (Eds.), *Family violence from a communication perspective* (pp. 151–176). London: Sage.

Schooler, C. (2007). Culture and social structure. In S. Kitayama & D. Cohen (Eds.), *Handbook of cultural psychology* (pp. 370–388). New York: Guilford.

Smith, M. D. (1987). The incidence and prevalence of woman abuse in Toronto. *Violence and Victims, 2,* 33–37.

Stevens, E. P. (1973). Machismo and marianismo. *Transaction Society, 10,* 57–63.

Stevens, E. P. (1994). Marianismo: The other face of machismo. In G. M. Yeager (Ed.), *Confronting change, challenging tradition: Women in Latin American history* (pp. 3–17). Wilmington, DE: SR Books.

Straus, M. A., & Gelles, R. (1986). Societal change and change in family violence from 1975 to 1985 as revealed by two national surveys. *Journal of Marriage and the Family, 48*, 465–480.

Sugihara,Y., & Warner, A. (2002). Dominance and domestic abuse among Mexican Americans: Gender differences in the etiology of violence in intimate relationships. *Journal of Family Violence, 17*, 315–340.

Thibaut, J., & Kelley, H. H. (1959). *The social psychology of groups.* New York: John Wiley.

Tjaden, P., & Thoennes, N. (1998). *Prevalence, incidence, and consequences of violence against women: Findings from the National Violence Against Women Survey* (NCJ Report No. 172837). Washington, DC: Department of Justice, National Institute of Justice.

Torres, S. (1987). Hispanic-American battered women: Why consider cultural differences? *Response, 10*, 20–21.

Triandis, H. (1994). *Culture and social behavior.* New York: McGraw-Hill.

UNESCO (1999). *Investing in education.* Retrieved November 28, 2007, from http://www.uis.unesco.org/template/pdf/wei/WEI1999InvestingInEducation.pdf

U.S. Census Bureau. (1999). *Statistical abstract of the United States: 1999.* Washington, DC: Author.

Vandello, J. A., & Cohen, D. (2003). Male honor and female fidelity: Implicit cultural scripts that perpetuate domestic violence. *Journal of Personality and Social Psychology, 84*, 997–1010.

Vandello, J. A., & Cohen, D. (unpublished document). *How cultural differences in female purity predict women's power, rights, and vulnerability to intimate partner violence.* University of South Florida.

Vandello, J. A., Cohen, D., & Ransom, S. (2008). U.S. Southern and Northern differences in perceptions of norms about aggression: Mechanisms for the perpetuation of a culture of honor. *Journal of Cross-Cultural Psychology, 39*, 162–177.

Van de Vijver, F. J. R., & Leung, K. (2001) Personality in cultural context: Methodological issues. *Journal of Personality, 69*, 1007–1031.

Walker, G., & Goldner, V. (1995). The wounded prince and the women who love him. In C. Burck & B. Speed (Eds.), *Gender, power, and relationships* (pp. 24–45). London: Routledge.

Wilson, C. R., & Ferris,W. (1989). *Encyclopedia of southern culture.* Chapel Hill: University of North Carolina Press.

Wilt, S., & Olson, S. (1996). Prevalence of domestic violence in the United States. *Journal of American Medical Women's Association, 51*, 77–82.

Wirt, F. (1989). The changing bases of regionalism. In P. Nadulli (Ed.), *Diversity, conflict, and state politics* (pp. 31–60). Urbana: University of Illinois Press.

Wood, J. T. (2001). The normalization of violence in heterosexual romantic relationships: Women's narratives of love and violence. *Journal of Social and Personal Relationships, 18*, 239–261.

Yost, M., & Zurbriggen, E. (2006). Gender differences in the enactment of sociosexuality. *Journal of Sex Research, 43,* 163–173.

Zurbriggen, E. (2000). Social motives and cognitive power-sex associations. *Journal of Personality and Social Psychology, 78*, 559–581.

Joseph A. Vandello, PhD, is an associate professor of psychology at the University of South Florida. He conducts research in the areas of conflict, aggression, gender, and culture. He received a BS in psychology from the University of Iowa and PhD in psychology from the University of Illinois at Urbana–Champaign.

Dov Cohen conducts research on cultural syndromes of honor, dignity, and face. He has been on faculty at the University of Waterloo and the University of Illinois, where he is currently a professor. He is coeditor of the Handbook of Cultural Psychology.

Ruth Grandon a psychotherapist in Kitchener, Ontario, Canada, has a special interest in issues of violence against women, political violence, and diversity. She has a BA in Psychology from the University of Waterloo, Waterloo, Ontario and a Master of Science in Couple and Family Therapy from the University of Guelph, Guelph, Ontario.

Renae Franiuk, PhD, is an associate professor of psychology at Aurora University. She conducts research in the areas of romantic relationships and relationship violence. She received her PhD in psychology from the University of Illinois at Urbana–Champaign.

Reconstruction of Automobile Destruction: An Example of the Interaction Between Language and Memory

Despite their persuasive impact on judges and juries, eyewitnesses to crimes are, in many ways, imperfect. As is discussed in Chapter 12 (Law), perceptions are limited by lighting, distance, and distraction; memories fade over time and as a result of interference; and the ability to retrieve a memory can be biased by suggestive questions, photographs, and lineups. In the following classic study, Loftus and Palmer (1974) began to develop what is now an important and well established theory: that eyewitness memories are constructed and then often reconstructed—not only on the basis of the observed event but from information obtained afterward, as from suggestive questions. As you read this article, ponder what it means about human memory and about the accuracy of eyewitness reports commonly used in criminal trials.

RECONSTRUCTION OF AUTOMOBILE DESTRUCTION: AN EXAMPLE OF THE INTERACTION BETWEEN LANGUAGE AND MEMORY*

Elizabeth F. Loftus and John C. Palmer

University of Washington

Two experiments are reported in which subjects viewed films of automobile accidents and then answered questions about events occurring in the films. The question, "About how fast were the cars going when they smashed into each other?" elicited higher estimates of speed than questions which used the verbs collided, bumped, contacted, or hit in place of smashed. On a retest one week later, those subjects who received the verb smashed were more likely to say "yes" to the question, "Did you see any broken glass?", even though broken glass was not present in the film. These results are consistent with the view that the questions asked subsequent to an event can cause a reconstruction in one's memory of the event.

How accurately do we remember the details of a complex event, like a traffic accident, that has happened in our presence? More specifically, how well do we do when asked to estimate some numerical quantity such as how long the accident took, how fast the cars were traveling, or how much time elapsed between the sounding of a horn and the moment of collision?

---

* SOURCE: Loftus, E. F. & Palmer, J.C. 1974. "Reconstruction of Automobile Destruction: An Example of the Interaction Between Language and Memory" *JOURNAL OF VERBAL LEARNING AND VERBAL BEHAVIOR*, *13*, 585–589, copyright © 1974 by Academic Press, Inc. Reprinted by permission of the publisher.

It is well documented that most people are markedly inaccurate in reporting such numerical details as time, speed, and distance (Bird, 1927; Whipple, 1909). For example, most people have difficulty estimating the duration of an event, with some research indicating that the tendency is to overestimate the duration of events which are complex (Block, 1974; Marshall, 1969; Ornstein, 1969). The judgment of speed is especially difficult, and practically every automobile accident results in huge variations from one witness to another as to how fast a vehicle was actually traveling (Gardner, 1933). In one test administered to Air Force personnel who knew in advance that they would be questioned about the speed of a moving automobile, estimates ranged from 10 to 50 mph. The car they watched was actually going only 12 mph (Marshall, 1969, p. 23).

Given the inaccuracies in estimates of speed, it seems likely that there are variables which are potentially powerful in terms of influencing these estimates. The present research was conducted to investigate one such variable, namely, the phrasing of the question used to elicit the speed judgment. Some questions are clearly more suggestive than others. This fact of life has resulted in the legal concept of a leading question and in legal rules indicating when leading questions are allowed (*Supreme Court Reporter*, 1973). A leading question is simply one that, either by its form or content, suggests to the witness what answer is desired or leads him to the desired answer.

In the present study, subjects were shown films of traffic accidents and then they answered questions about the accident. The subjects were interrogated about the speed of the vehicles in one of several ways. For example, some subjects were asked, "About how fast were the cars going when they hit each other?" while others were asked, "About how fast were the cars going when they smashed into each other?" As Fillmore (1971) and Bransford and McCarrell (in press) have noted, *hit* and *smashed* may involve specification of differential rates of movement. Furthermore, the two verbs may also involve differential specification of the likely consequences of the events to which they are referring. The impact of the accident is apparently gentler for *hit* than for *smashed*.

EXPERIMENT I

Method

Forty-five students participated in groups of various sizes. Seven films were shown, each depicting a traffic accident. These films were segments from longer driver's education films borrowed from the Evergreen Safety Council and the Seattle Police Department. The length of the film segments ranged from 5 to 30 sec. Following each film, the subjects received a questionnaire asking them first to, "give an account of the accident you have just seen," and then to answer a series of specific questions about the accident. The critical question was the one that interrogated the subject about the speed of the vehicles involved in the collision. Nine subjects were asked, "About how fast were the cars going when they hit each other?" Equal numbers of the remaining subjects were interrogated with the verbs *smashed, collided, bumped*, and *contacted* in place of *hit*. The entire experiment lasted about an hour and a half. A different ordering of the films was presented to each group of subjects.

Results

Table 1 presents the mean speed estimates for the various verbs. Following the procedures outlined by Clark (1973), an analysis of variance was performed with verbs as a fixed effect, and subjects and films as random effects, yielding a significant quasi F ratio $F'(5.55) = 4.65, p < .005$.

Some information about the accuracy of subjects' estimates can be obtained from our data. Four of the seven films were staged crashes; the original purpose of these films was to illustrate what can happen to human beings when cars collide at various speeds. One collision took place at 20 mph, one at 30, and two at 40. The means estimates of speed for these four films were: 37.7, 36.2, 39.7 and 36.1 mph, respectively. In agreement with previous work, people are not very good at judging how fast a vehicle was actually traveling.

TABLE 1

Speed Estimates for the Verbs Used in Experiment

Verb	Mean speed estimate
Smashed	40.8
Collided	39.3
Bumped	38.1
Hit	34.0
Contacted	31.8

Discussion

The results of this experiment indicate that the form of a question (in this case, changes of a single word) can markedly and systematically affect a witness's answer to that question. The actual speed of the vehicles controlled little variance in subject reporting, while the phrasing of the question controlled considerable variance.

Two interpretations of this finding are possible. First, it is possible that the differential speed estimates result merely from response-bias factors. A subject is uncertain whether to say 30 mph or 40 mph, for example and the verb *smashed* biases his response towards the higher estimate. A second interpretation is that the question form causes change in the subject's memory representation of the accident. The verb *smashed* may change a subject's memory such that he "sees" the accident as being more severe than it actually was. If this is the case, we might expect subjects to "remember" other details that did not actually occur, but are commensurate with an accident occurring at higher speeds. The second experiment was designed to provide additional insights into the origin of the differential speed estimates.

EXPERIMENT II

Method

One hundred and fifty students participated in this experiment, in groups of various sizes. A film depicting a multiple car accident was shown, followed by a questionnaire. The film lasted less than 1 min; the accident in the film lasted 4 sec. At the end of the film, the subjects received a questionnaire asking them first to describe the accident in their own words, and then to answer a series of questions about the accident. The critical question was the one that interrogated the subject about the speed of the vehicles. Fifty subjects were asked, "About how fast were the cars going when they smashed into each other?" Fifty subjects were asked, "About how fast were the cars going when they hit each other?" Fifty subjects were not interrogated about vehicular speed.

One week later, the subjects returned and without viewing the film again they answered a series of questions about the accident. The critical question here was, "Did you see any broken glass?" which the subjects answered by checking "yes" or "no." This question was embedded in a list totalling 10 questions, and appeared in a random position in the list. There was no broken glass in the accident but since broken glass is commensurate with accidents occurring at high speed, we expected that the subjects who had been asked the *smashed* question might more often say "yes" to this critical question.

Results

The mean estimate of speed for subjects interrogated with *smashed* was 10.46 mph; with *hit* the estimate was 8.00 mph. These means are significantly different, $t(98) = 2.00$, $p < .05$.

Table 2 presents the distribution of "yes" and "no" responses for the *smashed, hit*, and control subjects. An independence chi-square test on these responses was significant beyond the .025 level, $\chi^2(2) = 7.76$.

The important result in Table 2 is that the probability of saying "yes," P(Y), to the question about broken glass is .32 when the verb *smashed* is used, and .14 with *hit*. Thus *smashed* leads both to more "yes" responses and to higher speed estimates. It appears to be the case that the effect of the verb is mediated at least in part by the speed estimate. The question now arises: Is *smashed* doing anything else besides increasing the estimate of speed? To answer this, the function relating P(Y) to speed estimate was calculated separately for *smashed* and *hit*. If the speed estimate is the only way in which effect of verb is mediated, then for a given speed estimate, P(Y) should be independent of verb. Table 3 shows that this is not the case. P(Y) is lower for *hit* than for *smashed*: the difference between the two verbs ranges from .03 for estimates of 1–5 mph to .18 for estimates of 6–10 mph. The average difference between the two curves is about .12. Whereas the unconditional difference of .18 between the *smashed* and *hit* conditions is attenuated, it is by no means eliminated when estimate of speed is controlled for. It thus appears that the verb smashed has other effects besides that of simply increasing the estimate of speed. One possibility will be discussed in the next section.

TABLE 2

Distribution of "Yes" and "No" Responses to the Question, "Did you See Any Broken Glass?"

Response	Verb Condition		
	Smashed	Hit	Control
Yes	16	7	6
No	34	43	44

DISCUSSION

To reiterate, we have first of all provided an additional demonstration of something that has been known for some time, namely, that the way a question is asked can enormously influence the answer that is given. In this instance, the question, "About how fast were the cars going when they smashed into each other?" led to higher estimates of speed than the same question asked with the verb *smashed* replaced by *hit*. Furthermore, this seemingly small change had consequences for how questions are answered a week after the original event occurred.

As a framework for discussing these results, we would like to propose that two kinds of information go into one's memory for some complex occurrence. The first is information gleaned during the perception of the original event; the second is external information supplied after the fact. Over time, information from these two sources may be integrated in such a way that we are unable to tell from which source some specific detail is recalled. All we have is one "memory."

Discussing the present experiments in these terms, we propose that the subject first forms some representation of the accident he has witnessed. The experimenter then, while asking, "About how fast were the cars going when they smashed into each other?" supplies a piece of external information, namely, that the cars did indeed smash into each other. When these two pieces of information are integrated, the subject has a memory of an accident that was more severe than in fact it was. Since broken glass is commensurate with a severe accident, the subject is more likely to think that broken glass was present.

There is some connection between the present work and earlier work on the influence of verbal labels on memory for visually presented form stimuli. A classic study in psychology showed that when subjects are asked to reproduce a visually presented form, their drawings tend to err in the direction of a more familiar object suggested by a verbal label initially associated with the to-be-remembered form (Carmichael, Hogan, & Walter, 1932). More recently, Daniel (1972) showed that recognition memory, as well as reproductive memory, was similarly affected by verbal labels, and he concluded that the verbal label causes a shift in the memory strength of forms which are better representatives of the label.

TABLE 3

Probability of Saying "Yes" to, "Did You See Any Broken Glass?" Conditionalized of Speed Estimates

Verb Condition	Speed Estimate (mph)			
	1–5	6–10	11–15	16–20
Smashed	.09	.27	.41	.62
Hit	.06	.09	.25	.50

When the experimenter asks the subject, "About how fast were the cars going when they smashed into each other?", he is effectively labeling the accident a smash. Extrapolating the conclusions of Daniel to this situation, it is natural to conclude that the label, smash, causes a shift in the memory representation of the accident in the direction of being more similar to a representation suggested by the verbal label.

REFERENCES

Bird, C. The influence of the press upon the accuracy of report. *Journal of Abnormal and Social Psychology*, 1927, 22, 123–129.

Block, R. A. Memory and the experience of duration in retrospect. *Memory & Cognition*, 1974, 2, 153–160.

Bransford, J. D., & McCarrrell, N. S. A sketch of a cognitive approach to comprehension. Some thoughts about under-standing what it means to comprehend. In D. Palermo & W. Weiner (Eds.), *Cognition and the symbolic processes.* Washington, D.C.: V. H. Winston & Co., in press.

Carmichael, L., Hogan, H. P., & Walter, A. A. An experimental study of the effect of language on the reproduction of visually perceived form. *Journal of Experimental Psychology*, 1932, 15, 73–86.

Clark, H. H. The language-as-fixed-effect fallacy: A critique of language statistics in psychological research. *Journal of Verbal Learning and Verbal Behavior*, 1973, 12, 335–359.

Danill, T. C. Nature of the effect of verbal labels on recognition memory for form. *Journal of Experimental Psychology*, 1972, 96, 152–157.

Fillmore, C. J. Types of lexical information. In D. D. Steinberg and L. A. Jakobovits (Eds.), *Semantics: An interdisciplinary reader in philosophy, linguistics, and psychology.* Cambridge: Cambridge University Press, 1971.

Gardner, D. S. The perception and memory of witnesses. *Cornell Law Quarterly*, 1933, 8, 391–409.

Marshall, J. *Law and psychology in conflict.* New York: Anchor Books, 1969.

Ornstein, R. E. *On the experience of time.* Harmondsworth, Middlesex, England: Penguin, 1969.

Whipple, G. M. The observer as reporter: A survey of the psychology of testimony. *Psychological Bulletin*, 1909, 6, 153–170.

Supreme Court Reporter, 1973, 3: Rules of Evidence for United States Courts and Magistrates.

(Received April 17, 1974)

READING 16

The Social Psychology of False Confessions: Compliance, Internalization, and Confabulation

Confession to a crime is a potent and incriminating form of evidence. When a defendant confesses to the police, even if he or she later claims that the confession was coerced, judges and juries vote for guilt and conviction. Yet every now and then, there are documented reports about innocent people who confess to crimes they did not commit as a mean of compliance, in response to pressures exerted during a police interrogation. In some cases, innocent suspects actually come to believe they may be guilty, indicating an even stronger form of influence, internalization. Is it really possible to convince people that they are guilty of an act they did not commit? Based on an analysis of actual cases, Kassin and Kiechel (1996) theorized that two factors increase the risk: (1) a suspect who lacks a clear memory of the event, and (2) the presentation of false evidence, a common police trick. As you will see, these researchers tested and supported this hypothesis in a laboratory experiment on false confessions. While reading this article, think about how it illustrates processes not only relevant to the psychology of law (Chapter 12), but also to social influence (Chapter 9) and persuasion (Chapter 7) research as well.

THE SOCIAL PSYCHOLOGY OF FALSE CONFESSIONS: COMPLIANCE, INTERNALIZATION, AND CONFABULATION*

Saul M. Kassin and Katherine L. Kiechel

Williams College

An experiment demonstrated that false incriminating evidence can lead people to accept guilt for a crime they did not commit. Subjects in a fast- or slow-paced reaction time task were accused of damaging a computer by pressing the wrong key. All were truly innocent and initially denied the charge. A confederate then said she saw the subject hit the key or did not see the subject hit the key. Compared with subjects in the slow-pace/no-witness group, those in the fast-pace/witness group were more likely to sign a confession, internalize guilt for the event, and confabulate details in memory consistent with that belief. Both legal and conceptual implications are discussed.

Address correspondence to Saul Kassin, Department of Psychology, Williams College, Williamstown, MA 01267.

In criminal law, confession evidence is a potent weapon for the prosecution and a recurring source of controversy. Whether a suspect's self-incriminating statement was voluntary or coerced and whether a suspect was of sound mind are just two of the issues that trial judges and juries consider on a routine basis. To guard citizens against violations of due process and to minimize the risk that the innocent would confess to crimes they did not commit, the courts have erected guidelines for the admissibility of confession evidence. Although there is no simple litmus test, confessions are typically excluded from

* SOURCE: Kassin, S. I., & Kiechel, K.L. 1996. The Social Psychology of False Confessions: Compliance, Internalization, and Confabulation. *PSYCHOLOGICAL SCIENCE, 7*, 125–128. Reprinted by permission of Blackwell Science Ltd.

trial if elicited by physical violence, a threat of harm or punishment, or a promise of immunity or leniency, or without the suspect being notified of his or her Miranda rights.

To understand the psychology of criminal confessions, three questions need to be addressed: First, how do police interrogators elicit self-incriminating statements (i.e., what means of social influence do they use)? Second, what effects do these methods have (i.e., do innocent suspects ever confess to crimes they did not commit)? Third, when a coerced confession is retracted and later presented at trial, do juries sufficiently discount the evidence in accordance with the law? General reviews of relevant case law and research are available elsewhere (Gudjonsson, 1992; Wrightsman & Kassin, 1993). The present research addresses the first two questions.

Informed by developments in case law, the police use various methods of interrogation—including the presentation of false evidence (e.g., fake polygraph, fingerprints, or other forensic test results; staged eyewitness identifications), appeals to God and religion, feigned friendship, and the use of prison informants. A number of manuals are available to advise detectives on how to extract confessions from reluctant crime suspects (Aubry & Caputo, 1965; O'Hara & O'Hara, 1981). The most popular manual is Inbau, Reid, and Buckley's (1986) *Criminal Interrogation and Confessions*, originally published in 1962, and now in its third edition.

After advising interrogators to set aside a bare, soundproof room absent of social support and distraction, Inbau et al. (1986) describe in detail a nine-step procedure consisting of various specific ploys. In general, two types of approaches can be distinguished. One is *minimization*, a technique in which the detective lulls the suspect into a false sense of security by providing face-saving excuses, citing mitigating circumstances, blaming the victim, and underplaying the charges. The second approach is one of *maximization*, in which the interrogator uses scare tactics by exaggerating or falsifying the characterization of evidence, the seriousness of the offense, and the magnitude of the charges. In a recent study (Kassin & McNall, 1991), subjects read interrogation transcripts in which these ploys were used and estimated the severity of the sentence likely to be received. The results indicated that minimization communicated an implicit offer of leniency, comparable to that estimated in an explicit-promise condition, whereas maximization implied a threat of harsh punishment, comparable to that found in an explicit-threat condition. Yet although American courts routinely exclude confessions elicited by explicit threats and promises, they admit those produced by contingencies that are pragmatically implied.

Although police often use coercive methods of interrogation, research suggests that juries are prone to convict defendants who confess in these situations. In the case of *Arizona v. Fulminante* (1991), the U.S. Supreme Court ruled that under certain conditions, an improperly admitted coerced confession may be considered upon appeal to have been nonprejudicial, or "harmless error." Yet mock-jury research shows that people find it hard to believe that anyone would confess to a crime that he or she did not commit (Kassin & Wrightsman, 1980, 1981; Sukel & Kassin, 1994). Still, it happens. One cannot estimate the prevalence of the problem, which has never been systematically examined, but there are numerous documented instances on record (Bedau & Radelet, 1987; Borchard, 1932; Rattner, 1988). Indeed, one can distinguish three types of false confession (Kassin & Wrightsman, 1985): *voluntary* (in which a subject confesses in the absence of external pressure), *coerced-compliant* (in which a suspect confesses only to escape an aversive interrogation, secure a promised benefit, or avoid a threatened harm), and *coerced-internalized* (in which a suspect actually comes to believe that he or she is guilty of the crime).

This last type of false confession seems most unlikely, but a number of recent cases have come to light in which the police had seized a suspect who was vulnerable (by virtue of his or her youth, intelligence, personality, stress, or mental state) and used false evidence to convince the beleaguered suspect that he or she was guilty. In one case that received a great deal of attention, for example, Paul Ingram was charged with rape and a host of satanic cult crimes that included the slaughter of newborn babies. During 6 months of interrogation, he was hypnotized, exposed to graphic crime details, informed by a police psychologist that sex offenders often repress their offenses, and urged by the minister of his church to confess. Eventually, Ingram "recalled" crime scenes to specification, pleaded guilty, and was sentenced to prison. There was no physical evidence of these crimes, however, and an expert who reviewed the case for the state concluded that Ingram had been brainwashed. To demonstrate, this expert accused Ingram of a bogus crime and found that although he initially denied the charge, he later confessed—and embellished the story (Ofshe, 1992: Wright, 1994).

Other similar cases have been reported (e.g., Pratkanis & Aronson, 1991), but, to date, there is no empirical proof of this phenomenon. Memory researchers have found that misleading postevent information can alter actual or reported memories of observed events (Loftus, Donders, Hoffman, & Schooler, 1989; Loftus, Miller, & Burns, 1978; McCloskey & Zaragoza, 1985)—an effect that is particularly potent in young children (Ceci & Bruck, 1993; Ceci, Ross, & Toglia, 1987) and adults under hypnosis (Dinges et al., 1992; Dywan & Bowers, 1983; Sheehan, Statham, & Jamieson, 1991). Indeed, recent studies suggest it is even possible to implant false recollections of traumas supposedly buried in the unconscious (Loftus, 1993). As related to confessions, the question is, can memory of one's own actions similarly be altered? Can people be induced to accept guilt for crimes they did not commit? Is it, contrary to popular belief, possible?

Because of obvious ethical constraints, this important issue has not been addressed previously. This article thus reports on a new laboratory paradigm used to test the following specific hypothesis: The presentation of false evidence can lead individuals who are vulnerable (i.e., in a heightened state of uncertainty) to confess to an act they did not commit and, more important, to internalize the confession and perhaps confabulate details in memory consistent with that new belief.

METHOD

Participating for extra credit in what was supposed to be a reaction time experiment, 79 undergraduates (40 male, 39 female) were randomly assigned to one of four groups produced by a 2 (high vs. low vulnerability) × 2 (presence vs. absence of a false incriminating witness) factorial design.

Two subjects per session (actually, 1 subject and a female confederate) engaged in a reaction time task on an IBM PS2/Model 50 computer. To bolster the credibility of the experimental cover story, they were asked to fill out a brief questionnaire concerning their typing experience and ability, spatial awareness, and speed of reflexes. The subject and confederate were then taken to another room, seated across a table from the experimenter, and instructed on the task. The confederate was to read aloud a list of letters, and the subject was to type these letters on the keyboard. After 3 min, the subject and confederate were to reverse roles. Before the session began, subjects were instructed on proper use of the computer—and were specifically warned not to press the "ALT" key positioned near the space bar because doing so would cause the program to crash and data to be lost. Lo and behold, after 60 s, the computer supposedly ceased to function, and a highly distressed experimenter accused the subject of having pressed the forbidden key. All subjects initially denied the charge, at which point the experimenter tinkered with the keyboard, confirmed that data had been lost, and asked, "Did you hit the 'ALT' key?"

Two forensically relevant factors were independently varied. First, we manipulated subjects' level of *vulnerability* (i.e., their subjective certainty concerning their own innocence) by varying the pace of the task. Using a mechanical metronome, the confederate read either at a slow and relaxed pace of 43 letters per minute or at a frenzied pace of 67 letters per minute (these settings were established through pretesting). Two-way analyses of variance revealed significant main effects on the number of letters typed correctly ($Ms = 33.01$ and 61.12, respectively; $F[1, 71] = 278.93, p < .001$) and the number of typing errors made ($Ms = 1.12$ and 10.90, respectively; $F[1, 71] = 38.81, p < .001$), thus confirming the effectiveness of this manipulation.

Second, we varied the use of *false incriminating evidence*, a common interrogation technique. After the subject initially denied the charge, the experimenter turned to the confederate and asked, "Did you see anything?" In the false-witness condition, the confederate "admitted" that she had seen the subject hit the "ALT" key that terminated the program. In the no-witness condition, the same confederate said she had not seen what happened.

As dependent measures, three forms of social influence were assessed: compliance, internalization, and confabulation. To elicit *compliance*, the experimenter handwrote a standardized confession ("I hit the 'ALT' key and caused the program to crash. Data were lost") and asked the subject to sign it—the consequence of which would be a phone call from the principal investigator. If the subject refused, the request was repeated a second time.

To assess *internalization*, we unobtrusively recorded the way subjects privately described what happened soon afterward. As the experimenter and subject left the laboratory, they were met in the reception area by a waiting subject (actually, a second confederate who was blind to the subject's condition and previous behavior) who had overheard the commotion. The experimenter explained that the session would have to be rescheduled, and then left the room to retrieve his appointment calendar. At that point, the second confederate turned privately to the subject and asked, "What happened?" The subject's reply was recorded verbatim and later coded for whether or not he or she had unambiguously internalized guilt for what happened (e.g., "I hit the wrong button and ruined the program"; "I hit a button I wasn't supposed to"). A conservative criterion was employed. Any reply that was prefaced by "he said" or "I may have" or "I think" was not taken as evidence of internalization. Two raters who were blind to the subject's condition independently coded these responses, and their agreement rate was 96%.

Finally, after the sessions seemed to be over, the experimenter reappeared, brought the subjects back into the lab, reread the list of letters they had typed, and asked if they could reconstruct how or when they hit the "ALT" key. This procedure was designed to probe for evidence of *confabulation*, to determine whether subjects would "recall" specific details to fit the allegation (e.g., "Yes, here, I hit it with the side of my hand right after you called out the 'A'"). The interrater agreement rate on the coding of these data was 100%.

At the end of each session, subjects were fully and carefully debriefed about the study—its purpose, the hypothesis, and the reason for the use of deception—by the experimenter and first confederate. Most subjects reacted with a combination of relief (that they had not ruined the experiment), amazement (that their perceptions of their own behavior had been so completely manipulated), and a sense of satisfaction (at having played a meaningful role in an important study). Subjects were also asked not to discuss the experience with other students until all the data were collected. Four subjects reported during debriefing that they were suspicious of the experimental manipulation. Their data were excluded from all analyses.

RESULTS AND DISCUSSION

Overall, 69% of the 75 subjects signed the confession, 28% exhibited internalization, and 9% confabulated details to support their false beliefs. More important, between-group comparisons provided strong support for the main hypothesis. As seen in Table 1, subjects in the slow-pace/no-witness control group were the least likely to exhibit an effect, whereas those in the fast-pace/witness group were the most likely to exhibit the effect on the measures of compliance ($\chi^2[3] = 23.84$, $p < .001$), internalization ($\chi^2[3] = 37.61$, $p < .001$), and confabulation ($\chi^2[3] = 18.0$, $p < .005$).

Specifically, although 34.78% of the subjects in the slow-pace/no-witness group signed the confession, indicating compliance, not a single subject in this group exhibited internalization or confabulation. In contrast, the two in dependent variables had a powerful combined effect.

TABLE 1

Percentage of subjects in each cell who exhibited the three forms of influence

Form of influence	No witness		Witness	
	Slow pace	**Fast pace**	**Slow Pace**	**Fast pace**
Compliance	35a	65b	89bc	100c
Internalization	0a	12ab	44bc	65c
Confabulation	0a	0a	6a	35b

Note. Percentages not sharing a common subscript differ at p < .05 via chi-square test of significance.

Out of 17 subjects in the fast-pace/witness cell, 100% signed a confession, 65% came to believe they were guilty (in reality, they were not), and 35% confabulated details to support their false belief (via chi-square tests, the differences in these rates between the slow-pace/no-witness control group and fast-pace/witness group were significant at $ps < .001, .001$, and $.005$, respectively).

Additional pair-wise comparisons revealed that the presence of a witness alone was sufficient to significantly increase the rates of compliant and internalized confessions, even in the slow-pace condition ($\chi^2[1] = 12.18, p < .005$, and $\chi^2[1] = 16.39, p < .001$). There were no sex differences on any measures (i.e., male and female subjects exhibited comparable confession rates overall, and were similarly influenced by the independent variables).

The present study provides strong initial support for the provocative notion that the presentation of false incriminating evidence—an interrogation ploy that is common among the police and sanctioned by many courts—can induce people to internalize blame for outcomes they did not produce. These results provide an initial basis for challenging the evidentiary validity of confessions produced by this technique. These findings also demonstrate, possibly for the first time, that memory can be altered not only for observed events and remote past experiences, but also for one's own recent actions.

An obvious and important empirical question remains concerning the external validity of the present results: To what extent do they generalize to the interrogation behavior of actual crime suspects? For ethical reasons, we developed a laboratory paradigm in which subjects were accused merely of an unconscious act of negligence, not of an act involving explicit criminal intent (e.g., stealing equipment from the lab or cheating on an important test). In this paradigm, there was only a minor consequence for liability. At this point, it is unclear whether people could similarly be induced to internalize false guilt for acts of omission (i.e., neglecting to do something they were told to do) or for acts that emanate from conscious intent.

It is important, however, not to overstate this limitation. The fact that our procedure focused on an act of negligence and low consequence may well explain why the compliance rate was high, with roughly two thirds of all subjects agreeing to sign a confession statement. Effects of this sort on overt judgments and behavior have been observed in studies of conformity to group norms, compliance with direct requests, and obedience to the commands of authority. But the more important and startling result—that many subjects privately internalized guilt for an outcome they did not produce, and that some even constructed memories to fit that false belief—is not seriously compromised by the laboratory paradigm that was used. Conceptually, these findings extend known effects of misinformation on memory for observed events (Loftus et al., 1978; McCloskey & Zaragoza, 1985) and for traumas assumed to be buried in the unconscious (Loftus, 1993). Indeed, our effects were exhibited by college students who are intelligent (drawn from a population in which the mean score on the Scholastic Aptitude Test is over 1300), self-assured, and under minimal stress compared with crime suspects held in custody, often in isolation.

At this point, additional research is needed to examine other common interrogation techniques (e.g., minimization), individual differences in suspect vulnerability (e.g., manifest anxiety, need for approval, hypnotic susceptibility), and other risk factors for false confessions (e.g., blood alcohol level, sleep deprivation). In light of recent judicial acceptance of a broad range of self-incriminatory statements, increasing use of videotaped confessions at the trial level (Geller, 1993), and the U.S. Supreme Court's ruling that an improperly admitted coerced confession may qualify as a mere "harmless error" (*Arizona v. Fulminante*, 1991), further research is also needed to assess the lay jury's reaction to this type of evidence when presented in court.

Acknowledgments—This research was submitted as part of a senior honor's thesis by the second author and was funded by the Bronfman Science Center of Williams College.

REFERENCES

Arizona v. Fulminante, 59 U.S.L.W. 4235 (1991).

Aubry, A., & Caputo, R. (1965). *Criminal interrogation*. Springfield, IL: Charles C. Thomas.

Bedau, H., & Radelet, M. (1987). Miscarriages of justice in potentially capital cases, *Stanford Law Review, 40*, 21–179.

Borchard, E.M. (1932). *Convicting the innocent: Errors of criminal justice*. New Haven, CT: Yale University Press.

Ceci, S.J., & Bruck, M. (1993). Suggestibility of the child witness: A historical review and synthesis. *Psychological Bulletin, 113*, 403–439.

Ceci, S.J., Ross, D.F., & Toglia, M.P. (1987). Suggestibility of children's memory: Psycholegal implications. *Journal of Experimental Psychology: General, 116*, 38–49.

Dinges, D.F., Whitehouse, W.G., Orne, E.C., Powell, J.W., Orne, M.T., & Erdelyi, M.H. (1992). Evaluating hypnotic memory enhancement (hypermnesia and reminiscence) using multitrial forced recall. *Journal of Experimental Psychology: Learning, Memory, and Cognition, 18*, 1139–1147.

Dywan, J., & Bowers, K. (1983). The use of hypnosis to enhance recall. *Science, 222*, 184–185.

Geller, W.A. (1993). *Videotaping interrogations and confessions* (National Institute of Justice: Research in Brief). Washington, DC: U.S. Department of Justice.

Gudjonsson, G. (1992). *The psychology of interrogations, confessions, and testimony*. London: Wiley.

Inbau, F.E., Reid, J.E., & Buckley, J.P. (1986). *Criminal interrogation and confessions* (3rd ed.). Baltimore, MD: Williams & Wilkins.

Kassin, S.M., & McNall, K. (1991). Police interrogations and confessions: Communicating promises and threats by pragmatic implication. *Law and Human Behavior, 15*, 233–251.

Kassin, S.M., & Wrightsman, L.S. (1980). Prior confessions and mock juror verdicts. *Journal of Applied Social Psychology, 10*, 133–146.

Kassin, S.M., & Wrightsman, L.S. (1981). Coerced confessions, judicial instruction, and mock juror verdicts. *Journal, of Applied Social Psychology 11*, 489–506.

Kassin, S.M., & Wrightsman, L.S. (1985). Confession evidence. In S.M. Kassin & L.S. Wrightsman (Eds.), *The psychology of evidence and trial procedure* (pp. 67–94). Beverly Hills, CA: Sage.

Loftus, E.F. (1993). The reality of repressed memories. *American Psychologist, 48*, 518–537.

Loftus, E.F., Donders, K., Hoffman, H.G., & Schooler, J.W. (1989). Creating new memories that are quickly accessed and confidently held. *Memory and Cognition, 17*, 607–616.

Loftus, E.F., Miller, D.G., & Burns, H.J. (1978). Semantic integration of verbal information into visual memory. *Journal of Experimental Psychology: Human Learning and Memory, 4*, 19–31.

McCloskey, M., & Zaragoza, M. (1985). Misleading post-event information and memory for events: Arguments and evidence against memory impairment hypotheses. *Journal of Experimental Psychology, 114*, 3–18.

Ofshe, R. (1992). Inadvertent hypnosis during interrogation: False confession due to dissociative state; misidentified multiple personality and the satanic cult hypothesis. *International Journal of Clinical and Experimental Hypnosis, 40*, 125–156.

O'Hara, C.E., & O'Hara, G.L. (1981). *Fundamentals of criminal investigation*. Springfield, IL: Charles C. Thomas.

Pratkanis, A., & Aronson, E. (1991). *Age of propaganda: The everyday use and abuse of persuasion*. New York: W.H. Freeman.

Rattner, A. (1988). Convicted but innocent: Wrongful conviction and the criminal justice system. *Law and Human Behavior, 12*, 283–293.

Sheehan, P.W., Statham, D., & Jamieson, G.A. (1991). Pseudomemory effects and their relationship to level of susceptibility to hypnosis and state instruction. *Journal of Personality and Social Psychology, 60*, 130–137.

Sukel, H.L., & Kassin, S.M. (1994, March). *Coerced confessions and the jury: An experimental test of the "harmless error" rule*. Paper presented at the biennial meeting of the American Psychology-Law Society, Sante Fe, NM.

Wright, L. (1994). *Remembering Satan*. New York: Alfred A. Knopf.

Wrightsman, L.S., & Kassin, S.M. (1993). *Confessions in the courtroom*. Newbury Park, CA: Sage.

(Received 12/21/94; Accepted 2/22/95)

READING 17

Looking Deathworthy: Perceived Stereotypicality of Black Defendants Predicts Capital-Sentencing Outcomes

Should physical appearance be a determining factor in a jury's decision as to whether a convicted killer will live or die? Most people would rightfully say, "Of course, not." However, Eberhardt, Davies, Purdie-Vaughns, and Johnson found that Black defendants who have been found guilty of killing a White person were much more likely to receive the death penalty if they had stereotypically Black facial features (e.g., broad nose, thick lips, dark skin) than if they did not. The authors cite previous studies that have shown that stereotypically Black faces tend to be associated with criminality and that judges were more likely to mete out longer sentences to convicted felons with stereotypically Black features. In the present study, the finding that convicted defendants with stereotypically Black features were more likely to receive the death penalty did not extend to Black defendants accused of killing Blacks. The researchers speculate that the discrepancy is due to the fact that in cases where a Black person killed a White person, the race of the defendant became more salient, focusing jurors' attention on the defendant's racial characteristics. As you read this study, consider how it relates to the text's discussion of implicit racism in Chapter 5 (Stereotypes, Prejudice, and Discrimination). Think also about how it pertains to what you read in Chapter 4 (Perceiving Persons), with regard to how we tend to perceive and evaluate others based solely on their appearance.

LOOKING DEATHWORTHY: PERCEIVED STEREOTYPICALITY OF BLACK DEFENDANTS PREDICTS CAPITAL-SENTENCING OUTCOMES

Jennifer L. Eberhardt,[1] Paul G. Davies,[2] Valerie J. Purdie-Vaughns,[3] and Sheri Lynn Johnson[4]

[1]Department of Psychology, Stanford University; [2]Department of Psychology, University of California, Los Angeles; [3]Department of Psychology, Yale University; and [4]Cornell Law School

ABSTRACT—*Researchers previously have investigated the role of race in capital sentencing, and in particular, whether the race of the defendant or victim influences the likelihood of a death sentence. In the present study, we examined whether the likelihood of being sentenced to death is influenced by the degree to which a Black defendant is perceived to have a stereotypically Black appearance. Controlling for a wide array of factors, we found that in cases involving a White victim, the more stereotypically Black a defendant is perceived to be, the more likely that person is to be sentenced to death.*

Jennifer L. Eberhardt, Paul G. Davies, Valerie J. Purdie-Vaughns, and Sheri Lynn Johnson, "Looking Deathworthy: Perceived Stereotypicality of Black Defendants Predicts Capital-Sentencing Outcomes," Psychological Science, Vol. 17, No. 5, pp. 383-386. Reprinted with permission of Blackwell Publishing, Inc.

Address correspondence to Jennifer L. Eberhardt, Department of Psychology, Stanford University, Jordan Hall, Building 420, Stanford, CA 94305-2130, e-mail: jle@psych.stanford.edu.

Race matters in capital punishment. Even when statistically controlling for a wide variety of non-racial factors that may influence sentencing, numerous researchers have found that murderers of White victims are more likely than murderers of Black victims to be sentenced to death (Baldus, Pulaski, & Woodworth, 1983; Baldus, Woodworth, & Pulaski, 1985, 1990, 1994; Baldus, Woodworth, Zuckerman, Weiner, & Broffitt, 1998; Bowers, Pierce, & McDevitt, 1984; Gross & Mauro, 1989; Radelet, 1981; U.S. General Accounting Office (GAO), 1990). The U.S. GAO (1990) has described this race-of-victim effect as "remarkably consistent across datasets, states, data collection methods, and analytic techniques" (p. 5).

In one of the most comprehensive studies to date, the race of the victim and the race of the defendant each were found to influence sentencing (Baldus et al., 1998). Not only did killing a White person rather than a Black person increase the likelihood of being sentenced to death, but also Black defendants were more likely than White defendants to be sentenced to death.

In the current research, we used the data set from this study by Baldus and his colleagues (1998) to investigate whether the probability of receiving the death penalty is significantly influenced by the degree to which the defendant is perceived to have a stereo typically Black appearance (e.g., broad nose, thick lips, dark skin). In particular, we considered the effect of a Black defendant's perceived stereotypicality for those cases in which race is most salient—when a Black defendant is charged with murdering a White victim. Although systematic studies of death sentencing have been conducted for decades, no prior studies have examined this potential influence of physical appearance on death-sentencing decisions.

A growing body of research demonstrates that people more readily apply racial stereotypes to Blacks who are thought to look more stereotypically Black, compared with Blacks who are thought to look less stereotypically Black (Blair, Judd, & Fall-man, 2004; Blair, Judd, Sadler, & Jenkins, 2002; Eberhardt, Goff, Purdie, & Davies, 2004; Maddox, 2004; Maddox & Gray, 2002, 2004). People associate Black physical traits with criminality in particular. The more stereotypically Black a person's physical traits appear to be, the more criminal that person is perceived to be (Eberhardt et al., 2004). A recent study found that perceived stereotypicality correlated with the actual sentencing decisions of judges (Blair, Judd, & Chapleau, 2004). Even with differences in defendants' criminal histories statistically controlled, those defendants who possessed the most stereotypically Black facial features served up to 8 months longer in prison for felonies than defendants who possessed the least stereotypically Black features. The present study examined the extent to which perceived stereotypicality of Black defendants influenced jurors' death-sentencing decisions in cases with both White and Black victims. We argue that only in death-eligible cases involving White victims—cases in which race is most salient—will Black defendants' physical traits function as a significant determinant of death worthiness.

Phase I: Black Defendant, White Victim

Method

We used an extensive database (compiled by Baldus et al., 1998) containing more than 600 death-eligible cases from Philadelphia, Pennsylvania, that advanced to penalty phase between 1979 and 1999.

Fig. 1. Examples of variation in stereo typicality of Black faces. These images are the faces of people with no criminal history and are shown here for illustrative purposes only. The face on the right would be considered more stereotypically Black than the face on the left.

Forty-four of these cases involved Black male defendants who were convicted of murdering White victims. We obtained the photographs of these Black defendants and presented all 44 of them (in a slide-show format) to naive raters who did not know that the photographs depicted convicted murderers. Raters were asked to rate the stereo typicality of each Black defendant's appearance and were told they could use any number of features (e.g., lips, nose, hair texture, skin tone) to arrive at their judgments (Fig. 1).

Stanford undergraduates served as the raters. To control for potential order effects, we presented the photographs in a different random order in each of two sessions. Thirty-two raters (26 White, 4 Asian, and 2 of other ethnicities) participated in one session, and 19 raters (6 White, 11 Asian, and 2 of other ethnicities) participated in the second session. The raters were shown a black-and-white photograph of each defendant's face. The photographs were edited such that the backgrounds and image sizes were standardized, and only the face and a portion of the neck were visible. Raters were told that all the faces they would be viewing were of Black males. The defendants' faces were projected one at a time on to a screen at the front of the room for 4 s each as participants recorded stereo typicality ratings using a scale from 1 (*not at all stereotypical*) to 11 (*extremely stereotypical*). In both sessions, raters were kept blind to the purpose of the study and the identity of the men in the photographs. The data were analyzed for effects of order and rater's race, but none emerged.

Results

We computed an analysis of covariance (ANCOVA) using stereo typicality (low-high median split) as the independent variable, the percentage of death sentences imposed as the dependent variable, and six non racial factors known to influence sentencing (Baldus et al., 1998; Landy & Aronson, 1969; Stewart, 1980) as covariates: (a) aggravating circumstances, (b) mitigating circumstances, (c) severity of the murder (as determined by blind ratings of the cases once purged of racial information), (d) the defendant's socioeconomic status, (e) the victim's socioeconomic status, and (f) the defendant's attractiveness.[1] As per Pennsylvania statute (Judiciary and Judicial Procedure, 2005), aggravating circumstances included factors such as the victim's status as a police officer, prosecution witness, or drug-trafficking competitor; the defendant's prior convictions for voluntary manslaughter or violent

---

[1] With the exception of defendant's attractiveness, all of the covariates employed here were included in the Baldus database and have been described in detail elsewhere (e.g., see Baldus et al., 1998). We added defendant's attractiveness, basing this variable on 42 naive participants' ratings of the defendants' faces using a scale from 1 (*not at all attractive*) to 11 (*extremely attractive*).

felonies; and characteristics of the crime, such as torture, kidnapping, or payment for the murder. Mitigating circumstances included factors such as the defendant's youth or advanced age, extreme mental or emotional disturbance, lack of prior criminal convictions, minor or coerced role in the crime, and impaired ability to appreciate the criminality of his conduct. The Baldus database of death-eligible defendants is arguably one of the most comprehensive to date; using it allowed us to control for the key variables known to influence sentencing outcomes.

The results confirmed that, above and beyond the effects of the covariates, defendants whose appearance was perceived as more stereotypically Black were more likely to receive a death sentence than defendants whose appearance was perceived as less stereotypically Black, $F(1, 36) = 4.11, p < .05$, $\eta_p^2 = .10$ (Fig. 2a). In fact, 24.4% of those Black defendants who fell in the lower half of the stereotypicality distribution received a death sentence, whereas 57.5% of those Black defendants who fell in the upper half received a death sentence.

Phase II: Black Defendant, Black victim

Method

Using the same database and procedures described earlier, we examined whether this stereotypicality effect extended to cases in which the victims were Black. Of all cases that advanced to penalty phase, 308 involved Black male defendants who were convicted of murdering Black victims. The photographs for all of these defendants were obtained. The death-sentencing rate for these 308 defendants, however, was only 27% (as compared with 41% for the cases with White victims). Given both the low death-sentencing rate and the large number of cases involving Black defendants and Black victims, we selected 118 of these 308 cases randomly from the database with the stipulation that those defendants receiving the death sentence be oversampled. This oversampling yielded a subset of cases in which the death-sentencing rate (46%) was not significantly different from that for the cases with White victims (41%; $F = 1$). Using this subset provided a conservative test of our hypothesis. We then presented this subset of Black defendants who murdered Black victims to 18 raters (12 White and 6 Asian), who rated the faces on stereotypicality.[2]

Results

Employing the same analyses as we did for the cases with White victims, we found that the perceived stereotypicality of Black defendants convicted of murdering Black victims did not predict death sentencing, $F(1,110) < 1$ (Fig. 2b). Black defendants who fell in the upper and lower halves of the stereotypicality distribution were sentenced to death at almost identical rates (45% vs. 46.6%, respectively). Thus, defendants who were perceived to be more stereotypically Black were more likely to be sentenced to death only when their victims were White.

Although the two phases of this experiment were designed and conducted separately, readers may be interested in knowing whether combining the data from the two phases would produce a significant interactive effect of victims' race and defendants' stereotypicality on death-sentencing outcomes. Analysis confirmed that the interaction of victims' race (Black vs. White) and defendants' stereotypicality (low vs. high) was indeed significant, $F(1, 158) = 4.97, p < .05, \eta_p^2 = .03$.

---

[2] Faces of 15 of the Black defendants who murdered White victims were repeated in this session. Analysis of the ratings confirmed interrater reliability.

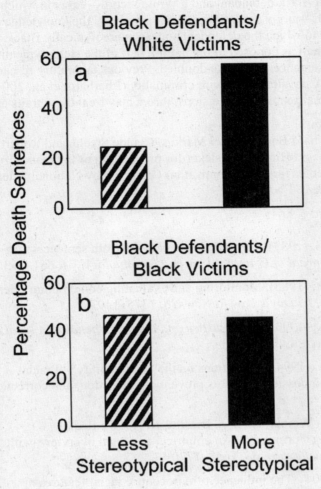

Fig. 2. Percentage of death sentences imposed in (a) cases involving White victims and (b) cases involving Black victims as a function of the perceived stereotypicality of Black defendants' appearance.

Discussion

Why might a defendant's perceived stereotypicality matter for Black murderers of White victims, but not for Black murderers of Black victims? One possibility is that the interracial character of cases involving a Black defendant and a White victim renders race especially salient. Such crimes could be interpreted or treated as matters of inter group conflict (Prentice & Miller, 1999). The salience of race may incline jurors to think about race as a relevant and useful heuristic for determining the blameworthiness of the defendant and the perniciousness of the crime. According to this racial-salience hypothesis, defendants' perceived stereotypicality should not influence death-sentencing outcomes in cases involving a Black defendant and a Black victim. In those cases, the intraracial character of the crime may lead jurors to view the crime as a matter of interpersonal rather than intergroup conflict (Prentice & Miller, 1999).

These research findings augment and complicate the current body of evidence regarding the role of race in capital sentencing. Whereas previous studies examined intergroup differences in death-sentencing outcomes, our results suggest that racial discrimination may also operate through intragroup distinctions based on perceived racial stereotypicality.

Our findings suggest that in cases involving a Black defendant and a White victim—cases in which the likelihood of the death penalty is already high—jurors are influenced not simply by the knowledge that the defendant is Black, but also by the extent to which the defendant appears stereotypically Black. In fact, for those defendants who fell in the top half as opposed to the bottom half of the stereotypicality distribution, the chance of receiving a death sentence more than doubled. Previous laboratory research has already shown that people associate Black physical traits with criminality (Eberhardt et al., 2004). The present research demonstrates that in actual sentencing decisions, jurors may treat these traits as powerful cues to death worthiness.

Acknowledgments—The authors thank R. Richard Banks, Hazel Markus, Claude Steele, and Robert Zajonc for comments on a draft of this article and Hilary Bergsieker for preparation of the manuscript. This research was supported by a Stanford Center for Social Innovation Grant and by National Science Foundation Grant BCS-9986128 awarded to J. L. Eberhardt.

REFERENCES

Baldus, D.C., Pulaski, C.A., & Woodworth, G. (1983). Comparative review of death sentences: An empirical study of the Georgia experience. *Journal of Criminal Law and Criminology, 74*, 661–753.

Baldus, D.C., Woodworth, G., & Pulaski, C.A. (1985). Monitoring and evaluating contemporary death sentencing systems: Lessons from Georgia. *U. C. Davis Law Review, 18*, 1375–1407.

Baldus, D.C., Woodworth, G., & Pulaski, C.A. (1990). *Equal justice and the death penalty: A legal and empirical analysis.* Boston: Northeastern University Press.

Baldus, D.C., Woodworth, G., & Pulaski, C.A. (1994). Reflections on the "inevitability" of racial discrimination in capital sentencing and the "impossibility" of its prevention, detection, and correction. *Washington and Lee Law Review, 51*, 359–419.

Baldus, D.C., Woodworth, G., Zuckerman, D., Weiner, N.A., & Broffitt, B. (1998). Racial discrimination and the death penalty in the post-Furman era: An empirical and legal overview, with recent findings from Philadelphia. *Cornell Law Review, 83*, 1638–1770.

Blair, I.V., Judd, C.M., & Chapleau, K.M. (2004). The influence of Afrocentric facial features in criminal sentencing. *Psychological Science, 15*, 674–679.

Blair, I.V., Judd, C.M., & Fallman, J.L. (2004). The automaticity of race and Afrocentric facial features in social judgments. *Journal of Personality and Social Psychology, 87*, 763–778.

Blair, I.V., Judd, C.M., Sadler, M.S., & Jenkins, C. (2002). The role of Afrocentric features in person perception: Judging by features and categories. *Journal of Personality and Social Psychology, 83*, 5–25.

Bowers, W.J., Pierce, G.L., & McDevitt, J.F. (1984). *Legal homicide: Death as punishment in America, 1864–1982.* Boston: Northeastern University Press.

Eberhardt, J.L., Goff, P. A., Purdie, V.J., & Davies, P.G. (2004). Seeing Black: Race, crime, and visual processing. *Journal of Personality and Social Psychology, 87*, 876–893.

Gross, S.R., & Mauro, R. (1989). *Death and discrimination: Racial disparities in capital sentencing.* Boston: Northeastern University Press.

Judiciary and Judicial Procedure, 42 Pa. Cons. Stat. § 9711 (2005).

Landy, D., & Aronson, E. (1969). The influence of the character of the criminal and his victim on the decisions of simulated jurors. *Journal of Experimental Social Psychology, 5*, 141–152.

Maddox, K.B. (2004). Perspectives on racial phenotypicality bias. *Personality and Social Psychology Review, 8*, 383–401.

Maddox, K. B., & Gray, S. A. (2002). Cognitive representations of Black Americans: Reexploring the role of skin tone. *Personality and Social Psychology Bulletin, 28*, 250–259.

Maddox, K.B., & Gray, S. A. (2004). Manipulating subcategory salience: Exploring the link between skin tone and social perception of Blacks. *European Journal of Social Psychology, 34*, 533–546.

Prentice, D.A., & Miller, D.T. (Eds.). (1999). *Cultural divides: Understanding and overcoming group conflict*. New York: Russell Sage Foundation.

Radelet, M.L. (1981). Racial characteristics and the imposition of the death penalty. *American Sociological Review, 46*, 918–927.

Stewart, J.E. (1980). Defendant's attractiveness as a factor in the outcome of criminal trials: An observational study. *Journal of Applied Social Psychology, 10*, 348–361.

U.S. General Accounting Office. (1990). *Death penalty sentencing: Research indicates pattern of racial disparities*. Washington, DC: Author.

(RECEIVED 7/27/05; REVISION ACCEPTED 10/20/05; FINAL MATERIALS RECEIVED 11/9/05

READING 18

Equity and Workplace Status: A Field Experiment

Being rewarded for one's work helps to maintain motivation and commitment, but, as Chapters 3 (The Social Self), 7 (Attitudes), and 13 (Business) make clear, the effects of reward on motivation are complex. According to *equity theory*, for example, people want rewards to be equitable so that the ratio between inputs and outcomes should be the same for the self as it is for co-workers. Thus, if you feel overpaid or underpaid and cannot change the situation, you will experience distress and try to restore equity—perhaps by working more or less. Studying workers in a large insurance firm, Greenberg (1988) measured changes in productivity among those who were temporarily moved to offices that were larger, smaller, or equal to their rank within the company. Did office size affect performance, as predicted by equity theory, in an actual office setting? As you read this article, think about the implications of equity theory for motivation not only in the workplace but in close relationships and educational settings as well.

EQUITY AND WORKPLACE STATUS: A FIELD EXPERIMENT[*]

Jerald Greenberg

Faculty of Management and Human Resources, The Ohio State University

In a field experiment, 198 employees in the underwriting department of a large insurance company were randomly reassigned on a temporary basis to the offices of either higher, lower, or equal-status coworkers while their own offices were being refurbished. The present study tested the hypothesis, derived from equity theory, that the status value of the temporary offices would create increases, decreases, or no change in organizational outcome levels. The resulting pattern of performance supported equity theory. Specifically, relative to those workers reassigned to equal-status offices, those reassigned to higher status offices raised their performance (a response to overpayment inequity) and those reassigned to lower status offices lowered their performance (a response to underpayment inequity). As hypothesized, the size of these performance changes was directly related to the magnitude of the status inconsistencies encountered. The value of these findings in extending equity theory to the realm of nonmonetary outcomes is discussed.

There can be little doubt about the existence of certain trappings of success in organizations—physical symbols (cf. Goodsell, 1977) reflecting the organizational status of job incumbents (Steele, 1973). Indeed, previous research has confirmed that certain indicators of status demarcation (cf. Konar & Sundstrom, 1985), such as large offices (Langdon, 1966), carpeting (Joiner, 1976), and proximity to windows (Halloran, 1978), are recognized as rewards symbolizing one's high standing in an organizational status hierarchy. Although these environmental rewards typically are associated with relatively high-status individuals, thereby reinforcing the social order of organizations (Edelman, 1978), there are some occasions in which the status of the job incumbent and the physical symbols associated with the status are not matched (Wineman, 1982). Such instances may be recognized as cases of status inconsistency (cf. Stryker & Macke, 1978) and, as such, reactions to them may be explained by equity theory (e.g., Adams, 1965; Walster, Walster, & Berscheid, 1978).

[*] Jerald Greenberg, "Equity and Workplace Status: A Field Experiment," Journal of Applied Psychology, 1988, Vol. 73, No. 4, pp. 606-613. Copyright (c) 1988 by the American Psychological Association. Reproduced with permission.

According to equity theory, workers who receive levels of reward (i.e., outcomes) higher or lower than coworkers who make equivalent contributions to their jobs (i.e., inputs) are considered overpaid and underpaid, respectively. Such inequitable states have been shown to result in dissatisfaction and to bring about increases and decreases, respectively, in job performance (for a review, see Greenberg, 1982). As such, the present investigation addresses whether the characteristics of an employee's workspace influence his or her perceptions of equitable treatment on the job. If the characteristics of one's work space are perceived as constituting part of one's work-related rewards, then it follows that receiving work-space-derived rewards greater or less than coworkers of equal status may create conditions of overpayment and underpayment inequity, respectively. The focal question of the present investigation is whether equity theory explains the reactions of persons encountering consistencies and inconsistencies between their job status and the rewards offered by their work space.

Although there is little direct evidence bearing on this question, managers have intuitively believed and long advocated the importance of basing office design decisions on employees' ranks in their organizations' status hierarchies as a mechanism for ensuring equitable treatment (Robichaud, 1958). According to equity theory, an employee's work space may be recognized as an element of equitable treatment insofar as it is perceived as a reward that reflects his or her organizational status. Indeed, previous research (e.g., Konar, Sundstrom, Brady, Mandel, & Rice, 1982) has shown that several elements of work space, such as the nature of the furnishings, amount of space, capacity for personalization, and the ability to control access by others, have been found to covary with workers' relative status rankings (for reviews, see Becker, 1981, 1982; Davis, 1984; Sundstrom, 1986).

Although previous researchers have not incorporated work-space elements into equity theory-based predictions directly, extrapolations from existing research suggest that reactions to work-space characteristics may be predictable from equity theory. For example, Burt and Sundstrom (1979) found in a field study that workers who were underpaid financially were less dissatisfied with their pay if they worked under conditions that were more environmentally desirable than those who did not receive additional work-space-related benefits. These results suggest that the desirable working conditions constituted an additional reward that offset the dissatisfaction created by inadequate monetary payment. Such a finding is consistent with the possibility that workers' reactions to their work spaces may be explained by equity theory. Inequities created by nonmonetary rewards have also been studied by Greenberg and Ornstein (1983), who found that experimental subjects who were overpaid by receiving an inappropriately high job title responded by increasing their job performance, as predicted by equity theory. Thus, much as an inappropriately high job title resulted in attempts to redress overpayment inequity by raising inputs, similar reactions may result from overpayments created by the introduction of work-space elements that are inappropriately lavish for one's organizational ranking.

On the basis of this logic, the present study tested hypotheses derived from equity theory in an organizational setting in which the refurbishing of offices necessitated the reassignment of employees to temporary offices. Specifically, I hypothesized that employees reassigned to offices of higher status workers (i.e., those who are overpaid in terms of office status) would be more productive than those reassigned to offices of other equal-status workers. Similarly, employees reassigned to offices of lower status worker (i.e., those who are underpaid in terms of office status) would be expected to be less productive than those reassigned to offices of other equal-status workers.

Following from equity theory's proposition that the magnitude of the inequity-resolution efforts will be proportional to the magnitude of the inequity (Adams, 1965; Walster et al., 1978), it was expected that improvements or decrements in performance would be greater the larger the over- or underpayments, respectively. Employees reassigned to offices of workers two levels above them would be expected to perform at a higher level than employees reassigned to offices of more modestly overpaid workers one level above them. Similarly, employees reassigned to offices of workers two levels below them would be expected to perform at a lower level than employees reassigned to offices of more modestly underpaid workers one level below them.

METHOD

Subjects

The 198 participants in the study (123 men and 75 women) were drawn from three groups of salaried employees in the life insurance underwriting department of a large insurance company. There were 91 underwriter trainees (Mdn age = 24 years; Mdn job tenure = 8 months), 60 associate underwriters (Mdn age = 28 years; Mdn job tenure = 1 year, 9 months), and 47 underwriters (Mdn age = 31 years; Mdn job tenure = 3 years, 2 months). All of these employees were charged with the responsibility for reviewing and either approving or disapproving applications for life insurance on the basis of the extent to which information uncovered in their investigations satisfied the company's criteria for risk. The primary difference in responsibility for the three groups was the monetary size of the policies they were permitted to approve.

Design

Because the offices of the underwriting department were being refurbished, an opportunity presented itself for studying the behavior of employees working temporarily (10 consecutive work days) in offices regularly assigned to higher, lower, or equally ranked coworkers in the underwriting department. With the cooperation of the participating organization, assignment to temporary office conditions was made at random.1 The reassignment made it possible to create conditions of potential overpayment (assignment to a higher status office), underpayment (assignment to a lower status office), or equitable payment (assignment to an equal-status office), as well as the degree of inequitable payment (office assignment either one or two levels above or below the worker's status). To create control groups, some workers in each employee group remained in their own permanent offices during the study period. Table 1 summarizes the experimental design and reports the number of subjects assigned to each condition.

In addition to these between-subjects elements, the design of the present study also included time as a within-subjects element. Repeated measures of the dependent variables were taken at six intervals; the second week before reassignment to a temporary office, the first week before reassignment, the first week during the reassignment period, the second week during reassignment, the first week back in one's permanent office after reassignment, and the second week after reassignment.

Procedure

Office assignment procedure Before the study began, workers (except those in the control groups) were informed that they would have to work for 2 consecutive 5-day work weeks in other offices while their own offices were being refurbished.[2] So as to not disrupt performance, but allowing ample time for workers to gather their belongings, workers were informed of the impending temporary move 2 workdays in advance. Workers drew lots to determine their temporary office assignments and were not permitted to switch these assignments. This procedure helped safeguard against the possibility that reactions to office assignments could be the result of perceived managerial favoritism or hostility resulting from an undisclosed (and potentially capricious) basis for the office assignments. The procedure also controlled against any possible self-selection bias in office reassignments.

TABLE 1
Summary of Study Design

Worker group/ temporary office	n	Payment condition
Trainee		
Other trainee	42	Equitably paid
Associate	18	One-step overpaid
Underwriter	12	Two-steps overpaid
Own	19	Control
Associate		
Trainee	18	One-step underpaid
Other associate	18	Equitably paid
Underwriter	12	One-step overpaid
Own	12	Control
Underwriter		
Trainee	12	Two-steps underpaid
Associate	12	One-step underpaid
Other underwriter	12	Equitably paid
Own	11	Control

Office characteristics The offices used in the study were those regularly assigned to either underwriter trainees, associate underwriters, or underwriters. In the organization studied, as in others (e.g., Harris, 1977; Kleinschrod, 1987), the offices of workers of different status-rankings differed along several predetermined, standardized dimensions. Consensual knowledge of such differences helped reinforce the status differences between the offices used in the study.[3] The key physical characteristics of the offices used in the experiment are described in Table 2. Although these dimensions were known within the host organization to reflect status differential, it is instructive to note that they are not idiosyncratic. Indeed, these dimensions are among those found in the survey study by Konar et al. (1982) to be associated with status differences among employees in other organizations.

As shown in Table 2, the offices of associate underwriters were shared by fewer office mates, allowed more space per person, and had larger desks than the offices of underwriter trainees. Underwriters' offices were always completely private (used by only one person), allowed the most space per person, and had the largest desks. In addition, the underwriters' offices had doors, whereas the offices of underwriter trainees and associate underwriters did not. The use of these status markers (cf. Konar & C Sundstrom, 1985) is in keeping with previous studies showing that higher status is associated with the use of unshared, private offices (Sundstrom, Burt, & Kamp, 1980), greater floorspace (Harris, 1977), larger desks (Wylie, 1958), and the option to limit access to oneself by the presence of doors (Geran, 1976).

Performance measure The principal dependent measure was job performance in reviewing applications for life insurance. It was the practice of the company studied to derive corrected performance scores for all underwriters. (Such measures typically were used, in part, as the basis for performance evaluations and pay raises.) Raw performance measures were computed weekly on the basis of the number of cases completed. These were then adjusted by supervisory personnel for decision quality, the complexity of the cases considered (both of which were based on predetermined criteria), and the number of hours spent reviewing application files, resulting in a corrected performance score. So as to provide a basis of comparison for interpreting these scores, the mean corrected performance scores of the workers studied in the 2 months prior to the present investigation was 49.2. Because this score was not significantly different than the two prereassignment scores observed in this investigation, $F < 1.00$, ns, there is no reason to believe that the study period was in any way atypical.

TABLE 2
Physical Characteristics of Offices

	Offices		
Physical characteristic	**Underwriter trainees** $(n = 15)$	**Associate underwriters** $(n = 30)$	**Underwriters** $(n = 47)$
No. of occupants per office	6a	2	1
Presence of door	No	No	Yes
Occupant space (m^2 per occupant)	21.34	29.87	44.81
Desk size (m^2)	1.14	1.32	1.53

Note. Because the host company standardized office characteristics as a function of employee status, there was very little or no variation in the values reported here.

[a] One of the 15 offices that was larger than the others housed seven underwriter trainees; the remaining 14 housed six.

Questionnaire measures To help explain the performance measure, questionnaire data were collected as supplementary measures. These questionnaires were administered at three times: one week before reassignment, one week into the reassignment period, and one week after reassignment.

To measure job satisfaction, the 20-item general satisfaction scale of the Minnesota Satisfaction Questionnaire (MSQ; Weiss, Dawis, England, & Lofquist, 1967) was used. It requires participants to indicate whether they are *very satisfied, satisfied, neither satisfied nor dissatisfied, dissatisfied,* or *very dissatisfied* with respect to a broad range of job dimensions, such as "the feeling of accomplishment I get from the job" and "the freedom to use my own judgment." This scale was chosen because it has excellent psychometric properties (Price & Mueller, 1986) and because its use enhances comparability with other tests of equity theory using the same measure (e.g., Pritchard, Dunnette, & Jorgenson, 1972). For the present sample, coefficient alpha was .88.

An additional set of questions was designed to determine the extent to which workers recognized the outcome value of their office environments. As such, a measure of environmental satisfaction was derived by asking subjects, "How pleased or displeased are you with each of the following aspects of your current work environment?": privacy, desk space, floorspace, noise level, lighting, furnishings, and overall atmosphere. Scale values could range from *extremely displeased* (1) to *extremely pleased* (7), Coefficient alpha was computed to be .82.

Finally, a separate item asked, "How would you characterize the overall level of rewards you are now receiving from your job?" Scale values could range from *extremely low* (1) to *extremely high* (7).

Manipulation checks As the basis for explaining performance differences in terms of the inequities caused by status differences in office assignments, it was necessary to establish that workers correctly perceived the status differences of their temporary offices and, also, had unaided and unimpaired opportunities to perform in their temporary offices. Accordingly, checklist questions addressing these matters were administered at the end of the first week in the temporary offices (at the same time as the second administration of the questionnaire measures). Because these questions were not applicable to workers in the control group, the checklist was not administered to them.

Specifically, to determine whether subjects recognized the status differences between their regular offices and their temporary offices, they were requested to respond to a checklist item that asked, "Is your temporary office usually assigned to a coworker of: lower status than you, equal status to you, or higher status than you?" An additional checklist item asked subjects, "Relative to your regular office, do the facilities found in your temporary office: help you do your job better, enable you to do your job equally well, or cause you to do your job more poorly?"

RESULTS

Manipulation Checks

Subjects' responses to the questionnaire item asking them to identify the relative status attached to their temporary offices showed that they were, in fact, aware of the similarities or differences between their own offices and their temporary ones. Virtually all of the subjects assigned to the offices of equal-status others recognized those offices as being of equal status. All of the subjects assigned to offices of higher and lower status others (whether one or two steps higher or lower) recognized the hierarchical level of those offices. This evidence supports the claim that subjects were aware of the status similarities or differences they encountered during the course of the study and that the manipulations of status were successful.

Another manipulation check sought to ensure that subjects' performance differences could not be attributed to differential opportunities to perform their jobs while in the temporary offices. In response to a checklist item, virtually all 198 participants reported that the facilities in their temporary offices enabled them to perform their jobs as well as they did in their regularly assigned offices. These data discount the possibility that performance increases or decreases noted while in the temporary offices were the result of opportunities provided by or thwarted by office conditions.

Preliminary Analyses

Prior to testing hypotheses, analyses were conducted on the work performance data to determine whether combining the various cells that composed the identically defined payment conditions shown in Table 1 was justified. This was done by including the identically defined groups (as a between-subjects factor) and the observation time (as a repeated measure) in mixed-design analyses of variance (ANOVAS). Justification for combining the responses of the identically defined groups required finding no significant differences between groups, either as main effects or in interactions with the observation time.

As shown in Table 1, four distinct payment conditions were identified by more than one group of workers. Specifically, three groups of workers (those reassigned to equal-status offices) were identified as equitably paid, three groups of workers (those who remained in their own offices) were identified as control subjects, two groups of workers (those assigned to offices one status level higher) were identified as one-step overpaid, and two groups of workers (those assigned to offices one status level lower) were identified as one-step underpaid. Separate ANOVAS for the groups defining each of these four payment conditions revealed no significant main effects of group membership and no interaction of group membership with time, all values of $F < 1.00$, *ns*. Accordingly, distinct payment conditions were created by combining the data for the identically defined groups.

Performance Measure

To test hypotheses regarding the effects of payment equity on task performance, a $6 \times (6)$ mixed-design ANOVA was used, in which the six payment conditions composed the between-subjects factor and the six observation periods composed the within-subjects factor. A significant interaction effect between these two factors was obtained, $F(25, 950) = 8.41$, $p < .001$; the corresponding means are displayed in Figure 1.

Simple effects tests were performed to compare the six payment groups at each of the time periods. These tests revealed no significant differences between groups during each of the two weeks before reassignment, in both cases, $F < 1.00$ *ns*, and also during the second week after reassignment, $F < 1.00$, *ns*. How ever, significant differences between groups were found as workers readjusted to their permanent offices during the first week after reassignment, $F(5, 192) = 2.85$, $p < .025$. Newman-Keuls tests (this and all subsequent Newman-Keuls tests are based on an alpha level of .05) revealed that significant differences existed between workers in the one-step overpaid group and the one-step underpaid group, whereas those in the remaining groups were not significantly different from each other.

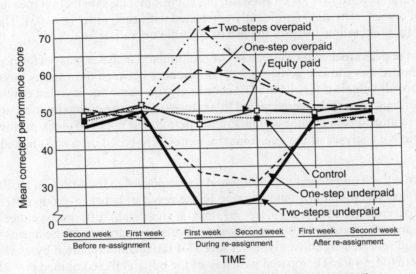

Figure 1. Mean job performance for each payment group over time.

Significant differences emerged in simple effects tests comparing payment groups during the first week of reassignment, $F(5, 192) = 13.99$, $p < .001$. Newman-Keuls tests revealed that the performance of the equitably paid group and the control group did not differ significantly. However, compared with this base level, the one-step overpaid group was significantly more productive and the one-step underpaid group was significantly less productive. Additional comparisons showed that those who were two-steps overpaid were significantly more productive than those who were one-step overpaid, and that those who were two-steps underpaid were significantly less productive than those who were one-step underpaid. Thus, for the first week during reassignment, all hypotheses were supported.

During the second week of reassignment, a significant simple effect of payment group was found as well, $F(5, 192) = 11, 60$, $p < .001$. As in the first week of reassignment, Newman-Keuls tests showed the equivalence of the control group and the equitably paid group. Also, as in the first week of reassignment, those who were one-step overpaid and underpaid performed significantly higher and lower than these base levels, respectively. The magnitude of inequity hypothesis was only partially supported during the second week of reassignment: Those who were two-steps underpaid were less productive than those who were one-step underpaid, but those who were two-steps overpaid did not perform at significantly higher levels than those who were one-step overpaid (although the difference between the means was in the predicted direction).

This finding is the result of a significant drop in performance from the first week during reassignment to the second week among those who were two-steps overpaid, $t(11) = 5.56$, $p < .001$ (this and subsequently reported t tests are two-tailed), indicating that the extreme initial reaction to gross overpayment was not sustained. By contrast, the failure to find significant differences between the first and second reassignment weeks for the one-step overpaid group, $t(29) = 1.98$, *ns*, the one-step underpaid group, $t(29) = .76$, *ns*, and the two-steps underpaid group, $t(11) = .88$, *ns*, suggests that the impact of these inequities was relatively stable over time.

Questionnaire Measures

Correlations between the questionnaire measures were uniformly low. Specifically, the MSQ scores were not significantly correlated with either the environmental satisfaction measures ($r = .04$) or the self-reports of overall reward ($r = .07$). Likewise, the environmental satisfaction measure and the self-reports of overall reward were not significantly correlated with each other ($r = .03$). The statistical independence of these measures justifies the use of separate univariate analyses.

As in the case of the performance measure, a set of preliminary analyses was performed for each questionnaire measure that showed nonsignificant differences between the various groups defining each payment condition, all values of $F < 1.00$, ns. Accordingly, the same six payment conditions that were used for the performance measure were created in analyses of the questionnaire measures. However, because there were three questionnaire-administration periods (as opposed to six performance-measurement periods), analyses of the questionnaire items were based on $6 \times (3)$ mixed-design ANOVAS.

A significant Payment × Time interaction was found for responses to the MSQ, $F(10, 389) = 3.01$, $p < .005$. A simple effects test found this interaction to be the result of between-group differences during the reassignment period, $F(5, 192) = 2.59$, $p < .01$, and no significant differences either before or after the reassignment, in both cases $F < 1.00$, ns. Newman-Keuls comparisons of the means within the reassignment period revealed significantly lower levels of satisfaction reported by workers who were two-steps underpaid ($M = 44.15$) compared with any of the other cells (combined $m = 75.50$), none of which were significantly different from each other.

Analyses of the environmental satisfaction questionnaire also revealed a significant interaction effect, $F(10, 389) = 3.65$, $p < .001$. Simple effects tests found that both the prereassignment and the postreassignment levels of satisfaction were not significantly different from each other, in both cases, $F < 1.00$, ns, although significant differences emerged during the reassignment period, $F(5, 192) = 3.18$, $p < .01$. Newman-Keuls tests showed that compared with the equitably paid group and the control group (which were not significantly different from each other; combined $M = 29.75$), the two overpaid groups were significantly higher (although not significantly different from each other; combined $M = 40.50$) and the two underpaid groups were significantly lower (although not significantly different from each other; combined $M = 18.10$).

Self-reports of overall reward received also revealed a significant Payment × Time interaction, $F(10, 389) = 3.74$, $p < .001$. Although perceived reward levels were not significantly different at the prereassignment and postreassignment sessions, in both cases, $F < 1.00$, ns, significant differences emerged during the reassignment period, $F(5, 192) = 3.61$, $p < .005$. Newman-Keuls tests comparing these means revealed that those who were two-steps overpaid ($M = 5.90$) reported significantly higher reward levels than either those who were only one-step overpaid, equitably paid, or in the control group (the means for which were not significantly different from each other; combined $M = 4.33$). The means for these groups, however, were significantly higher than the means for those who were either one- or two-steps underpaid (which were not significantly different from each other; combined $M = 2.75$).

DISCUSSION

The results of the present study provide strong support for hypotheses concerning the status value of offices (Edelman, 1978; Konar &: Sundstrom, 1985) as outcomes amenable to analysis by equity theory (e.g., Adams, 1965). The performance increases demonstrated by overpaid workers and the decreases demonstrated by underpaid workers in the present study take their place among many other studies that successfully support equity theory predictions (see reviews by Greenberg, 1982, 1987). The unique contribution of the present work, however, is the finding that conditions of overpayment and underpayment were able to be created by manipulating nonmonetary outcomes—elements of the work environment associated with organizational status.

Implications

As such, these findings support Adams's (1965) claim that "job status and status symbols" (p. 278) constitute outcomes in the equity equation, a notion that is just beginning to receive empirical support (e.g., Greenberg &. Ornstein, 1983). This is in contrast to the well-established impact of monetary outcomes demonstrated in the equity theory literature (Greenberg, 1982, 1987). The specific vehicle of status examined in the present work, the physical environment of offices, although previously recognized by students of office design (e.g., Becker, 1981, 1982; Steele, 1973), heretofore has received scant attention as a possible determinant of workers' equity perceptions (e.g., Burt & Sundstrom, 1979). The present work extends the findings of research by Konar et al. (1982), which demonstrated that certain physical features of offices are related to organizational status by showing that these physical symbols of status demarcation operate as outcomes amenable to equity theory analysis. As such, the present findings provide a useful complement to the accumulated literature on office design (e.g., Davis, 1984; Konar et al., 1982; Sundstrom, 1986) by providing an explanatory mechanism that may account for employees' reactions to their work environments (e.g., Wineman, 1982).

The present investigation also supports equity theory's prediction that the reaction to an inequity will be proportional to the magnitude of the inequity experienced (Adams, 1965, p. 281). Specifically, underpaid workers were found to reduce their performance (i.e., lower their inputs) more when they were extremely underpaid (i.e., assigned offices of others two steps below them) than when they were more moderately underpaid (i.e., assigned offices of others one step below them). Likewise, workers who were more overpaid (i.e., assigned to offices of others two steps above them) raised their performance more than those who were more moderately overpaid (i.e., assigned to offices of others one step above them). This set of findings is particularly noteworthy in that it is one of only a few studies (e.g., Leventhal, Allen, & Kemelgor, 1969) that directly manipulate the magnitude of the inequity encountered. As such, it is notable in attempting to reverse a trend toward the "striking absence of attempts to quantify the magnitude of inputs and outcomes, and thus inequities in the research literature on equity" (Adams & Freedman, 1976, p. 52).

Of particular interest in the present research is observed tendency for overpayment inequity to bring about overall lower levels of performance increments than did underpayments bring about performance decrements. Such a finding is in keeping with Adams's (1965) supposition that the threshold for experiencing overpayment inequity is higher than that for underpayment inequity. Similarly, several studies (see review by Walster et al., 1978) have shown that reactions to underpayment are more pronounced than reactions to overpayment. The overall weaker effects of overpayment demonstrated in the present study appear to be the result of lower performance levels in the second week of overpayment than in the first week. Similar temporary effects of overpayment have been demonstrated in both laboratory (e.g., Greenberg & Ornstein, 1983) and field (e.g., Pritchard et al., 1972) settings. Such findings are in keeping with theoretical assertions that reactions to in equity may be moderated by the passage of time (Cosier & Dalton, 1983). Knowing that their overpayment was only going to be temporary, workers may have had little motivation to redress the inequity they experienced by sustaining high levels of performance (Greenberg, 1984). In contrast to the sustained effects of underpayment, more precise explanations for the diminished effects of overpayment over time are lacking and should be recognized as a topic in need of future research.

Further evidence for the less potent effects of overpayment relative to underpayment are provided by the job satisfaction data. Significantly lower levels of satisfaction were found only for the most extremely underpaid workers, but not for overpaid workers, thereby corroborating the weaker effects of overpayment demonstrated by Pritchard et al. (1972). In this regard, it is essential to note that the failure to find more pronounced differences on the job satisfaction measure does not weaken the equity-theory-based interpretation of the present findings. Although equity theory postulates that behavioral reactions to inequity are driven by attempts to alleviate feelings of dissatisfaction (Walster et al., 1978), it has been argued elsewhere (Greenberg, 1984) that such affective mediation has not been clearly demonstrated in previous research and may not be a necessary precondition for behavioral reactions to inequity.

Indeed, an equity theory analysis of the pattern of observed performance differences is supported by other questionnaire findings. Specifically, during the reassignment period, extremely overpaid workers reported receiving higher rewards and extremely underpaid workers reported receiving lower rewards than equitably paid workers. Apparently the office-assignment manipulation was successful in getting workers to perceive changes in their outcome levels. Specific evidence attesting to the fact that these overall rewards were the result of the work environment is provided by the findings of the environmental satisfaction questionnaire: During the reassignment period, overpaid workers reported greater satisfaction, and underpaid workers reported less satisfaction, compared with equitably paid workers (and compared with their reactions to their permanent offices). Such evidence not only shows that workers were aware of the differences in their work environments, but also that changes in environmental satisfaction levels (outcomes) may account for the observed performance differences (inputs).[4]

Limitations and Future Research Directions

Prompted by the diminished impact of overpayment overtime found in the present study, one cannot help but wonder how long the observed effects of status-based inequities would persist. Before managers can be advised to manipulate workplace elements as a tactic for improving subordinates' attitudes or job performance (cf. Goodsell, 1977; Ornstein, in press), future longitudinal investigations need to be conducted to determine the persistence of the presently observed effects (or any reactions to inequity; Cosier & Dalton, 1983). Previous research suggesting that workers suspecting such manipulative intent might actually lower their performance (Greenberg & Ornstein, 1983) would dictate against intentional manipulations of inequity for instrumental purposes (Greenberg, 1982; Greenberg & Cohen, 1982). Clearly, future research is needed to determine the long-term reactions to inequities.

Additional future research is needed to help determine the relative contributions of the specific environmental elements manipulated in the present study. Indeed, the complex set of manipulations that defined relative status in the present study makes it impossible to determine which specific features may have had the greatest impact on the results. For example, we cannot determine from the present study whether the results were due to subjects' knowledge of the status of the office's permanent resident or of the status value of any of the furnishings or design (cf. Davis, 1984; Sundstrom, 1986). Although the inherent confounding of these features was necessary to enhance the validity of this field experiment, it would appear useful to isolate these factors in future laboratory experiments to determine their individual contributions (as outcomes) to inequity effects.

CONCLUSION

Given the importance of the workplace environment as a determinant of workers' job attitudes (Oldham & Fried, 1987; Sundstrom et al., 1980), it should not be surprising to find that workers' assignment to offices was related to their perceived level of job rewards and to their actual job performance. In this regard, equity theory proved to be a useful mechanism for explaining workers' reactions to temporarily encountered environmental conditions. As such, this work broadens the potential horizons of research and theory on organizational justice (Greenberg, 1987), as well as that on workplace environments (Becker, 1981; Sundstrom, 1986). As the rapprochement between these lines of investigation develops, we may well begin to understand the potential of the work environment as a tool for use by practicing managers (cf. Goodsell, 1977; Ornstein, in press; Steele, 1973).

REFERENCES

Adams, J. S. (1965). Inequity in social exchange. In L. Berkowitz (Ed.), *Advances in experimental social psychology* (Vol. 2, pp. 267–299). New York: Academic Press.

Adams, J. S., & Freedman, S. (1976). Equity theory revisited: Comments and annotated bibliography. In L. Berkowitz & E. Walster (Eds.), *Advances in experimental social psychology* (Vol. 9, pp. 43–90). New York: Academic Press.

Becker, F. D. (1981). *Workspace*. New York: Praeger.

Becker, F. D. (1982). *The successful office*. Reading, MA: Addison-Wesley.

Burt, R. E., & Sundstrom, E. (1979, September). Workspace and job satisfaction: Extending equity theory to the physical environment. In H. M. Parsons (Chair), *Physical environments at work*. Symposium presented at the 87th Annual Convention of the American Psychological Association, New York.

Cosier, R. A., & Dalton, D. R. (1983). Equity theory and time: A reformulation. *Academy of Management Reviews*, 8, 311–319.

Davis, T. R. V. (1984). The influence of the physical environment in offices. *Academy of Management Review*, 9, 271–283.

Edelman, M. (1978). *Space and social order*. Madison, WI: University of Wisconsin, Institute for Research on Poverty.

Geran, M. (1976). Does it work? *Interior Design*, 47(2), 114–117.

Goodsell, C. T. (1977). Bureaucratic manipulation of physical symbols: An empirical study. *American Journal of Political Science*, 21, 79–91.

Greenberg, J. (1982). Approaching equity and avoiding inequity in groups and organizations. In J. Greenberg & R. L. Cohen (Eds.), *Equity and justice in social behavior* (pp. 389–435). New York: Academic Press.

Greenberg, J. (1984). On the apocryphal nature of inequity distress. In R. Folger (Ed.), *The sense of injustice: Social psychological perspectives* (pp. 167–186). New York: Plenum Press.

Greenberg, J. (1987). A taxonomy of organizational justice theories. *Academy of Management Review*, 12, 9–22.

Greenberg, J., & Cohen, R. L. (1982). Why justice? Normative and instrumental interpretations. In J. Greenberg & R. L. Cohen (Eds.), *Equity and justice in social behavior* (pp. 437–469). New York: Academic Press.

Greenberg, J., & Ornstein, S. (1983). High status job title as compensation for underpayment: A test of equity theory. *Journal of Applied Psychology*, 68, 285–297.

Halloran, J. (1978). *Applied human relations: An organizational approach*. Englewood Cliffs, NJ: Prentice-Hall.

Harris, T. G. (1977, October 31). Psychology of the New York work space. *New York*, pp. 51–54.

Joiner, D. (1976). Social ritual and architectural space. In H. Proshansky, W. Ittleson, & L. Rivlin (Eds.), *Environmental psychology: People and their physical settings* (2nd ed., pp. 224–241). New York: Holt, Rinehart & Winston.

Kleinschrod, W. A. (1987, July). A balance of forces. *Administrative Management*, 48(7), 18–23.

Konar, E., & Sundstrom, E. (1985). Status demarcation in the office. In J. Wineman (Ed.), *Behavioral issues in office design* (pp. 48–66). New York: Van Nostrand.

Konar, E., Sundstrom, E., Brady, C., Mandel, D., & Rice, R. W. (1982). Status demarcation in the office. *Environment and Behavior*, 14, 561–580.

Langdon, F. J. (1966). *Modern offices: A user survey* (National Building Studies Research Paper No. 41, Ministry of Technology, Building Research Station). London: Her Majesty's Stationery Office.

Leventhal, G. S., Allen, J., & Kemelgor, B. (1969). Reducing inequity by reallocating rewards. *Psychonomic Science*, 14, 295–296.

Louis Harris & Associates, Inc. (1978). *The Steelcase national study of office environments: Do they work?* Grand Rapids, MI: Steelcase.

Oldham, G. R., & Fried, Y. (1987). Employee reactions to workspace characteristics. *Journal of Applied Psychology*, 72, 75–80.

Ornstein, S. (in press). Impression management through office design. In R. Giacolone & P. Rosenfeld (Eds.), *Impression management in organizations*. Hillsdale, NJ: Erlbaum.

Price, J. L., & Mueller, C. W. (1986). *Handbook of organizational measurement*. Marshfield, MA: Pitman.

Pritchard, R. D., Dunnette, M. D., & Jorgenson, D. O. (1972). Effects of perceptions of equity and inequity on worker performance and satisfaction. *Journal of Applied Psychology*, 56, 75–94.

Robichaud, B. (1958). *Selecting, planning, and managing office space*. New York: McGraw-Hill.

Steele, F. (1973). *Physical settings and organizational development*. Reading, MA: Addison-Wesley.

Stryker, S., & Macke, A. S. (1978). Status inconsistency and role conflict. In R. H. Turner, J. Coleman, & R. C. Fox (Eds.), *Annual review of sociology* (Vol. 4, pp. 57–90). Palo Alto, CA: Annual Reviews.

Sundstrom, E. (1986). *Work places*. New York: Cambridge University Press.

Sundstrom, E., Burt, R., & Kamp, D. (1980). Privacy at work: Architectural correlates of job satisfaction and job performance. *Academy of Management Journal*, 23, 101–117.

Walster, E., Walster, G. W., & Berscheid, E. (1978). *Equity: Theory and research*. Boston: Allyn & Bacon.

Weiss, D. J., Dawis, R. V., England, G. W., & Lofquist, L. H. (1967). *Manual for the Minnesota Satisfaction Questionnaire*. Minneapolis: University of Minnesota, Industrial Relations Center.

Wineman, J. D. (1982). Office design and evaluation: An overview. *Environment and Behavior*, 14, 271–298.

Wylie, H. L. (1958). *Office management handbook* (2nd ed.). New York: Ronald Press.

NOTES

1. The number of employees within each worker group assigned to each condition was predetermined by the number of available offices and the number of desks per office. To maintain the characteristics of the permanent offices while they were used as temporary offices, the number of temporary residents assigned to an office was kept equal to the number of its permanent residents. Further stimulating the permanent characteristics of the offices, while also avoiding possible confoundings due to having mixed-status office mates, all multiple-employee offices were shared by equal-status coworkers.

2. To keep constant the amount of time that all of the workers spent in their temporary offices, none were allowed to return to their permanent offices in advance of the 2-week period, even if the work was completed ahead of schedule. The physical separation of the various offices and the

placement of construction barriers made it unlikely that workers could learn of any possible early completions. Because the 2 weeks allowed for completion of the offices was liberally budgeted, no delays in returning to permanent offices were necessitated.

3.   A preexperimental questionnaire conducted among employees of the host organization indicated strong consensual agreement about the existence and nature of symbols of status demarcation in their organization. In responding to an open-ended question, 222 employees surveyed identified the four dimensions listed in Table 2 most frequently (from 75% to 88%) as reflective of status differences in their organization. Such findings are in keeping with those reported in more broad-based survey research (Louis Harris & Associates, 1978).

4.   Unfortunately, however, because these questionnaires were administered only once during the reassignment period, the responses cannot be used to gauge changes in affective reactions within this critical period.

Received September 15, 1987

Revision received December 18, 1987

Accepted February 17, 1988

READING 19

Sociability and Susceptibility to the Common Cold

What determines your susceptibility to the common cold virus? Lately, there has been much research into the role that social relationships play in predicting people's health. However, according to researchers Cohen, Doyle, Turner, Alper, and Skoner, it is not social relationships, per se, that need to be examined, but, rather, the personality traits that facilitate social interactions. Specifically, their study demonstrated that sociable people are less likely than unsociable people to catch a cold when exposed to a rhinovirus. The researchers defined "sociable" to mean people who seek others and are agreeable. They rated participants' sociability levels and then exposed them to the virus and proceeded to objectively and subjectively measure their rates of infection. They found that the higher their sociability score, the less likely people were to develop a cold. As for how sociability might be related to resistance to colds, the researchers propose that sociability is genetically determined and that those same genes might be contributing to biological processes that play a role in the body's ability to fight infection. See Chapter 14 (Health) of the text for other aspects of personality that have been found to influence health.

SOCIABILITY AND SUSCEPTIBILITY TO THE COMMON COLD

Sheldon Cohen,[1] William J. Doyle,[2] Ronald Turner,[3] Cuneyt M. Alper,[2] and David P. Skoner[2]

[1]Carnegie Mellon University, [2]University of Pittsburgh School of Medicine and Children's Hospital of Pittsburgh, and [3]University of Virginia Health Sciences Center

Abstract—*There is considerable evidence that social relationships can influence health, but only limited evidence on the health effects of the personality characteristics that are thought to mold people's social lives. We asked whether sociability predicts resistance to infectious disease and whether this relationship is attributable to the quality and quantity of social interactions and relationships. Three hundred thirty-four volunteers completed questionnaires assessing their sociability, social networks, and social supports, and six evening interviews assessing daily interactions. They were subsequently exposed to a virus that causes a common cold and monitored to see who developed verifiable illness. Increased sociability was associated in a linear fashion with a decreased probability of developing a cold. Although sociability was associated with more and higher-quality social interactions, it predicted disease susceptibility independently of these variables. The association between sociability and disease was also independent of baseline immunity (virus-specific antibody), demographics, emotional styles, stress hormones, and health practices.*

Sheldon Cohen, William J. Doyle, Ronald Turner, Cuneyt M. Alper, andDavid P. Skoner, "Sociability and Susceptibility to the Common Cold," Psychological Science, September 2003, Vol. 14, No. 5, pp. 389-395. Reprinted with permission of Blackwell Publishing, Inc.
Address correspondence to Sheldon Cohen, Department of Psychology, Carnegie Mellon University, Pittsburgh, PA 15213; e-mail: scohen@cmu.edu.

There has been much recent emphasis on the role of social relationships in health (e.g., Cohen, Gottlieb, & Underwood, 2000; Uchino, Cacioppo, & Kiecolt-Glaser, 1996). The structure of people's social networks (Brissette, Cohen, & Seeman, 2000), the support they receive from others (Helgeson & Gottlieb, 2000; Wills & Shinar, 2000), and the quality and quantity of their social interactions (Kiecolt-Glaser & Newton, 2001; Reis & Collins, 2000) have all been identified as potential predictors of their health and well-being. Although these various indicators of people's social lives are to some extent molded by their personalities, there has been much less interest in the role of socially relevant dispositions in health.

This article focuses on sociability, a disposition that is generally recognized as a determinant of quality and quantity of social interaction. We define sociability as the quality of seeking others and being agreeable (Liebert & Spiegler, 1994; Reber, 1985). We assume that sociability plays a role in the development and maintenance of social networks, intimate relationships, and social supports. If our assumption is correct, one would expect that more sociable people would be healthier than less sociable people. This could occur because better and closer relationships might increase positive and decrease negative affect, promote positive health practices, help regulate health-relevant biological systems, or provide social support in the face of stressful events (Cohen, 1988; Cohen et al., 2000; Uchino et al., 1996).

The first question we raise in this article is whether those individuals who seek out interactions and are generally agreeable and genial in company are somehow protected from illness. Two factors of the Big Five personality factors can be viewed as combining to represent the central components of sociability: extraversion, the personality dimension that reflects an individual's preferences for social settings, and agreeableness, the dimension of personality that underlies geniality (Costa & McCrae, 1992). Of these, only extraversion has been seriously considered in terms of its implications for health. Eysenck (1967) proposed that extraversion is characterized by low resting levels of electrocortical and sympathetic nervous system (SNS) activity (Geen, 1997). Because activation of these systems is related to suppression of immune function, low activation would be expected to reduce risk for developing disease when exposed to infectious agents. Three studies of susceptibility to infection by common cold viruses found that extraversion is related to reduced susceptibility (Broadbent, Broadbent, Phillpotts, & Wallace, 1984; Cohen, Doyle, Skoner, Rabin, & Gwaltney, 1997; Totman, Kiff, Reed, & Craig, 1980). None of these studies addressed the potential psychological or biological pathways through which extraversion might influence disease susceptibility.

The second question we address is how sociability might get inside the body. On the psychological side, we were interested in whether associations of sociability and health are mediated through interpersonal behavior. Are sociable people healthier than others because they interact more often or with more people, have fewer conflicts or more satisfactory interactions, and have more social support? More and better interactions could facilitate the regulation of emotions and provide the motivation and opportunity to take better care of oneself. In turn, helping regulate emotional response contributes to the regulation of emotion-related biological systems that have implications for immune competence. These systems include the SNS and the hypothalamic-pituitary-adrenal-cortical (HPA) axis. In the study we report here, we tested whether sociability is associated with the ability to resist infectious illness and examined plausible explanations for how such an association might occur. Social, psychological, and biological data were collected from volunteers who were subsequently exposed to one of two rhinoviruses that cause common colds. The major outcome was whether or not volunteers developed verifiable disease.

Method

Participants

Data were collected between 1997 and 2001. The participants were 159 men and 175 women, ages 18 to 54 years, who responded to newspaper advertisements and were judged to be in good health after a medical examination. They were paid $800 for their participation.

Procedure

Table 1 summarizes the sequence of the study.

Table 1. *Temporal sequence of a trial*

2 months before quarantine
  Eligibility screening:
    Physical exam
    Blood for preexisting antibody to virus
    Extraversion and agreeableness questionnaires (first
      administration)
    Social-network questionnaire
    Demographics
2 to 4 weeks before quarantine
  Daily interviews:
    6 daily assessments of social interactions and affect
Quarantine Day 0
  Extraversion and agreeableness questionnaires (second
    administration)
  Positive Relationship With Others Scale
  Social-support questionnaire
  Health-practice questionnaires
  Saliva cortisol and urine epinephrine samples
  Nasal secretions for virus culture
  Baseline signs and symptoms of respiratory illness
  Daily affect assessment
End of Day 0
  Inoculation with virus
Quarantine Days 1 through 5
  Nasal secretions for virus culture
  Signs and symptoms of respiratory illness
4 weeks after virus challenge
  Blood for antibody to virus

Eligibility screenings

At the onset of the study, all volunteers underwent medical-eligibility screenings. They were excluded from the study if they had a history of any psychiatric or chronic physical disease, had abnormal blood or urine profiles, were pregnant or currently lactating, had antibody for HIV, or were on a regular medication regimen. In addition, during the first 24 hr of quarantine (Day 0, before virus exposure), volunteers had a nasal examination. They were excluded from the study at this point if they had symptoms of a cold.

Data collected before exposure to the virus

Demographics, all psychological data, immunity to the experimental virus (levels of preexisting antibody), weight and height, SNS and HPA hormones, and health practices were assessed during the 8-week period before exposure to the virus. Baseline symptoms and objective signs of illness were assessed during the day (Day 0) before virus exposure.

Virus exposure and assessments of illness

Volunteers were quarantined in separate rooms and exposed (after 24 hr) to one of two types of rhinovirus, RV39 ($n = 228$) or RV23 ($n = 106$). On each of the 5 days after exposure, they reported their respiratory symptoms and were assessed for objective indicators of infection (virus culture of nasal secretions) and illness. Four weeks after virus exposure, a blood sample was collected to test for an additional marker of infection—increases (from baseline) in level of antibody to the virus. Investigators were blinded to all psychological and biological measures.

Psychological Measures

Sociability

We used three measures to assess sociability: extraversion, agreeableness, and positive relationship style. Extraversion and agreeableness were assessed twice (8-week interval) before virus exposure; positive relationship style was assessed on the day before exposure (Day 0). Extraversion and agreeableness were each measured with an eight-item subscale from a short version of the Goldberg Big Five Questionnaire (Cohen et al., 1997; Goldberg, 1992). Each item on these subscales is a trait (e.g., extraversion: talkative, bashful; agreeableness: generous, unsympathetic), and respondents indicated how accurately the trait described how they "typically are," on a scale ranging from 0 (*not at all accurate*) to 4 (*extremely accurate*). The nine-item Positive Relationship With Others Scale (Ryff, 1989) is intended to more broadly tap sociability. Participants indicated their agreement that each item described them, using a 6-point scale ranging from 1, *strongly disagree*, to 6, *strongly agree*. An example of an item from this scale is "Most people see me as loving and affectionate." For all three scales, the appropriate items were reversed, and the scale scores were summed. The test-retest correlations were .79 for extraversion and .69 for agreeableness (all $ps < .001$). The internal reliabilities were .83 to .85 for extraversion, .76 to .79 for agreeableness, and .78 for positive relationships. To obtain final scale scores for extraversion and agreeableness, we averaged the scores from the two assessments.

We then entered the three final scale scores into a principal component factor analysis. All three scales loaded on the first principal component (.69, .64, and .80, respectively). To create a single sociability scale, we transformed the final scale scores into z scores and added the three scores together.

Social interactions

We used telephone interviews to assess daily social interactions. Volunteers were interviewed on 3 evenings a week (2 weekdays and 1 weekend day) for 2 weeks during the month before quarantine. The interview included a review of the interpersonal interactions participants had over the day and was modeled after the Rochester Interaction Record (Reis & Wheeler, 1991). An interaction was defined as spending time with one or more persons for 10 consecutive minutes or longer. For each one-on-one or group interaction, participants indicated with whom they interacted, when the interaction started and ended, how pleasant it was (from 1, *unpleasant*, to 7, *pleasant*), and the level of disagreement or conflict (none, mild, moderate, severe).

We derived a number of scores from the 6 days of interaction interviews, including total number of interactions; average number of people interacted with per day; average pleasantness of interactions; and percentage and number of interactions that were pleasant (≥ 5 on the 7-point scale), were unpleasant (≤ 3), or involved moderate to severe conflict.

Social network and social support

We administered two standardized questionnaires. The Social Network Index (SNI; Cohen et al., 1997) assessed the number of social roles regularly engaged in (e.g., spouse, friend, family member, worker) and the number of people talked to (in person or on the phone) within these roles in a 2-week period. Marital status was also recorded. The 12-item version of the Interpersonal Support Evaluation List (ISEL; Cohen, Mermelstein, Kamarck, & Hoberman, 1985) assessed participants' perception that others would provide them with support in the face of stressful events. Internal reliability for the ISEL was .87.

Emotional styles

Data on emotional style were collected during the six interviews described earlier, as well as on the evening of the Day 0 (before virus exposure) of quarantine. Each evening, participants were asked how accurately (from 0, *not at all accurate*, to 4, *extremely accurate*) each of nine positive and nine negative mood adjectives described how they felt during the last day (Cohen, Doyle, Turner, Alper, & Skoner, in press). The positive adjectives included *lively, happy*, and *relaxed*. The negative adjectives included *sad, on edge*, and *angry*. Daily positive-mood scores were calculated by summing the ratings of the nine positive adjectives, and daily negative-mood scores were calculated by summing the ratings of the nine negative adjectives. The internal reliabilities (alphas) for the seven interviews ranged from .89 to .93 for the positive-mood scale and .87 to .92 for the negative-mood scale. To form measures of emotional style, we averaged daily mood scores (separately for positive and negative) across the seven interviews.

Control Variables

We examined eight control variables that might provide alternative explanations for the relation between sociability and illness. These included levels of antibody to the experimental virus before challenge (titer of ≤ 4 or ≥ 8), age (18–21, 22–32, 33–54), body mass index (weight in kilograms/height in meters^2), race (Caucasian, other), gender, and virus type (RV23 or RV39). Also included were month of exposure (March, May, July, September, or December) and education level (high school graduate, high school graduate with less than 2 years of college, and high school graduate with 2 or more years of college).

Pathways Linking Sociability to Susceptibility

Health practices

Smoking rate was defined as the number of cigarettes smoked a day. In calculating the average number of alcoholic drinks per day, we treated a bottle or can of beer, glass of wine, or shot of whiskey as a single drink. Exercise was measured by the number of days per week engaged in an activity long enough to work up a sweat, get the heart thumping, or get out of breath (Paffenbarger, Blair, Lee, & Hyde, 1993) multiplied by a rating, from 0 (*no effort*) to 10 (*maximum effort*), of the associated level of exertion. Assessments of sleep quality included subjective quality, efficiency (percentage of time in bed sleeping), and duration (Buysse, Reynolds, Monk, Berman, & Kupfer, 1989). Dietary intake of vitamin C and zinc was assessed by standard questionnaire (Block, Hartman, & Naughton, 1990).

Endocrine hormones

Samples for hormone assessments were collected on the 1st day of quarantine. The SNS hormones epinephrine and norepinephrine were assessed in a 24-hr urine sample and assayed using high-performance liquid chromatography with electrochemical detection. To assess the release of the HPA hormone cortisol, we collected 12 saliva samples via salivettes (cotton rolls). Approximately 1 sample was collected per hour between 5:45 a.m. and 4:00 p.m., with others collected at 6:30 and 10:30 p.m. Levels of salivary cortisol were determined via time-resolved immunoassay with fluorometric end-point detection. Area under the curve was calculated to measure total free-cortisol release.

Infections and Colds

Infectious diseases result from the growth and action of microorganisms or parasites in the body. Infection is the multiplication of an invading microorganism. Clinical disease occurs when infection is followed by the development of signs and symptoms characteristic of the disease.

Infection

The presence of an infectious agent can be established directly through the use of culturing techniques (in this case, finding the virus in nasal secretions). Nasal secretion samples collected daily in a saline wash of the nose were frozen and later cultured for rhinovirus using standard techniques (Gwaltney, Colonno, Hamparian, & Turner, 1989). Infection can also be detected indirectly by examining changes in specific antibody to the infectious agent. When exposed to foreign agents, the immune system produces protein molecules (antibodies) that help mark and destroy invading microorganisms. The production of antibodies to a specific infectious agent is evidence for the presence of that agent. Hence, we compared virus-specific antibody levels measured in serum collected before and 28 days after exposure (Gwaltney et al., 1989).

Signs and symptoms

At the end of each day of quarantine, participants rated the severity of eight respiratory symptoms (congestion, runny nose, sneezing, cough, sore throat, malaise, headache, and chills) during the previous 24 hr (Jackson et al., 1960). Ratings ranged from 0 (*none*) to 4 (*very severe*) for each symptom. Ratings of the eight symptoms were summed to create daily symptom scores. Participants were also asked each day if they had a cold.

We assessed daily mucus production by collecting used facial tissues in sealed plastic bags (Doyle, McBride, Swarts, Hayden, & Gwaltney, 1988). The bags were weighed and the weight of the tissues and bags subtracted. Nasal mucociliary clearance function is an objective measure of what is experienced as congestion. Specifically, it refers to the effectiveness of nasal cilia in clearing mucus from the nasal passage toward the throat. Clearance function was assessed as the time required for a dye administered in the nostrils to reach the throat (Doyle et al., 1988).

To create baseline-adjusted daily scores for each measure, we subtracted the appropriate baseline score (day before challenge) from each of the five post-challenge daily scores. Adjusted daily scores that were negative were rescored as 0. We then summed the appropriate adjusted daily scores across the 5 days to create total adjusted symptoms, mucus weight, and mucociliary clearance scores.

Definition of a cold

Volunteers were considered to have a clinical cold if they both were infected and met illness criteria. They were classified as infected if the challenge virus was isolated on any of the 5 post-challenge study days or there was at least a 4-fold rise in virus-specific serum antibody titer from before exposure to 28 days after exposure. We used two alternative illness criteria. The objective criterion required a total adjusted mucus weight of at least 10 g or total adjusted mucociliary nasal clearance time of at least 35 min (Cohen et al., 1997). The subjective criterion (modified Jackson criterion) required a total adjusted symptom score of 6 or higher, in addition to either reporting having a cold or reporting runny nose on 3 or more days (e.g., Cohen et al., 1997).

Table 2. *Control variables associated with risk of common cold*

Control measure	Objective	Subjective
	Illness criterion	
Preexisting antibody	$b = -0.65 \pm 0.28, p < .02$	$b = -0.80 \pm 0.26, p < .002$
Virus type (RV23 or 39)	$b = -0.82 \pm 0.30, p < .006$	$b = -0.74 \pm 0.28, p < .007$
Age	n.s.	$b = -0.66 \pm 0.29, p < .05$

Note. Each result is from a separate equation in which the individual control variable was the only predictor.

Note. Each result is from a separate equation in which the individual control variable was the only predictor.

Statistical Analyses

Body mass index, total symptom scores, mucus weight, mucociliary clearance scores, cortisol level, epinephrine and norepinephrine levels, number of cigarettes per day, number of alcoholic drinks per day, and zinc and vitamin C intake were all log-transformed (base 10) to better approximate a normal distribution. We used stepwise logistic regression to predict the binary outcome presence/absence of a cold. Sociability measures were treated as continuous variables, and we report the regression coefficients, with standard errors and probability levels. In several cases, we also provide an estimate of relative risk—the ratio of risk (odds ratio and 95% confidence interval, CI) of participants with lower levels of sociability (each of the bottom 4 quintiles) relative to participants with the highest sociability (top quintile). We sequentially added variables to the first step of regression analyses in order to determine whether the association between sociability (entered alone in the second step) and susceptibility to colds is substantially reduced after controlling for the contribution of other variables. All analyses we report included the eight control variables. Interaction terms were entered together in a third step of the equation.

Results

Table 2 presents the significant associations between control variables and frequency of colds. Having previous antibody and being exposed to RV23 rather than RV39 were both associated with fewer colds by both the objective and the subjective illness criteria. For the subjective criterion only, being 18 to 21 years old was associated with fewer colds than being older. None of these variables, however, were associated with sociability.

We examined the association of each of the components of sociability with frequency of colds. As is apparent from Table 3, higher scores for extraversion, agreeableness, and positive relationships were all associated with decreased risk for colds, irrespective of the illness criterion. To simplify presentation, for the remaining analyses we use the sociability index. This index provides a broader conceptual scope and better reliability than the three individual measures. As is apparent from Figure 1, increases in sociability were associated in an approximately linear manner with decreases in the rate of illness defined by both criteria (statistics for sociability treated as a continuous variable are in Table 3). The adjusted odds ratios were 2.9 (CI = 1.12, 7.37), 3.0 (CI = 1.22, 7.47), 2.2 (CI = 0.89, 5.34), 1.4 (CI = 0.52, 3.66), and 1 (reference group) for objectively defined colds and 4.4 (CI = 1.76, 11.16), 4.8 (CI = 2.00, 11.74), 2.3 (CI = 0.96, 5.58), 1.0 (CI = 0.38, 2.70), and 1 (reference group) for subjectively defined colds.

Table 3. *Associations (adjusted for controls) between continuous sociability measures and risk of common cold*

Sociability measure	Illness criterion	
	Objective	Subjective
Extraversion	$b = -0.06 \pm 0.03, p < .03$	$b = -0.10 \pm 0.03, p < .001$
Agreeableness	$b = -0.07 \pm 0.04, p < .06$	$b = -0.11 \pm 0.04, p < .005$
Positive relationships	$b = -0.04 \pm 0.02, p = .05$	$b = -0.05 \pm 0.02, p < .006$
Sociability index	$b = -0.19 \pm 0.07, p < .006$	$b = -0.30 \pm 0.07, p < .001$

Note. Each result is from a separate equation.

Note. Each result is from a separate equation.

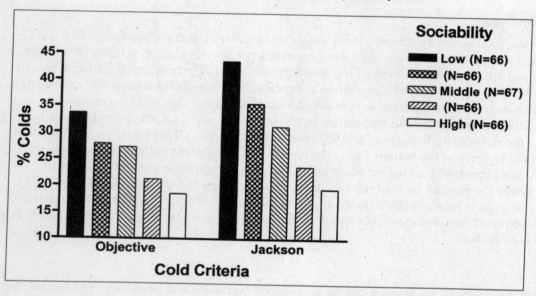

Fig. 1. Rate of developing colds (adjusted for controls) as a function of sociability quintile. Colds were defined either as infection plus objective signs of illness or as infection plus subjective symptoms of illness (modified Jackson criterion).

There were no statistically reliable interactions between control variables and sociability in predicting objective clinical colds. There was a sociability-by-sex interaction predicting subjective colds. Rates of colds decreased with sociability for both sexes, although low sociability was associated with a greater risk among women than men ($b = -0.34 \pm 0.14, p < .02$). Hence, the reported associations were similar across pre-challenge antibody levels, age, race, sex (for the objective criterion), education, body mass index, month of exposure, and virus type.

We proposed that associations between sociability and risk for colds might be attributable to the ability of sociable people to develop and maintain relationships, particularly supportive ones. The correlations between sociability and the questionnaire and interview variables were consistent with this proposal (see Table 4). Marital status was not associated with sociability. However, none of the relationship or support variables were themselves associated with colds. Moreover, when we entered them all in the first step of the equation, they did not reduce the association between sociability and colds ($b = -0.19 \pm$

0.09, $p < .03$, for the objective criterion; $b = -0.35 \pm 0.09$, $p < .001$, for the subjective criterion). Hence they were not, alone or in combination, responsible for the sociability-illness link.

In an analysis reported elsewhere (Cohen et al., in press), we found that positive emotional style was associated with lower risk of developing a cold. In the present study, sociability was associated with increased positive emotional style ($r = .45$, $p < .001$) and decreased negative emotional style ($r = < -.29$, $p < .001$). Adding positive and negative emotional style to the equation, however, also had only a minimal effect on the sociability-cold relation ($b = -0.17$, ± 0.08, $p < .05$, for the objective criterion; $b = -0.33 \pm 0.09$, $p < .001$, for the subjective criterion).

Finally, health practices and endocrine measures were assessed as possible pathways linking sociability to illness. Correlations indicated that sociability was associated with better sleep quality (.20, $p < .001$) and sleep efficiency (.15, $p < .006$), but not sleep duration (.02, n.s.), and with more vitamin C (.12, $p < .03$), but not dietary zinc (.06, n.s.) or exercise (.05, n.s.). Sociability was also related to lower cortisol levels (−.15, $p < .009$) and to lower levels of epinephrine (−.11, $p < .05$), but not to norepinephrine (.01, n.s.). Sociability was not associated with smoking or alcohol use. When the five variables associated with sociability were entered into an equation predicting colds, better sleep efficiency ($p < .04$) and higher cortisol levels ($p < .05$) were associated with less risk.

Table 4. *Correlations between sociability and questionnaire and interview measures of social interaction*

Measure of social interaction	Correlation
Interview	
Total number of interactions	.29*
Average number of people interacted with per day	.21*
Average pleasantness of interactions	.29*
Percentage of interactions that were pleasant	.31*
Number of interactions that were pleasant	.39*
Percentage of interactions that were unpleasant	−.12*
Number of interactions that were unpleasant	−.05
Percentage of interactions that involved moderate to severe conflict	−.14*
Number of interactions that involved moderate to severe conflict	−.01
Questionnaire	
Number of social roles	.18*
Number of people interacted with within social roles	.23*
Perceived availability of social support	.55*

*$p < .001$

However, adding all five variables to the equation (including the control variables) did not decrease the relation between sociability and colds ($b = -0.22 \pm 0.08$, $p < .004$, for the objective criterion; $b = -0.30 \pm 0.08$, $p < .001$, for the subjective criterion; $n = 315$ because of missing data). Hence, none of these five variables were mediators.

Discussion

We found that sociability was associated with greater resistance to developing colds when persons were experimentally exposed to a cold virus. Although this association was found individually for extraversion, agreeableness, and positive relationships, the largest association was found when these variables were combined to form a single sociability score. The relation between sociability and disease susceptibility was found irrespective of whether colds were defined as infection and self-reported symptoms or as infection and objective signs of illness. In both cases, the relation was approximately linear, with increases in sociability associated with decreases in disease susceptibility. That these associations were found after entering eight control variables is notable. In particular, by controlling for preexisting antibody (immunity) to the virus, we excluded as a possible explanation the idea that sociable people had more social contact and hence were more likely to have been infected in the past and have developed immunity to the virus. The association also was equal (no interactions) across pre-challenge virus-specific antibody levels, age, race, sex (for the objective criterion), education, body mass index, season, and virus type. The consistency of associations for the two different viruses is especially important in that it indicates the biological generality of the association. We did find, however, that low levels of sociability produced a greater risk for women than men when the subjective definition of illness was employed.

How does sociability get inside the body? On the psychological side, we were interested in whether associations of sociability and health are mediated through interpersonal behavior. In fact, sociability was moderately associated with both increased rate and increased quality of interactions. Sociable people also had more diverse and larger networks, and perceived greater availability of social support. Sociability was similarly associated with better sleep and diet, and more positive and less negative emotions. However, our analyses failed to support any of these as potential mediators. The sociability index was associated with colds even after controlling for these alternatives.

On the biological side, we were interested in whether sociability might modulate emotion-related biological systems, like the SNS and the HPA axis, that are known to influence immune response. Sociability was associated with lower concentrations of the HPA hormone cortisol and the SNS hormone epinephrine. However, these hormones failed to meet the criteria for mediation of the sociability-cold relation.

How could perceived measures of sociability predict colds when behavioral measures of social interaction do not? One possibility is that perceived measures are partly determined by individual differences that bias people's estimates of their own sociability. In turn, it might be that it is these individual differences, not true (measured without error) social dispositions, that predict health. Alternatively, it is possible that our behavioral assessment was not optimal. We defined interactions in terms of minimal time (10 min). More meaningful ways of breaking up the stream of behavior (e.g., specific activities such as eating a meal or watching television together) might provide an assessment more highly correlated with sociability questionnaires and with health.

Why can we not explain the association between sociability and colds in terms of health practices or endocrine variables? Few of these proposed mediators themselves predicted susceptibility to colds in this study. This is puzzling because several were predictive in previous studies (Cohen et al., 1997). However, a lower rate of illness than we expected (usually 37% for the objective criterion, but 25.7% in this study) may have resulted in insufficient power for detecting these effects. Even so, one would expect that the effect sizes of putative mediators would be at least as great as that of sociability. Reliability of measurement and sensitivity to the dynamics of mediators could be improved by measuring mediators multiple times. Moreover, broader views of the relevant biological systems (e.g., shape of diurnal rhythms, stress reactivity, and binding affinity) may tap important aspects of regulatory response not picked up by hormone concentrations.